Authors

James L. Kinneavy, the Jane and Roland Blumberg Centennial Professor of English at The University of Texas at Austin, directed the development and writing of the composition strand in the program. He is the author of *A Theory of Discourse* and coauthor of *Writing in the Liberal Arts Tradition*. Professor Kinneavy is a leader in the field of rhetoric and composition and a respected educator whose teaching experience spans all levels—elementary, secondary, and college. He has continually been concerned with teaching writing to high school students.

John E. Warriner developed the organizational structure for the Handbook of Grammar, Usage, and Mechanics in the book. He coauthored the *English Workshop* series, was general editor of the *Composition: Models and Exercises* series, and editor of *Short Stories: Characters in Conflict*. He taught English for thirty-two years in junior and senior high school and college.

W9-AKV-772

Writers and Editors

Ellen Ashdown has a Ph.D. in English from the University of Florida. She has taught composition and literature at the college level. She is a professional writer of educational materials and has published articles and reviews on education and art.

Jan Freeman has an M.A. in English from New York University. She has taught college composition classes. A published poet, she is a contributing editor to *The American Poetry Review* and the director of Paris Press.

Mary Hix has an M.A. in English from Wake Forest University. She has taught freshman composition courses. She is a professional writer and editor of educational materials in language arts.

Madeline Travers-Hovland has an M.A. in Teaching from Harvard University. She has taught English in elementary and secondary school and has been an elementary school librarian. She is a professional writer of educational materials in literature and composition.

Alice M. Sohn has a Ph.D. in English Education from Florida State University. She has taught English in middle school, secondary school, and college. She has been a writer and editor of educational materials in language arts for seventeen years.

Raymond Teague has an A.B. in English and journalism from Texas Christian University. He has been children's book editor for the *Fort Worth Star-Telegram* for more than fifteen years and has been a writer and editor of educational materials for twelve years.

Acknowledgments

We wish to thank the following teachers, who participated in field testing of pre-publication materials for this series:

Susan Almand-Myers
Meadow Park
  Intermediate School
Beaverton, Oregon

Theresa L. Bagwell
Naylor Middle School
Tucson, Arizona

Ruth Bird
Freeport High School
Sarver, Pennsylvania

Joan M. Brooks
Central Junior High
  School
Guymon, Oklahoma

Candice C. Bush
J. D. Smith Junior High
  School
N. Las Vegas, Nevada

Mary Jane Childs
Moore West Junior High
  School
Oklahoma City,
  Oklahoma

Brian Christensen
Valley High School
West Des Moines, Iowa

Lenise Christopher
Western High School
Las Vegas, Nevada

Mary Ann Crawford
Ruskin Senior High
  School
Kansas City, Missouri

Linda Dancy
Greenwood Lakes
  Middle School
Lake Mary, Florida

Elaine A. Espindle
Peabody Veterans
  Memorial High School
Peabody, Massachusetts

Joan Justice
North Middle School
O'Fallon, Missouri

Beverly Kahwaty
Pueblo High School
Tucson, Arizona

Lamont Leon
Van Buren Junior High
  School
Tampa, Florida

Susan Lusch
Fort Zumwalt South
  High School
St. Peters, Missouri

Michele K. Lyall
Rhodes Junior High
  School
Mesa, Arizona

Belinda Manard
McKinley Senior High
  School
Canton, Ohio

Nathan Masterson
Peabody Veterans
  Memorial High School
Peabody, Massachusetts

Marianne Mayer
Swope Middle School
Reno, Nevada

Penne Parker
Greenwood Lakes
  Middle School
Lake Mary, Florida

Amy Ribble
Gretna Junior-Senior
  High School
Gretna, Nebraska

Kathleen R. St. Clair
Western High School
Las Vegas, Nevada

Carla Sankovich
Billinghurst Middle School
Reno, Nevada

Sheila Shaffer
Cholla Middle School
Phoenix, Arizona

Joann Smith
Lehman Junior High
  School
Canton, Ohio

Margie Stevens
Raytown Middle School
Raytown, Missouri

Mary Webster
Central Junior High
  School
Guymon, Oklahoma

Susan M. Yentz
Oviedo High School
Oviedo, Florida

We wish to thank the following teachers who contributed student papers for this Revised Edition of *Elements of Writing, Introductory Course.*

Peter J. Caron
Cumberland Middle School
Cumberland, Rhode
  Island

Steve Funnell
Trafalgar Middle School
Cape Coral, Florida

Susan Gordon
Randolph Middle School
Randolph, New Jersey

Becky Holditch
Deerpark Middle School
Round Rock Independ-
  ent School District
Austin, Texas

Marcelle LaRose
School No. 5, Cliffside
  Park High School
Cliffside Park, New
  Jersey

Contents in Brief

Table of Contents

What Lava Is

2

magma = hot liquid rock deep in earth
lava = magma when it erupts from volcano—
mixed with gas & steam
1,300°–2,200° F. Glows red to white.

Mask, Bassa Peoples, Liberia. Wood, pigment, bone or ivory, iron. H. 9 1/2" W. 5 3/4" D. 4 1/2", NMAfA, 88-5-1. Photograph by Franko Khoury. National Museum of African Art, Eliot Elisofon Archives, Smithsonian Institution.

▶ CHAPTER *15* **THE PREPOSITIONAL PHRASE** 418

Adjective Phrases and Adverb Phrases

▶ CHAPTER 20 **USING MODIFIERS CORRECTLY**   525

Comparison of Adjectives and Adverbs

▶ CHAPTER 21 **A GLOSSARY OF USAGE**   543

Common Usage Problems

CHAPTER 25 SPELLING 636

Improving Your Spelling

Good Spelling Habits 636

Spelling Rules 637

Words Often Confused 648

CHAPTER 26 CORRECTING COMMON ERRORS 662

Key Language Skills Review

Grammar and Usage 663

Mechanics 679

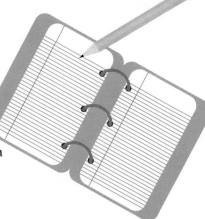

CHAPTER **29** THE LIBRARY/MEDIA CENTER   716

CHAPTER **30** THE DICTIONARY   726

Fiction

Rudolfo A. Anaya, *Tortuga*
Terry Brooks, *The Sword of Shannara*
Beverly Cleary, *Ramona Forever*
Ernest J. Gaines, "The Sky Is Gray," *Bloodline*
Edward Hoch, "Zoo," *Sudden Twists*
Julius Lester, "Brer Billy Goat Tricks Brer Wolf,"
    Further Tales of Uncle Remus
Keith Robertson, *Henry Reed, Inc.*
Cynthia Rylant, "Boar Out There," *Every Living
    Thing*
Lee Smith, *Oral History*
Eva-Lis Wuorio, "You Can't Take It with You,"
    Escape If You Can

Nonfiction

Isaac Asimov, *How Did We Find Out About Coal?*
James Axtell, "Massasoit," *The World Book
    Encyclopedia*, 1996 ed.
Beverly Cleary, *A Girl from Yamhill: A Memoir*
Joanna Cole, *A Cat's Body*
Kathy Darling, *Manatee on Location*
Margery Facklam, *Wild Animals, Gentle Women*
Harry Gersh, *Women Who Made America Great*
Don Herbert, "Banana Surprise," *Mr. Wizard's
    Supermarket Science*
Cheng Hou-tien, *Scissor Cutting for Beginners*

Tatsuo Ishimoto, *The Art of the Japanese Garden*
Patricia Lauber, *Volcano: The Eruption and
    Healing of Mount St. Helens*
Barry Lopez, *Arctic Dreams*
"Lava and Magma," *Compton's Interactive
    Encyclopedia*, 1996 ed.
Paula Morrow, "Making a Flying Fish," *Faces*
Huynh Quang Nhuong, *The Land I Lost*
Joanne Settel and Nancy Baggett, "How Can
    Water Striders Walk on Water?," *How Do
    Ants Know When You're Having a Picnic?*
"The Sinking of the *Titanic*: An Eyewitness
    Account from a Lifeboat," *The New York
    Times*
Paul Robert Walker, *Pride of Puerto Rico—The
    Life of Roberto Clemente*
Ralph Whitlock, *Rabbits and Hares*
Laurence Yep, *The Lost Garden*

Poetry

A Limerick, *Beastly Boys and Ghastly Girls*
James Berry, Riddle #11, *When I Dance*
William Blake, "A Poison Tree"
Langston Hughes, "Poem"
Edward Lear, *A Book of Nonsense*
Naomi Shihab Nye, "The Rider"
James Reeves, "The Sea"

PART ONE

WRITING

INTRODUCTION TO WRITING
The Magician's Wand

THE MAGICIAN'S WAND

James L. Kinneavy

The tall, mysterious magician strides onto the stage, silk cape swirling. Suddenly, he stretches out his arm and points a slender wand at a dirt-filled flower pot. Presto! Flowers bloom. He shakes out a silk handkerchief, rolls it up, points the magic wand. Eureka! Birds fly from the silk. His assistant disappears into a small box. The **magician** waves the magic **wand** and points to the back of the auditorium. Presto! There's the assistant!

What amazing powers magicians appear to have. But did you know that some of the world's most powerful magicians don't wear capes or perform on stage? Yet they make things happen all around you. With their magic wands they explain mysteries (even magic tricks), build whole cities, fill theaters with laughter. Astounding!

Who are these people? What are their magic wands?

Who Are These Magicians?

These magicians are writers and their magic wands are words. Their words give them the power to make things happen and appear. What things? All the things that fill your life.

With their magic wands they tell how to build a skyscraper and how to repair your bike. They give instructions for new video games and explain black holes in space. They scare you and delight you with movies and TV shows. They convince you to recycle cans and buy new jeans. They say what mattered to them when they were your age.

Take a quick look around you. These word magicians have been at work everywhere. They've created computer software, dictionaries, and newspaper comics. They've made all sorts of things appear: textbooks, billboards, magazines, the song lyrics for your favorite hits—even baseball cards!

How important are these word magicians? Just stop for a minute and imagine the world without a single written word. It's a very empty stage, isn't it? Thank goodness for the people who fill our world with the power of words!

What's the Magic?

Writers really do have a special power: the power of communication. They have something to write about (a *subject*), someone to say it to (an *audience*), and a way to say it (a *language*). You can have this power, too. Think of these magic elements as a communication triangle. Notice that language—both written and spoken—is at the center of the triangle.

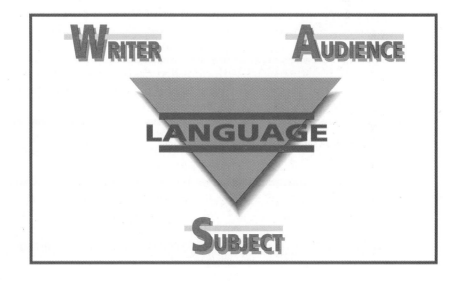

How Do Writers Write?

The Writing Process

Writers even have a magic formula for what they do. But this formula is not a trick, and it's not a secret. It's a series of steps called the *writing process.* It helps writers develop their ideas and communicate them clearly. Different writers use the process in different ways, but it's a basic formula for making things happen on paper.

Prewriting	Thinking and planning; thinking of a subject to write about, a purpose, and an audience; collecting ideas and details; making a plan for presenting ideas
Writing	Writing a first draft; putting ideas into sentences and paragraphs; following the writing plan
Evaluating and Revising	Reading the draft closely; deciding what to keep and what to take out; making changes to make the draft better
Proofreading and Publishing	Looking for and fixing mistakes; writing a final copy; finding ways to share it with an audience

Why Do Writers Write?

The Aims of Writing

Writers have four main reasons, or *aims*, for writing. They write to inform someone, to persuade someone, to express themselves, or to be creative. Sometimes a writer has only one aim, but other times a writer might combine two or more aims. Part of a writer's power comes from knowing the basic aim before starting to write.

To Inform	Writers give facts and other information, or explain something.
To Persuade	Writers also try to convince others to think or act in a certain way.
To Express Themselves	Writers sometimes just want to express their own thoughts and feelings.
To Be Creative	Writers may also write to create something new with language. They create stories, poems, songs, and plays.

Next you'll read four models about a man named Basil. Each model has a different aim. As you read, think about each writer's reason for writing.

INFORMATIVE WRITING

Local Millionaire Dies

Basil Northampton, 72, of 12 Axminster Court, died Tuesday of natural causes. He was born and lived most of his life in Surrey.

The son of working-class parents, Mr. Northampton made a fortune mining gold in the Transvaal. He was one of the ten richest men in England and was well known in financial circles for his wise investment decisions.

Mr. Northampton never married. Surviving family members include sisters Clotilda Greystone, Bernice Walton, and Maud Scarborough; brothers Cecil, Charles, and Lionel Northampton; and several nieces and nephews. At Mr. Northampton's request, family members will attend a private funeral. Distribution of his vast estate is not known.

READER'S RESPONSE

1. Why do you think newspapers print obituaries (death notices)? Do you think it's natural, or odd, to read obituaries about people you *don't* know? Why?
2. Can you think of any information to add to this obituary? Can you tell from reading it what the writer thinks and feels? Explain your answers.

EXPRESSIVE WRITING

July 1—The whole bunch of phony money-grabbers was here today for my birthday. Ha! What they'd really like to celebrate is my death day. I hope I live forever just to spite them.

That lazy wimp Percival had the nerve to ask me to buy him some fancy new car. Why should it be up to me to give him a car he'd probably just wreck? I told him to get a job and buy his own car. "You can't take it with you, you know," he whined. That's all he knows.

They think I can't hear. They go around acting all lovey-dovey even while they're saying mean things about me. They call me names and say I'm stingy. Why shouldn't I be stingy with them? Not one of them deserves even a part of what I have. Letitia's still pouting because I won't buy her a new fur coat. They never ask for anything sensible. Well, it's my fortune. I earned it. I'll decide where it goes.

Thanks to Verner, my plan is working. He's the only relative who doesn't want to bleed me dry. And he's the only one who never says I can't take it with me. We will see, won't we? Ha!

READER'S RESPONSE

1. Who do you think wrote this journal entry?
2. What is on the writer's mind? What feelings does the writer express?

PERSUASIVE WRITING

Dear Charles,

As you know, Basil has announced that he won't split up his fortune when he dies. Of course, this means that one of us will get millions and the rest of us will get nothing. This is a situation that could hurt <u>any one</u> of us very much. But I have a plan that will help us all. We should draw up an agreement stating that whoever receives the money will share it equally with the rest. Anyone interested in fairness will surely sign it.

We have all been equally kind and loyal to Basil. We deserve to be rewarded. We also have to admit that Basil has gotten a little odd in recent years. He may have decided who should get the money when he wasn't thinking clearly. I'm sure he really wants all of us to share it. Most important, there is plenty of money to go around. Everyone will benefit from sharing it, and no one will be hurt.

I will have my lawyer write the agreement. To protect your interests, you should sign it. It's completely to your advantage.

Your loving sister,
Bernice

READER'S RESPONSE

1. Someone could leave a fortune to a goldfish. Should a person's decisions in a will *always* be honored? Or can that be unfair? What do you think?
2. If you were Charles, would Bernice's letter convince you to sign the agreement? Why or why not? What do you think is Bernice's strongest reason?

You Can't $ Take It with You

by Eva-Lis Wuorio

There was no denying two facts. Uncle Basil was rich. Uncle Basil was a miser.

The family were unanimous about that. They had used up all the words as their temper and their need of ready money dictated. Gentle Aunt Clotilda, who wanted a new string of pearls because the one she had was getting old, had merely called him Scrooge Basil. Percival, having again smashed his Aston Martin for which he had not paid, had declared Uncle Basil a skinflint, a miser, tightwad, churl, and usurer with colorful adjectives added. The rest had used up all the other words in the dictionary.

"He doesn't have to be so parsimonious, that's true, with all he has," said Percival's mother. "But you shouldn't use rude words, Percival. They might get back to him."

"He can't take it with him," said Percival's sister Letitia, combing her golden hair. "I need a new fur but he said, 'Why? it's summer.' Well! He's mingy, that's what he is."

"He can't take it with him" was a phrase the family used so often it began to slip out in front of Uncle Basil as well.

"You can't take it with you, Uncle Basil," they said. "Why don't you buy a sensible house out in the country, and we could all come and visit you? Horses. A swimming pool. The lot. Think what fun you'd have, and you can certainly afford it. You can't take it with you, you know."

Uncle Basil had heard all the words they called him because he wasn't as deaf as he made out. He knew he was a mingy, stingy, penny-pinching screw, scrimp, scraper, pinchfist, hoarder, and curmudgeon (just to start with). There were other words, less gentle, he'd also heard himself called. He didn't mind. What galled him was the oft repeated warning, "You can't take it with you." After all, it was all his.

He'd gone to the Transvaal when there was still gold to be found if one knew where to look. He'd found it. They said he'd come back too old to enjoy his fortune. What did they know? He enjoyed simply having a fortune. He enjoyed also saying no to them all. They were like circus animals, he often thought, behind the bars of their thousand demands of something for nothing.

Only once had he said yes. That was when his sister asked him to take on Verner, her somewhat slow-witted eldest son. "He'll do as your secretary," his sister Maud had said. Verner didn't do at all as a secretary, but since all he wanted to be happy was to be told what to do, Uncle Basil let him stick around as an all-around handyman.

Uncle Basil lived neatly in a house very much too small for his money, the family said, in an unfashionable suburb. It was precisely like the house where he had been born. Verner looked after the small garden, fetched the papers from the corner tobacconist, and filed his nails when he had time. He had nice nails. He never said to Uncle Basil, "You can't take it with you," because it didn't occur to him.

Uncle Basil also used Verner to run messages to his man of affairs, the bank, and such, since he didn't believe either in the mails or the telephone. Verner got used to carrying thick envelopes back and forth without ever bothering to question what was in them. Uncle Basil's lawyers, accountants, and bank managers also got used to his somewhat unorthodox business methods. He did have a fortune, and he kept making money with his investments. Rich men have always been allowed their foibles.

Another foible of Uncle Basil's was that, while he still was in excellent health he had Verner drive him out to an old-fashioned carpenter shop where he had himself measured for a coffin. He wanted it roomy, he said.

The master carpenter was a dour countryman of the same generation as Uncle Basil, and he accepted the order matter-of-factly. They consulted about woods and prices, and settled on a medium-price, unlined coffin. A lined one would have cost double.

"I'll line it myself," Uncle Basil said. "Or Verner can. There's plenty of time. I don't intend to pop off tomorrow. It would give the family too much satisfaction. I like enjoying my fortune."

Then one morning, while in good humor and sound mind, he sent Verner for his lawyer. The family got to hear about this and there were in-fights, out-fights, and general quarreling while they tried to find out to whom Uncle Basil had decided to leave his money. To put them out of their misery, he said, he'd tell them the truth. He didn't like scattering money about. He liked it in a lump sum. Quit bothering him about it.

That happened a good decade before the morning his housekeeper, taking him his tea, found him peacefully asleep forever. It had been a good decade for him. The family hadn't dared to worry him, and his investments had risen steadily.

Only Percival, always pressed for money, had threatened to put arsenic in his tea but when the usual proceedings were gone through Uncle Basil was found to have died a natural death. "A happy death," said the family. "He hadn't suffered."

They began to remember loudly how nice they'd been to him and argued about who had been the nicest. It was true too. They had been attentive, the way families tend to be to rich and stubborn elderly relatives. They didn't know he'd heard all they'd said out of his hearing, as well as the flattering drivel they'd spread like soft butter on hot toast in his hearing. Everyone, recalling his own efforts to be thoroughly nice, was certain that he and only he would be the heir to the Lump Sum.

They rushed to consult the lawyer. He said that he had been instructed by Uncle Basil in sane and precise terms. The cremation was to take place immediately after the death, and they would find the coffin ready in the garden shed. Verner would know where it was.

"Nothing else?"

"Well," said the lawyer in the way lawyers have, "he left instructions for a funeral repast to be sent in from Fortnum and Mason. Everything of the best. Goose and turkey, venison and beef, oysters and lobsters, and wines of good vintage plus plenty of whiskey. He liked to think of a good send-off, curmudgeon though he was, he'd said."

The family was a little shaken by the use of the word "curmudgeon." How did Uncle Basil know about that? But they were relieved to hear that the lawyer also had an envelope, the contents of which he did not know, to read to them at the feast after the cremation.

They all bought expensive black clothes, since black was the color of that season anyway, and whoever inherited would share the wealth. That was only fair.

Only Verner said that couldn't they buy Uncle Basil a smarter coffin? The one in the garden shed was pretty tatty, since the roof leaked. But the family hardly listened to him. After all, it would only be burned, so what did it matter?

So, duly and with proper sorrow, Uncle Basil was cremated.

The family returned to the little house as the house-keeper was leaving. Uncle Basil had given her a generous amount of cash, telling her how to place it so as to have a fair income for life. In gratitude she'd spread out the Fortnum and Mason goodies, but she wasn't prepared to stay to do the dishes.

They were a little surprised, but not dismayed, to hear from Verner that the house was now in his name. Uncle Basil had also given him a small sum of cash and told him how to invest it. The family taxed him about it, but the amount was so nominal they were relieved to know Verner would be off their hands. Verner himself, though mildly missing the old man because he was used to him, was quite content with his lot. He wasn't used to much, so he didn't need much.

The storm broke when the lawyer finally opened the envelope.

There was only one line in Uncle Basil's scrawl.

"I did take it with me."

Of course there was a great to-do. What about the fortune? The millions and millions!

Yes, said the men of affairs, the accountants, and even the bank managers, who finally admitted, yes, there had been a very considerable fortune. Uncle Basil, however, had drawn large sums in cash, steadily and regularly, over the past decade. What had he done with it? That the men of affairs, the accountants, and the bank managers did not know. After all, it had been Uncle Basil's money, ergo, his affair.

Not a trace of the vast fortune ever came to light.

No one thought to ask Verner, and it didn't occur to Verner to volunteer that for quite a long time he had been lining the coffin, at Uncle Basil's behest, with thick envelopes he brought back from the banks. First he'd done a thick layer of these envelopes all around the sides and bottom of the coffin. Then, as Uncle Basil wanted, he'd tacked on blue sailcloth.

He might not be so bright in his head but he was smart with his hands.

He'd done a neat job.

READER'S RESPONSE

1. Basil's family considered him mean and stingy. How would you describe him? Why?
2. Stories with a surprise ending, or twist, are popular. Do you like them? Did you guess the ending? (If so, what clues did you use?) Besides the ending, what was your favorite part of the story?

Writing and Thinking Activities

1. Discuss these questions with two or three classmates.
   a. In which model does the writer try to convince the reader to do something? How?
   b. Which model is mostly about the writer's own thoughts and feelings?
   c. Which model gives mostly factual information about Basil?
   d. Which model tells a story? What creative ending does the story have?
2. Did you ever think about the ways you communicate? On one ordinary day of your life, jot down the ways you use language. Make a note when you write, read, speak, and listen to words. Decide what your aim is each time: to inform, persuade, express yourself, be creative—or some mixture? Then talk over your day with two or three classmates. Which aims appear most often for each of you?
3. Bring a magazine or newspaper to class. With a group, try to find examples of the four types of writing: informative, persuasive, self-expressive, and creative. Which type do you find most often? Compare your findings with another group's. Do different publications focus on different types of writing?
4. What do you think of as creative writing? Probably novels, short stories, poems, and plays. They take a lot of imagination. But can other writing be creative, too? What about Bernice's letter to Charles? Or Uncle Basil's journal entry? In what ways are Bernice and Basil being creative in those writings? Find something you've written that is not a story or poem but that you feel is creative in some way. Explain why.

1 WRITING AND THINKING

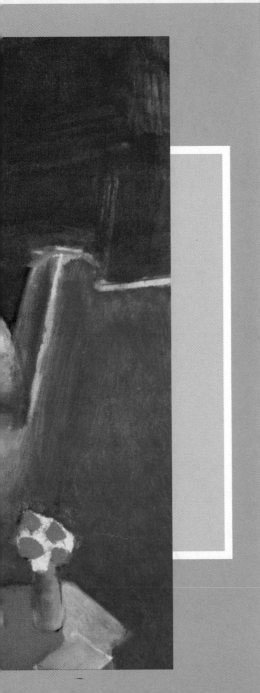

Looking at the Process

What's your reaction to writing? Maybe you're not sure. You don't *love* writing and you don't *hate* writing. It's just that sometimes the **process** of writing isn't easy.

Writing and You. Maybe it takes you forever to get an idea for writing. Or, you have great ideas but get stuck when you're choosing the right words. Well, you're not alone. Every writer faces trouble like that. It's all part of the *writing process:* the steps that you take to get from blank paper to finished paper. Did you realize that you and "real writers"—even *poets*—go through the same process?

As You Read. In her reflections about writing, Naomi Shihab Nye says that poets are "regular people." Read her poem and her thoughts about writing. Where does she get her ideas? What does she think of blank paper?

The RIDER

by

NAOMI SHIHAB NYE

A boy told me
if he rollerskated fast enough
his loneliness couldn't catch up to him,

the best reason I ever heard
for trying to be a champion.

What I wonder tonight
pedaling hard down King William Street
is if it translates to bicycles.

A victory! To leave your loneliness
panting behind you on some street corner
while you float free into a cloud of sudden azaleas,
luminous pink petals that have never felt loneliness,
no matter how slowly they fell.

"For me poetry has always been a way of paying attention to the world. We hear so many voices every day, swirling around us, and a poem makes us slow down and listen carefully to a few things we have really heard, deep inside. For me poems usually begin with 'true things'—people, experiences, quotes—but quickly ride off into that other territory of imagination, which lives alongside us as much as we will allow in a world that likes to pay too much attention to 'facts' sometimes. I have always had a slight difficulty distinguishing where the 'true' part ends and the 'made-up' part begins, because I think of dreaming and imagining as being another kind of *true*. Once I made up a song that ends, 'You tell me what's real, what I see or what I feel?', and I think that corresponds to the poems we make out of our lives."

"...a poem makes us slow down and listen carefully to a few things we have really heard, deep inside."

"Sometimes there's no one to listen to what you really might like to say at a certain moment. The paper will always listen. Also, the more you write, the paper will begin to speak back and allow you to discover new parts of your own life and other lives and feel how things connect.**"**

"Poets are explorers, pilgrims. Most of the poets I know are not in the least bit frilly. Poets are also regular people who live down the block and do simple things like wash clothes and stir soup. Sometimes students ask, 'Are you famous?', as if fame is what would make a poet happy. I prefer the idea of being invisible, traveling through the world lightly, seeing and remembering as much as I can.**"**

READER'S RESPONSE

1. Naomi Shihab Nye's poem puts into words what it feels like to ride (or run or skate or swim) *very hard.* When you're moving all-out, do you leave "loneliness panting behind"? Do you "float free"? What words would you use to describe how you feel when you do the following:

    When I ride my bike I _____.
    When I swim I _____.
    When I skate I _____.

2. Writing ideas come from "people, experiences, quotes" for Naomi Shihab Nye. Where do you get your best ideas?

3. She also says that dreaming and imagining are "another kind of *true.* " What do you think she means? In your writing, how do you use your imagination? Give an example.

4. Nye says "the paper will always listen" and after a while it will "speak back." Have you ever tried writing out your thoughts, just for yourself? Do you sometimes surprise yourself when writing—maybe coming up with a word or idea you didn't expect?

5. Do you agree that being invisible would be good for your writing? Why or why not?

LOOKING AHEAD

In this chapter you'll learn some writing techniques. They'll help you with your own writing process. And many of them are fun. You'll get to practice all parts of writing, from finding topics to publishing. As you try out your writing, remember that

- writing and thinking go together
- the writing process isn't just rules— you'll be able to make the process fit *you*

Aim—The "Why" of Writing

It may seem like there should be as many individual purposes for writing as there are people who write. But there are really just a few.

WHY PEOPLE WRITE	
To express themselves	To explore their ideas and feelings; to learn more about themselves
To share information	To tell others about things they need or want to know; to give knowledge and information to others
To persuade	To cause others to think or do something
To create literature	To write something creative or unique

Whatever people write has one of these four purposes. However, sometimes more than one of these four purposes shows up in a single piece of writing at the same time. For example, a writer may want to express himself or herself, to persuade you to think a certain way about a topic, and to create a piece of literature—all at the same time.

No matter what country or language a writer writes in, every time a writer writes, it's for at least one of these same four purposes.

Process—The "How" of Writing

Wouldn't it be great if you had an Instant Perfect Writing pen? You could sit right down and turn out a guaranteed "A" paper in five minutes. And the pen would do all the work. Unfortunately, there's no such magic writing tool. Good writing takes time and a great deal of thinking.

Most writers go through a whole process, or series of steps, shown in the following diagram. Notice that each stage in the writing process requires thinking.

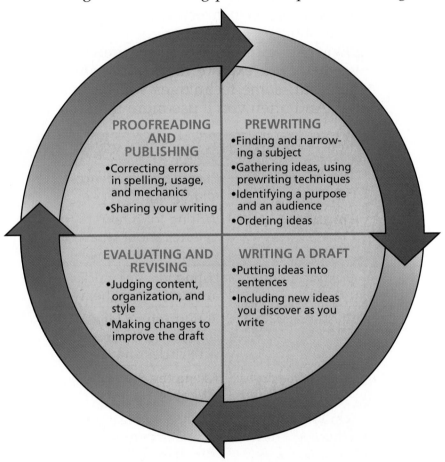

Each time you write, the process may be a little different. Sometimes you work straight through the stages, but at other times you may go back and forth between stages. Suppose you're entering a Mother's Day writing contest. You write an entry that gives three reasons why your mom should win. But when you reread it, you decide it needs examples of what your mom does and says. Then you would go back to the prewriting stage to think of examples.

Prewriting

Finding Ideas for Writing

The first problem every writer faces is "What will I write about?" Your experiences and interests make good writing topics. These six prewriting techniques will help you explore ideas for writing. As you try them out, some techniques will become your favorites. And often you'll use more than one for a paper.

PREWRITING TECHNIQUES		
Writer's Journal	Recording experiences and thoughts	Page 26
Freewriting	Writing for a few minutes about whatever comes to mind	Page 27
Brainstorming	Listing ideas as quickly as you think of them	Page 29
Clustering	Brainstorming ideas and connecting the ideas with circles and lines	Page 30
Asking Questions	Asking the *5W-How?* and "What if?" questions	Page 32
Reading and Listening	Reading and listening to find information	Page 34

Writer's Journal

Fill your *writer's journal* with experiences, feelings, and thoughts. You can have a section called "Things I Like." You can put in cartoons, quotations, song lyrics, and poems that have special meaning for you. Keep your journal in a notebook or file folder.

- Try to write every day, and date your entries.
- Write as much or as little as you want. Don't worry about spelling, punctuation, or grammar.
- Give your imagination some space. Write about dreams, daydreams, and far-out fantasies.

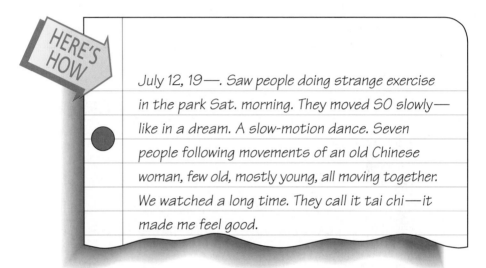

HERE'S HOW

July 12, 19——. Saw people doing strange exercise in the park Sat. morning. They moved SO slowly— like in a dream. A slow-motion dance. Seven people following movements of an old Chinese woman, few old, mostly young, all moving together. We watched a long time. They call it tai chi—it made me feel good.

EXERCISE 1 ▶ **Starting a Writer's Journal**

You can write about anything, but here's one possible idea: your early-morning routine. Do you jump right out of bed in the morning? Or do you want to keep snoozing? Are you organized or always searching for your shoes? Describe how you got ready and came to school this morning.

Freewriting

Freewriting means just that—writing freely. You begin with a word or phrase and then write whatever comes to mind. Time yourself for three to five minutes, and keep writing until the time is up.

- Write your topic first. Then write whatever the topic makes you think of.
- Don't stop or pause. If you can't think of anything to write, keep writing the same word or phrase until something pops into your head.
- Don't worry about spelling, punctuation, or complete sentences.

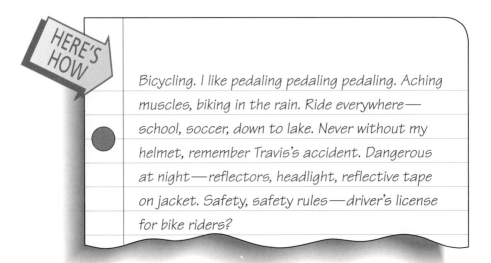

HERE'S HOW

Bicycling. I like pedaling pedaling pedaling. Aching muscles, biking in the rain. Ride everywhere—school, soccer, down to lake. Never without my helmet, remember Travis's accident. Dangerous at night—reflectors, headlight, reflective tape on jacket. Safety, safety rules—driver's license for bike riders?

In *focused freewriting* (or *looping*), you begin with a word or phrase from freewriting you've already done. You might choose "biking in the rain," for instance, and do three minutes of freewriting on this limited topic.

EXERCISE 2 ▶ **Using Freewriting**

Think of six activities you really like to participate in or watch. (Consider bicycling, dancing, listening to music, skating, reading, or playing ball.) Choose one activity, and freewrite for three minutes about it.

Brainstorming

When you **brainstorm**, your thoughts fly out in all directions. You start with a subject. Then you quickly list everything the subject makes you think of. You can brainstorm alone, but it's also fun to brainstorm ideas with a group.

- Write any subject at the top of a piece of paper or on a chalkboard.
- Write down every idea that occurs to you. If you're brainstorming in a group, one person should record the ideas.
- Don't stop to judge what's listed.
- Don't stop until you run out of ideas.

Here are some brainstorming notes on the subject "astronauts." Notice the silly ideas. When you're brainstorming, it's OK to list silly ideas. You can always cross them off your list later.

Astronauts	
Sally Ride	space explorers
Neil Armstrong	floating without gravity
walking on the moon	cramped space, food in
space shuttle	tubes
spacesuits, diving suits	Challenger explosion
Astroturf	man in the moon
astrodome	woman in the moon
"lunar rover" vehicles	

EXERCISE 3 ▶ **Using Brainstorming**

Brainstorming is like flipping through the files in your brain to see what's stored there. With two or three classmates, choose one of the following subjects or one of your own. Brainstorm as fast as you can and have someone record every idea.

1. movies
2. musical groups
3. brothers and sisters
4. summer vacations
5. computer games
6. scary experiences

Clustering

Clustering is sometimes called *mapping* or *webbing* (because the diagram looks like a spider web). It's a visual kind of brainstorming.

- Write your subject in the center of your paper, and then circle it.
- Around the subject, write related ideas that you think of. Circle these, and draw lines to connect them with the subject or with each other.
- Keep going. Write new ideas, circle them, and draw lines to show connections.

Here's a cluster diagram on the topic of Hispanic grocery stores, or *bodegas.*

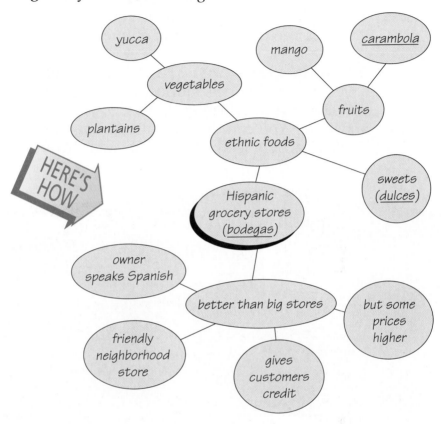

EXERCISE 4 ▶ **Using Clustering**

See if you can make a cluster diagram that has enough ideas and connections to look like a spider web. First, select a subject. You might use one of the subjects that were listed for Exercise 3 (page 30) but that you didn't use for that activity. You could also think of a subject of your own that you could use to develop ideas and connections.

COMPUTER NOTE: Create tables or cluster diagrams within your word-processing program, and use them to organize your prewriting notes.

Asking Questions

Do you ever talk to yourself? Do you ever answer? You can find facts and ideas for writing by asking yourself two different kinds of questions.

5W-How?* Questions.**   To gather information when they write their news stories, reporters often ask the ***5W-How? questions: *Who? What? Where? When? Why?* and *How?* You can do the same for any topic.

Here are some *5W-How?* questions about the photographs below.

HERE'S HOW		
WHO?	<u>Who</u> lived in these cliff dwellings?
WHAT?	<u>What</u> was their daily life like?
WHERE?	<u>Where</u> are cliff dwellings found?
WHEN?	<u>When</u> did people live in cliff dwellings? <u>When</u> did they abandon their villages?
WHY?	<u>Why</u> did they build their villages on or into cliffs? <u>Why</u> did they leave their villages?
HOW?	<u>How</u> did they get food and water?

"What if?" Questions.   What if you could be any-one you wanted to be for a day? What if you could travel through time into the future or past? What if you happened to find a diamond ring on the seat beside you in a movie theater or on a city bus? Asking questions like these can help you think of creative writing ideas.

- *What if I could change one thing in my life?* (What if I could make myself invisible? What if I had a car and a driver's license?)
- *What if some everyday thing did not exist?* (What if the earth had no moon? What if radios hadn't been invented?)
- *What if I could change one thing about the world?* (What if everyone in the whole world had enough food and a home? What if animals could really talk with people?)

EXERCISE 5 ▶   **Asking *5W-How?* Questions**

You've been chosen to interview an athlete for an article for the school paper. Choose a real athlete, and write some *5W-How?* questions you would ask him or her.

EXERCISE 6 ▶   **Asking "What if?" Questions**

You and a partner are writing a short story for a magazine contest. Here's your idea: Two friends are helping a neighborhood group with a project to clean up a vacant lot. Write four "What if?" questions to develop this story idea.

EXAMPLES   *What if the friends found a box full of money?*
What if they argued about what to do with the money?

Reading and Listening

Suppose you need to write about what it was like for immigrants to arrive at Ellis Island, New York, in the 1890s. How can you find out? For a topic like this, you'll *read* or *listen* to gather information.

Reading with a Focus.   When you look for information in books, magazines, and newspapers:

- Find your topic in a book's table of contents or index. Turn to the pages listed.
- Don't read every word. Skim pages quickly, looking for your topic.
- When you find information on your topic, slow down and read carefully.
- Take notes on main ideas and important details.

E X E R C I S E 7 ▶ **Reading with a Focus**

Do you recognize any of these names: Mauna Loa, Mount Saint Helens, Mount Fuji, Krakatau, Mount Vesuvius, Tambora, Mount Pelée, Nevado del Ruiz? If you lived near one, you would—they're all volcanoes. Choose one volcano, and look it up in an encyclopedia, almanac, or other source. Find and write down answers to these questions.

1. Where is the volcano?
2. How tall is it?
3. When did it last erupt?
4. What danger resulted from the last eruption?

Peanuts reprinted by permission of United Feature Syndicate, Inc.

Listening with a Focus. You can find information by listening to radio and TV programs, audiotapes, and videotapes. You may even be able to interview someone who knows something about your topic. Before you listen, write out some questions about your topic. Then listen for answers to your questions and take notes.

☞ REFERENCE NOTE: For more information on listening, see pages 706–711. See pages 708–709 for more about interviewing.

CRITICAL THINKING
Observing Details

If you watch and listen carefully, you can collect information from educational programs and videotapes. A videotape can show you details you can't learn from a book. For example, if you watch a videotape on alligators, you can see how they swim and listen to the sounds they make.

CRITICAL THINKING EXERCISE:
Watching and Listening for Details

With a partner, decide on an educational TV show you are both going to watch this week—a program about nature, science, or history. As you watch and listen, take notes on important details. Write at least five new facts you learned. Then compare your notes with your partner's.

 *Prewriting*

Thinking About Purpose and Audience

What do you want your writing to *do*? If you don't have a clear idea of the *purpose* for your writing, it may not have the effect you want. Here are the basic writing purposes and some forms you might use.

MAIN PURPOSE	FORMS OF WRITING
To express yourself	Journal entry, letter, personal essay
To be creative	Short story, poem, play
To explain, inform, or explore	Science or history report, news story, biography
To persuade	Persuasive composition, letter to the editor, advertisement

The readers of your writing—your *audience*—are also important to think about. When you express your ideas on a specific topic to your friends at school, you probably talk differently than you do when you're talking to your parents about the same topic. Most of us do this automatically, adjusting what we're saying to fit whoever we're talking to.

You'll need to think about your audience when you're writing, too. For example, a letter you might write to your six-year-old cousin would use different vocabulary than a letter you might write to a future supervisor. The topics would also differ. When you write, ask yourself these questions about your audience:

- What do my readers already know about the topic? What will I need to explain?
- What will interest them?
- What kinds of words should I use?

EXERCISE 8 ▸ **Thinking About Purpose and Audience**

You're writing a factual report on Chamizal National Memorial in El Paso, Texas. It will be part of a travel guidebook for your school library. Which sentences are appropriate for your report? Which ones aren't?

1. The park honors the Chamizal Treaty of 1963.
2. The treaty settled a 99-year-old boundary dispute between the United States and Mexico.
3. Two years ago my uncle went to the Border Folk Festival in Chamizal. He met his wife-to-be there.
4. More than 225 different fine arts and folk art programs are held in Chamizal each year.
5. My favorite Mexican foods are tacos and burritos.

 *Prewriting*

Arranging Ideas

If you were writing the report on Chamizal National Memorial, what would you discuss first? As soon as you had gathered some details and ideas, you would need to choose what order to put them in. Deciding what will come first, second, and third in your paper is the next writing step.

Types of Order

Here are four common ways that you can arrange information. The chart below shows you each of these four ways to arrange ideas and tells you some of the kinds of writing that use each method.

ARRANGING IDEAS		
TYPE OF ORDER	DEFINITION	EXAMPLES
Chronological Order	Describes events in the order they happen	Story, narrative poem, "how-to" paper
Spatial Order	Describes details according to their location (near to far, left to right, top to bottom, and so on)	Description of place, room, object
Order of Importance	Gives details from least to most important, or the reverse	Persuasive writing, description, book report
Logical Order	Groups related details together	Definition, comparison and contrast

CRITICAL THINKING

Arranging Ideas

How do you choose an order for your writing? Let your subject, purpose, and details guide you.

Suppose you're writing about Sacagawea, the Shoshone woman who guided the Lewis and Clark expedition. Your purpose is to inform your classmates about her life. It's natural to tell about a person's life from birth to death, so you arrange your details in *chronological order,* the order that they happened.

But suppose your purpose is to explain how Sacagawea helped the expedition. In that case, you might use *order of importance.* First, you could discuss the most important thing she did. Then you could tell the next most important, and so on.

 CRITICAL THINKING EXERCISE:
Deciding How to Arrange Information

Study the writing examples below. Think about each topic, purpose, and audience. Next, imagine the kinds of details you'd probably include. Last, use the chart on page 39 to decide the order you'd use.

1. You are writing a letter to the editor of your local paper. You give three reasons why your city should have a new park with a zoo and recreational facilities.
2. You're writing a letter to a friend. You describe the stage setting you helped create for a school skit.
3. In your journal, you're writing about how you spent your birthday.
4. For a social studies report, you're comparing and contrasting two women governors.

Using Visuals

"A picture is worth a thousand words," the old saying goes. And sometimes a chart or diagram can even help you see the meaning of your own notes better.

Charts. A *chart* groups together details that are alike in some way. Look at your notes, and decide which details belong together. Write a heading for each group. Here's an example.

HERE'S HOW

Inuit Stone Prints		
History	How They're Made	What They Show
Cape Dorset, Canada Long history of sculpture and carving, no experience with printing In 1950s taught about printing by James Houston	Carve slabs of native stone. Ink the surface. Press paper against stone.	Scenes of daily life Animals Dreams and visions Myths

Shoroshiluto/Reproduced with permission of West Baffin Eskimo Co-Operative Ltd., Cape Dorset, NWT.

Venn Diagrams.   A *Venn diagram* uses circles to show how two subjects are alike (comparison) and different (contrast). Each subject has its own circle, but the circles overlap. In the overlapping part, you write details that are the same for both subjects. In the parts that don't overlap, you write details that make these subjects different.

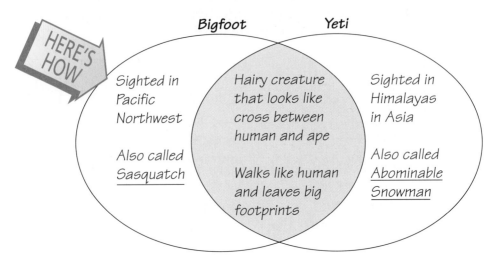

HERE'S HOW

Bigfoot   Yeti

Sighted in Pacific Northwest

Also called Sasquatch

Hairy creature that looks like cross between human and ape

Walks like human and leaves big footprints

Sighted in Himalayas in Asia

Also called Abominable Snowman

EXERCISE 9 ▶ **Making a Chart**

Study the following notes about "Nessie," a mysterious monster. Nessie supposedly lives in Loch Ness, a deep lake in northern Scotland. Organize the following notes under these two headings: Description and Sightings.

Has long neck and small head

First sighting in A.D. 565; hundreds of
    sightings since

Sonar investigations—large, moving object in
    Loch Ness

One or two humps on its back

1960 film shows dark shape moving in lake

About 30 feet long

1970s—researchers took photographs

Writing a First Draft

Remember the magic Instant Perfect Writing pen that doesn't exist? At this stage in the writing process, any old pen, pencil, typewriter, or word processor will do. That's because you already have everything you need to write your first draft.

Some people write quickly, zapping their notes into sentences. Others write more slowly, laboring over each sentence. Whatever works for you is fine.

- Follow your prewriting plans as you write.
- If you come up with new ideas, include them.
- Don't worry about spelling and grammar; you'll correct mistakes later. Just keep writing.

WRITING NOTE Beginning writers sometimes try to use difficult-sounding words and long sentences. That's a mistake. Your writing should sound like your own voice—not someone else's. Try to express your ideas clearly, simply, and naturally.

On the next page is a first draft of a paragraph from a paper about Thurgood Marshall, the first African American Supreme Court Justice. The paragraph tells a family story about Justice Marshall's grandmother. You'll see that the paragraph isn't perfect. The writer will make changes later.

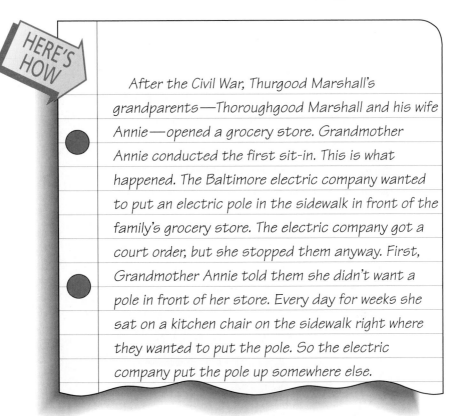

After the Civil War, Thurgood Marshall's grandparents—Thoroughgood Marshall and his wife Annie—opened a grocery store. Grandmother Annie conducted the first sit-in. This is what happened. The Baltimore electric company wanted to put an electric pole in the sidewalk in front of the family's grocery store. The electric company got a court order, but she stopped them anyway. First, Grandmother Annie told them she didn't want a pole in front of her store. Every day for weeks she sat on a kitchen chair on the sidewalk right where they wanted to put the pole. So the electric company put the pole up somewhere else.

CRITICAL THINKING
Synthesizing Ideas

Synthesizing means creating something new from separate parts. Musicians can use an electronic synthesizer to put sounds together and create music. Songs, salads, patchwork quilts, paragraphs—all these are new wholes made from separate parts. To synthesize a paragraph:

- Look over your prewriting notes. Think about your main idea, and then write a sentence that states this main idea.

- Choose the details that best support your main idea. List the details in an order that makes sense to you.
- Write a draft of the paragraph. Express your ideas as clearly and naturally as you can.

CRITICAL THINKING EXERCISE:
Writing a First Draft

Draft a paragraph based on these prewriting notes about the albatross, the largest of all sea birds. Make your topic "the albatross's flying abilities." You won't use all the information.

Lives on oceans; goes to land to lay single egg

Eats squid and small sea creatures; drinks salt water

Long flights—months—with brief rests

Wingspan of six to eleven feet

Glides on nearly constant air currents

Alternates flapping and gliding

Glides for hours without flapping its wings

Zigzags against wind currents to reach a certain spot

Can fly hundreds of miles

Evaluating and Revising

Until they figure out what's wrong, doctors can't cure patients and mechanics can't repair cars. The same is true for writing. Before you can improve your first draft, you have to decide what needs fixing.

Evaluating

Evaluating means judging. You evaluate writing by judging what's good and what needs improving. You'll evaluate your own writing and that of your classmates.

Self-Evaluation.   Try these techniques whenever you evaluate your own writing.

- Take some time. Set the draft aside for a day or two. You'll be able to see it from a fresh viewpoint.
- Read and reread. Read your paper carefully more than once. Focus on both ideas and wording.
- Read your paper aloud. Listen for awkward or unclear spots.

Peer Evaluation. A peer is someone who is your equal. In this case, it's your classmate. When you do peer evaluation, you trade papers with one of your classmates. You read the paper carefully and take notes about it. Then you tell your classmate what you think was good about the paper and what parts could be improved.

When you do peer evaluation, you'll have two roles. You'll be a writer (listening to your classmate's evaluations of your writing). And you'll also be a reader (evaluating your classmate's writing).

GUIDELINES FOR PEER EVALUATION

Tips for the Writer

1. List some questions for the reader. Ask about parts of your paper that you feel especially unsure about.
2. Take your classmate's comments seriously, but don't get hurt feelings. Everyone's writing can be improved.

Tips for the Reader

1. First, remember to tell the writer what's good about the paper.
2. Make suggestions and criticisms politely. Asking questions is usually a good way. For example, you might say, "Can you give a specific example here?"
3. Suggest something specific the writer can do to improve the paper.

Revising

Once you figure out what needs fixing, do it. You'll use these four basic revision techniques: *adding, cutting, replacing,* and *reordering.*

On the following page are some general guidelines that fit all types of writing.

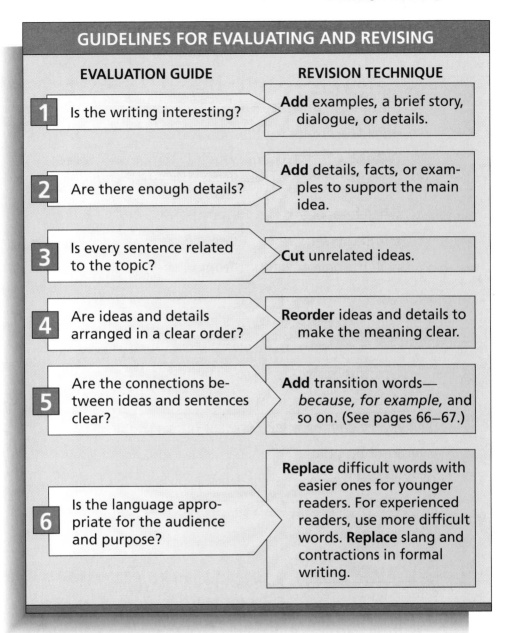

GUIDELINES FOR EVALUATING AND REVISING

EVALUATION GUIDE	REVISION TECHNIQUE
1 Is the writing interesting?	**Add** examples, a brief story, dialogue, or details.
2 Are there enough details?	**Add** details, facts, or examples to support the main idea.
3 Is every sentence related to the topic?	**Cut** unrelated ideas.
4 Are ideas and details arranged in a clear order?	**Reorder** ideas and details to make the meaning clear.
5 Are the connections between ideas and sentences clear?	**Add** transition words—*because, for example*, and so on. (See pages 66–67.)
6 Is the language appropriate for the audience and purpose?	**Replace** difficult words with easier ones for younger readers. For experienced readers, use more difficult words. **Replace** slang and contractions in formal writing.

Now take another look at the draft paragraph about Thurgood Marshall's grandmother. It's been revised using the four revision techniques. To understand what the handwritten marks mean, see the chart of proofreading and revising symbols on page 54. To understand why the writer made the changes, use the guidelines in the chart on page 49.

After the Civil War, Thurgood

Marshall's grandparents—Thorough-

good Marshall and his wife Annie—

opened a grocery store. (in Baltimore) (Justice Marshall says that) Grandmother   **add/add**

Annie conducted the first (successful) sit-in (in Maryland). This is ~~what happened.~~   **add/add/cut**

The Baltimore electric   **cut/cut**

company wanted to put an electric

pole in the sidewalk in front of the

family's grocery store. The electric

company got a court order, but

Annie Marshall wouldn't be stopped.
~~she stopped them anyway. First,~~   **replace/cut**

Grandmother Annie told them she   **reorder**

didn't want a pole in front of her store.

Every day for weeks she sat on a

kitchen chair on the sidewalk right

where they wanted to put the pole. ~~So~~   **cut**

the electric company (finally gave up and) put the pole ~~up~~   **add/cut**

somewhere else.

EXERCISE 10 ▶ **Evaluating and Revising a Paragraph**

With a partner, evaluate the paragraphs you wrote about the albatross (page 46). Write some evaluation comments for each other. (Review the guidelines on page 48.) Take turns telling the comments, then discuss them. Later, evaluate your paragraph on your own. Using your partner's suggestions along with your ideas, revise your paragraph.

Proofreading and Publishing

After you've revised your paper, it's time to give your writing its finishing touches. Then you can share it with an audience.

Proofreading

Give yourself a break. A little time away from your writing usually makes it easier to come back to it later with fresh eyes. Then you can proofread your paper. When you proofread, you read your paper carefully to spot any mistakes in spelling, grammar, usage, and punctuation.

The secret of proofreading is to slow your reading down to a crawl. Focus on one line at a time, and read it word by word. If you find something that you think looks wrong, check it in a dictionary or grammar handbook (see pages 336–691). Double-check your proofreading by exchanging papers with a classmate.

GUIDELINES FOR PROOFREADING

1. Is every sentence a complete sentence? (See pages 303–305.)
2. Does every sentence begin with a capital letter and end with the correct punctuation mark? (See pages 564–565 and 587–591.)
3. Do singular subjects have singular verbs? And do all plural subjects have plural verbs? (See pages 456–470.)
4. Are verb forms and tenses used correctly? (See pages 476–495.)
5. Are the forms of personal pronouns used correctly? (See pages 503–520.)
6. Are all words spelled correctly? (See pages 636–661.)

EXERCISE 11 ▶ Proofreading a Paragraph

What's wrong with this paragraph? Work with a partner to find and correct five mistakes. Use a dictionary and the **Handbook** on pages 336–691.

> Have you ever thought of makeing a mobile for your room? a mobile is made of hanging shapes that move in a current of air. You can use any shape, though many people likes fish, birds, butterflys, or other animal shapes. As the shapes move, they come close and then pass each other, The shapes seem to dance in a wobbly sort of way.

Publishing

Now you're ready to publish or share your writing. Here are a few of the many ways to find an audience.

- Start a class newspaper with news, brief reports, and creative writing. It can be handwritten, typed, or done on a computer.
- Post class writing on a bulletin board in the classroom or in the hall. Change the writing every week.
- Create a class booklet with one piece of writing from each student. Lend your book to other classes and the school library.

When you publish your writing, it should look good. Be sure to proofread your final copy.

CRITICAL THINKING

Reflecting on Your Writing

A **portfolio** is a collection of your writing. During the year, you do many different kinds of writing, such as stories, essays, and reports. Which papers will you add to your portfolio? Consider adding papers with weaknesses as well as strengths. These papers may reflect your progress.

When you keep a paper, write the date on it. Dating helps both your teacher and you track your progress. You'll be asked to reflect on each piece of writing in your portfolio. You reflect in two ways. First, you analyze your writing by breaking it down into stages. How did you choose a topic? What changes did you make during revision? Then, you evaluate each piece of writing by forming your own judgments. How pleased are you with your paper? What changes would you make next time? Write your reflections, and include them in your portfolio.

CRITICAL THINKING EXERCISE:
Reflecting on Your Writing

Think about the writing you have done recently. If you have saved some of your papers, reread them now. Then, reflect on your writing by answering these questions.

1. Which part of the writing process is most helpful for you? least helpful? Why?
2. Which paper are you least pleased with? Suppose you write that kind of paper again. What would you do differently?
3. What did you discover about yourself by writing these papers?

GUIDELINES FOR THE FORM OF A PAPER

1. Use only one side of a sheet of paper. Write in blue or black ink, or type. Double-space if you type.
2. Leave margins of about one inch at the top, sides, and bottom of each page.
3. Include your name, the date, your class, and the title of your paper. Your teacher will tell you where to place this information.
4. Indent the first line of each paragraph.

EXERCISE 12 ▶ **Publishing Your Writing**

Brainstorm ideas for sharing or publishing your writing. Research information (addresses, requirements, deadlines) about contests or magazines that publish student writing.

SYMBOLS FOR REVISING AND PROOFREADING

SYMBOL	EXAMPLE	MEANING OF SYMBOL
≡	spanish class	Capitalize a lowercase letter.
/	my older Brother	Use lowercase letter.
∧	by ^the front door	Add a word, letter, or punctuation mark.
ℐ	"Hi," he ~~he~~ said.	Leave out a word, letter, or punctuation mark.
∩	eas|il|y	Change the order of the letters or words.
¶	¶The street was empty.	Begin a new paragraph.
⊙	Mrs⊙Martinez	Add a period.
⋏	Yes∧I'll go with you.	Add a comma.

MAKING CONNECTIONS

Spell-Checking with a Computer

Every writer makes mistakes. Good writers take time to check for mistakes and to correct them. One way to check for misspelled words in a draft is to look up in a dictionary every word you aren't sure you've spelled correctly. This can take a lot of time.

A faster way to find errors is to proofread using a spell-checker. A spell-checker is a computer program, or a part of a program, that quickly searches a document for misspelled words and then suggests replacements for them. The best reason to use a spell-checker is that it speeds up proofreading.

Another reason to use a spell-checker is that it may catch mistakes you wouldn't have caught on your own. When you use a dictionary to check spelling, you don't look up every word you've written. You skip words that you're pretty sure you spelled correctly. Sometimes, though, a word you skip may actually be misspelled. The spell-checker will catch the error because it checks every word, including ones you might skip.

Remember, though, that a spell-checker cannot tell the difference between words that sound the same but are spelled differently. If you use the word *their* in a draft when you meant to use the word *there*, your spell-checker won't catch your error.

Use a computer to create a "Spelling Practice List" file, and add to it the words your spell-checker seems to catch often. If you don't have access to a computer, look through some catalogs or computer magazines for information on software that checks spelling. Give your class a summary of the information you find.

2 LEARNING ABOUT PARAGRAPHS

Looking at the Parts

Have you flown a kite? A kite has several **parts.** It has a frame and paper stretched over it. It also has some kind of a tail. But kites aren't all alike. Some are big, and some are small. Some have fancy designs, and others don't.

Paragraphs are like kites. They may have the same parts but be very different. Some are long, and some are short. Some can stand alone, and others can't.

Writing and You. Writers usually connect paragraphs together in a story, an article, a letter, or even a book. When you write, you may use paragraphs this way, also. Do you think about paragraphs as you read and write?

As You Read. The following paragraphs are about a volcano named Mount Saint Helens. As you read, look for different kinds of paragraphs.

Dragon puzzle © Stave Puzzles Inc., Norwich, Vt. Photo © 1990 Richard Howard.

FROM

VOLCANO

By Patricia Lauber

Mount Saint Helens erupted on May 18, 1980. These paragraphs describe the mountain as it appeared a few months later.

In early summer of 1980 the north side of Mount St. Helens looked like the surface of the moon—gray and lifeless. The slopes were buried under mud, ground-up rock, pumice, and bits of trees. Ash covered everything with a thick crust. The eruption had set off thunderstorms that wet the falling ash. The ash became goo that hardened into a crust. The slopes looked like a place where nothing could be alive or ever live again. Yet life was there.

With the coming of warm weather, touches of green appeared among the grays and browns. They were the green of plants that had survived the force and heat of the eruption.

Some plants had still been buried under the snows of winter on May 18 [when the volcano had erupted].

Huckleberry and trillium sprang up among the fallen forest trees. So did young silver firs and mountain hemlocks.

In other places, where the snow had melted, the blast swept away the parts of plants that were aboveground. But roots, bulbs, and stems remained alive underground. They sprouted, and hardy shoots pushed up through the pumice and ash. Among these was fireweed, one of the first plants to appear after a fire.

A few plants were even growing in blocks of soil that had been lifted from one place and dropped in another.

"The slopes looked like a place where nothing could be alive or ever live again. Yet life was there."

READER'S RESPONSE

1. Would you like to visit Mount Saint Helens? Explain why or why not.
2. The author describes Mount Saint Helens after the volcano erupted. What is a place, person, or object that you've seen and remember well? Write several sentences about it in your journal.

WRITER'S CRAFT

3. The first paragraph has seven sentences in it. How many sentences does the shortest paragraph have?
4. These few paragraphs come from a book. What do you think the rest of the book is about?
5. Some paragraphs can be as short as one or two words. Look for some really short paragraphs in stories or magazine articles. How do they work?

LOOKING AHEAD

In this chapter, you'll learn what paragraphs do and how they're put together. As you work, keep in mind that a paragraph

- is usually part of a longer piece of writing
- usually has a main idea
- may have supporting details to explain or prove the main idea
- may be developed in one of four basic ways

The Parts of a Paragraph

Paragraphs aren't all alike, but many of them have the same three parts. One part is the *main idea.* This is the big idea of the paragraph. Most paragraphs have a main idea. The main idea may be in a *topic sentence,* which is the second part of some paragraphs. A third part consists of the *supporting sentences.* These sentences add details about the main idea. Here's an example of a paragraph with all three parts.

Topic sentence
Main idea
Supporting sentences

Chimpanzees are very social animals. They enjoy being with each other. When they meet, they greet each other with kisses, hugs, pats on the back, and hand-holding. Grooming—the gentle parting of the hair, combing, and touching—is an important social function. It is peaceful, relaxing, friendly physical contact.

Margery Facklam, *Wild Animals, Gentle Women*

The Topic Sentence

When a paragraph has a topic sentence, it is often the first or second sentence. But not always. Sometimes it comes in the middle or at the end. In the following paragraph, the topic sentence comes at the end. Notice how the other sentences all support the main idea in the topic sentence.

He thought he had failed in his life's work. Others agreed with him. He died poor and bitterly disliked. To us today, this rejection seems strange. He had helped to free five South American countries from Spanish rule. He had won major victories on the battlefield. He was anything but a failure. Over time, people began to accept the truth. Monuments were built to honor him. People started to celebrate his birthday. Today, Simón Bolívar is regarded as one of Latin America's greatest heroes.

A topic sentence helps a writer stick to the topic. But remember that not all paragraphs have topic sentences. You'll see many good paragraphs that don't. Often a paragraph has a main idea but no topic sentence. The details all fit together, however, and support, or prove, the main idea.

EXERCISE 1 ▶ **Identifying Main Ideas and Topic Sentences**

How good are you at identifying main ideas and topic sentences? Each of the following paragraphs has one main idea. Read each paragraph, and try to identify its main idea. If the paragraph has a topic sentence, tell what it is. If there isn't a topic sentence, state the main idea in your own words.

1.   Whenever cats are together, they have ways of communicating with each other. They make faces to express feelings like anger, fear, and contentment. They also use body language. Switching the tail can mean "I am annoyed." Holding the tail straight up means "I am happy and friendly." Cats also "talk" to each other with sounds. They meow, hiss, growl, chirp. These noises can mean many things, from "hello" to "don't come any closer."

Joanna Cole, *A Cat's Body*

2.   It was a warm tropical evening in Puerto Rico. Roberto Clemente was playing with a group of boys on a muddy field in Barrio San Antón. It was nothing at all like the great stadium in San Juan. There were bumps and puddles, and the outfield was full of trees. The bat in Roberto's hand was a thick stick cut from the branch of a guava tree. The bases were old coffee sacks. The ball was a tightly-knotted bunch of rags.

Paul Robert Walker, *Pride of Puerto Rico*

3.   Some types of wood gave more light than others did. There were the kinds that contained soft, gummy substances called *resin*. Such wood burned with a brighter flame that made it possible to see at night. The wood of certain evergreen trees such as pines and cedars burned brightly for this reason and such wood was used as torches.

Isaac Asimov, *How Did We Find Out About Coal?*

Supporting Sentences

Supporting sentences have details that support, or prove, the main idea. These may be facts, examples, or other kinds of details. In the following paragraph, notice how the supporting sentences reinforce the main idea. This idea is stated in the first sentence.

Topic sentence

Details

Example/Facts

Icebergs come in different shapes and sizes. An iceberg may be domed, with a rounded top like that of an old mountain. It may be blocky, a great squared slab of floating ice. Or it may be tabular, almost like a tombstone on its side adrift at sea. Some icebergs are small, but many are huge. In 1956, a naval icebreaker in the Antarctic measured a tabular iceberg at about 12,500 square miles. That's two and a half times the size of the state of Connecticut.

EXERCISE 2 ▶ **Collecting Details**

Perhaps you collect details about the life of your favorite movie or TV star. In the same way, you can collect details about your main idea for a paragraph. Choose one of the following main ideas. Then make a list of three or four details that support it.

EXAMPLE *Main Idea:* *Stamp collecting is a useful hobby.*
Details: *(1) It makes geography interesting. (2) Stamps teach you something about history. (3) The value of your stamps may go up in time.*

1. Skateboarding (or another sport) requires skill.
2. My room is always messy.
3. Snakes (or spiders, worms, lightning storms) are one thing I can't stand.

Words That Connect Ideas. A good paragraph makes sense. When you read it, you see that all its details relate to the main idea.

Sometimes you can easily tell how ideas are related. In a story, for example, one event usually follows another. This order helps you understand what happens in the story.

But many times, special words help to show how ideas are related. These words are called *transitional words and phrases.* They are *connectors.* They may connect one idea to another, one sentence to another, or one paragraph to another.

TRANSITIONAL WORDS AND PHRASES		
Showing Likenesses	Showing Differences	Showing Causes and Effects
also like and too another in addition	although but however instead	as a result because since so
Showing Time	Showing Place	Showing Importance
after next before second finally then first when	above down across into around there behind under	first last mainly most important

The following paragraph is about Babe Didrikson Zaharias, a great athlete. In 1932, she was the entire winning track "team" for an insurance company in Dallas, Texas. Notice how transitional words connect ideas in this paragraph.

Even as they entered the stadium, the loud-speakers were calling the teams for the parade onto the field. <u>When</u> the Illinois Women's Athletic Club was called, twenty-two athletes marched forward. A <u>second</u> club fielded fifteen girls, <u>another</u> twelve. All in all there were more than 200 female athletes on the field. <u>Then</u> they called the team of the Employers' Casualty Insurance Company of Dallas, Texas. <u>And</u> one lonely girl marched bravely down the field. The crowd roared.

Harry Gersh, *Women Who Made America Great*

| E X E R C I S E 3 ▶ | **Identifying Transitions** |

How do you bake a potato? Why might a polar bear's fur look green? The transition words in the following paragraphs can help you answer those questions. Find and list the transitions in each of the paragraphs. Use the chart on page 66 to help you.

1.   It's easy to bake a potato. First, preheat the oven to 425° F. Then, choose a potato that's the right type for baking, such as an Idaho. Next, wash and scrub it thoroughly. Dry the potato, and grease it lightly with butter. Puncture the skin with a fork to allow steam to escape while baking. Bake the potato for approximately one hour. When it's done, serve it with a topping. For a healthful dish, use yogurt or cottage cheese.

2.   A polar bear's fur looks white, but it isn't. Instead, each hair is a transparent tube. When the hairs are clear, the bear appears to be white. But sometimes tiny green plants called algae grow inside the hairs. As a result, the bear looks green.

Ways to Develop Paragraphs

You often use the same parts (main idea, topic sentence, and supporting sentences) in writing paragraphs. But you don't develop all paragraphs the same way. For example, the way you develop paragraphs for your teachers might differ from the way you will develop your writing in the workplace. Here are four ways to develop a paragraph.

WAYS TO DEVELOP PARAGRAPHS	
Description	Looking at details about a person, place, or thing
Narration	Looking at changes over time in a person, place, or thing
Comparison/ Contrast	Finding likenesses and differences between people, places, or things
Evaluation	Judging the value of someone or something

Description

What does your street look like when it rains or snows? What's your lunch like today?

When you want to tell what something is like or looks like, you use description. *Description* calls for details. Sometimes they are *sensory details*. *Sensory details* come from your five senses: sight, hearing, smell, taste, touch. You may describe how the bakery smells or how a peach tastes.

Details for a description are often arranged in spatial order. With *spatial order,* you organize details by their location. To describe a scene, for example, you might give details as your eyes move from left to right or right to left. You might also arrange details from far away to close up or from close up to far away.

The description in the next paragraph begins in the mountains and moves down to the lowlands.

Mountains dominate the landscape. Down their slopes rush many swift streams and rivers, cascading in waterfalls, pausing in hillside pools and small lakes. The mountains are not only forested, they are rocky. In the high mountains are stands of fir, larch, hemlock, spruce—also azaleas, dwarf bamboo, dwarf birch and dwarf pine. On the lower slopes grow oak, elm, magnolia, also linden, birch, cherry—all trees familiar to Americans although the species differ from the native species of the United States. In the lowlands are the gardener's favorites—black pine and red pine and the tall bamboos. And always, not far away, is the sea.

Tatsuo Ishimoto, *The Art of the Japanese Garden*

EXERCISE 4 ▶ Using Description to Develop Paragraphs

How would you describe the lizard that slithers across your driveway? Choose one of the following subjects. Then list the details you would use to describe it. Try to use sensory details of sight, sound, smell, taste, and touch. Arrange the details in spatial order.

1. what you think the planet Mars is like
2. one person or creature in your favorite video game
3. a shopping mall when it's very busy
4. a city (or country) street in the middle of the day
5. your dirty tennis shoes

Narration

What happens to the characters in your favorite movie? How does an eagle build its nest?

When you answer these questions, you're narrating. *Narrating* means telling what happens over time. You may tell a story. You may tell how to do something or explain a process.

When you narrate, you often arrange events in chronological order. With *chronological order,* you put events in the order in which they happen.

Telling a Story. Some stories are true, and some are made up. Either kind of story is a narrative. The following narrative paragraph is from a book of fiction.

> Strangely, when Ramona's heart was heavy, so were her feet. She trudged to the school bus, plodded through the halls at school, and clumped home from the bus after school. The house felt lonely when she let herself in, so she turned on the television set for company. She sat on the couch and stared at one of the senseless soap operas Mrs. Kemp watched. They were all about rich people—none of them looking like Howie's Uncle Hobart—who accused other people of doing something terrible; Ramona didn't understand exactly what, but it all was boring, boring, boring.
>
> Beverly Cleary, *Ramona Forever*

WRITING NOTE Paragraphs that tell a story usually don't have a main idea. But events in the paragraph do follow one another. That makes the paragraph easy to understand.

Explaining a Process. When your friend explains how to make a dog sit, she's explaining a process. She puts her instructions in step-by-step order. It's the same as chronological order.

Notice how the writer uses chronological order in the following paragraph. He explains how to begin the Chinese art of paper cutting.

> First, cut up paper squares about the size of the palm of your hand. Make a model using any paper. When you have the right size, use it to cut colored paper. If you are going to cut a word, make sure the squares are all the same size.
>
> Cheng Hou-tien, *Scissor Cutting for Beginners*

| EXERCISE 5 | **Using Narration to Develop Paragraphs** |

It's fun to tell a story. It's easy to explain a process. In these exercises you will develop those skills.

1. Write a group story. Work as a whole class or in smaller groups. Begin with one of the following "starters" or with one of your own. Then, take turns adding a sentence to the story. Be sure the events of the story are in chronological order.

   a. Every day promptly at 5:00 P.M., Ms. Arrigo set the burglar alarm on the main bank vault.
   b. The long gray car came sputtering into the gas station. A white poodle climbed out from behind the steering wheel.

2. Choose one of the following processes. Then, list three or more steps in doing it. List the steps in chronological order (in the order they happen).

   c. how to get to the library from your classroom
   d. how to use the telephone to report an emergency
   e. how to choose a pair of sneakers

 COMPUTER NOTE: If the computers at your school are arranged in a network, you may be able to use them to do collaborative prewriting or drafting.

Comparison and Contrast

How are you and your brother or sister alike? What's the difference between football and soccer?

To answer these questions, you need to *compare* or *contrast* things. You tell how they are alike and how they are different. When you compare and contrast, you use logical order. With **logical order,** you group related ideas in a way that makes sense.

Read the following two paragraphs. How are rabbits and hares alike? How are they different?

Comparison

To look at, rabbits and hares are very like each other. Both have long ears, big eyes and short, white, tufty tails which show up when they are running away. Both live by eating plants. Both can run very fast.

Contrast

Their habits, however, are very different. Hares live alone in open fields. Rabbits are gregarious, which means that they like crowding together. They dig a maze of underground tunnels, in which lots of them live.

Ralph Whitlock, *Rabbits and Hares*

EXERCISE 6 ▶ **Using Comparison or Contrast to Develop Paragraphs**

Think about yourself one year ago. How are the two "you's" alike? How are they different? Try the same thing with one of the following topics. First, make a list of likenesses between the two animals, pizzas, or movies. Then make another list of differences.

1. a dog and a cat as pets
2. the best and the worst pizza you've ever had
3. movies on television and movies in a theater

Evaluation

What's the best dish your school lunchroom serves? What movie is a waste of time? When you answer these questions, you're *evaluating.* You're deciding the value, or worth, of things.

When you evaluate, it's important to give reasons to support your opinion. You can organize your reasons by *order of importance.* You can either begin or end with the most important reason.

In the following paragraph, the writer gives an opinion about bottled apple juice. Notice the reasons the writer gives for this opinion. Where is the most important reason?

Opinion
Reason

Reason

Reason

> I love apples, but not bottled apple juice. My opinion is based mainly on taste. This juice tastes like sugar, not like apples. Secondly, there isn't much nutrition in bottled apple juice. About all a glass of it offers is a hundred empty calories. Finally, most bottled apple juice just doesn't *look* very good. Its pale yellow color is sickly compared to the color of orange juice or grape juice. For apple lovers like me, the choice is fresh-pressed apple cider.

EXERCISE 7 ▶ **Speaking and Listening: Evaluating a Food**

President George Bush once made headlines by declaring, "I hate broccoli!" Choose a food that you like or dislike very much. Then list at least three reasons for your opinion. Begin with the most important reason. Share your evaluation with your class in a two-minute talk. Compare your evaluation with those of your classmates. Which foods do your classmates like most? least?

MAKING CONNECTIONS

In this chapter you've learned what makes a paragraph. Now you can try making your own. Remember that the basic purposes of writing are to express yourself, to inform, to persuade, and to be creative.

WRITING PARAGRAPHS FOR DIFFERENT PURPOSES

Writing a Paragraph to Express Yourself

Writing about your own thoughts and feelings is called personal, or *expressive*, writing. Expressive writing is often private. For example, you might write about your private thoughts and feelings in a diary or journal.

Write a paragraph telling how you feel or think about something. Use one of the following sentence starters or create one of your own.

- My favorite time of the day (week, year) is ___.
- I've always thought it would be fun to ___.
- A person who seems like a real hero to me is ___.
- Something that always annoys me is ___.

Prewriting. To make a plan for your paragraph, you might start by freewriting, clustering, or brainstorming for ideas. (For more help with these prewriting techniques, see pages 27–31.)

Writing, Evaluating, and Revising. If you're only writing for yourself, write just one draft. But if you'd like to share your paragraph, reread it first. Did you express your thoughts and feelings clearly? Did you arrange your ideas in an order that makes sense? Make changes to improve your paragraph.

Proofreading and Publishing. If you share your paragraph, proofread it first. Correct any mistakes. (See the Guidelines for Proofreading on page 51.)

Writing a Paragraph to Inform

You get and give information all the time. For example, you get information from books, newspapers, and magazines. You also get information from television and radio. You give information when you give directions to your house or explain how to fold a paper crane.

The following chart gives information about life spans for different animals. Use this information to write a paragraph for your classmates. You might not use all the information in the chart. You can use the following topic sentence.

Topic Sentence: Large animals often have longer life spans than small ones.

LIFE SPANS	
Animal	Longest Life Span
mosquito	30 days
rat	3 years
dog	12–15 years
gorilla	50 years
whale	60 years
elephant	65 years

Prewriting. Start with the topic sentence on page 78. Decide how you will use the figures in the chart. Will you use them all? Will you summarize some of the information? You might write, for example, "The biggest animals, such as the elephant and the whale . . . "

Writing, Evaluating, and Revising. Write two or three supporting sentences to go with the topic sentence. Then write a sentence that sums up what you have said; just say the topic sentence in different words. Are your details clearly arranged? Do you use transitional words to show how the details are related? After you have written your paragraph, evaluate it and revise it.

Proofreading and Publishing. Check over your writing one last time. Look for mistakes in spelling, punctuation, or usage. Share your writing with the other students in your science class. Can the science teacher help you find out why larger animals usually live longer?

Writing a Paragraph to Persuade

People use persuasion all the time. You persuade a friend to lend you a new CD. A teacher persuades you to join the computer club at your school. In order to persuade, you need to give reasons to support your belief.

In most schools, students take physical education. Suppose you want to persuade your school board to change some P.E. (physical education) classes in your school. You think everyone should take swimming. Here are possible reasons:

Swimming is a good choice for P.E. because it
- exercises every muscle in the body
- can be a year-round activity with an indoor pool
- could save your life some day

Write a paragraph to persuade your school board to add a specific activity to your school's P.E. program. Begin by writing a topic sentence like this one. Just substitute your activity for *swimming*.

> The school board should add swimming to the school's P.E. program.

Prewriting. List three reasons that might persuade the school board to add the activity.

Writing, Evaluating, and Revising. Are your reasons the best ones? Are they clearly arranged? Revise your paragraph to make it more persuasive.

Proofreading and Publishing. Be sure to correct any errors in usage, spelling, or punctuation. Ask other readers if your paragraph is convincing.

Writing a Paragraph That Is Creative

When you create, you use your imagination. You invent something that didn't exist before. To make up your own creative paragraph, start by imagining that you're in the picture of the stairwell at the top of page 81, standing at the base of the steps, looking upward. Write a paragraph that tells what you see and what happens next.

Prewriting. Think about what might happen.

- Is there a strange figure at the top of the steps?
- At the top of the steps, do you open an old, creaky door?
- Do you try to walk away but find that you can't move?

Use your imagination! Think about what might happen on or near these steps. Jot down your ideas.

 Writing, Evaluating, Revising. Write a narrative paragraph telling what happens. Put in lots of action. Then, exchange papers with a classmate. What ideas does your classmate have for improving your paragraph?

 Proofreading and Publishing. Correct any errors in spelling, punctuation, or usage. Read your paragraphs aloud in a group. Whose is the most exciting?

Reflecting on Your Writing

Date the paragraphs that you want to add to your **portfolio.** Use these questions to write your reflections, and attach them to your papers.

1. Which way of gathering ideas was most helpful?
2. Was it difficult or easy to write a topic sentence? Explain.
3. What kinds of errors did you find when you proofread? Were you surprised at the errors? Explain.

---

3 EXPRESSIVE WRITING: NARRATION

Discovering Yourself

Remember when you learned to ride a bicycle? You thought you'd never keep that wobbly bike straight. But you did. You've discovered you can do many things. And there's more you can **discover about yourself.** You can do this with expressive writing.

Writing and You. People often write about familiar experiences. For example, did you know that Bill Cosby writes about his own family? He tells about funny things that happen between parents and children. He expresses himself in writing. When have you put your feelings in writing?

As You Read. The author of the following selection writes about a scary experience. What are his thoughts and feelings?

Vincent van Gogh, *The Starry Night* (1889). Oil on canvas, 29″ × 36¼″. Collection, The Museum of Modern Art, New York. Acquired through the Lillie P. Bliss Bequest.

83

from

T H E

L A N D

I L O S T

by *Huynh Quang Nhuong*

During the six-month rainy season, most of the river fish swim into the shallow water of the rice field and live there, feeding on all kinds of insects. Then during the dry season they return to the river. In addition most of the tropical fish in the area also have the ability to live out of the water for more than two hours, staying on paths and dikes where they can find more insects at night.

My cousin and I liked to go out into the field and catch fish at

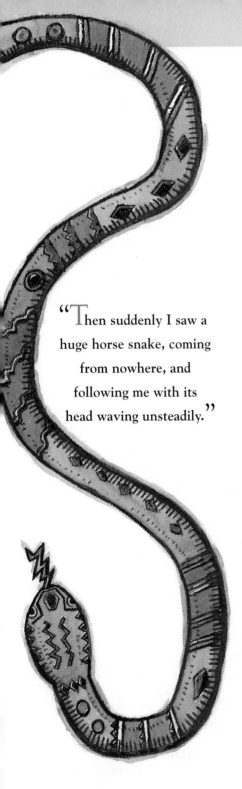

"Then suddenly I saw a huge horse snake, coming from nowhere, and following me with its head waving unsteadily."

night. Whenever we went out we always carried a hogfish oil lamp. Since I could not catch fish as well as my cousin, who was ten years older, I carried the lamp and a bucket to put the fish in, and my cousin carried a long knife to kill any fish that we found near the edge of the water. But he preferred to catch them alive.

One evening when we were in the field, my cousin began teasing me, saying that since I carried the hogfish oil lamp, a horse snake would follow us home. I knew that he was teasing, but I was frightened and looked back every so often to make sure that there was no horse snake following us. Then suddenly I saw a huge horse snake, coming from nowhere, and following me with its head waving unsteadily. I was so terrified that I couldn't speak; I could barely drag my feet. Luckily my cousin stopped and tried to catch a fish lying in the middle of the path. I bumped into him and almost knocked him over. Surprised at my unusual clumsiness, he looked back and saw the horse snake behind me. He was terrified too, but instinctively he swung his knife and struck the snake in the head. We dropped everything and ran home as fast as we could, more frightened than ever by the great noise the snake made behind us.

"The snake was so heavy that it took eight men to carry it home."

When we reached home my father gathered all his friends to search for the snake. He felt that since it had been discovered so nearby they ought to try to destroy it as soon as possible.

When we returned to the place where my cousin and I had encountered the snake, we saw, to our great surprise and relief, that the snake was lying there dead. With extraordinary luck, my cousin had hit the snake right in the middle of its head and split its brain.

The snake was so heavy that it took eight men to carry it home. The next day it was on display in front of our house. Everybody was impressed by its size. To fight against a snake of this length twenty men usually were needed.

My cousin put some coconut oil on his hair to make it shinier and he stayed around near the snake. The young girls smiled at him a little bit more than usual, and the young men seemed jealous.

My cousin was a hero!

READER'S RESPONSE

1. This narrative is about the writer's experiences in the jungles of Vietnam. How are they different from your experiences? How are they similar?
2. Have you ever been frightened by something? How did you behave?

WRITER'S CRAFT

3. In a good narrative, the writer shows you the experience. What are some details that show you how the horse snake looks?
4. What are some details that show how frightened the writer is?

Ways to Express Yourself

You express yourself in letters to friends and relatives, in messages on greeting cards, in notes to classmates, and in journal entries. Writing is expressive when you focus on your own experiences, thoughts, and feelings. Huynh Quang Nhuong expresses his feelings in a narrative. A narrative is just one way to develop expressive writing. Here are other examples.

- in a letter to a friend, telling what happened on your first day of school
- in your journal, writing about a time when you were sick
- in a diary entry, describing the unusual snakes your science teacher has in a terrarium
- in your journal, describing your brand-new soccer uniform and how proud it makes you feel
- in an article for the school newspaper, expressing your thoughts about an environmental issue
- in a letter to your cousin, comparing your feelings about two friends
- in a company newsletter, expressing your feelings that your business is the perfect place to work

LOOKING AHEAD

In the main part of this chapter, you'll use narration to write about a personal experience. In the workshop, you'll use description to write about a special place. Keep in mind that a good personal narrative

- tells about events in a clear order
- has details that show the experience
- tells why the experience is important

Writing a Personal Narrative

Prewriting

Choosing an Experience

Did you ever sprain an ankle and go to the emergency room? Maybe you sat, frightened, until a doctor could see you. Or did you ever earn an A on a big test or make the soccer or baseball team? Have you ever been lost and scared?

You don't have to be chased by a snake to have something important to write about. What's happened that's changed your life? or changed the way you feel about yourself or others? What experience have you had that sticks out strongly in your memory? What experience would you like to share with others? Here are some points to help you choose an experience for your narrative.

- *Choose an experience you remember.* You'll have details about the experience stored in your memory. (Remember that you want to tell your readers about your experience. You can't if you don't remember details about it.)
- *Choose an experience that's important to you.* You probably haven't ridden your skateboard around the world. But the small, quiet things you do are important, too. (Remember that you don't have to write about a big adventure—just an experience that means something to you.)
- *Choose an experience you can share.* If the experience is private, write about it in your journal. (Remember that you want to be comfortable sharing the experience with your readers.)

| **WRITING** ASSIGNMENT | PART 1:
Choosing a Topic for a
Personal Narrative |

Have you climbed a mountain? Or have you climbed the stairs to receive an award? If you still don't have a topic idea, try brainstorming to draw out what's stored in your own mind. Talk to friends, family, and classmates to recall experiences you have shared. Write down your topic ("the day my family moved to El Paso"; "the scariest storm I ever saw"). You can change it later if you think of a better one. It's not carved in stone!

Prewriting

Planning Your Personal Narrative

When you write a science report about penguins, you have to look for facts. Then you have to develop ideas about how to present the facts you've found. But for a personal narrative, ideas are already in your mind. Should you just start writing? Minds are funny, and your memories probably aren't in an order that makes sense. Spend some time planning before you write.

Peanuts reprinted by permission of United Feature Syndicate, Inc.

Thinking About Purpose and Audience

Have you ever had a nightmare? Didn't it feel good to tell someone about it and feel the fear going away? That's the *purpose* of a personal narrative—to share an experience with others. And writing about it helps you understand your feelings.

Your first *audience* will probably be your teacher and classmates. To understand your experience, what details do they need? What details will make the experience seem interesting to them?

Recalling Details

Think of watching a movie with half the screen blank. You wouldn't enjoy it as much because many details would be left out. That's how readers feel when a personal narrative lacks details.

There are many ways you can recall details for your narrative. You can brainstorm or cluster. You can talk to others who were part of the experience. Or you can close your eyes and replay the time in your mind. Think about two kinds of details: *sensory details* and *action details.*

Sensory details help you relive the experience so that you almost see, taste, smell, hear, and touch again.

> my baby sister's <u>tiny</u> feet, the <u>hot</u> and <u>melting</u> cheese, the <u>rotten</u> garbage, the <u>sharp</u> cries, a <u>cool</u> fall day

Action details tell what happened and how it happened.

> I rushed to the bus and climbed on board. Two minutes later I noticed we were going down a strange street. I was on the wrong bus.

Action details may also be the words that people say. These words are called *dialogue.*

> Crying, I asked the driver, "Would you please help me?"

☞ REFERENCE NOTE: For more help on writing and punctuating dialogue, see pages 157 and 615–621.

Sensory and action details about people, places, and events will make your personal narrative livelier. You might use a chart like this one as you try to recall details.

Topic: The day I took the wrong bus	
<u>ACTION DETAILS</u>	<u>SENSORY DETAILS</u>
At age 8 took bus downtown alone for first time	inside bus—hot, humid, noisy; whoosh of electric door opening and closing
Got on wrong bus coming home; crying; saying to driver, "Would you please help me?"	smell of wet clothes; people pushing; tears stinging chapped face
Changed buses and got home; people probably thinking, "Dumb kid"	best sight ever was my snow-covered street

COMPUTER NOTE: Use your word-processing program's thesaurus function (or a standalone thesaurus program) to look for the best words to describe sensory and action details that you plan to use in your draft.

Think about a time you told a friend about a movie. You probably said what happened first, second, next, and so on. You used *chronological,* or *time, order* to tell about events. Events in a narrative are often arranged in time order. You might want to use time order for events in your own narrative.

| EXERCISE 1 ▶ | **Speaking and Listening: Practice in Writing Dialogue** |

As you try to recall your experience, you may not be able to remember exactly what people said. When that happens, it's important to try to recreate what was said. You may have to use a little imagination or guesswork. To practice your guesswork, get together with two or three classmates. Then choose one of the situations in the following list. Work together to write the words the people in the situation might say. Think about *how* they speak, as well as *what* they say. When you finish, share your dialogue with the rest of the class.

EXAMPLE

Situation   Jesse, Cari, and Jon plan to start a band. Jesse and Cari have been working on their music all summer. Jon has been playing baseball instead. Cari is angry.

Dialogue   "How can we start a band if you goof off all the time?" Cari shouted.

"I know it was stupid," Jon yelled back. "But it'll be okay. We can still make the talent show."

1. Your parents don't like big dogs very much. A friend of yours is moving. She needs to find a home for her black Labrador. You really like the dog and want to adopt it. Write what you and your parents might say.

2. You and your brother are exploring the attic in your grandmother's house. The wind blows the attic door shut and it locks. It's dark and creepy, and you're both scared. Write what the two of you might say.
3. You're trying to teach your five-year-old cousin how to ride a bike. Things aren't going too well. Write what you and your cousin might say.

CRITICAL THINKING

Evaluating Details

If you look at bikes to buy, you think what's good and bad about each one. You decide which one has more value for you. Judging the value of something is called *evaluating.*

After you jot down details for your narrative, evaluate them. Begin by asking yourself what was important about your experience. Suppose you went on a camping trip with your family. Maybe the most important part was seeing animals like deer and bears. Or, maybe it was learning to have fun without watching TV and playing video games.

fawns on hillside

stories around campfire

water fight in stream

Now you can evaluate your details. You can decide which details show readers what was important about the experience. If the most important part of a camping trip is the animals, most of your details should be about animals. If the most important part is having fun without TV, details may be about many different activities.

CRITICAL THINKING EXERCISE:
Evaluating Details

On the next page there are some details about a visit to the Tigua Indian Reservation near El Paso, Texas. The most important part of the visit is learning about the history and culture of the Tiguas. Discuss the details with two or three classmates. Which details show the important part of the visit? Which details don't? Make a list of the details that show the most important part of the visit—what the writer learned about the history and culture of the Tiguas.

Action Details
    took tour of reservation
    saw an old mission church
    brother sprained his foot
    had Indian bread at lunch
    car had flat tire on way home

Sensory Details
    delicious hamburger on the way home
    smooth pottery decorated with designs
    soft voice of woman making pottery
    warm taste of Indian bread
    bright sun hitting on adobe houses
    sound of my favorite rock music on car radio

 **WRITING ASSIGNMENT**

PART 2:
Recalling Details

Elephants may never forget, but humans often do. Try to recall both sensory details and action details about your experience. Collect them in a chart like the one above. If you recall some dialogue, put it in the chart, too. After you've collected several details, take time to evaluate them. Cross out any details that are not really important to your experience.

How our brain loses things along the way.

Writing Your First Draft

The Parts of a Personal Narrative

A personal narrative may be one paragraph or several. That's up to you. But most personal narratives have these parts:

- a **beginning** that grabs the reader's interest and tells the topic
- a **body** that presents the events in an order that makes sense (usually time order)
- an **ending** that tells why the experience was important

Writers don't usually wait until the end to tell their thoughts and feelings. They include them in the body of the narrative. Sometimes they tell them directly.

> I was really afraid.

Sometimes they reveal them by their words or actions—what they say or do.

> I shivered and pulled my coat tighter around me. "What's going on?" I asked. Was my voice really shaking?

The following passage is from a memoir (a kind of autobiography) by Beverly Cleary. In this passage, Cleary tells about something that happened to her when she was a small child. Even though this is a part of a book, it has the three basic parts of a narrative—a beginning, a middle, and an end.

A PASSAGE FROM A BOOK

from A Girl from Yamhill: A Memoir
by Beverly Cleary

BEGINNING

Sensory details

At Christmas I was given an orange, a rare treat from the far-off land of California. I sniffed my orange, admired its color and its tiny pores, and placed it beside my bowl of oatmeal at the breakfast table, where I sat raised by two volumes of Mother's *Teacher's Encyclopedia.*

BODY
Dialogue

Action details

Father picked up my orange. "Did you know that the world is round, like an orange?" he asked. No, I did not. "It is," said Father. "If you started here" — pointing to the top of the orange — "and traveled in a straight line" — demonstrating with his finger — "you would travel back to where you started." Oh. My father scored my orange. I peeled and thoughtfully ate it.

Thoughts

Events in order

Sensory details

I thought about that orange until spring, when wild forget-me-nots suddenly bloomed in one corner of our big field. The time had come. I crossed the barnyard, climbed a gate, walked down the hill, climbed another gate, and started off across the field, which was still too wet to plow. Mud clung to my shoes. I plodded on and on, with my feet growing heavier with every step. I came to the fence that marked the boundary of our land and bravely prepared to climb it and plunge into foreign bushes.

ENDING

Dialogue

Sensory and action details

My journey was interrupted by a shout. Father came striding across the field in his rubber boots. "Just where in Sam Hill do you think you're going?" he demanded.

"Around the world, like you said."

Father chuckled and, carrying me under his arm, lugged me back to the house, where he set me on the back porch and explained the size of the world.

Mother looked at my shoes, now gobs of mud, and sighed. "Beverly, what will you think of next?" she asked.

EXERCISE 2 ▶   **Analyzing a Personal Narrative**

Get together with two or three classmates, and talk over these questions.

1. Beverly Cleary understands her father when he compares the earth to an orange. But he forgets to tell her how big the earth is. Can you remember a time when you misunderstood something about the world? What was it?
2. What sensory details does Cleary use in this narrative? How does she describe the orange? How does she describe her walk across the field?
3. Does Beverly Cleary's experience seem real to you? Why or why not?
4. Since this passage is part of a whole book, Cleary doesn't stop at the end and tell us how she felt about the experience. However, she does tell us some of her thoughts and feelings earlier in the passage. What are they?

A Writer's Model for You

Beverly Cleary is a professional writer. She wrote her narrative as an adult. Your writing might be more like the following shorter model. As you read, notice that this writer's model has the same parts as Cleary's narrative. It also has the same purpose.

A WRITER'S MODEL

BEGINNING **Attention grabber/Topic**	I was so scared my legs were shaking. It was my first day at Oakridge School. As a "new kid," I was afraid to speak to anyone. No one spoke to me either, but two girls smiled at me.
BODY **Action details**	The principal gave me a class schedule and a locker number. Then she called a boy

Dialogue

into her office and said, "Sam will be your guide today, Rosa. He lives in your apartment building. I thought you'd like to meet a new

Feelings

friend and neighbor." I was embarrassed and

Sensory details

couldn't speak because my throat felt so dry. Sam rescued me by asking which apartment I lived in and if I had any brothers or sisters. It felt good to meet someone who wanted to know me.

ENDING

Now Sam is one of my best friends. I have

Meaning of experience

many other friends, too. Being a "new kid" is painful for a while, but it doesn't last very long. Then the hurt goes away. I guess everyone's a new kid some time.

The narrative you've just read uses this framework. You might want to follow it as you write your own first draft.

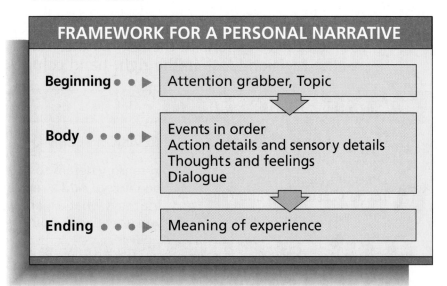

FRAMEWORK FOR A PERSONAL NARRATIVE

Beginning • • ▶ | Attention grabber, Topic

Body • • • • ▶ | Events in order
Action details and sensory details
Thoughts and feelings
Dialogue

Ending • • • ▶ | Meaning of experience

Reminder

As you write your draft, remember to

- use action details, sensory details, and dialogue
- put events in order
- tell the meaning the experience has for you

WRITING ASSIGNMENT

PART 3:
Writing Your First Draft

It's time to turn your notes (from Writing Assignment, Part 1, page 90, and Part 2, page 97) into sentences and paragraphs. If you have trouble getting your ideas on paper, try telling your experience to a friend or classmate. Ask him or her to ask questions about the experience. Then use your answers to develop your narrative.

Evaluating and Revising

This chart will help you improve your first draft. Ask yourself the questions in the left-hand column. Then use the revision ideas in the right-hand column.

EVALUATING AND REVISING PERSONAL NARRATIVES

EVALUATION GUIDE	REVISION TECHNIQUE
1 Does the beginning get readers' attention and tell the topic?	**Add** sensory details to the beginning. **Add** a sentence that says what experience you are telling about.
2 Do action and sensory details show readers the experience?	**Add** details about people, places, and actions. **Add** dialogue to show what you and other people said.
3 Does the writer tell or show the meaning of the experience?	**Add** your thoughts and feelings to the body. **Add** a sentence or two at the end that tells the meaning of the experience to you.

EXERCISE 3 ▶ **Analyzing a Writer's Revisions**

The following sentences from the narrative about being the new kid at school show changes the writer made. See if you can figure out why the writer made the changes. Then answer the questions.

I was so scared my legs were shaking.

∧It was my first day at Oakridge   **add**

School. ~~The name Oakridge is from the~~   **cut**

~~streets, Oak and Ridge.~~ As a "new kid,"

No one spoke to me either, but

I was afraid to speak to anyone. ∧Two   **add**

girls smiled at me.

1. Why did the writer add a new beginning sentence?
2. Why did the writer cut the second sentence? [Hint: Review pages 95–97.]
3. Why did the writer add *No one spoke to me either, but* to the last sentence?

PART 4:

Evaluating and Revising Your Personal Narrative

You probably made some changes as you wrote your first draft. Now, think about your finished draft. How can you improve it? Start by using the evaluating and revising chart on page 104. You might also exchange papers with a classmate and evaluate each other's narrative. Think about your evaluation and your classmate's. Finally, make changes that will improve your narrative.

Proofreading and Publishing

Proofreading.   What if you got an award, and your name was misspelled on it? You'd wish the mistake had been found before the award was given to you. Readers will feel the same way if they find errors in your paper. That's why proofreading is important. It's your chance to find and correct grammar, usage, and mechanics mistakes your readers won't want to see.

USAGE HINT

Using Personal Pronouns

When you write about yourself, you use the pronoun *I.* This pronoun has a subject form and an object form.

Use the subject form when the pronoun is the subject of the sentence.

> I didn't realize the mountain was so high.
> I am always ready to climb, as my friends will tell you.

Use the object form when the pronoun is an object.

Direct object:	The climb exhausted **me.**
Indirect object:	The ledge gave **me** a place to rest.
Object of a preposition:	My parents bought a little trophy for **me.**

👉 REFERENCE NOTE: For more about personal pronouns, see pages 374–376 and 503–517.

Publishing. After proofreading, the final step is *publishing*—sharing your narrative with the class. Or you might want to share it only with a trusted friend or adult. Here are two ideas.

■ Use the experience you wrote about in a short story. You can change the experience any way you want. You can change the time and place. You can change the outcome. You can even make the characters Martians, if you want to. You'll have fun writing when you use your imagination.
■ Share your narrative with yourself a year from now. Put it in a box in the back of a closet. One year later, read it again. Or put it in your writing portfolio, and pull it out in three or four months. How have you changed? Does the experience still have the same meaning for you?

WRITING ASSIGNMENT

PART 5:
Proofreading and Publishing Your Personal Narrative

Make your writing shine! Check it carefully for errors. Then, choose a way to share it. Use one of the ideas above or one of your own.

 Reflecting on Your Writing

Will you add your personal narrative to your **portfolio**? If so, reflect on your writing by answering these questions, and attach the answers to your paper.

■ How did you choose the experience you wrote about?
■ How easy was it to recall sensory details? action details? dialogue? Explain your responses.
■ What important changes did you make to your narrative during revision?

A STUDENT MODEL

*In the following narrative, Anthony C. Rodrigues—
a student at Cumberland Middle School in
Cumberland, Rhode Island—writes about winning
and losing. Anthony suggests that writers should
make "an organizational chart" of sensory details
to re-create the experience.*

In the Net
by Anthony C. Rodrigues

It was two o'clock on a Sunday afternoon and I was
on my way to my championship soccer game. As I drove
up to the field and entered the parking lot, I wondered if
this game was going to be like the other years when our
team made it to the semifinals but then lost in the
championship game. I looked at the field and I remembered seeing the pine trees in the background, but I
couldn't concentrate on their beauty because I was so
nervous. One by one the players arrived and the coach
told us to begin our warm-up drills and to take shots on
our goaltender. I wondered if during the game I was
going to shoot as well as I had in warm-ups.

Finally, it was time. I was in the starting lineup,
playing halfback. The whistle blew and the game had
officially started. In the first half our team played excep-
tionally well, but at half time the score was 0–0 and we
were all exhausted and cold. In the beginning of the
second half we scored a goal. The crowd went up with a
roar and the players were running down the field
yelling and screaming. I started to believe that maybe
we would win. The second half went on and on. We
maintained our 1–0 lead. We went on to win the game
1–0. I was so excited that I had won my first championship game in all of my six years playing soccer. I learned
that anything is possible if I put my mind and soul into it.

WRITING WORKSHOP

A Journal Entry

Personal narratives are expressive writing that you usually share with someone. A journal entry is a form of private expressive writing. It's a chance to explore your ideas and feelings without worrying about other people. That also means you don't have to worry about correct usage and punctuation unless you just want to.

Here's a journal entry about a favorite place in a city park. As you read, notice the details the writer uses to describe the park. Notice how the writer's feelings are part of the entry, too.

I had a bad day today. I made a D on that dumb test. This afternoon, I sat at the fountain in Fairmont Park. It has trees and benches all around it. The sun was shining, and lots of people were there. Mothers and fathers and kids walk around. The kids like to stick their hands and feet in the fountain. Today, I saw a big black dog jump in. When he jumped out, he shook water all over everybody. Just being there made me feel better. There's more to life than a D on a test. But I'll try harder next time.

Thinking It Over

1. How does this writer feel about his day? Have you ever felt the way he does? When?
2. Suppose the writer rereads this paragraph ten or fifteen years from now. What details will help him recall what his day was like?

Writing a Journal Entry

Prewriting. What's a special place to you? What do you do at your special place? Why is it special? Do you share it with others, or is it a private place? Write a journal entry about this special place. Use sensory details to describe it.

Writing, Evaluating, and Revising. A journal can be anything you write in. People have kept journals on scraps of paper, on walls, even on the backs of their own hands. A journal is different from a personal narrative. You don't have to write about events in order. You can skip around if you want to.

Proofreading and Publishing. You don't have to share your journal entries. But remember how fun it is to look at photographs of yourself when you were younger. A journal can be like those photographs. It gives you a record of yourself through the years. If you add your journal entry to your **portfolio,** date it, and attach written responses to these questions: How did you choose a place to write about? If you were to publish this entry, what changes would you make to it?

MAKING CONNECTIONS

WRITING ACROSS THE CURRICULUM

A Day in the Life of a Historical Figure

What if George Washington really did cut down the cherry tree? What would he have written in his journal? Use your skills in expressive writing to "capture" a famous moment from history. Begin by choosing a famous person you know about. Think of a major event in his or her life, such as the day Guion S. Bluford, Jr., becomes the first African American to go into space, or the day Amelia Earhart becomes the first woman to fly alone across the Atlantic Ocean. "Step into the shoes" of the person you want to write about. Write a journal entry about the event.

MASS MEDIA

A Comic Strip About Your Own Life

Artists who draw comic strips often use them to tell about funny stories from their own lives. Think of a funny experience you've had. Decide how many comic strip panels you will need to tell your readers about it. (Comic strips in daily newspapers may have just four or five panels, but those in the Sunday "funny pages" often use many more.) Then, sketch a comic strip based on the experience, using a pencil so you can erase mistakes and add changes. Leave room in each panel and add dialogue balloons that show what each of the characters is saying or thinking. When you're done, go over the pencil lines in ink.

4 Using Description

Creating Pictures and Images

Sparkling fireworks: Can you see them? The drone of an airplane: Can you hear it? Writers use words to create **pictures and images** in your mind.

Writing and You. A reporter describes a tornado so realistically that you are afraid of it. A sports writer describes an Olympic event so vividly that you want to be there. These writers don't **tell** you about their subjects; they **show** them to you. When have you used words to show a subject to readers?

As You Read. The following description is Mrs. D. H. Bishop's eyewitness account of the sinking of the *Titanic*. On April 15, 1912, the huge ocean liner struck an iceberg in the North Atlantic Ocean. From a lifeboat, Mrs. Bishop watched the ship sink. What images do you see as you read her account?

Carmen Lomas Garza, *Barbacoa para cumpleaños* (1994). Alkyds on canvas, 36 × 48". © 1993 Carmen Lomas Garza (reg. 1994). Photo credit: M. Lee Fatherree. Collection of the Federal Reserve Bank of Dallas.

113

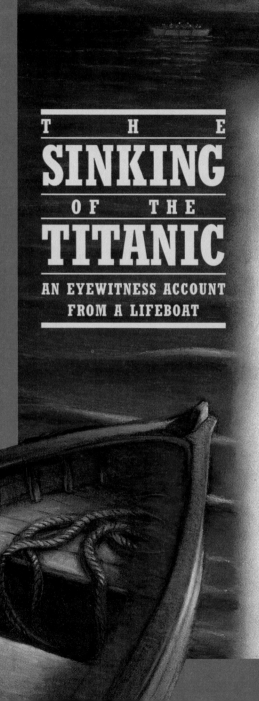

THE SINKING OF THE TITANIC

AN EYEWITNESS ACCOUNT FROM A LIFEBOAT

We did not begin to understand the situation till we were perhaps a mile or more away from the *Titanic*. Then we could see the rows of lights along the decks begin to slant gradually upward from the bow. Very slowly the lines of light began to point downward at a greater and greater angle. The sinking was so slow that you could not perceive the lights of the deck changing their position. The slant seemed to be greater about every quarter of an hour. That was the only difference.

In a couple of hours, though, she began to go down more rapidly. Then the fearful sight began. The people in the ship were just beginning to realize how great their danger was. When the forward part of the ship dropped suddenly at a faster rate, so that the upward slope became marked, there was a sudden rush of passengers on

all the decks toward the stern. It was like a wave. We could see the great black mass of people in the steerage sweeping to the rear part of the boat and breaking through into the upper decks. At the distance of about a mile we could distinguish everything through the night, which was perfectly clear. We could make out the increasing excitement on board the boat as the people, rushing to and fro, caused the deck lights to disappear and reappear as they passed in front of them.

This panic went on, it seemed, for an hour. Then suddenly the ship seemed to shoot up out of the water and stand there perpendicularly. It seemed to us that it stood upright in the water for four full minutes.

Then it began to slide gently downward. Its speed increased as it went down head first, so that the stern shot down with a rush.

The lights continued to burn till it sank. We could see the people packed densely in the stern till it was gone. . . .

> "...we could hear the screaming a mile away."

As the ship sank we could hear the screaming a mile away. Gradually it became fainter and fainter and died away. Some of the lifeboats that had room for more might have gone to their rescue, but it would have meant that those who were in the water would have swarmed aboard and sunk [them].

from *The New York Times*, April 19, 1912

READER'S RESPONSE

1. What image or picture in this selection do you remember best?
2. How did the passengers' reactions change as the ship gradually went under? Write down words that you think might describe their thoughts and feelings.

WRITER'S CRAFT

3. To describe the event, the writer uses some factual details. What are they?
4. The writer also uses sensory details, especially those that appeal to the senses of sight and hearing. What are some of these details?

> Find details that are significant. They may be important to your narrative; they may be unusual, or colorful, or comic, or entertaining. But make sure they are details that do useful work.
>
> William Zinsser

Uses of Description

All writers of description want to plant an image in your mind. They want you to see, hear, feel, taste, or smell what they describe. But writers use description for many reasons. Here are some purposes you might have for writing description.

- in a journal entry, describing a severe thunderstorm
- in a letter to a friend, describing your weird party costume
- in a notice on a bulletin board, describing your lost baseball glove so others can help you find it
- in a memo, describing the track team's performance at the track meet to persuade the principal to provide more funding
- in your school newsletter, describing a parade celebrating Black History Month
- in an essay, telling about a favorite dish your grandparent makes
- in a short story, creating a picture of a haunted house
- in a poem, describing the shining green eyes of a cat

Descriptions are everywhere: in newspapers, books, magazines, or even menus. Descriptions are used to create a clear picture in your mind.

LOOKING AHEAD

In the main assignment in this chapter, your basic purpose will be to inform readers about an event you saw. As you plan and write your description, remember to

- use factual and sensory details
- use exact words, and dialogue, if possible
- organize your ideas so they're easy to follow

Writing an Eyewitness Description

Prewriting

Planning an Eyewitness Description

Perhaps you've seen an exciting parade. You enjoyed the unusual costumes, the colorful floats, and the marching bands. When you observe an event like this firsthand, you are an eyewitness. You can share the event with others by writing an eyewitness description. Careful planning will help you write your description.

Thinking About Subject, Purpose, and Audience

Subject. If you saw a fire on your way to school, wouldn't you describe it to a friend? You don't have to think about finding a *subject* at a time like that. You already know what subject you want to describe.

When you write an eyewitness description in school, though, you may wonder at first what you could possibly describe. Just think about events in your everyday life. They may happen at home, at school, or in your neighborhood.

Purpose. Your *purpose* in this chapter is to inform readers about an event that you have observed first-hand. As you describe the event, you want to answer questions like these:

- What happened?
- Where did the event take place?
- When did the event take place?
- Who took part in the event?

Audience. Your *audience* is important, too. Think about what your readers need to know. For example, perhaps you watched an air show featuring biplanes. If your readers have already seen a biplane, they probably know about its design. But if they have never seen a biplane, they will probably need to know that biplanes are planes used in World War I that have two sets of wings.

WRITING ASSIGNMENT

PART 1:
Choosing a Subject

You may already have observed an event that you can describe. Or perhaps you can observe one now. You can choose one of the following kinds of events or brainstorm for ideas of your own. Then, decide on one particular event. When you have made a choice, write down the name of the event.

1. a natural event, such as a storm or flood
2. a sports event, such as a baseball or soccer game
3. a neighborhood event, such as a street festival
4. a family event, such as a wedding or birthday
5. an event with animals, such as a circus performance

Gathering Details

Some descriptions sizzle. Others just simmer. The details make the difference. You can gather details by observing your subject. You can also recall it.

When you *observe* an event, look carefully. Perhaps you have watched a school's marching band perform. How many musicians were there? Who marched at the front? What outfits did the performers wear? What did the band play? If you witnessed the event long ago, take time to *recall* it. Close your eyes and picture the event as it happened; jot down what you recall. As you observe or recall, think about factual details, sensory details, and dialogue.

Factual Details.   Factual details can be checked in reference books or through firsthand observation. They often include numbers and figures.

> There are two elephants and four tigers in the circus parade. The parade began at Fourth Street at about 10 a.m. More than three hundred spectators lined the streets.

Sensory Details.   Sensory details are details that you see, hear, taste, touch, or smell. They help readers share the experience of the event. You *see* the velvety coat on the tiger and *hear* the lions roar. You *taste* the crunchy, salty popcorn. You *feel* the moist, hot air. You *smell* the sawdust.

Dialogue.   The words people actually say are called *dialogue.* A well-chosen quotation can add spice to the description of an event. For example, suppose you observe a low-flying plane in an air show. At that moment, someone in the crowd yells, "Oh, no! It's going to crash!" Dialogue such as this helps readers share in the event.

CRITICAL THINKING

Observing Sensory Details

Sensory details—details of sight, sound, taste, touch, and smell—make descriptions come alive. What noises did you hear at the event? Were there smells? What did you touch? What did you taste? Try to use at least two or three of your senses when you describe an event.

You could make a chart of details as you observe them. Here's a chart one writer created after observing the children's play period at a playground.

SIGHT	TOUCH	SOUND
swings	rough canvas seats	"Higher! Higher!"
monkey bars	sticky metal	laughing
seesaw	sharp splinters	creaky
water fountain	icy water	gurgling

 CRITICAL THINKING EXERCISE:
Observing Sensory Details

What can you see in this picture? What might you hear, feel, taste, and smell? Make a chart like the one above. Fill in as many details as you can. Then, get together with a partner and compare your lists.

Including Thoughts and Feelings

When you write an eyewitness description, you want
your readers to share your experience—to see what
you saw. Sometimes, your own reactions are an
important part of your experience. For that reason,
you may want your description to include thoughts
and feelings along with factual and sensory details. In
the example of the marching band, you might want to
tell how excited you were as you watched it perform.
Or, you might want to reflect on how the band's
performance showed good teamwork. However,
remember that your basic purpose is to describe
details that you see, hear, taste, touch, or smell.
When you write an eyewitness description, your
focus is on presenting the actual experience.

| EXERCISE 1 ▶ | **Speaking and Listening:**
 Observing Sounds |

Writers train their senses to be alert. They don't just
see a cat; they see a jet-black Persian with a twitching
tail. They don't just hear the drone of noises in a
classroom; they hear the squeak of chalk on the chalkboard and the buzz of a pesky fly.

   You can do the same thing. Practice on just one
sense for now: your hearing. During lunchtime at
your school cafeteria, list at least ten sounds that you
hear. Afterward, share your list with a classmate. In
what ways do your lists differ? If you put your lists
together, how many sounds are there?

WRITING
 ASSIGNMENT

PART 2:
Gathering Details

How good an observer are you? Observe firsthand
the event you chose in Writing Assignment, Part 1
(page 119) or call it to mind. First, write down details
that tell facts about the event. Then, let each of your

senses "check it out." Write down details that tell what your eyes see, what your nose smells, what your ears hear, and so on. It may help to write your details in a chart like the one on page 121. Finally, write down a thought or feeling you had about the event.

Choosing and Organizing Details

Choosing Details.   Now you have a list of details. But you might not need to use all of them. To choose which details to use, ask yourself: What do I want readers to know and remember about the event I witnessed? Choose details that will help readers focus on the event as you experienced it.

Organizing Details.   You usually list details as you think about them. You may have details about the number of riders in a parade and then details about the sounds of the crowd. To help readers follow your description, arrange details in a certain order. Arrange details about the event itself in *chronological order*. Arrange sensory details that describe people, places, and objects, in *spatial order*.

With ***chronological order,*** list details in the order in which they happened. Tell what happened first, second, third, and so on.

Spatial order arranges details according to their location. For example, your eyes might move from the tip of a horse's muzzle to its tail. In your description, you'd arrange details about the horse this way: muzzle, head, eyes, mane, body, tail.

WRITING NOTE

As you write your eyewitness description, remember that the basic structure is your narrative of the event. Descriptive details are what you add once you have the narrative skeleton of what happened first, next, and so on.

Here's how one writer chose details for a description. Notice how details that don't focus on the event itself were crossed out. Other details were then numbered in the order in which they would be used.

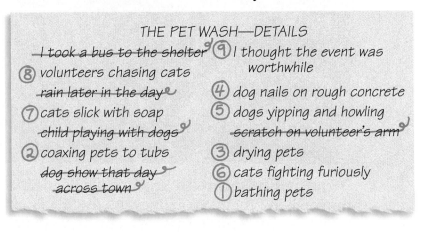

THE PET WASH—DETAILS

~~I took a bus to the shelter~~ ⑨ I thought the event was worthwhile

⑧ volunteers chasing cats

~~rain later in the day~~

⑦ cats slick with soap

~~child playing with dogs~~

② coaxing pets to tubs

~~dog show that day~~
~~across town~~

④ dog nails on rough concrete

⑤ dogs yipping and howling

~~scratch on volunteer's arm~~

③ drying pets

⑥ cats fighting furiously

① bathing pets

WRITING ASSIGNMENT

PART 3:
Choosing and Organizing Details

Read over the list of details you gathered for Writing Assignment, Part 2 (page 122). Which details will tell readers what you want them to know? Next, arrange and number details in chronological order.

Writing Your First Draft

Have you ever seen a 3-D movie? You wear a special pair of glasses. Then people and places seem so real they almost come off the screen. You can make your descriptions as real as a 3-D movie if you choose your words carefully.

Using Exact Words.   A camera that's not in focus takes a blurry picture. As you focus the lens, the picture becomes sharper. Using exact words is like putting a camera in focus. Vague words create blurry images. But exact words create bright, clear pictures: They show just what you want to get across.

An exact word to describe the color of a person's eyes might be *chocolate* or *sandy*, not just *brown*. You might describe a *bald eagle* or a *sparrow*, not just a *bird*. You show what a snake does, not by saying that it *moves* through the grass but that it *slithers* or *glides*.

Sometimes it's hard to come up with the exact word that says what you mean. Using a word bank can help. In your journal, you might want to start a word bank like the one on page 126. Then you'll have a list of words when you need them. Don't forget to leave room for more words.

WORD BANK	
Sight Words	shiny, golden, freckled, torn, short, wrinkled, bumpy, narrow, plastic
Touch Words	fuzzy, slippery, hard, lumpy, scratchy, cool, damp, dry, rough
Sound Words	shriek, blare, whisper, shout, cry, moan, cackle, screak, whoop
Smell Words	smoky, fresh, spicy, spoiled, stink, perfumy, reek, sniff, decaying
Taste Words	sweet, salty, greasy, sour, sugary, rotten, syrupy, cool, bitter

WRITING NOTE

A *thesaurus* can help you find the exact words you want. Every library has at least one. When you want to replace a vague word, look it up in the thesaurus. You'll find an entire list of words that you can choose from. For example, if you look up the word *fast*, a thesaurus might offer you words like these: *swift, rapid, dashing, snappy, zippy, like a flash, like greased lightning, supersonic.* Take your pick!

Born Loser reprinted by permission of
Newspaper Enterprise Association, Inc.

Using Similes and Metaphors. You can make an event more real to readers by comparing parts of it to things they know. *Similes* and *metaphors* help you make these comparisons. A **simile** uses *like* or *as*.

His hair was as orange *as apricots.*
He snuck away *like an alley rat.*

Metaphors make a direct comparison. They don't use the word *like* or *as*.

Her long brown hair was *a veil she hid behind.*
The dog, far ahead, was *just a black dot on the horizon.*

Here's an eyewitness account of a surprise encounter between a man and an animal. As you read, look for factual details, sensory words, and exact words.

A PASSAGE FROM A BOOK

from Arctic Dreams
by Barry Lopez

Factual details

Exact words

Sensory words, simile

Once in winter I was far out on the sea ice north of Melville Island in the high Arctic with a drilling crew. I saw a seal surface at some hourless moment in the day in a moon pool, the open water directly underneath the drilling platform that lets the drill string pass through the ice on its way to the ocean floor. The seal and I regarded each other in absolute stillness, I in my parka, arrested in the middle of an errand, the seal in the motionless water, its dark brown eyes glistening in its gray, catlike head. Curiosity held it. What held me was:

**Thought/
Feeling**

Metaphor

**Thought/
Feeling**

how far out on the edge of the world I am. A movement of my head shifted the hood of my parka slightly, and the seal was gone in an explosion of water. Its eyes had been enormous. I walked to the edge of the moon pool and stared into the dark ocean. I could not have been more surprised by the seal's appearance if it had fallen out of the winter sky overhead, into the spheres of light that embraced the drill rig and our isolated camp.

EXERCISE 2 ▶ Analyzing a Description

Get together with two or three classmates. Then, answer these questions about the above description.

1. You might have had the experience of unexpectedly coming face to face with an animal. Was your experience like what the writer describes? Explain.
2. What factual details help you see the encounter between the writer and the seal?
3. What are some of the sensory details that help you see the event the writer describes?
4. Would you have enjoyed this piece more or less if the writer had not included his thoughts and feelings? Explain your response.

A Writer's Model for You

You might not be quite ready to match the skill of Barry Lopez. But here's a model you could match. It's about an event you may have seen.

A WRITER'S MODEL

Event—place and time	The City Animal Shelter on Third Street held a pet wash on Saturday, June 3. Seven volunteers bathed twenty-three dogs and seventeen cats. Some of the volunteers coaxed
Metaphor	the pets to tubs filled with soapsud mountains. Others bathed the pets. Still more dried the
Sensory details	animals with large, fluffy towels. The dogs were bathed first. Most dogs tried to dig their nails into the rough concrete, making noises
Simile	like nails on a chalkboard. Some of them
Exact words	yipped and howled. The last dog to be bathed pulled the volunteer into the tub. The volunteer came up soaked, but smiling. The cats were bathed last. Most of them fought furiously.
Exact words	Two of the cats, slick with soap, squeezed out of the volunteers' arms and dashed for safety. Laughing, the volunteers chased after
Dialogue	them. "Thanks to all of you volunteers," the director said, "the day was a great success." I
Thought/Feeling	left with the feeling that the event had been both successful and worthwhile.

 *Reminder*

When you write your description

- choose factual and sensory details, and possibly thoughts and feelings, so that readers can share your experience
- organize details so your readers can follow your description
- use specific details and exact words
- include dialogue if possible

 **WRITING** ASSIGNMENT

PART 4:
Writing a Draft of Your Description

Now re-create your event with words. Using your prewriting notes, write the first draft of your description. Begin by naming the event. Then, use specific details and exact words to show it to readers. Focus on what you want readers to know and remember.

Peanuts reprinted by permission of United Feature Syndicate, Inc.

Evaluating and Revising

It's important to evaluate and revise your description, and the chart below can help you do it. To use the chart, ask yourself each question in the left-hand column. If you find a problem, the ideas in the right-hand column will show you how to fix it.

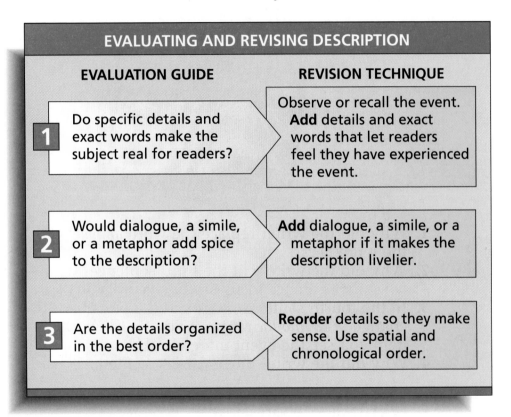

EVALUATING AND REVISING DESCRIPTION

EVALUATION GUIDE	REVISION TECHNIQUE
1 Do specific details and exact words make the subject real for readers?	Observe or recall the event. **Add** details and exact words that let readers feel they have experienced the event.
2 Would dialogue, a simile, or a metaphor add spice to the description?	**Add** dialogue, a simile, or a metaphor if it makes the description livelier.
3 Are the details organized in the best order?	**Reorder** details so they make sense. Use spatial and chronological order.

EXERCISE 3 ▶ **Evaluating a Writer's Revisions**

The following sentences are from the description of the pet wash on page 129. Try to figure out why the writer made the changes you see. Use the evaluating and revising chart, above, to help you decide.

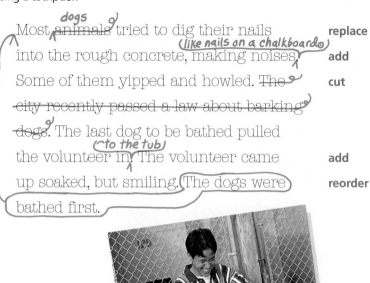

Most ~~animals~~ *dogs* tried to dig their nails   **replace**
into the rough concrete, making noises*(like nails on a chalkboard.)*   **add**
Some of them yipped and howled. ~~The~~   **cut**
~~city recently passed a law about barking~~
~~dogs.~~ The last dog to be bathed pulled
the volunteer in. *(^to the tub)* The volunteer came   **add**
up soaked, but smiling. (The dogs were)   **reorder**
bathed first.

1. Why did the writer replace the word *animals* with the word *dogs*?
2. Why did the writer cut the third sentence? (Hint: Does the sentence focus on the event itself?)
3. In the fourth sentence, why did the writer change *in* to *into the tub*? How do these words help you see the event more clearly?
4. Why did the writer move the last sentence?

PART 5:
Evaluating and Revising Your Description

Use the chart on page 131 to help evaluate your draft. Then, trade descriptions with a classmate, and evaluate each other's work. Think about your own and your classmate's evaluations. Finally, make changes that will *show* the events to readers.

Proofreading and Publishing

Proofreading. When you proofread, you look for mistakes in capitalization, punctuation, spelling, or usage. Once you've corrected any errors, your readers will be able to read your description more easily.

MECHANICS HINT

Using Commas with Adjectives

You often use adjectives to make a subject seem real. Separate two or more adjectives before a noun with commas.

> Large, colorful slogans decorated the biplane.
> I hear the low, steady sound of the propeller.

Don't separate an adjective and the noun it describes with a comma.

INCORRECT   An old, mangy, dog slept in the corner.
CORRECT   An old, mangy dog slept in the corner.

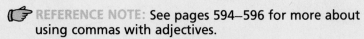 REFERENCE NOTE: See pages 594–596 for more about using commas with adjectives.

Publishing. Now it's time to share your eyewitness account. Here are two publishing ideas.

- With your classmates, produce a class "radio show" by taping all of your descriptions. Speak slowly so your audience won't miss any details.

- Illustrate your work with drawings or other artwork or with magazine photos. Your teacher might display your work in the classroom, or you might get together with some classmates and bind your work together in a booklet.

 COMPUTER NOTE: Word-processing programs allow you to set titles and other words in real italic type instead of using underlining.

WRITING ASSIGNMENT

PART 6:
Proofreading and Publishing

A diamond doesn't shine brightly until it's properly cut and polished. Proofread your description, and correct any errors to make it shine. Then, use one of the ideas you have read about to publish it. Or use an idea of your own.

📁 Reflecting on Your Writing

To add your paper to your **portfolio,** date it. Then, attach your answers to these questions about your work.

- Did you observe your event, or did you recall it? How hard was it to gather details?
- Which details were harder to gather: factual or sensory? Why?
- How was your process for writing an eyewitness account different from that for other kinds of writing you've done?

A STUDENT MODEL

You can be an eyewitness to almost anything—including important family events. Here Loucas Tasigiannis describes a brother's graduation. Loucas, a student at Cliffside Park No. 5 School in Cliffside Park, New Jersey, says the most important things to remember when writing eyewitness accounts are to proofread the paper and to "have fun writing it."

Graduation Day
by Loucas Tasigiannis

On one of the most important days of my brother's life he couldn't behave. It was his nursery school graduation. He was playing with the kid next to him. They were both hitting each other lightly. Mrs. Chris, the teacher, told them to behave but they didn't. They were talking and laughing. My mother even tried to tell them to stop, but they didn't hear. They finally stopped when they all started singing.

My brother only knew a few words. Instead, he mumbled and looked at the other children. I felt sorry for him.

At the end all the children got paint sets. Then the children and the adults got treats. Finally, everybody said goodbye and they headed for their houses.

WRITING WORKSHOP

A Poem That Describes

Writing an eyewitness account is one way to describe, but poems can also describe. In a descriptive poem, you need to use sensory details, just as you used them in your descriptive paper. In addition, descriptive poems sometimes use word sounds. The following poem uses sensory details and word sounds—rhyming words—to describe the sea.

from The Sea
by James Reeves

The sea is a hungry dog,
Giant and gray.
He rolls on the beach all day.
With his clashing teeth and shaggy jaws
Hour upon hour he gnaws
The rumbling, tumbling stones,
And "Bones, bones, bones!"
The giant sea dog moans,
Licking his greasy paws.

And when the night wind roars
And the moon rocks in the stormy cloud,
He bounds to his feet and snuffs and sniffs,
Shaking his wet sides over the cliffs,
And howls and hollos long and loud.

Think about the sensory details in this poem. The words *giant* and *gray* help you see a large body of water. The words *howls* and *hollos* help you hear the sound of the waves breaking on the shore. Try writing a poem that describes an object. If you like, start your poem as this one starts: "The _____ is a _____."

Writing a Descriptive Poem

Prewriting. Think of some common object, such as your bicycle or closet. Imagine this object as a creature. Brainstorm for sensory details. How might it look or sound? smell or taste? How does it feel to touch it?

Writing, Evaluating, and Revising. Now use the details you listed to write your poem. For example, you might describe the space under your bed as this poem does:

> I see you there beneath my bed,
> A hungry space I've always fed
> With crumpled clothes and other stuff
> Until my room is clean enough
> 　　　O helpful beast, that likes to eat,
> 　　　O hidden friend, keep my room neat!

You can make any lines rhyme in your poem. Or you can decide to have no words that rhyme. Just revise the poem until it sounds good.

Proofreading and Publishing. Commas and periods don't always go at the end of lines in poetry. Put them where your voice pauses or stops. To share your poem, write or type it in the center of unlined paper. For the final touch, draw a picture of the object or creature. If you add your poem to your **portfolio,** date it. Include your answer to this question: Would you rather write a poem or a paragraph? Explain why.

MAKING CONNECTIONS

DESCRIPTIONS IN CREATIVE WRITING

When you wrote your eyewitness description, you focused on presenting the actual experience to your readers. In creative writing, however, the focus is usually on the writer's thoughts and feelings. Here's a description of a tortoise, or turtle, from a short story. What thoughts and emotions does the writer tell you about?

from Tortuga
by Rudolfo A. Anaya

There in the middle of the narrow path lay the biggest tortoise any of us had ever seen. It was a huge monster which had crawled out of the dark river to lay its eggs in the warm sand. I felt a shiver when I saw it, and when I breathed, I smelled the spoor of the sea. The taste of copper drained in my mouth and settled in my queasy stomach.

The giant turtle lifted its huge head and looked at us with dull, glintless eyes. The tribe drew back. Only I remained facing the monster from the water. Its slimy head dripped with bright green algae. It hissed a warning, asking me to move. It had come out of the water to lay its eggs; now it had to return to the river. Wet, leathery eggs fresh from the laying clung to its webbed feet, and as it moved forward it crushed them into the sand. Its gray shell was dry, dulled by the sun, encrusted with dead parasites and green growth; it needed the water.

Do this writer's reactions remind you of a time when you came upon something unexpected? Imagine a surprising incident that you could write about. You might start with an idea drawn from an event you saw or heard about, or you might make up an event. Write a short description of the incident. Your description should include sensory details that will show the narrator's feelings about the experience.

DESCRIPTION AND PERSUASION

Writing a Travel Description

Have you ever noticed the travel section of the Sunday newspaper? Take a look sometime. You'll find all kinds of ads, and you'll also find some articles written by travel writers. Travel writers describe places they have visited. Sometimes they just share information, but often they try to persuade their readers to visit the sites they're describing. Here's an example of a persuasive description of the Grand Canyon. Does it make you want to go there?

If you're interested in time and space travel, visit Grand Canyon National Park in Arizona. A good way to start is floating down the Colorado River on a raft. It took the river millions of years to carve out the canyon. Or take a ride on a mule, down six or seven thousand feet from the rim to the bottom of the canyon. While there, take another look at the past and visit the ruins of adobe houses built hundreds of years ago by the Pueblo Indians. From the rim itself, look out over the canyon and watch the colors of the rocks change with the varying light of the sun. And if you want to get a true sense of space, rent a seat on one of the planes that fly out over the canyon. Its vastness and majesty are unforgettable.

Now it's your turn to be a travel writer. Pick some place you've visited and enjoyed. You can even use your own town if you'd like. Write a paragraph describing its most interesting features. Convince your readers it's a great place to visit.

5 CREATIVE WRITING: NARRATION

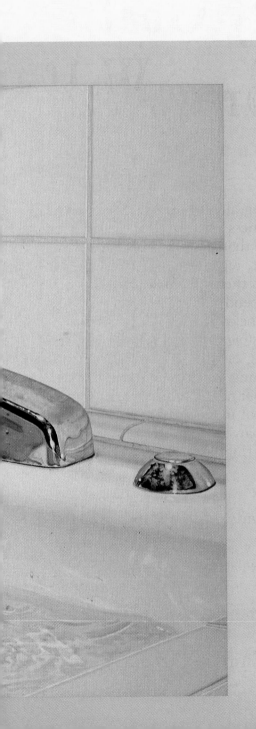

Imagining Other Worlds

Quick! Think of the perfect world. Would rutabaga be the national vegetable? Or would stuffed animals do chores for their owners? You've just **imagined another world.**

Writing and You.   That's what writers of stories, poems, plays, and TV shows do. They create other worlds with their imaginations. Their worlds may be unusual—like the world of *Star Trek Voyager*. Or they may be scary—like Frankenstein's creepy world. But all writers try to make the people, places, and events of their worlds seem real. Have you noticed that an imaginary world can even help explain the real world?

As You Read.   The world in the following African American folk tale is make-believe. But it seems real, too. What could the folk tale explain about life?

Doug Webb, *Kitchenetic Energy*. © 1988, Martin Lawrence Limited Editions.

Brer Billy Goat Tricks Brer Wolf

as told by Julius Lester

Brer Wolf was going along the road one day and Ol' Man Hungriness was on him. Brer Wolf made up his mind that the first thing he saw, he was going to eat it, regardless.

No sooner was the thought thunk than Brer Wolf rounded a bend and there was Brer Billy Goat standing on top of a rock. This was not one of your little rocks. This rock was as big and broad as a house, and Brer Billy Goat was standing on the top like he owned it and was thinking about turning it into a condominium.

Brer Wolf didn't care about none of that. He charged up the rock to find out what goat meat tasted like.

Brer Billy Goat didn't pay him no mind. He put his head down and went to acting like he was chewing on

---

"Brer Wolf made up his mind that the first thing he saw, he was going to eat it, regardless."

something. Brer Wolf stopped. He stared at Brer Billy Goat, trying to figure out what he was eating. Brer Billy kept on chewing.

Brer Wolf looked and looked.

Brer Billy Goat chewed and chewed.

Brer Wolf looked close. He didn't see no grass. He didn't see no corn shucks. He didn't see no straw and he didn't see no leaves.

Brer Billy Goat chewed and chewed.

Brer Wolf couldn't figure out to save his life what Brer Billy Goat was eating. Didn't nothing grow on a rock like that. Finally Brer Wolf couldn't stand it any more.

"How do, Brer Billy Goat? I hope everything is going well with you these days."

Brer Billy Goat nodded and kept on chewing.

"What you eating, Brer Billy Goat? Looks like it tastes mighty good."

Brer Billy Goat looked up. "What does it look like I'm eating? I'm eating this rock."

Brer Wolf said, "Well, I'm powerful hungry myself, but I don't reckon I can eat rock."

"Come on. I'll break you off a chunk with my horns. There's enough here for you, if you hurry."

Brer Wolf shook his head and started backing away. He figured that if Brer Billy Goat could eat rock, he was a tougher man than Brer Wolf was. "Much obliged, Brer Billy Goat. But I got to be moving along."

"Don't go, Brer Wolf. This rock is fresh. Ain't no better rock in these parts."

Brer Wolf didn't even bother to answer but just kept on going. Any creature that could eat rock could eat wolf too.

Of course, Brer Billy Goat wasn't eating that rock. He was just chewing his cud and talking big.

You know something? There're a lot of people like that.

READER'S RESPONSE

1. Do Brer Wolf and Brer Billy Goat remind you of real people? Why? What words would you use to describe them?
2. Brer Billy Goat was "talking big" to save himself from Brer Wolf. Can you think of a time when you saw someone talking big? How did it turn out? In your journal, write about what happened.

WRITER'S CRAFT

3. In most stories, a problem makes the characters act. What is the problem in this story?
4. The place where Brer Billy Goat is standing is very important to the story. What details describe this place?
5. What do you think was the most convincing thing Brer Billy Goat said to fool Brer Wolf?

Ways to Write Creatively

In this chapter, you'll write a story and a poem, two types of creative writing. Creative writing always starts with imagination, but it can have many different forms. Writers create plays, song lyrics, movie scripts, and fairy tales. They use words in many different ways—like musicians playing different instruments. Here are some ways writers use words and imagination to write creatively.

- in a movie script, telling what happens to a child who gets separated from her parents at a circus
- in a story, telling about a boy who trains his dogs for a dog-sled race in Alaska
- in a poem, describing how a kitten's fur looks and feels
- in a paragraph for a short story, describing a log cabin at a summer camp
- in a song, showing how a father and son are different
- in a poem, comparing fog to "little cat feet"
- in a play, showing how hard work leads to an athlete's victory
- in a poem, stating the qualities that you think a best friend should have

LOOKING AHEAD

In the main assignment in this chapter, you'll use narration to create a story. As you think and write, keep in mind that a good short story

- entertains the reader
- includes a problem, or conflict
- presents lifelike characters, clearly described places, and interesting events

Writing a Story

Prewriting

Finding a Story Idea

Have you ever seen two kids whispering to each other and imagined what they were saying? Maybe they're deciding where to bury a treasure. What about seeing a car stranded with a flat tire? You might imagine it's Michael Jordan—on his way to a big Bulls game! Will he make it in time?

These are great starting ideas for stories. And how did you get them? Just notice any person or problem. Then let your imagination take off.

Starting with People.   Think about people you see on the news, read about in the newspaper, or see on the street. Imagine them as *characters* in a story. What problems might they have? You see an article about your town's mayor and imagine that she's being held hostage by a creature from another planet. You notice the big ring on your next-door neighbor's finger and imagine that it suddenly disappears.

Starting with Problems. Listen to friends, family, or people on the news talk about *problems.* Are you curious about how the problems might turn out? One of your friends has to move to another state, and you imagine a teenager having trouble making friends. You read about a two-year-old trapped in a well and imagine a boy coming to the rescue.

EXERCISE 1 ▶ **Exploring Story Ideas**

It's time to rev up your imagination! Following are three story starters—details about a possible character or about a problem someone has. With each story starter, there is a question for you to answer about the problem or the characters. Work with a small group and brainstorm as many ideas as you want.

EXAMPLE 1. **A Person**: A twelve-year-old boy who is small for his age and not very strong.
What is the problem?

1. *Chim will be grounded if he's late getting home. He can make it if he takes the shortcut through the alley. But he's scared of the dark alley and a big mean dog.*

1. **A Person**: A teenage circus performer who has never lived outside the circus. Her parents are great acrobats with the circus.

What is the problem?

2. **A Problem**: The lights suddenly go off in a noisy, crowded food court at the mall on a Friday evening.

Who is (are) the character(s)?

3. **A Problem**: A big storm develops on a camping trip. The tent begins to leak and fall down.

Who is (are) the character(s)?

WRITING ASSIGNMENT

PART 1:
Finding a Story Idea

Now you're ready to find your own story ideas. Brainstorm until you find an idea for your story. Your idea should include a problem and at least one character. Remember: You might pick up a hint of an idea from a real person or problem, but you need to use your imagination to go beyond that hint to an original story idea.

Prewriting

Planning Your Story

Now you can think about your purpose and audience and can gather material for your characters, setting, and events.

Thinking About Purpose and Audience. When you write a story, one *purpose* is to be creative. Another purpose is to entertain your *audience*. Maybe you'll write a scary story about aliens or a funny story about talking ducks. Just think about what your readers would enjoy.

Imagining Characters. You may start with an idea drawn from a real person and experience—for example, your neighbor and the ring on her finger. But how do you go from there to the characters in your story? Try to form a mental picture. Will they have black shiny hair like your friend Wen Yu? Maybe they'll dress like your favorite band. Use the following questions to bring your characters to life.

- How old is my character?
- What does she or he look like? dress like? talk like?
- How does the character act—mean? silly? brave? kind?

HERE'S HOW

Main character: monster

looks: big, scary, <u>lots</u> of eyes, big fangs, no
        clothes, just lots of blue slime

talks: no words—loud roaring noises

acts: mean, angry, not afraid to fight

Imagining Setting.   The place and time of your story are the *setting.* A setting can create a problem or a mood. Suppose your setting is a burning building with people inside. That's quite a problem! A dark cave in a storm would also create a mood of fear.

The setting doesn't always create a problem or a mood. Maybe it's as ordinary as the school ball field. But your readers will need to see the setting in their minds so they can understand your story. Use these questions to plan your setting.

- Where will my story take place—in a house or a bus? under the sea? in a city or on a farm?
- When will my story take place? at what time of day? during the spring, summer, fall, or winter?

| WRITING ASSIGNMENT | PART 2:
Imagining Characters and Setting |

Can you close your eyes and picture your characters? How about your setting? To spark your imagination, use the questions on pages 151 and above. Write your ideas down.

Exploring Your Plot. All stories have *plots,* and they start with a *problem* (sometimes called a *conflict*). The problem sets a *series of events* in motion. These events happen in chronological order, with one event causing the next.

The events build in excitement or interest to the reader until they reach a *high point.* That's when the problem is settled, one way or another.

The part of the story that occurs after the problem is settled is called the *outcome.* It shows how everything works out and answers all the questions readers might have.

When you developed your original story idea, you built it around a problem. Now, all you have to do is take that problem and build the rest of your plot. To plan your plot, ask yourself these questions:

- What series of events does my problem begin?
- What happens first, second, later?
- What event will settle the problem (the high point)? How will it be settled?
- Will my readers have any questions about what happened at the end of the story? How could I answer those questions (the outcome)?

One way to plan a story is to complete a map. Here is how a writer did a map of a story about a monster.

HERE'S HOW

	Plot Map
<u>Conflict</u>	Tyrel needs to get rid of the monster and save Great Aunt Bernice.
<u>Events</u>	1. He can't find Great Aunt Bernice. 2. He finds the monster in the kitchen after it's shrunk Great Aunt Bernice. 3. He gets Great Aunt Bernice outside.
<u>High point</u>	4. He goes back to the monster and destroys it.
<u>Outcome</u>	5. It's a dream.

To plan a good story

- use your imagination to develop your characters
- imagine a setting that creates a problem or a mood, or that helps your readers understand the story
- explore the conflict or problem and map out a series of events, a high point, and an outcome

CRITICAL THINKING

Analyzing Causes and Effects

When you analyze causes and effects, think about how one thing leads to another. In a story one event should cause another event. If something happens without an obvious cause, the story seems fake. Have you ever seen a movie where the hero crawls out of a flooding river and then pulls a dry match out of his pocket to light a fire? How did he happen to have that dry match? To write a good story, you have to connect effects with causes.

CRITICAL THINKING EXERCISE:
Analyzing Causes and Effects

Figure out causes and effects with a little help from your imagination. Look at the following example and notice how it begins with one event that causes a chain of events. After studying the example, get together with a partner and create a cause-and-effect chain for the three events listed below the example. Then compare your chains with those of other students. Is there an obvious cause for every effect?

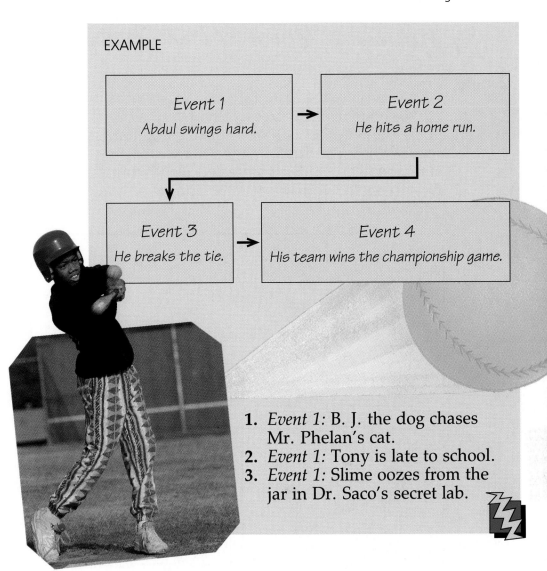

EXAMPLE

Event 1 Abdul swings hard.	→

Event 2
He hits a home run.

Event 3
He breaks the tie.

Event 4
His team wins the championship game.

1. *Event 1:* B. J. the dog chases Mr. Phelan's cat.
2. *Event 1:* Tony is late to school.
3. *Event 1:* Slime oozes from the jar in Dr. Saco's secret lab.

WRITING ASSIGNMENT

PART 3:
Planning Your Story

Gather together the main events for your story. Then make your own plot map just like the one on page 153. Put this map together with the notes you made about your characters and setting in Writing Assignment, Part 2 (page 152). That's it—you have a good plan for your story!

Writing Your First Draft

As you write your first draft, you may feel as if part of you is living in the secret world of your story. That's a good sign. It shows that your imagination is taking over. Wherever your imagination leads you, make sure you keep readers interested. Following are some tips to make your story's beginning, middle, and ending strong.

Peanuts reprinted by permission of United Feature Syndicate, Inc.

Combining the Basic Parts of a Story

Beginning. Get your reader hooked right away. Introduce the conflict early, so the reader wants to find out what happens. Gabriella loses her sister Elena's new bracelet. Can she find it before Elena misses it?

Middle.   Use *suspense* to keep your readers wondering what will happen next. Elena says she can't wait to show her bracelet to a friend. How will Gabriella stall Elena?

Also keep events and characters lively with these two techniques:

- **Use description.** Don't just say, "Gabriella acted nervous." Does she jump up from the table and talk in a loud voice? Is her face red? Remember to *show*, not tell, your readers what's happening.
- **Use dialogue.** The words a character uses add life, too. "Gabriella tried to stop her sister" is pretty dull. See how much better this dialogue is: "Wait, wait!" she shouted. "You can't, I mean, don't get the bracelet. Not yet, OK? Have more spinach!" Try to make dialogue sound natural, as people actually talk. You can use short phrases, contractions, and slang.

👉 REFERENCE NOTE: For help in punctuating dialogue, see pages 615–621.

Ending.   Solve your conflict, and tie up any loose ends. Make the outcome believable. If Gabriella finds the bracelet before Elena discovers it's missing, the conflict is over. But have you explained how and where Gabriella found it? Be sure to satisfy your readers' curiosity.

EXERCISE 2 ▶	**Speaking and Listening: Using Description and Dialogue**

Working with a group, rewrite the following passages. Use description and dialogue to make them come alive. Working with another group, take turns reading your passages aloud. What are your favorite parts?

1. Angela's mother told her to get off the phone. Angela ignored her and kept talking. Then her mother got mad.
2. The coach called Deven off the bench as relief pitcher. The other players shouted support as he ran to the mound. Deven felt nervous.

Looking at a Short Story

No two stories are exactly the same. Writers use characters, setting, and plot in many different ways. The following science fiction story begins with a description of the setting. It also starts off with strong suspense. Can you guess the ending as you read?

A SHORT STORY

Zoo
by Edward D. Hoch

BEGINNING

Setting
Main character

The children were always good during the month of August. This was especially so when it began to get near the twenty-third. For every year on the twenty-third of August, Professor Hugo's Interplanetary Zoo came to the Chicago area. The great silver spaceship would settle down in a huge parking area. It would remain there during its annual six-hour visit.

Long before daybreak large crowds would gather. Lines of children and adults, each one clutching his or her dollar, would wait restlessly to see the Professor's Interplanetary Zoo. Everyone was eager to see what race of strange creatures the Professor had brought this year.

In the past they had been treated to three-legged creatures from Venus. Or tall, thin men from Mars. Or snake-like horrors from some even more distant planet.

This year, as the large silver spaceship settled down to earth in the huge parking area just outside of Chicago, the children watched with awe. They saw the sides of the spaceship slide up to reveal the usual cages made of thick bars. Inside the cages were some wild, small, horse-like animals that moved with quick, uneven motions and kept chattering in a high-pitched tone.

The citizens of Earth clustered around as Professor Hugo's crew quickly collected a dollar from everyone in the audience. Soon the good Professor, himself, made an appearance. He was wearing his many-colored cape and top hat.

Suspense

Characters

MIDDLE
Event 1

Setting

Description

Description

Dialogue

"Peoples of Earth," he called into his microphone.

The crowd's noise died down and he continued. "Peoples of Earth," he went on, "this year we have a real treat for your dollar. Here are the little-known horse-spider people of Kaan — brought to you across a million miles of space at great expense. Gather around the amazing horse-spider people of Kaan. See them, study them, listen to them. Tell your friends about them. But hurry! My spaceship can remain here for only six hours!"

Conflict/
Suspense

Event 2

And the crowds slowly filed by, horrified and fascinated by these strange creatures that looked like horses, but ran up the walls of their cages like spiders. "This is certainly worth a dollar," one man remarked. "I'm going home to tell my wife."

Dialogue

All day long it went like that. Finally, ten thousand people had filed by the barred cages which were built into the side of the spaceship. Then, as the six-hour time limit ran out, Professor Hugo once more took the microphone in his hand.

Event 3

Dialogue

"We must go now," said the Professor, "but we will return again next year on this date. And if you enjoyed Professor Hugo's Interplanetary Zoo this year, phone your friends in other cities. Tell them about it. We will land in New York tomorrow. Next week we go on to London, Paris, Rome, Hong Kong, and Tokyo. Then we must leave for other worlds!"

He waved farewell to them. And, as the ship rose from the ground, the Earth peoples agreed that this had been the very best Zoo yet. . . .

ENDING
Event 4

Setting

Description

Two months and three planets later, the silver spaceship of Professor Hugo settled at last onto the familiar jagged rocks of Kaan. The horse-spider creatures filed quickly out of their cages. Professor Hugo was there to say a few parting words to them. Then the horse-spider creatures scurried away in a hundred different directions as they began seeking their homes among the rocks.

Event 5

**Dialogue/
Suspense**

**Description/
Dialogue**

In one, the she-creature was happy to see the return of her mate and little one. She babbled a greeting in the strange Kaan language. Then she hurried to embrace them. "You were gone a long time," she said. "Was it good?"

The he-creature nodded. "Our little one enjoyed it especially," he said. "We visited eight worlds and saw many things."

The little one ran up the wall of the cave. "The place called Earth was the best.

Conflict

High point

Outcome/Surprise
Ending

The creatures there wear garments over their skins, and they walk on two legs."

"But isn't it dangerous?" asked the she-creature.

"No," the he-creature answered. "There are bars to protect us from them. We stay right in the ship. Next time you must come with us. It is well worth the nineteen commocs it costs."

The little one nodded. "It was the very best Zoo ever. . . ."

| EXERCISE 3 | **Analyzing the Parts of the Short Story** |

Think about the parts of "Zoo." Then, with a partner, answer the following questions.

1. Do you like this story? What is your favorite part of the story?
2. Is the setting of the story important? Why or why not?
3. Who are the characters in the story?
4. "Zoo" is unusual because there is a small conflict—whether everyone in line can see the horse-spider people—that is solved pretty easily. But then, POW! A surprise ending makes you see the events in a different way. What do you learn at the end?

Using a Story Framework

"Zoo" is filled with odd characters, strong descriptions, and a funny surprise ending. Your own story may not be as long and tricky, but it can be just as entertaining. Read the following Writer's Model and notice how the writer gets right to the conflict. Does the beginning make you curious? Does it make you want to keep on reading?

A WRITER'S MODEL

Soap to the Rescue

BEGINNING
Characters/
Setting

Event 1

After school Tyrel went to his Great Aunt Bernice's house. He went there every Tuesday to see if she needed anything. She was his favorite relative. When he knocked on the door, he heard a weird roaring noise. He opened the door and looked around. He didn't see Great Aunt Bernice anywhere. He did see tons of gigantic blue footprints.

Conflict/Suspense
Description

Event 2

Tyrel went down the hall and saw a huge space monster standing in the kitchen. He didn't see Great Aunt Bernice anywhere. The monster looked very fierce. It had five gigantic eyes that popped out of its head. It had two fangs sticking out of its mouth. It was covered in blue slime, and it smelled bad.

Character/Description

MIDDLE
Event 3

Dialogue/
Suspense

Tyrel was about to run for help. Then suddenly one of the monster's eyes shot out of its head and saw him. Tyrel said, "Yi! Yi! Yi!" He jumped into the air and zoomed to the other side of the kitchen. Suddenly he saw a little glass jar on the table. Great Aunt Bernice was inside it. She was trying to jump out of the jar.

Event 4

Tyrel grabbed the jar and jumped out the kitchen window. He put Great Aunt Bernice on the ground. Then he ran around and went back inside the house. In science class he had learned that space monsters were scared of soap. He filled a bucket with soapy water and ran back to the kitchen.

ENDING
High point/
Description

Outcome

The monster was roaring, and blue slime was all over. Tyrel said, "Take this, Stinky!" He threw the soapy water onto the monster. It roared even louder, and all its eyes popped out. Then it shrank to the size of a bug. When Tyrel looked up, he saw Great Aunt Bernice. She was shaking him. He had dreamed the whole thing.

WRITING ASSIGNMENT

PART 4:
Writing Your First Draft

Now it's your turn. Use your notes and plot map to guide your writing. But don't try to stop your frisky mind. If you have new ideas for characters, setting, or plot, use them. Be creative with the outcome of your story. The model used a dream. What other kind of ending could you try?

Evaluating and Revising

One tough part of writing a story is over. You made it all the way through! Now you can do some finishing touches. Could you make your characters more real? your plot more exciting? By evaluating your story, you'll find spots that could be better. When you revise, you'll fix those weak spots, so your story will be really fantastic.

The chart on the next page will help you evaluate and revise. If you answer no to any of the questions in the left-hand column, try out the suggestions in the right-hand column.

WRITING NOTE Don't forget an important finishing touch to your story: the title. The title is an invitation to the reader. If it's snazzy in some way, the reader may accept the invitation and start reading. You can create an inviting title by thinking about an important character, the setting, or the plot. The writer focused on the way Tyrel destroyed the monster. Doesn't "Soap to the Rescue" make you curious about how and what soap could rescue? Try to create a title your reader can't resist.

EVALUATING AND REVISING SHORT STORIES

EVALUATION GUIDE	REVISION TECHNIQUE
1 Does the story grab the reader's attention right away?	**Add** sentences that make the conflict stand out. **Add** specific details about characters and setting.
2 Are events tied together? Do they make the reader curious?	**Cut** events that don't show cause and effect. **Add** events that create suspense.
3 Do the characters seem real?	**Add** details about how characters look, act, think, and feel. **Add** dialogue that sounds natural.
4 Is the setting clear?	**Add** details about time of day, time of year, and place.
5 Is the conflict solved? Does the end of the story make sense?	**Add** a high point, in which the conflict is settled. **Add** details to show how everything works out.

HAVE YOU FINISHED YOUR CREATIVE WRITING ASSIGNMENT, SKYLER?

NOT YET.

© 1990 Tribune Media Services, Inc. All Rights Reserved

WHILE WORKING ON MY FINAL DRAFT, I LEFT MY MANUSCRIPT NEAR AN OPEN WINDOW. I GOT UP TO DO SOME RESEARCH IN MY UNCLE'S LIBRARY...

WHILE I WAS GONE, A BAND OF FERRETS CAME THROUGH THE WINDOW AND ATE THE LAST THREE PAGES...

GOOD GRIEF...

MY EXCUSES ARE GETTING MORE CREATIVE THAN MY WRITING.

GRAMMAR HINT

Using Verb Tenses

To describe action in a story, you usually use the past tense: "They **slurped** and **burped**." Be careful not to switch from past tense to present tense. Be consistent by using one tense. (Remember that past tense shows what has already occurred. Present tense shows what is occurring now.)

TENSES SWITCHED   The monkey **threw** the coconut out of the tree. It **hits** the sand and **rolls** down to the water. The fisherman **picked** it up and **puts** it in his sack.

TENSES CONSISTENT   The gigantic bug **crawled** to the door and **pushed** it open. It **knocked** over a table and **moved** toward the cat food. The cat **scrambled** out of the way.

☞ REFERENCE NOTE: For more help with verb tenses, see pages 489–490.

E X E R C I S E 4 ▶ Analyzing a Writer's Revisions

Here is a draft of the last paragraph of "Soap to the Rescue." It shows the changes the writer made to revise the first draft. Working with a classmate, take turns reading the paragraph aloud. Study the writer's changes. Then answer each of the questions about the writer's revisions. Your answers may help you revise your own story.

The monster was roaring, and blue

slime was all over. Tyrel said, "Take

(He threw the soapy water onto the monster.)

this, Stinky!" It roared even louder,   **add**

and all its eyes popped out. Then it ~~got~~

shrank to the size of a bug.

~~very small~~. When Tyrel looked up, he   **replace**

saw Great Aunt Bernice. She was

shaking him. He had dreamed the

whole thing.

1. Why did the writer add a sentence between the second and third sentences? How does this help the story?
2. Do you think replacing *got very small* with *shrank to the size of a bug* is a good change? Why?

WRITING ASSIGNMENT

PART 5:
Evaluating and Revising Your Story

It's time to evaluate and revise your own story. Read it over carefully and use the evaluating and revising chart on page 166 to help you out. When you're finished, trade stories with a classmate. Read each other's stories and give each other a few good suggestions about how to revise. (Remember to give helpful feedback.)

Proofreading and Publishing

Now that you've revised your story, it's time to clean it up. Are words spelled correctly? Are verb tenses consistent? Correct all the errors you can find.

Then, get together with classmates, and make a list of ideas for publishing or sharing your story. Here are two ideas to get you started.

- During lunchtime, read your stories aloud to other students.
- Make your own book, and illustrate the important events in your story. When you're finished, give the book to someone special.

 COMPUTER NOTE: Create eye-catching pages by using a word-processing program to add lines, borders, and boxes between different parts of your document.

 PART 6:
Proofreading and Publishing Your Story

Carefully proofread your revised story. Then, share your story with classmates or family members.

 Reflecting on Your Writing

If you like, date your story and add it to your **portfolio.** Then, use these questions to reflect on your writing. Attach your answers to your story.

- What details did you use to make your characters seem real?
- During revision, what events did you add to create suspense?
- What would you do differently the next time you write a story?

A STUDENT MODEL

"Never make the story unreasonable, and have fun with it." This advice comes from Melanie Scheidler, a student at Deerpark Middle School in Austin, Texas. Notice how Melanie develops her characters as you read this passage from her story.

from The Great Fall
by Melanie Scheidler

Everybody scurried to the low beams. Unfortunately, Casee got there last and had to use the high beam used for competition. She kicked her leg over the four-foot high beam and pulled her body up straight into a gymnast's lunge. Casee lost her balance, wobbled, and fell from the sky like a duck with a broken wing.

Ready to mount the beam again, Casee looked around at her teammates. They were all doing perfect cartwheels, keeping their bodies straight and tall, and landing without a wobble on their feet, not on the ground. Casee wished she could be like them. She shoved her leg over the top of the beam, pushing herself into another lunge.

As Casee's first foot landed, her right foot landed way too close, and she had not swiveled her hips enough. Casee tripped over her feet, immediately knowing this wasn't good news. Her arms slashed through the air, struggling to keep her balance. As she fell head first toward the floor, her left arm, still swinging, hit the rock-hard beam. The pain shot up her arm like a bullet. Her feet, trying to land, reached the floor but missed. As in slow motion, her broken arm, her hips, her legs, and finally, her head landed, making separate thumps on the hard, badly matted area. Not breathing, she got up and started limping, searching for oxygen; gasping for air, tears streaming down her face.

WRITING WORKSHOP

A Limerick

A *limerick* is a funny rhyming poem that tells a story. Most limericks are about characters who do very silly things, like the ones in this limerick:

> There was a Young Lady of Bute,
> Who played on a silver-gilt flute;
>   She played several jigs
>   To her Uncle's white Pigs:
> That amusing Young Lady of Bute.
>
> Edward Lear, *A Book of Nonsense*

All limericks have five lines. The first, second, and fifth lines rhyme with each other. The third and fourth lines also rhyme with each other.

Each line in a limerick has a certain number of stresses. A *stress* is a strong beat—an emphasis in your voice. In the next limerick, the stresses are shown with capital letters. Read the limerick aloud. You'll hear that the first, second, and fifth lines have three stresses. The third and fourth lines have two stresses.

Many limericks are like jokes. They travel all around the world by word of mouth. Have you heard the one about the girl who threw eggs?

> There WAS a young GIRL of AsTURias,
> Whose TEMper was FRANtic and FURious.
>   She USED to throw EGGS
>   At her GRANDmother's LEGS—
> A HABit unPLEASant, but CURious.
>
> Anonymous

Thinking It Over

1. What makes this limerick funny?
2. Does this girl seem real?
3. What words rhyme at the end of lines one, two, and five?
4. What words rhyme at the end of lines three and four?

Writing a Limerick

Prewriting. Can you think of a silly character for your limerick? You might begin by finishing this line: "There once was a . . ." Brainstorm a few ideas.

Writing, Evaluating, and Revising. Listen to the limerick rhythm a few times. Get the singsong beat in your head. Then, start writing. When you've finished writing your limerick, read it to yourself aloud. Is it silly enough? Do the right words rhyme? Swap limericks with a classmate, and give each other a few helpful suggestions. Then, revise your limerick.

Proofreading and Publishing. Proofread your limerick carefully to catch mistakes. Then, publish your limerick. Perhaps you can read it aloud for a "Who Can Be Silliest?" contest. Do you want to add your limerick to your **portfolio**? If so, date the paper, and attach written responses to these questions: What story does your limerick tell? What was easy about creating a limerick?

MAKING CONNECTIONS

WRITING A SKIT

Another good way to tell a story is to act it out. You can do that by writing a *skit,* or very short play, which tells a story through dialogue and action.

Try writing a skit to perform for your class based on "Brer Billy Goat Tricks Brer Wolf" on pages 144–146. With other students as co-writers, read the story again. Try to picture how you could act it out. Ask yourself these questions before writing.

- Can we use all the dialogue that's in the story?
- Will we need to write more dialogue for the characters?
- What can we show through action?

WRITING ACROSS THE CURRICULUM

Writing Sports Stories

Many of the things you learned about writing make-believe stories can be used to write stories about real people and real events. To write a true story about a real sports hero, you need to

- show how the person walks, talks, and acts
- show how the person faces a real problem
- create suspense for the reader
- let the reader know the outcome of the story

Think of a great athlete you admire. Then, read something about your sports hero. After reading about the obstacles this person faced, write a story showing how your hero overcame them.

6 WRITING TO INFORM: EXPOSITION

MATERIALS:
8½ × 11 IN. PAPER
(LIGHT WEIGHT)
SCISSORS

FLYING TIPS:
ADJUSTING FLAPS
CHANGES FLIGHT
PATTERN.

STUNT FLYER

Working and Playing

Have you asked any questions today? Have you gotten any answers? Have you found out something? You probably have. We want and get information every single day of our lives. And because **working and playing** fill so many hours, we're often finding out about *processes* — how to do something or how something works.

Writing and You. Writers give you information about processes all the time. One tells you how to build a model plane. Another explains how to perform a certain job. What processes have you read about lately? Did you learn to do something new?

As You Read. Mr. Wizard, whose real name is Don Herbert, explains "how-to" processes in science and makes them fun. As you read "Banana Surprise," notice that his information contains careful steps.

BANANA SURPRISE

BY DON HERBERT

MAGINE the amazement of a friend when you hand him a banana, which he peels only to find it has already been sliced into pieces! How can you slice the inside of a banana and not the outside?

INSERT a threaded needle into one of the ridges on the peel and push it through under the skin to the next ridge. Pull the needle through, leaving a few inches of the tail end of the thread sticking out of the banana. Reinsert the needle into the same hole, and run it under the skin again to the next ridge. Pull the needle through again, leaving the thread in both the first and second holes. Continue around the banana like this until the needle comes out of the first hole you made. The thread now circles the banana under the skin. Gently pull the two ends of the thread, slicing the banana as neatly as with a knife. The more cuts like this you make, the more surprised your friend will be to find the banana sliced under the skin.

from *Mr. Wizard's Supermarket Science*

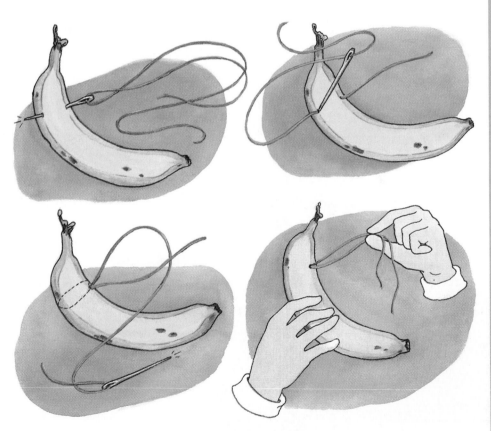

READER'S RESPONSE

1. Would you like to do this trick? Would you want it done *to* you? Describe how you think you would react to Banana Surprise.
2. In your journal, describe the funniest trick you ever played on someone—or someone played on you. If you like, swap stories with others. You may get ideas!

WRITER'S CRAFT

3. When you give information about a "how-to" process, materials and tools are usually important. What "tool" do you need for Banana Surprise?
4. The steps of a process should be given in the order you do them in—one, two, three, and so on. Are the steps of this trick in order? Give numbers to them.
5. Mr. Wizard ends his explanation with a final hint. What is it?

Ways to Inform

Your main writing assignment in this chapter will be explaining a process. To do that, you tell about something as it happens, step by step. But you often share information in other ways, too. Here are examples of other ways you can inform in writing.

- in a note to a friend, giving her directions so that she can find a new library
- in a science report, describing the preparations for the first Apollo moon landing
- in a field guide for hikers, describing how to recognize and avoid poisonous oleander
- in a classified ad, describing a bicycle you're selling
- in a report for a health class, explaining how martial arts and gymnastics are alike and how they are different
- in a life science report, comparing the songs of various birds in your neighborhood
- in a memo to a boss, explaining your opinion on your company's plan to offer new services
- in a book review, judging how realistic the book's setting is

LOOKING AHEAD

In the main assignment in this chapter, you'll be writing a paper telling how to do something. Your basic purpose will be to inform. As you prepare to write, keep in mind that a "how-to" paper

- includes all of the necessary materials, tools, and steps
- gives the steps in the order that you need to do them in

Writing a "How-to" Paper

Prewriting

Choosing a Process to Explain

All day long you learn how to do things. Here's your chance to teach other people how to do something.

Start by brainstorming a list of things you do well. Are you good at a certain game? Can you cook?

Choose something your *audience,* or readers, will want to learn. Remember that the *purpose* of a "how-to" paper is to explain an interesting process. Let's say you want to write about how to double Dutch jump rope. Some readers will be very interested, but others may not be at all. If you don't think your readers will want to learn how to jump rope, you might want to write about a process they will find more interesting.

COMPUTER NOTE: Use the multiple-window feature of your word-processing program to view two or three documents, such as your notes, your process ideas, and an outline, at one time.

EXERCISE 1 ▶ **Exploring Possible Topics**

Get together with two or three classmates to brain-storm ideas for "how-to" papers. You may have a million ideas, but if you're feeling blank, start with subjects like "games," "crafts," and "cooking." Then narrow the subject to a specific process like "how to play chess" or "how to make a pizza." When you have some topics, talk about them. Would you like to learn one of these processes? Can it be covered in a paragraph or two?

 **WRITING ASSIGNMENT**

PART 1:
Choosing a Process to Explain

The group brainstorming may have given you the perfect topic. But if not, think about your skills and thrills. Are you good at something other people might not know how to do? What's really fun to do? After you've picked your topic, write one sentence telling what it is.

Gathering and Organizing Information

What happens if you forget to tell your readers to put soap in the water? They can't blow bubbles. To make sure you don't forget any necessary information, plan carefully. Identify every important step, the materials you will need, and the best way to arrange the information.

Listing Important Steps and Materials

In a "how-to" paper, you need two types of information: the steps in the process and the materials and tools you need for the process.

Here's one way to gather the information. Imagine yourself doing the process on a "how-to" TV program. You do each step carefully and with great skill. You yourself didn't know you could do it so well! As you watch yourself, jot down two things: what each step is and what materials you need for it.

Arranging Your Information

Usually, the first thing your readers want to know is what materials or tools they'll need. Then they need the steps of the process in the order in which they need to be done. That's usually *chronological order,* or time order. Always check to be sure you don't put a step too early or too late. That might confuse your readers.

Remember, too, that every detail you use should help your readers understand the process. This is a good time to cross out any details that just get in the way.

On the next page is an example showing how one writer listed information for a paper about teaching a dog to heel. Notice that the steps are in the order you have to do them in.

How to Teach Your Dog to Heel on a Leash

Materials: six-foot leash and a training collar
Steps:
1. Get a leash and a training collar called a choke chain.
2. Put the training collar on your dog.
3. Get into the correct starting position.
4. Say "Heel," and start walking.
5. Jerk the collar when the dog makes a mistake.

Reminder

To plan a "how-to" paper

- list the steps in the process
- jot down the materials needed for each step
- make sure the steps are in chronological order
- take out details that aren't necessary

 **EXERCISE 2** ▶ **Listing Steps and Materials**

Here is a list of steps for making a Chinese papercut. Only the first two steps are in the right order. Working with a partner, number the other steps in order. Finally, list the materials and tools needed for this process.

1. Using tracing paper, copy your design.
2. Put the traced design on top of two or three sheets of colorful tissue paper.
   Tape your papercuts to a window, so light will shine through them.
   Last of all, cut the outline of the design.
   Staple around the edges of the sheets so they can't move.
   Using a sharp scissors, start cutting from the center of the design.

CRITICAL THINKING

Evaluating Details

When you write a "how-to" paper, it's easy to get carried away. Sometimes you know so much about the topic that many more details than you need crowd into your mind. It's important to get rid of unneeded details. They just confuse your readers. To *evaluate*, or judge, whether to keep a detail, ask yourself:

- Is this information that my audience already knows? (If it is, cross it out!)
- Is this detail a helpful hint? Does it keep readers from making a mistake? (If it does, keep it!)

CRITICAL THINKING EXERCISE:
Evaluating Details

One writer jotted down the following notes for making salsa, a Mexican sauce. The audience is a class of sixth-graders. Which details do you think could be crossed out?

You need 1 ripe tomato, 1 small onion, 1 peeled garlic clove, 1 or 2 chile peppers, 1/2 teaspoon salt, and 1 teaspoon lime juice.

Use serrano or jalapeño peppers. I like jalapeños best.

Also find measuring spoons, a knife, a cutting board, a mixing spoon, and a bowl.

My grandmother has a mixing bowl she bought in San Diego.

Chop the tomato, onion, garlic, and peppers very finely. Be careful not to cut yourself while you're chopping. You may want an adult to help you.

You can chop all the vegetables on the same cutting board since they'll be mixed up together anyway.

Put the chopped vegetables in a bowl and mix in the salt and lime juice.

Let the mixture sit for about half an hour, so the flavors can combine.

Serve with fajitas, tacos, or eggs. Salsa makes a plain egg fantastic.

WRITING ASSIGNMENT	PART 2: **Gathering and Organizing Information for Your Paper**

Now you're ready to plan your own "how-to" paper. First, create a chart like the one on page 183. Remember to double-check for chronological order and to cross out details readers don't need.

Writing Your First Draft

Here are some tips for writing your first draft.

- In the very beginning, try to catch your readers' interest. [Hint: Why is this process fun or important?]
- List the materials.
- Discuss the steps in order.
- End with a helpful tip or another example showing why the process is fun or important.

The explanation that follows tells one way to celebrate Children's Day. It's a national holiday in Japan. Do you think you could follow the writer's directions?

A MAGAZINE ARTICLE

Making a Flying Fish
by Paula Morrow

Attention grabber

Japanese boys and girls have their own special day each year on May 5. It is called Children's Day and is a national holiday. This is a time for families to celebrate having children by telling stories, feasting, going on picnics, or visiting grandparents. . . .

Process to be explained

A special feature of Children's Day is the *koinobori* that families display in their yards—one for each child in the family. A tall pole is placed in the garden. . . . Fish made of cloth or strong paper are attached to the pole. Each fish has a hoop

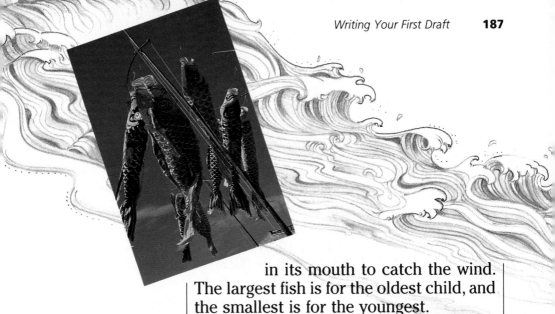

in its mouth to catch the wind. The largest fish is for the oldest child, and the smallest is for the youngest.

These fish represent a kind of carp known as a strong fighter. These carp battle their way upstream against strong currents. When the koinobori dance in the wind, they remind the children of carp leaping up a waterfall. This is supposed to inspire children to be equally brave and strong.

Reason for learning process

You can make your own koinobori and fly it from a pole or hang it from your window on May 5. In that way, you can share Children's Day with the boys and girls of Japan.

List of materials

You need an 18- by 30-inch piece of light-weight cloth (cotton, rayon, or nylon), felt-tip markers, a needle and thread, scissors, a narrow plastic headband, and string.

Step 1

First, choose a piece of cloth with a bright, colorful pattern or decorate it yourself with felt-tip markers. Fold the fabric in half lengthwise, with the bright side on the inside. Sew a seam 1/2 inch from the long (30-inch) edge, making a sleeve.

Step 2

Step 3

Step 4

Explanation

Step 5
Explanation

Step 6

Step 7

Step 8

Repeat of
reason

On one end of the sleeve, make a 1-inch-wide hem by turning the right side of the fabric over the wrong side. Then, sew the hem, leaving three 1-inch-wide openings about 5 inches apart.

Make cuts 5 inches deep and 1 inch apart all around the unhemmed end of the sleeve to form a fringe. This is the fish's tail.

Next, turn the sleeve right side out. With . . . a felt-tip marker, add eyes near the hemmed (head) end (away from the fringed tail).

Thread the narrow plastic headband into the hem through one of the openings. Continue threading it until the open part of the headband is hidden.

Then, tie a 12-inch-long piece of string to the headband at each of the three openings. Tie the loose ends of the strings together.

Finally, hang your windsock from the strings on a tree limb, a clothes pole, or the eaves of your house. On windy days, it will dance like a carp swimming upstream against a waterfall!

Faces

EXERCISE 3 ▶ **Analyzing a "How-to" Explanation**

Before you make your own flying fish, take a closer look at the process. Get together with a partner to discuss the following questions.

1. Paula Morrow writes a long introduction before talking about the "how-to" steps. What interesting details does she give?
2. What are the basic steps in making koinobori? Can you follow all of them? If not, where do you need help?
3. Do the pictures help you understand the process better? Explain.

WRITING NOTE

Think about drawing pictures for your "how-to" paper. Sometimes they make following a process easier.

Following a Basic Framework for a "How-to" Paper

Don't think you have to write a "how-to" paper like Paula Morrow's. The following writer's model is more like what you'll write. Your paper may even be shorter than the model. You may need only one or two paragraphs to explain your process.

A WRITER'S MODEL

Attention grabber

Reason

List of materials

Is your dog a daredevil? Does it chase cars or fight other dogs? To control your daredevil, train it to "heel" on a leash.

You will need a six-foot leash. You'll also need a special training collar called a choke

Step 1
Helpful hint

Explanation
Step 2

Step 3

Helpful hint
Step 4

Step 5

Step 6

Explanation
Helpful hint

Repeat of reason

chain. Before you get the collar, measure your dog's neck. The best collar size is about two inches longer than the dog's neck.

A choke chain has a ring at each end. To make it work, attach the leash to one ring. Hold the other ring in your right hand. With your left hand, double the chain. Then put the doubled chain through the ring you're holding. This makes a loop. To start training, put the loop over your dog's head.

The starting position is important. Stand with your dog at your left. Hold the end of the leash in your right hand. Your left hand holds the leash close to the choke chain. Say "Heel" in a firm voice, and begin walking, left foot first.

If the dog gets ahead or behind, jerk the leash with your left hand. Say "Heel." Your dog will learn that a tight collar means "Uh, oh, mistake!" Of course, be sure to say "Good dog" when your dog walks right.

That's one way to be your dog's best friend. Teach it to heel!

Transition words like *before, first, next,* and *then* signal a new step. They help your readers follow along, as these examples show.

Before you get the collar, measure your dog's neck.
First attach the leash to one ring.

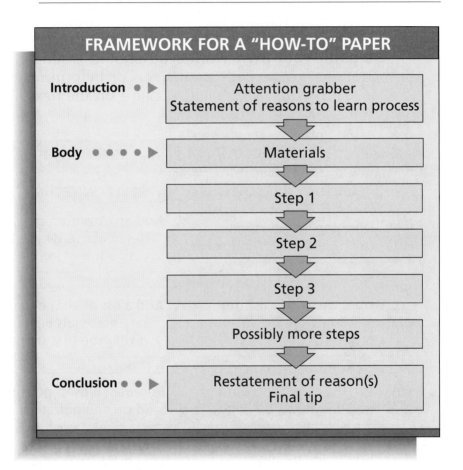

FRAMEWORK FOR A "HOW-TO" PAPER

Introduction ● ▶
Attention grabber
Statement of reasons to learn process

Body ● ● ● ● ▶
Materials

Step 1

Step 2

Step 3

Possibly more steps

Conclusion ● ● ▶
Restatement of reason(s)
Final tip

WRITING ASSIGNMENT

PART 3:
Writing a Draft of Your "How-to" Paper

Put your own process on paper, using your chart of steps and materials as a guide. Look at the framework above whenever you need to know what comes next.

Evaluating and Revising

Use the chart below to look more closely at your paper. Ask yourself each question on the left. When you honestly answer a question no, use the technique in the right-hand column.

Because you may skip over missing or confusing steps in your own work, you should evaluate your "how-to" paper with a partner. For helpful feedback on your paper, also use Exercise 4 on the next page.

EVALUATING AND REVISING PROCESS PAPERS

EVALUATION GUIDE	REVISION TECHNIQUE
1 Does the introduction catch the readers' interest?	**Add** an attention-getting detail about why the process is fun or important.
2 Does the writer list the materials needed for the process?	**Add** a list of all the necessary materials before giving the first step.
3 Are the steps in the order that they must be done?	**Reorder** steps to put them in chronological order.
4 Are all the details necessary and helpful?	**Cut** unneccessary details.
5 Is there a conclusion?	**Add** a sentence that gives a final hint or a reason for learning the process.

EXERCISE 4 ▶ **Speaking and Listening: Explaining and Following a Process**

Will your process make sense to readers? Let's find out. Get together with two classmates and read your draft aloud. One classmate will be the "actor" who performs your process as you read. The other will be the "director." The director first jots down the list of materials as you read it. If the actor needs an item you haven't listed, the director stops the process. The director also stops the process whenever a step doesn't work correctly, makes notes of problems, and gives a final evaluation of how clearly your paper describes the process. After you've finished reading your draft aloud, switch roles and perform your classmates' processes. Make sure everyone has a chance to be reader, actor, and director.

GRAMMAR HINT

Using Different Kinds of Sentences

When you write a "how-to" paper, it's easy to use too many *imperative sentences*. **Imperative sentences** give commands: Do this! Do that! To avoid sounding too pushy, try to vary your sentences.

IMPERATIVE SENTENCES	Don't let your pet decide where you go. Don't let it get ahead or behind. Jerk the leash with your left hand.
VARIED SENTENCES	You shouldn't let your pet decide where you go. If it gets ahead or behind, jerk the leash with your left hand.

 REFERENCE NOTE: For more information on sentence variety, see pages 311–318.

EXERCISE 5 ▶ **Analyzing a Writer's Revisions**

Here's the way the writer revised the fourth paragraph in the model on pages 189–190. After you've studied the changes, answer the questions that follow the paragraph.

> The starting position is important.
> Hold the end of the leash in your right
> hand. ~~You may be left-handed, but~~   cut
> ~~that doesn't matter.~~ Hold the leash   add
> close to the choke chain ~~in~~ your left   add/cut/reorder
> hand. Stand with your dog at your left.   reorder
> Say "Heel" *(in a firm voice,)* and begin walking, left foot   add
> first.

1. Why did the writer move the fifth sentence to the beginning of the paragraph?
2. Why did the writer cut the third sentence?
3. What's the reason for changing the fourth sentence to begin *Your left hand holds . . .*? [Hint: See page 182.]
4. At the end, is *in a firm voice* a good detail to add? Why or why not?

WRITING ASSIGNMENT

PART 4:
Evaluating and Revising Your "How-to" Paper

You probably have some ideas for improving your paper from the actor-director exercise (page 193). Now, use the evaluating and revising chart on page 192 for more help. After you've made all your changes, make a clean copy. Then, have your partners evaluate the paper one final time.

Proofreading and Publishing

Proofreading. You should always proofread a "how-to" paper carefully. A tiny mistake can ruin the description of a whole process and lead to undesired results.

Publishing. "How-to" papers are meant to be put to use. Here are some suggestions for sharing a "how-to" paper with people who might find it helpful.

- If you are explaining how to do a science project, give a copy to your science teacher.
- If you are explaining how to cook something, get together with a friend to try out the recipe.

| WRITING ASSIGNMENT |
PART 5:
Proofreading and Publishing Your Paper

After you've checked your paper for mistakes, make a clean copy of it. Then, find a way to share it.

 Reflecting on Your Writing

If you add your "how-to" paper to your **portfolio,** date it and attach responses to the following questions.

- Was it easy or hard to describe your process? Why?
- What did you do to get your reader's attention?

A STUDENT MODEL

The following excerpt is from a "how-to" paper written by Victor Chiang, a student in Randolph, New Jersey. As the excerpt shows, not all "how-to" papers are meant to be taken seriously. Victor advises other students to "try exaggerating" if they want to write amusing papers.

How to Watch Television
by Victor Chiang

Watching television is a favorite pastime of many Americans. You can watch TV, too. First, you need to get your materials. The first thing you need for watching television is--you guessed it--a television! Get a big-screen TV--projection is OK.

With your television, there should be a remote control. You'll need this valuable tool when watching all kinds of television. If the spacing between the channel up/down and the previous channel buttons on your remote control is not comfortable for your hand, then I suggest you get a new control. (The previous channel button allows you to flip between two channels by just pressing one button.) You will not need a number pad on your control for channels--use of the number pad is strictly forbidden. You must use either the channel up/down or the previous channel button.

You will also need to get popcorn, tissues (optional, see Watching Soap Operas and Watching Movies), your favorite sports team's hat, jackets, jerseys, your pajamas, and a jumpsuit. Your jumpsuit must be in a neon color that will practically blind someone. It must be either too big or too small, and it must have reflective tape on it, even if you don't plan on going outside. If your jumpsuit does not meet these requirements, it is not officially a jumpsuit.

WRITING WORKSHOP

Travel Directions

You can give different kinds of information in process papers—such as explaining how to do something. You can also explain how to get from one place to another using landmarks. A landmark is anything that can be seen easily—a big tree, a street corner, or a high building. In travel directions, words like *right*, *north*, *up*, and *near* help people understand where to go. They are *geographical* directions. Details about the distance between landmarks can help, too.

JumpStart reprinted by permission of United Feature Syndicate, Inc.

In the following passage from a fantasy adventure book, three characters are on a journey. Menion is giving his friends directions for getting to the Anar Forests. What landmarks does he mention?

from The Sword of Shannara
by Terry Brooks

"Well, at least we've made it this far," he declared cheerfully. "Now for the next leg of the trip!"

He sat up and began to sketch a quick map of the area in the dry earth. Shea and Flick sat up with him and watched quietly.

"Here we are," Menion pointed to a spot on the dirt map representing the fringe of the Black Oaks. "At least that's where I think we are," he added quickly. "To the north is the Mist Marsh and farther north of that the Rainbow Lake, out of which runs the Silver River east to the Anar Forests. Our best bet is to travel north tomorrow until we reach the edge of the Mist Marsh. Then we'll skirt the edge of the swamp," he traced a long line, "and come out on the other side of the Black Oaks. From there, we can travel due north until we run into the Silver River, and that should get us safely to the Anar."

Thinking It Over

1. How does the map help Shea and Flick understand Menion's directions?
2. Find some details that give you information about geographical directions and landmarks.
3. Which part of this trip would you enjoy? Can you find hints that the journey will be dangerous?

Writing Travel Directions

Prewriting. Like Menion, you will tell how to get from one place to another. You might tell how to get from home to school, or from a park to a friend's house. Or you can give directions to a made-up place. If you do that, make a map first. Your friends and teacher will need it to see whether your directions work!

Writing, Evaluating, and Revising. Your beginning should briefly describe the place you're writing directions for and name the starting place. Then, organize your directions in chronological order. Be sure to include details about landmarks, geographical directions, and distance. To evaluate your directions, ask a friend to draw a map as you read the directions aloud. Look at your friend's map, and see how well it matches yours. How can you change your directions to make them clearer?

Proofreading and Publishing. Be sure to check your punctuation, capitalization, and spelling before setting someone off on a journey. Is your landmark a *hill* or a *mill*? It makes a difference! You could swap neighborhood directions with others who live near you. Or you could play a draw-the-map game.

Do you plan to add your travel directions to your **portfolio**? If you do, date your paper and include your response to the following questions: What details did you add, and why did you add them? How did you revise your directions to make them clearer?

MAKING CONNECTIONS

PROCESS IN LITERATURE

Riddle Poems

Here's a riddle from *When I Dance* by Jamaican writer James Berry. Can you figure out the answer?

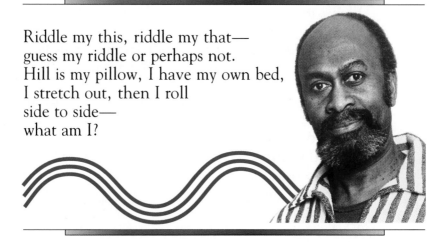

Riddle my this, riddle my that—
guess my riddle or perhaps not.
Hill is my pillow, I have my own bed,
I stretch out, then I roll
side to side—
what am I?

"What am I?" riddles like this often describe a process. When you figure out the process, you know the riddle's answer. But the process may be written in a tricky way! Words may have more than one meaning, like river *bed* in James Berry's riddle poem.

You can find many other riddles that make you figure out a process. Ask people in your family if they know any riddles, or look for "What am I?" riddles in the library. Choose the process riddle you like best. Then see if your classmates can guess the answer.

Answer: A river from its source to meeting and mixing with the sea.

SPEAKING AND LISTENING

Science and Health: First Aid

In emergencies, you hope that someone knows how to give first aid. If no one else knows what to do, *your* first-aid skills may save someone's life.

Most first-aid instruction is a clear list of steps. For example, here's what to do if someone is choking.

1. Stand behind the person.
2. Put your arms around the person's waist.
3. Place your fist against the middle of the person's waist. The right place is just below the ribs.
4. With your other hand, grab your fist.
5. Pull your fist in. Use a quick, upward motion.

Fortunately for Sparky, Zeke knew the famous "Rex maneuver."

Get together with two classmates. Choose one of the following emergencies: burn, sprain, cut, nosebleed, or bee sting. Together, find out the first-aid process for helping the injured person. You can look for information in scout handbooks, Red Cross manuals, health books, and encyclopedias. Write down the first-aid steps for the emergency, and prepare a class demonstration.

PROTECT
OUR
WILDLIFE

Taking a Stand

When you feel strongly about something, you **take a stand.** You say, "Listen. This is what I believe, and why I believe it." Then you try to persuade others to think or feel the same way. Notice how the poster on these pages tries to persuade you.

Writing and You. There are different ways to persuade. You can give logical reasons. Or you can try to use words that will affect people's feelings. Usually, people do a little of both. The government urges you to recycle; advertisers try to convince you to buy a certain brand of hair gel or jeans; your parents try to get you to study harder; and you try to convince them to let you go to a party. Have you taken a stand lately?

As You Read. In the following story passage, Midge Glass tries to persuade Henry Reed that her brains will help him with his business.

from

HENRY REED, INC.

by Keith Robertson

"Why should I?"

"Teamwork," she answered. "Teamwork's the thing these days in research. My father says things have gotten so complicated that one man alone can't discover much any more."

I thought this over for a minute while I kept working on my sign. If her father was a research chemist like she said, she probably knew quite a bit about how research organizations work, and also with the whole summer ahead of me I figured it might be nice to have someone to talk to, even if it was a girl a year and a half younger than I. I turned around and sat down on the ladder.

"What are you going to put into the business?" I asked. "I've got the property here, the building, a lot of pigeons which are inside, and one turtle." I waved my hand up at the half-finished sign, which was pretty good. "I'm even furnishing the sign."

"I'll furnish brains," she said.

Even though I always try to be polite, I laughed out loud at that, but she didn't seem to mind.

"Brains are the most important part of any research organization. My father says so."

"He's probably right," I admitted. "But the question is who has them? What grade are you in?"

"Seventh," she replied.

"There you are," I said. "I'm in the eighth grade so I've had more education. I've had more experience, too. I'm a teen-ager and you're only twelve."

"That's no advantage," she said. "Who are all these delinquent children you read about in the papers? Teen-agers—that's you. Me, I'm not a teen-ager so I must be a respectable, law-abiding citizen."

She started laughing like an idiot again. I don't know what about, since her remark didn't even make any sense. I climbed down the ladder and put my can of paint and brush on a box. I sharpened my pencil and started toward the ladder again.

"I could also contribute a pair of rabbits," she said. "We could raise rabbits, and they use a lot of rabbits in research to test serum and drugs and feeds and things like that."

I thought this over for a minute. I've never had any rabbits because we have never lived anyplace where there was room enough. "What kind of rabbits?" I asked.

"Checkered Giants," Midge replied. "They're great big white rabbits with black spots."

"That might not be a bad idea," I said, "to have a few rabbits."

"You could just make that 'Reed and Glass, Inc.,'" she said, pointing up at my sign.

I had just finished painting the words "Henry Reed" and I didn't care much for the idea of changing my sign before it was half finished. "Let's see the rabbits first," I suggested.

READER'S RESPONSE

1. If you were Midge, would you give different answers to "Why should I?" If you were Henry, would you ask Midge other questions? Pretend you are either character, and freewrite what you would say to the other. You could also work up a skit with a friend.
2. Can you think of a time when you wanted someone to let you join in or tag along or share something? What did you say or do? What do you *wish* you had said or done? Write about it in your journal.

WRITER'S CRAFT

3. What reasons does Midge give Henry to convince him?
4. He thinks two of the reasons are pretty good ones. One reason makes him laugh. Explain his reactions.
5. Persuasion that asks you to do something ends with a **call to action:** a suggestion for a specific act. What does Midge try to get Henry to do (probably so he can't easily change his mind)?

Ways to Persuade

Persuasion has many different forms and messages. You can recognize it in television commercials and songs as well as in articles and books. The goal is always the same, though: to convince someone to believe or act a certain way. Here are some examples of ways to persuade.

- in a flyer, describing a dramatic chess game to persuade students to join a chess club
- in a letter, telling a story about your grandmother to get your cousin to come to a family reunion
- in a report for an art class, describing a piñata to persuade your art teacher to let you make one
- in an "items for sale" notice for the classified advertisements section of your local newspaper, describing a bicycle to persuade a reader to buy it
- in a cover letter for a job application, classifying your skills to persuade an employer to hire you
- in a letter to the editor, defining the word *art* to persuade other readers to support local art projects
- in a report for a health class, comparing foods to persuade readers that some are more nutritious
- in a newspaper article, reviewing a TV show and trying to persuade your readers to watch it
- in an oral report, evaluating a tutoring program to persuade your classmates to volunteer as tutors

LOOKING AHEAD

In this chapter, you will write a persuasive composition and a persuasive letter. As you develop your writing assignments, keep in mind that effective persuasion

- states an opinion clearly
- gives convincing support for the opinion

Writing a Persuasive Paper

 *Prewriting*

Choosing a Topic

You hear on the news that the city council is considering this law: No one under the age of fourteen can be on the street after 9 P.M. on school nights. You don't want this curfew law to be passed, but some other people think it's a good idea. This would be a good topic for persuasion.

Finding a Topic That Matters. What makes you mad? Litter on your street? What do you think should be changed in your school? Dress rules? If you care about something and have a strong opinion about what should be done, you can write about it.

Of course, it's also important that some other people disagree with you. If everyone has the same opinion about litter, you don't have anyone to persuade. Make sure you choose a topic about which people have different opinions.

Focusing Your Opinion. Sometimes you're not sure exactly what you think until you try to put something into writing. What do you really think should be done about your school's dress rules? No rules at all? Rules for Friday but not for Monday? To focus your opinion, write a sentence saying exactly what you believe. This *opinion statement* is the starting point of your paper. Here are some examples:

> The curfew law should not be passed.
> Our school lunchroom should have a salad bar.
> Writing a pen pal is a great way to learn about another country.

CRITICAL THINKING

Identifying Facts and Opinions

A *fact* is a statement that can be tested and proved true. Facts can be checked in books and other sources.

FACTS   The moon has many craters on its surface.
Nolan Ryan is the third pitcher in baseball history to strike out three hundred men in back-to-back seasons.

An *opinion* states a personal belief. Opinions can't be proved or checked in books. Notice that opinions often contain "judgment words," such as *good, best, worst, least, most, should, ought*.

OPINIONS   The United States should build a space station on the moon.
The best name for our new ball field is Nolan Ryan Park.

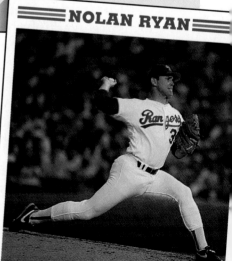

NOLAN RYAN

In persuasion, you need to be able to tell facts from opinions. Here's why:

- Your opinion statement expresses a belief. You aren't trying to persuade others of facts.
- You support your opinion statement with facts. These facts help you convince other people that your opinion is right.

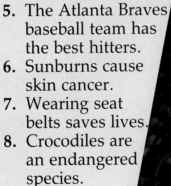 CRITICAL THINKING EXERCISE:
Identifying Facts and Opinions

Decide which statements below are facts and which are opinions. Then decide whether each statement would make a good topic for persuasive writing. Explain your thinking.

1. Dogs make the best pets.
2. Bicycles produce less air pollution than cars.
3. Our club should sell tacos at the Spring Fair.
4. Zoos are cruel to animals and should be closed.
5. The Atlanta Braves baseball team has the best hitters.
6. Sunburns cause skin cancer.
7. Wearing seat belts saves lives.
8. Crocodiles are an endangered species.

Reminder

When you choose a topic for persuasive writing

- find a topic you care about
- make sure everyone doesn't already have the same opinion about it
- write one sentence that clearly states your opinion

EXERCISE 1 ▶ **Exploring Possible Topics**

In a small group, brainstorm possible persuasion topics. (You can start with general subjects like the environment, schools, the homeless, movies, and TV. But also remember that you'll need to narrow down any general subjects.) Each person then chooses two of the topics and writes opinion statements for them. Discuss your statements. Who disagrees? Which topics create interest?

WRITING ASSIGNMENT

PART 1:
Choosing a Topic

Will you write about a topic from the brainstorming you did in your small group? Will you take a stand on something else? Your journal and newspapers are also sources for topics you care about. Choose one and write your opinion statement.

Planning Your Paper

Suppose you're facing your audience in person. You have stated your opinion. But the people in the audience just sit there, looking doubtful. "Why should we believe you?" they ask. To persuade them, you have to build a convincing answer.

Thinking About Purpose and Audience

Your *purpose* is always to persuade your *audience* to agree with you. You want your readers to think or to feel the same way you do about something. Sometimes, too, you'll add a *call to action* that asks them to do something. For instance, you may want them to vote for building a school taco stand or to volunteer for cleaning the schoolyard.

Think ahead about your audience. Ask yourself, *What do my readers think about my topic? What reasons will appeal to them? Will I ask them to take an action?*

Finding Support for Your Opinion

Suppose you've been studying about nutritious meals and you think people shouldn't eat doughnuts for breakfast every day. You can't just write "Don't do it. It's bad for you." To support your opinions, you can use *reasons*, *facts*, and *the opinions of experts*. Here are some examples:

- **Reasons:** Doughnuts are fattening.
- **Facts:** A yeast doughnut has about 235 calories. That's more than four times the calories in a serving of strawberries.
- **Expert opinions:** Mrs. Capo, the cafeteria manager, says that doughnuts are high in sugar and fat, not protein.

Sometimes you'll be able to think of reasons and facts by yourself. For some topics, though, you'll need to find support in books, magazines, and other library resources. These sources will also give you expert opinions to quote. But don't forget about people in your school or community who know something about your topic. You can quote them, too.

There's no magic number of reasons when you're writing persuasion. But two or three items of support are probably fine for a short paper. Here's how one writer gathered reasons, facts, and expert opinions for a paper.

HERE'S HOW

OPINION:	Our city should have a tree-planting program.
AUDIENCE:	The city council

SUPPORT:
1. Trees are pretty.
2. Trees give off oxygen (helps fight pollution).
3. Trees make shade.
4. They lower traffic noise that can damage hearing. (Yori Matsuo, pres. Arbor Club)

Organizing Your Ideas

Some reasons and facts are more convincing than others. Look at these reasons for not riding your bicycle into a wall:

1. You could leave a scuff mark on the wall.
2. You could bend your wheel.
3. You could break your head.

Probably the first reason is totally unimportant to you—hardly worth mentioning. The second reason is more important, and the last one is most important of all.

A good way to arrange your support is *order of importance:* from least important reason to most important, or the opposite. Either will work. In persuasion, you can start with a strong punch or end with one.

Reminder

To plan a persuasive paper

- support your opinion with reasons, facts, expert opinions
- choose support you think will convince your audience
- arrange your support in order of importance

EXERCISE 2 ▶   **Using Order of Importance**

"Just *try* to convince me," says the audience. Think about the following opinion statement, specific audience, and support. Choose the reasons you think will be most convincing to this audience. Then number the reasons in order of importance, with 1 as most important. Be ready to explain your thinking.

OPINION: Neighborhood businesses should hire kids to pick up litter from the streets.
AUDIENCE: Neighborhood Merchants Association
REASONS: 1. City employees will have less work to do.
           2. People like to shop in an area with clean streets.
           3. Picking up litter teaches kids good citizenship habits.
           4. Kids will have more money to spend in the neighborhood stores.

WRITING ASSIGNMENT

PART 2:
Supporting Your Opinion

Use a chart like the one on page 214 to gather support for your opinion. Be sure to identify your audience. Then ask yourself, *Why should they believe me?* Jot down all the reasons and facts you can think of. If your support seems weak, use the library or talk to experts on your topic. Finally, number your support in the order of importance to your audience.

EXERCISE 3

Speaking and Listening: Testing Your Support

In a small group, test the strength of your supporting ideas. First, identify your audience. Your listeners will then pretend to be that audience. Read your opinion statement and list of support once. Next, read everything again. This time your audience can stop you to ask questions or even to argue! Answer as best you can, and also make notes about good ideas. Finally, before you change roles, discuss which parts of your support were strong and which seemed weak. And don't forget what the "arguers" said—you may get ideas for other support.

Writing Your First Draft

The Basics of Persuasion

To put together your opinion statement and support in a persuasive essay, keep these basic parts in mind:

- **The Beginning.** Open with a surprising fact or question. Give your opinion statement.
- **The Middle.** Present support in a convincing way. Place your strongest support right after the introduction or just before the conclusion.
- **The Ending.** Close powerfully. Restate your opinion or call your readers to action.

COMPUTER NOTE: When you're writing the first draft of your essay, use bold, italic, or underline styling to mark sentences you think you might want to move or revise later.

The following example is from a book about a sea mammal, the manatee. What is the writer trying to persuade you to do or to think? Is she successful?

A PASSAGE FROM A BOOK

from Manatee on Location
by Kathy Darling

Opinion statement

Reason

Facts

aving the manatee is an American challenge—one that we should be able to meet.
Manatees are adaptable. They can live in fresh or salt water. They can eat a variety of plants. They do not require big wilderness areas. Where they are not hunted, they have no fear of humans and can coexist even in heavily populated areas.

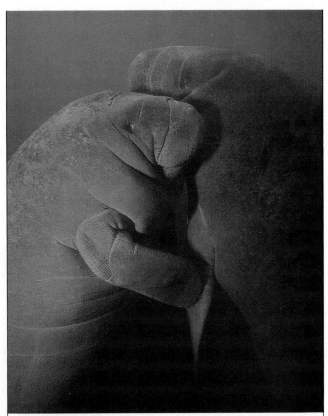

Reason//Fact

But it is beyond their power to adapt to speeding boats and crushing barges, which account for one third of all deaths. Only humans can prevent boat collisions or accidents in flood-control gates.

Reason

Not as dramatic, but perhaps the biggest threat of all, is the increasing destruction of the sea-grass beds the manatees need for food.

Opinion

Laws prohibiting dumping, dredging, or filling of these underwater pastures are urgently needed.

Opinion statement

With our help the manatees can survive.

Reason

By saving an endangered species in our own country, we can help the world to see how important—and effective—animal protection can be.

E X E R C I S E **4** ▶   **Analyzing Persuasive Writing**

Discuss the excerpt from *Manatee on Location* with two or three classmates. Then answer the following questions.

1. What did you know about manatees before you read this material? How did you feel about them?
2. Kathy Darling's opinion—what she's trying to convince you to believe and do—has three parts. One part is that we should save the manatees, even though she never says this directly. What are the other two parts of her opinion?
3. What reasons does she give to support her opinion? What facts does she give to support her opinion?
4. Does the support convince you? Explain why or why not.

   WRITING NOTE   The words you choose are important in persuasion. You can appeal to your readers' emotions with words like "hottest hockey star" or "unfair curfew." But don't go overboard. If you're too negative ("lousy idea") or excited ("worldwide favorite"), readers may not trust your opinion.

A Simple Framework for Persuasion

On the next page is a persuasive paper that follows a simple plan. You might want to organize your own first draft in the same way. The writer's audience is the city council.

A WRITER'S MODEL

Trees Help Humans

Attention grabber

Opinion statement

When you think of a city, do you picture buildings, concrete, and cars? Trees belong in that picture, too. Our city council needs to start a tree-planting program.

Reason

Reason

Reason

Expert opinion

Fact

Fact

Everybody agrees that trees are pretty, but they have other benefits, too. For one thing, their shade makes the city cooler in the summer. They also cut traffic noise and help people's health. Yori Matsuo, president of the Arbor Club, says trees lower loud traffic sounds that raise people's blood pressure and even damage their hearing. Most important, trees actually fight pollution by giving off oxygen. That's a great benefit for streets full of car fumes.

Summary of reasons

Call to action

The city council can help make our city prettier and healthier this spring. Please vote to start a tree-planting program at your meeting on February 11.

The writer's model you've just read follows the framework given below. You might want to refer to this framework as you write your first draft.

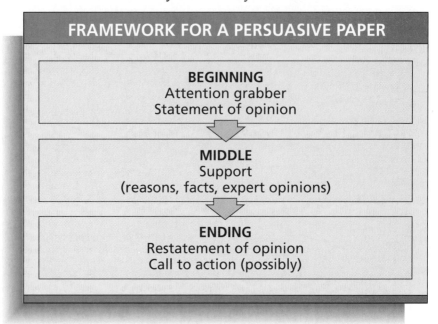

FRAMEWORK FOR A PERSUASIVE PAPER

BEGINNING
Attention grabber
Statement of opinion

MIDDLE
Support
(reasons, facts, expert opinions)

ENDING
Restatement of opinion
Call to action (possibly)

WRITING NOTE   In persuasive writing, it's important for your readers to follow your reasoning. Transitional words will help them follow along. Try using words like *first, next, also, finally, most important,* and *for example* to guide your readers through your paper.

WRITING ASSIGNMENT   PART 3:
Writing a Draft of Your Persuasive Paper

Use your planning chart to draft a convincing paper. Don't waste words. Be as clear and as forceful as you can. This is a good time to choose a title for your paper. Think of one that will interest your audience in your topic and will make them want to read on.

Evaluating and Revising

How often have you come away from an argument thinking, "I *should* have said . . . ?" By then, of course, it's too late. When you write a persuasive paper, however, it's not too late. You can take time to get your reasoning just right.

You can try your persuasion out on other people. Then you can use the evaluating and revising chart on page 224 to help you find problems in your paper and fix them. Ask yourself each question in the left-hand column. When you answer no to a question, use the revision technique in the right-hand column.

EXERCISE 5 ▶ **Analyzing a Writer's Revisions**

Here is a draft of the second paragraph in the writer's model on page 221. Study the changes with a partner. Use the evaluating and revising chart on page 224 to help you answer the questions that follow.

> Everybody agrees that trees are
> pretty, but they have other benefits,
> *[For one thing]*
> too. Their shade makes the city cooler   **add**
> *Most important,*
> in the summer. Trees actually fight   **add/reorder**
> pollution by giving off oxygen. That's a
> great benefit for streets full of car
> fumes. They also cut traffic noise and
> *[Yori Matsuo, president of the Arbor Club, says]*
> help people's health. Trees lower loud   **add**
> traffic sounds that raise people's blood
> pressure and even damage their
> hearing.

1. Why did the writer move the third and fourth sentences to the end of the paragraph?
2. Is *Most important* a good addition? Why or why not?
3. How does the addition about Yori Matsuo help make the paper more convincing?

EVALUATING AND REVISING PERSUASIVE WRITING

EVALUATION GUIDE	REVISION TECHNIQUE
1 Do the first one or two sentences grab the reader's interest?	**Add** (or **replace** your first-draft sentences with) a question or a surprising fact.
2 Is the writer's opinion stated early in the paper?	**Add** a clear statement of your opinion in the first two or three sentences.
3 Is there enough convincing support for the writer's opinion?	**Add** reasons, facts, or expert opinions.
4 Is support arranged in an effective order?	**Reorder** your support in order of importance to your audience.
5 Is the ending strong?	**Add** a restatement of your opinion or possibly a call to action.

GRAMMAR HINT

Combining Sentences with *Because* and *Since*

When you give reasons in persuasion, you are trying to show your readers *why* they should accept your opinion. Often you can combine sentences that explain *why* by using the words *since* or *because*. The new sentence makes your idea clearer and your writing smoother.

TWO SENTENCES	In-line skating is good for you. The movements tone your muscles.
	I'll do better in math. Mr. García will be tutoring me.
COMBINED SENTENCE	In-line skating is good for you **because** the movements tone your muscles.
	I'll do better in math, **since** Mr. García will be tutoring me.

☞ REFERENCE NOTE: For more information on combining sentences, see pages 311–318.

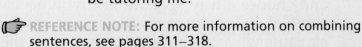

WRITING ASSIGNMENT	PART 4 **Evaluating and Revising Your Persuasive Paper**

Read your first draft aloud to yourself, and try to hear it as your audience would. To check your paper carefully, use the guidelines on page 224. If you answer no to questions on the left, use the techniques on the right to make improvements in your paper.

Proofreading and Publishing

On a radio, static can drown out the music. In a paper, annoying errors can interfere with your message. Proofread your paper carefully to find and fix all mistakes in punctuation, spelling, and usage.

Here are some ways to publish your paper:

- Mount your paper on construction paper, and hang it where your audience is sure to see it. You might hang it on a class bulletin board or on your family refrigerator.
- Give (or send) a copy of your paper to someone who could do what you would like to have done—the mayor, the school principal, or the President of the United States, for example.

WRITING ASSIGNMENT

PART 5:
Proofreading and Publishing Your Paper

Proofread your paper carefully. Try having a partner read it aloud while you follow along silently and look for errors. Make a clean copy of your corrected paper, and choose a way to share it. If you decide to mail a copy of it to someone, include a cover letter that explains why you have sent him or her the paper.

 Reflecting on Your Writing

If you plan to add your persuasive paper to your **portfolio,** date the paper and attach your responses to the following questions.

- How did you shape your supporting sentences so that they would appeal to your audience?
- What important changes did you make during the revision stage? Why did you make them?

A STUDENT MODEL

You can be convincing about all kinds of topics, as Cameron Kuehne shows in his persuasive paragraph. Cameron, a student at Sunnyside Elementary School in Clackamas, Oregon, supports a four-day workweek for students and teachers. To Cameron, "picking which topic to write about was easy because I knew exactly what I wanted." Does Cameron convince you?

A Four-day Workweek
by Cameron Kuehne

Which would you rather have, a four-day workweek, or a five-day workweek? I know a four-day workweek would be better for teachers and students, and even for the schools! Teachers would get more rest and have more time to prepare better lessons. Students would have resting time, time to practice extra on instruments, more study time, and more time for classroom reports. The schools would save energy, and the buses would save a tank of gas a week. There would be less garbage from school lunches, and there wouldn't be as much stress or pressure on students. Students could even improve in grades! Better grades, better lessons, more rest, and even helping to save the earth—let's have a four-day workweek!

WRITING WORKSHOP

A Persuasive Letter

Letter writing is often persuasive writing. You may write a friend to convince her you *didn't* blab a certain secret that everybody now knows. You may write a clothing company with a good reason for a refund: After washing, your new shirt is small enough to fit your hamster.

Then there are public letters—ones published in magazines and newspapers. These "letters to the editor" are really written for readers. Often they give opinions. The writer wants a specific group of readers to believe a certain idea or take a certain action. Here's a letter published in a local newspaper.

To the Editors:

This year the School Board will vote on whether students can wear shorts. We believe the change in the dress code should be approved.

First, shorts aren't really different from other clothes now allowed. Some people say shorts are too casual. But they're no more casual than jeans, which kids wear all the time. Also, there's no rule about the length of skirts. If girls can wear short skirts, why can't people wear shorts?

But the main reason to let students wear shorts is that they're cooler. It gets very hot in Florida, and shorts are more comfortable than pants. Some classes are air-conditioned, but some are not. When you're hot, it's hard to concentrate.

Changing the dress code is fair and will actually help students at our school. We hope you'll agree and call the School Board at 555-3261.

Mr. Deloach's Sixth-Grade Class

Thinking It Over

1. Who is the audience for this letter?
2. Which sentence gives the writers' statement of opinion? What is the writers' call to action?
3. Summarize the support for the opinion.
4. Do you think the letter will convince people to call? Which parts of it do you think are strongest?

Writing a Persuasive Letter

Prewriting. You have a choice of audiences in the letter you will write. Do you want to write about a topic that is between you and one other person? Maybe you want your cousin to come visit over the Thanksgiving holiday. Or do you want to write about a topic that is important to many people? Perhaps you want the police department to give tickets to people who speed near your school. First, decide on your topic and the person or people you want to convince.

Now, find your support. What facts or reasons will be convincing, and how will you arrange them?

Writing, Revising, and Evaluating. Be sure you state your opinion and support it clearly. If you're writing a letter to the editor, be *brief*. Newspapers and magazines may shorten long letters. Then, have someone else read your letter to help you evaluate it. You can ask each other the following questions.

1. What is the writer's opinion? Who is the audience?
2. What reasons does the writer give? In what order does he or she present them?
3. If the letter contains a call to action, what is it?

Proofreading and Publishing. After you correct any errors, make a clean copy. Follow the personal letter format if you're writing to a friend or relative. Follow the business letter format if you're writing to a business or to an editor (see pages 741–745). Mail your letter to the person or group you're trying to persuade.

You may decide to add your persuasive letter to your **portfolio.** If you do, date your letter and include a note that responds to these questions: Which part of your letter is the best? Why do you think so?

MAKING CONNECTIONS

PERSUASION IN ADVERTISING

Language Arts

Reasons and facts appeal to your brain. Emotional appeals are aimed at your feelings. Advertisers are good at emotional appeals. They try to persuade you that their brand of soap, jeans, and sneakers will make you happy and popular. Following are two ways they do it.

- **Bandwagon.** The idea behind the bandwagon appeal is "Everybody loves it, so join the crowd." If you *don't* "jump on the bandwagon," you'll feel left out, different, and peculiar.

EXAMPLE Rubber socks! The fashion craze that's bouncing across the nation!

■ **Testimonial.** This appeal uses a famous person to "testify" that a product is good. Because you like the person, you're supposed to like the product.

EXAMPLE   What keeps Wanda Wonder going when she's on a concert tour? A big bowl of Breakfast Chunks every morning.

Can you spot bandwagon and testimonial appeals in ads? For a week collect examples of ads from television or magazines. Cut out the magazine ads if you can; make notes on the TV ads. Try to find ten ads that show either bandwagon or testimonial appeals. Share your ads in a small group, and see if you agree on the emotional appeals used in each one.

PERSUASION ACROSS THE CURRICULUM

Social Studies

Should your community build a historical museum? You think so, but city voters have to decide. You need to convince them that your community has a history worth preserving and sharing.

With a group of classmates, create a presentation to convince the voters. Begin by digging up some unusual facts about the history of your community. Look in the library, write to state historical societies, and interview older residents. You might find facts in the earliest issues of a local newspaper.

Present the history you find in a persuasive way. You might tell stories, read from old letters, and play taped interviews. You might show photographs and present skits. Use any format you like. Just prove that your community has a fascinating history worth celebrating in a museum.

8 WRITING ABOUT LITERATURE: EXPOSITION

Reading and Responding

When you're **reading and responding,** thoughts and feelings are perking inside you. You respond to everything you see and hear, too. A cartoon makes you laugh—or yawn. This year's most popular song puts you to sleep. "But wait a minute," someone might say, "that's a *good* song." Each person's response is different.

Writing and You.   You talk to friends about songs and TV shows. You can also talk on paper. Writing down your response helps you understand it. What good—or bad—song, book, or comic strip could you write about?

As You Read.   The author of the following excerpt writes about the kinds of books he used to like. As you read, see if you can tell how he felt about the books.

Jacob Lawrence, *Libraries Are Appreciated* (1943). Gouache and watercolor on paper. Philadelphia Museum of Art: The Louis E. Stern Collection.

from The Lost Garden

by Laurence Yep

Though I really couldn't have put my feelings into words at the time, I think I loved the Oz books because they seemed far more real to me than the Homer Price books. The Oz books gave me a way to think about myself.

In the Oz books, you usually have some child taken out of his or her everyday world and taken to a new land where he or she must learn new customs and adjust to new people. There was no time for being stunned or for complaining. The children took in the situation and adapted. Unlike the Homer Price books, the Oz books talked about survival.

They dealt with the real mysteries of life—like finding yourself and your place in the world. And that was something I tried to do every day I got on and off the bus.

From fantasy, it was natural to begin reading science fiction. At that time, every science-fiction book was marked by a rocket ship on the spine; and I would go through the children's room at the Chinatown and North Beach branches as well as the Main Library, looking for anything with a blue rocket on its spine. I moved quickly on to the young adult science-fiction books. Robert Heinlein was an author I liked because his characters were so funny and memorable.

However, Andre Norton was a special favorite because she could evoke whole new worlds with a kind of sadness and wonder. Up until then, I had not really thought that much about stars because I saw only a few in the night sky. San Francisco's lights were too bright and hid most of them. On some of our expeditions, my mother had taken me to Morrison Planetarium in the park to see stars; but I did not see the real thing until my first trip to Disneyland. We took the train, called the Lark, to Los Angeles and slept in a Pullman car. Kept awake by the clackety-clack of the train wheels, I leaned over from my berth and peeked out under the shade. For the first time in my life, I saw a blaze of stars spilled out over the black sky. I didn't sleep

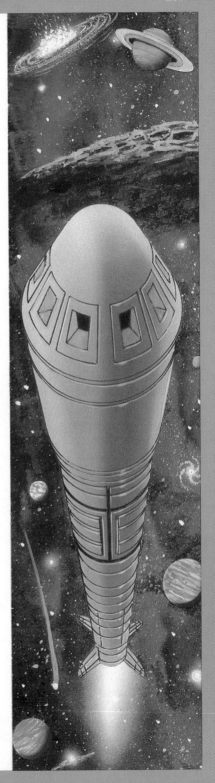

much that night between the noise, the excitement of seeing Disneyland, and the display of stars.

Unfortunately, stars were something that people had to drive to see. I only saw them when I went on camping trips, either with my parents to Yosemite or with the Boys' Club.

Anyway, the real appeal of Norton's books was not the stars themselves but the exotic worlds she created with their mysterious, half-ruined cities. I already knew what it was like to see an area that had been abandoned. Half the fun of her books wasn't so much the plot or the characters but the universe itself she created. And through that sad, tragic landscape ran outlaws and outcasts with whom I could identify.

"The Oz books gave me a way to think about myself."

THE WIZARD of OZ

L. FRANK BAUM
ILLUSTRATED BY MICHAEL HAGUE

Ballantine/35311 (Canada $6.50) U.S. $4.95

Robert A. HEINLEIN

Matt Dodson's dreams were simple—he desperately wanted to join the Solar Patrol's Space Academy and begin training as a

SPACE CADET

"Robert Heinlein was an author I liked because his characters were so funny and memorable."

READER'S RESPONSE

1. Laurence Yep liked fantasy and science fiction. What's your favorite kind of book? Tell why you like it.
2. Have you read an Oz book, a Homer Price book, or anything by Andre Norton? If you have, tell why you like or don't like that kind of story.

WRITER'S CRAFT

3. Did Laurence Yep like the Oz books or the Homer Price books better? How do you know?
4. Why does the author like science fiction by Andre Norton?

"...Andre Norton was a special favorite because she could evoke whole new worlds with a kind of sadness and wonder."

Author Laurence Yep

Purposes for Writing About Literature

Laurence Yep wrote about the kinds of books he liked when he was growing up. You write about literature, too—and not just in English class. Here are some other ways to write about literature.

- in a journal entry, comparing yourself to a character in a TV show or movie
- in a letter to your favorite author, telling why you like his or her books
- in an e-mail message to a friend, telling why you think he or she should read your favorite book
- in a note to your school librarian, explaining why you think the library should order more copies of a popular book
- in a letter to your grandfather, describing what you learned about the Cherokees from reading a story by an American Indian author
- in a posting for a message board at work, telling your co-workers about a book they might enjoy
- in a new ending for a novel, imagining what happens to the characters after the real novel ends
- in a script for a skit, showing a character from one story reacting to a character from another story

LOOKING AHEAD

In the main assignment in this chapter, you'll evaluate a story. Your purpose will be to inform your readers. As you work, remember that a good evaluation

- evaluates one or more story elements, or parts
- gives details to support the evaluation

Writing a Story Evaluation

 *Prewriting*

Starting with Personal Response

You're crazy about rock music. Your best friend loves Top-40 songs. Some people are die-hard fans of country, rap, metal, reggae, or soul. Each person responds in a different way to music.

Each person responds differently to stories, too. One reader loves a detective story. She says, "It was fun to figure out 'whodunit' before I got all the clues." That same story bores another reader. "I had to force myself to finish it," he says. Ask ten other readers how they feel about that story. You're likely to get ten different responses. When it comes to personal response, there's no right or wrong.

Here's a story about a girl and a wild boar. Read it and see how you respond.

"When I write...I think of the books on library shelves, without their jackets, years old, and a countryish teen-aged boy finding them, and having them speak to him."

John Updike

A SHORT STORY

Boar Out There

by Cynthia Rylant

Everyone in Glen Morgan knew there was a wild boar in the woods over by the Miller farm. The boar was out beyond the splintery rail fence and past the old black Dodge that somehow had ended up in the woods and was missing most of its parts.

Jenny would hook her chin over the top rail of the fence, twirl a long green blade of grass in her teeth and whisper, "Boar out there."

And there were times she was sure she heard him. She imagined him running heavily through the trees, ignoring the sharp thorns and briars that raked his back and sprang away trembling.

She thought he might have a golden horn on his terrible head. The boar would run deep into the woods, then rise up on his rear hooves, throw his head toward the stars and cry a long, clear, sure note into the air. The note would glide through the night and spear the heart of the moon. The boar had no fear of the moon, Jenny knew, as she lay in bed, listening.

One hot summer day she went to find the boar. No one in Glen Morgan had ever gone past the old black Dodge and beyond, as far as she knew. But the boar was there somewhere, between those awful trees, and his dark green eyes waited for someone.

Jenny felt it was she.

Moving slowly over damp brown leaves, Jenny could sense her ears tingle and fan out as she listened for thick breathing from the trees. She stopped to pick a teaberry leaf to chew, stood a minute, then went on.

Deep in the woods she kept her eyes to the sky. She needed to be reminded that there was a world above and apart from the trees—a world of space and air, air that didn't linger all about her, didn't press deep into her skin, as forest air did.

Finally, leaning against a tree to rest, she heard him for the first time. She forgot to breathe, standing there listening to the stamping of hooves, and she choked and coughed.

Coughed!

And now the pounding was horrible, too loud and confusing for Jenny. Horrible. She stood stiff with wet eyes and knew she could always pray, but for some reason didn't.

He came through the trees so fast that she had no time to scream or run. And he was there before her.

His large gray-black body shivered as he waited just beyond the shadow of the tree she held for support. His nostrils glistened, and his eyes; but astonishingly, he was silent. He shivered and glistened and was absolutely silent.

Jenny matched his silence, and her body was rigid, but not her eyes. They traveled along his scarred, bristling back to his thick hind legs. Tears spilling and flooding her face, Jenny stared at the boar's ragged ears, caked with blood. Her tears dropped to the leaves, and the only sound between them was his slow breathing.

Then the boar snorted and jerked. But Jenny did not move.

High in the trees a bluejay yelled, and, suddenly, it was over. Jenny stood like a rock as the boar wildly flung his head and in terror bolted past her.

Past her. . . .

And now, since that summer, Jenny still hooks her chin over the old rail fence, and she still whispers, "Boar out there." But when she leans on the fence, looking into the trees, her eyes are full and she leaves wet patches on the splintery wood. She is sorry for the torn ears of the boar and sorry that he has no golden horn.

But mostly she is sorry that he lives in fear of bluejays and little girls, when everyone in Glen Morgan lives in fear of him.

What was your personal response to "Boar Out There"? You can respond to a story in different ways.

WAYS TO RESPOND PERSONALLY

- Pretend you're the main character in the story. Write about what happens to you after the story ends.

- Make up some details about the main character. What does he or she do for fun? What's the character's favorite food? How does he or she feel about school?

- How does the ending of the story make you feel? You don't like the ending? Make up a new one.

- Think about what happens in the story. Pretend it's made into a TV movie. You're in charge of finding background music for it. What music would you pick?

EXERCISE 1 ▶   **Responding to a Story**

How did you like "Boar Out There"? Do you think Jenny was foolish to go into the woods? Would you rather the story ended in a different way? Pick one of the personal-response ideas you read about on page 245. Then write your response in your journal, or share it with a classmate.

EXERCISE 2 ▶   **Speaking and Listening: Making Up Dialogue**

You're the author! Here are three events that might have happened in "Boar Out There." With two or three classmates, choose one event. Make up the words the two characters say to each other. Have one classmate write down the lines. When you finish, share your work with the rest of the class.

1. Jenny takes a friend into the woods with her and they are together when the boar runs toward them. What do they say to each other?
2. At school the next day, Jenny tells her best friend about her experience. What do Jenny and her friend say to each other?
3. Twenty-five years have gone by and Jenny tells the story of the boar to her twelve-year-old daughter. What do they say to each other?

WRITING ASSIGNMENT

PART 1:
Choosing a Story for Response

Choose a story in your literature book. Or look for stories in the library, and choose one of those. (And remember: If you still can't think of a story to read, one of your friends might be able to suggest one to you.) Read the story, and then write your response in your journal. Tell how the story makes you feel.

 *Prewriting*

Looking Closely at a Story

You read some stories just for fun. Then, your personal response is all you care about. Sometimes, though, you need to read a story more closely. Your teacher may ask you to write about a story for English class. Maybe you want to tell someone why you loved a story—or why it put you to sleep.

Understanding the Elements of Stories

To talk or write about a story, you need to know about its elements. *Elements* are what something is made of. They are like the materials—wood, paint, metal, and nails—that make up a skateboard.

The following chart gives you three important elements that make up a story. You can refer to this chart as you work through this chapter.

ELEMENTS OF STORIES

CHARACTERS. The people and animals in a story are its *characters.* Sometimes, even plants or things or imaginary creatures can be characters. Heth, a bronze dragon, is an important character in the science fiction story "The Smallest Dragonboy."

SETTING. The *setting* is the place and time of the story. For example, a story's setting may be a city in an African country during the 1300s. Another story's setting might be a Caribbean island in the 1980s.

PLOT. What happens in a story is called the *plot.* In a good story, one event leads to another. What makes a plot interesting is *conflict.* That's some kind of problem or fight. There is *suspense:* you keep wondering and worrying how the conflict will turn out. By the end of the story, you know how the problem is solved or who wins the conflict.

Taking Notes on a Story

Taking notes while you read a story helps you write about it later. Following are some notes you might take while reading part of Cynthia Rylant's story "Boar Out There." Each of the notes is about character, setting, or plot. Some of the notes are questions that you might ask yourself. As you read, try to answer your questions.

A MODEL OF NOTE TAKING

Reading Passage

Close-Reading Notes

Everyone in Glen Morgan knew there was a wild boar in the woods over by the Miller farm. The boar was out beyond the splintery rail fence and past the old black Dodge that somehow ended up in the woods and was missing most of its parts.

A wild boar?
Is this the conflict?

Are the woods the setting?

Jenny would hook her chin over the top rail of the fence, twirl a long green blade of grass in her teeth and whisper, "Boar out there."

And there were times she was sure she heard him. She imagined him running heavily through the trees, ignoring the sharp thorns and briars that raked his back and sprang away trembling.

She thought he might have a golden horn on his terrible head. The boar would run deep into the woods, then rise up on his rear hooves, throw his head toward the stars and cry a long, clear, sure note into the air. The note would glide through the night and spear the heart of the moon. The boar had no fear of the moon, Jenny knew, as she lay in bed, listening.

Who's Jenny? I wonder why she's so interested in the boar. A conflict between Jenny and the boar?

Jenny must be the main character. There aren't any other characters yet.

She's really curious about the boar, fascinated even.

I think Jenny's going to run into this boar someplace. How? Will she get hurt?

Like the reader of this passage, you can ask and answer questions as you read along.

CRITICAL THINKING

Making Inferences

Inferences are educated guesses. When you read a story, you need to make educated guesses about the characters, the setting, and the plot. To make inferences, you look for clues that the writer gives you. Sometimes these clues are in the actions or words of the character. They may also be in details or words that describe the setting or the action in the story.

 CRITICAL THINKING EXERCISE:
Making Inferences

To practice the critical thinking skill of making inferences, look back at "Boar Out There." Then answer the following questions to make inferences about the story.

1. From the first sentence of the story, "Everyone in Glen Morgan knew there was a wild boar in the woods. . . ," you can infer that
   a. the people in Glen Morgan like to gossip
   b. Glen Morgan will be important in the story
   c. the boar will be important in the story
2. When you read that Jenny looks over the fence and whispers, "Boar out there," you can infer that she
   a. has had a bad experience with a wild boar
   b. is curious about the wild boar
   c. likes wild animals
3. When you read that the "pounding was horrible" and Jenny "stood stiff with wet eyes," you can infer
   a. that Jenny is frightened
   b. that the boar is going to hurt Jenny
   c. that Jenny thinks her father will be angry

4. When Jenny notices the boar's "scarred" back and "ragged ears, caked with blood," you can infer that she
   a. is beginning to feel sorry for the boar
   b. knows that the boar has been in a fight with the dog her neighbor owns
   c. is terrified of the wild boar

PART 2:

Looking Closely at a Story

You wrote your personal response to the story you picked. Now, take a closer look. Read the story again. This time take notes on it. Try to have notes about each element: character, setting, and plot.

Prewriting

Planning a Story Evaluation

You've read a story and thought about it carefully. Now it's time to plan the paper you're going to write.

Thinking About Purpose and Audience

The *purpose* of a story evaluation is to tell how well you think the story is written. Evaluating a story helps you think more deeply about it. You may evaluate a story just for yourself—to help you understand it better—or for an *audience* such as your teacher, classmates, co-workers, relatives, pen pals, or friends who are looking for a good story.

Evaluating a Story

To **evaluate** something, you rate it. That means you judge it against a set of standards. For instance, judges at a dog show look closely at each dog's coat. A thick, healthy coat is one of the standards used to evaluate dogs. There are also standards for rating such things as TV shows, video games, bicycles, clothes, and restaurants.

People use standards to evaluate stories, too. The standards for stories are based on the elements. Here are some questions about story elements. You can use the questions to evaluate a story.

- Do the characters act and talk like real people?
- What details about the setting do you notice? Do these details make the story seem real?
- Is the plot believable? Is there a problem or a conflict? Does the author create suspense and make you wonder what will happen next?

WRITING NOTE Most stories are not all bad or all good. A story may have great characters that are really believable. Yet that same story may not have a very interesting plot. Don't be surprised if you find that the author has done a better job with some story elements than others.

EXERCISE 3 ▶ **Evaluating a Story**

Get together with some classmates to evaluate "Boar Out There." Use the questions given above. After you have answered the questions, decide on your overall evaluation of the story. Is it great, average, weak—or something else? Does everyone in the group agree on the evaluation?

Calvin & Hobbes copyright 1987 Watterson. Distributed by Universal Press Syndicate. Reprinted with permission. All rights reserved.

Deciding on Your Main Idea

By now you've made a judgment about the story. You probably think it's great, terrible, or something in between. Now you need to write a main idea statement that expresses your evaluation of the story. Here are some example main idea statements about "Boar Out There."

> "Boar Out There," by Cynthia Rylant, is one of the best stories I have ever read.
>
> The plot of "Boar Out There," by Cynthia Rylant, has suspense and an interesting conflict.
>
> In "Boar Out There," by Cynthia Rylant, the character is interesting and believable.

Notice that two of these main idea statements are about only one story element. They are more realistic for a short paper. It would be difficult to write about all the story elements in a paragraph or two.

Once you've written your main idea statement, you can use it as a guide for planning. Later you may use it, or some version of it, in your paragraph.

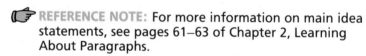 REFERENCE NOTE: For more information on main idea statements, see pages 61–63 of Chapter 2, Learning About Paragraphs.

WRITING ASSIGNMENT

PART 3:
Evaluating Your Story

Are you ready to evaluate the story you picked? Get set by looking back at the close-reading notes you took. Jot down answers to the questions on page 253. Use your answers to help you decide which element to write about. Then write a sentence that states your main idea—for example, "The characters seem like real people." Or you might write, "The plot is interesting and suspenseful."

Supporting Your Evaluation with Details

To back up your evaluation, you need details from the story. You'll need to read the story again. This time, keep your main idea statement in mind. Hunt for details in the story that support it. Here are examples of three kinds of details from "Boar Out There." They support this main idea statement: In "Boar Out There" the plot has suspense and a strong conflict.

Action (what characters do)	"One hot summer day she went to find the boar."
Dialogue (what characters say)	"Jenny would . . . whisper, 'Boar out there.' "
Description	"Jenny stood like a rock as the boar wildly flung his head and in terror bolted past her."

On the next page you'll see notes one writer jotted down to support an evaluation of the plot in "Boar Out There." Notice that the writer uses a quotation from the story, and that most notes are in the writer's own words.

Main idea:	The plot has suspense and an interesting conflict.
Details:	First sentence hints at danger of wild boar. Jenny looks over fence and whispers "Boar out there." Makes you think she's going to have a problem with the boar. (Page 242) When she goes into the woods you worry even more. (Page 243) Boar runs through trees; worry about Jenny. (Page 244)

Reminder

To plan a paper evaluating a story

- evaluate the characters, setting, and plot
- decide which element to write about
- write a main idea statement of your evaluation
- take notes on the story to support your main idea

WRITING ASSIGNMENT

PART 4:
Gathering Details to Support Your Evaluation

It's time for the final prewriting step. Get out the evaluation and main idea statement you wrote in Writing Assignment, Part 3. Now, read the story one more time. Look for description, actions, and dialogue that support your evaluation. You're judging. Make notes about each of these elements like the notes you've just read.

Writing Your First Draft

You're just about ready to write your first draft. The paper you write about the story you've read will have these four parts:

- the story's title and author
- a sentence or two telling your readers what the story is about
- your evaluation of an element in the story (your main idea)
- details from the story that support your evaluation

If you like, you can also give your personal response to the story. (In fact, your response might give your readers some new ideas or feelings about the story.) Here's a model paragraph that evaluates the plot in "Boar Out There." As you read, look for the four parts.

A WRITER'S MODEL

A Frightening Meeting

Title/Author
Summary
Main idea/Evaluation

"Boar Out There," by Cynthia Rylant, is about a young girl who faces a wild boar. The plot of this story keeps you interested and in suspense. The suspense starts with the beginning of the first sentence: "Everyone in Glen Morgan knew there was a wild boar in the

Details to
support
evaluation

woods. . . ." You soon start to wonder if Jenny, the young girl, will look for the boar. She keeps looking over the fence and whispering "Boar out there." When she goes into the woods, you are afraid she will meet the boar; and she does. He comes running through the trees and she doesn't have "time to scream or run." Then, just as you think the boar will charge, he runs past her. The

Personal response story is exciting, but it made me feel sorry for wild animals. The boar was scared, too.

 PART 5:
WRITING **Writing Your First Draft**
ASSIGNMENT

You already have most of the information you need for your first draft. All you need to do is shape your notes into sentences. You're writing about one element, so you may have just one paragraph. As you work, remember what you've learned about writing paragraphs. (For more information about the parts of paragraphs, see Chapter 2.)

Evaluating and Revising

Once you've written your draft, you need to start thinking about how to improve it. This evaluating and revising chart can help you. Ask yourself the questions in the left-hand column. If you find problems, try the ideas in the right-hand column.

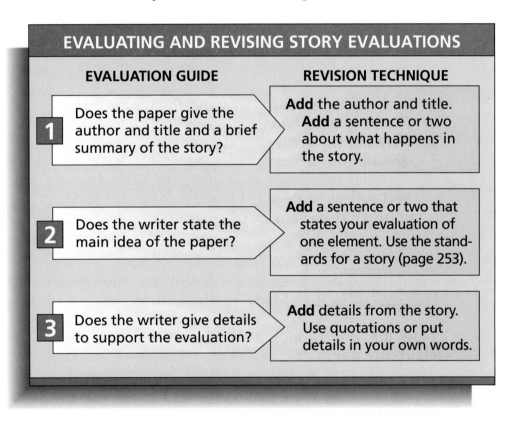

EVALUATING AND REVISING STORY EVALUATIONS

EVALUATION GUIDE	REVISION TECHNIQUE
1 Does the paper give the author and title and a brief summary of the story?	**Add** the author and title. **Add** a sentence or two about what happens in the story.
2 Does the writer state the main idea of the paper?	**Add** a sentence or two that states your evaluation of one element. Use the standards for a story (page 253).
3 Does the writer give details to support the evaluation?	**Add** details from the story. Use quotations or put details in your own words.

EXERCISE 4 ▶ Analyzing a Writer's Revisions

The following rough draft shows how the writer revised the beginning of the evaluation of "Boar Out There." Working with a partner, answer the questions to tell why the writer made the changes. Use the evaluating and revising chart to help you.

"*Boar Out There,*"

~~This story~~, by Cynthia Rylant, is   **replace**

about a young girl who faces a wild

boar. The plot of this story keeps you

interested and in suspense. ~~I've never~~   **cut**

~~seen a real wild boar.~~ The suspense

starts with the beginning of the first

: "Everyone in Glen Morgan knew there was a wild boar in the woods...."

sentence. You soon start to wonder if   **add**

Jenny, the young girl, will look for the

boar.

1. In the first sentence, why did the writer replace *This story* with *"Boar Out There"*?
2. Why did the writer cut the sentence *I've never seen a real wild boar*?
3. Why did the writer add the quotation in the next-to-last sentence? How does that addition improve the evaluation?

WRITING ASSIGNMENT

PART 6:

Evaluating and Revising Your Story Evaluation

Now it's time to look at your own writing. Use the chart on page 259 to do a self-evaluation. Then, exchange papers with a partner and evaluate each other's work. (See page 48 for guidelines on peer evaluation.) After you've thought about your partner's suggestions, make changes to improve your paper.

COMPUTER NOTE: Before you print a copy of a draft you plan to proofread or revise, adjust the line spacing and margins to make room for handwritten corrections on the printout. Use double- or triple-spacing and a wide right margin. When you want to print a final draft, reset the spacing and margins.

Proofreading and Publishing

Proofreading. Don't let your audience read your paper now! You still have to *proofread* it. Check your work for errors in grammar, usage, and mechanics.

MECHANICS HINT

Using Quotation Marks

In a story evaluation, put quotation marks around the title of the story and before and after a quotation from the story. Add single quotation marks for a quotation within a quotation.

EXAMPLES *Story Title:* **"Boar Out There"** has a strong, suspenseful plot.

Quotations from Story: The suspense builds when you read that the boar **"**came through the trees so fast that she had no time to scream or run.**"**

Quotation Within a Quotation: **"**Jenny would hook her chin over the top rail of the fence, twirl a long green blade of grass in her teeth and whisper, **'**Boar out there.**' "**

 REFERENCE NOTE: For more information on quotation marks, see pages 615–622.

Publishing. Here's how to share your evaluation:

- Make a bookmark for the book that has your story in it. Write your evaluation on the bookmark.
- Display your paper on a bulletin board. Add pictures that illustrate parts of the story.

WRITING ASSIGNMENT

PART 7:
Proofreading and Publishing Your Story Evaluation

You're almost finished with your assignment! Just proofread your final draft carefully and correct your mistakes. Finally, share it with others.

Reflecting on Your Writing

Before adding your story evaluation to your **portfolio,** date the paper and attach responses to these questions.

- Was it harder for you to state your main idea or to find details from the story to support it? Explain.
- What problems did you have while writing? How can you avoid these problems on your next paper?

A STUDENT MODEL

What you say about a story sometimes makes other people want to read it. David Sierra, a student at Hillview Junior High School in Pittsburg, California, writes about Mark Twain's story "Dentistry." Here's what David suggests when you're writing about a story: "Take notes as you go along and write little comments to put in your essay." He also says, "Don't rush it."

"Dentistry"
by David Sierra

The story I evaluated was "Dentistry" by Mark Twain. I enjoyed reading it. At first it was boring, but toward the middle it became great. It was great how Twain expressed how Tom Sawyer felt. The story also gave me the feeling that I was right at the bedside with Tom when his aunt pulled out his tooth. It really caught my attention when Tom was trying to find a way to stay home from school. I think it reminded me of myself. Twain made Tom's aunt sound really mean because of how she pulled out his tooth, but I guess they didn't have dentists like us. I think Twain used very good dialogue and really made the characters come to life. I would highly recommend this story to people who like to laugh.

WRITING WORKSHOP

A Scene for a Play

One way to respond to literature is to be creative yourself. Have you ever tried turning a story into a play? Stories and plays have many things (characters, settings, and plots) in common. Here's an example of a scene for a play. It's based on the story you read earlier in this chapter, "Boar Out There." (The words in brackets are stage directions.)

Scene 1: [The front porch of a house]

[The wooden porch has a railing around it. At the top of the stairs is a middle-aged man wearing jeans, a light-weight jacket, and boots. He has a water jug in his hand and a blanket thrown over his arm. He looks frantic as he starts to run down the porch stairs. Then a young girl runs on stage from the right.]

> **Mr. Carmona:** [in a panicked voice] Jenny! Where have you been? I've been looking everywhere for you!

> **Jenny:** [almost breathless from running] Dad, you'll never guess--just saw. . .

> **Mr. Carmona:** [angrily] Jenny, I've been scared to death! Where were you for the last four hours?

> **Jenny:** In the woods. I saw the wild boar.

> **Mr. Carmona:** You saw the boar? He didn't hurt you?

> **Jenny:** [sadly] No, Dad. He ran past me when he heard a bluejay yell. He was afraid of me.

Thinking It Over

1. Where does the writer tell what the setting is?
2. Where does the writer describe the characters?
3. How does the writer tell what the characters are doing?
4. What does this scene have in common with the story? How is it different?

Writing a Scene for a Play

Prewriting. Find a story you like, or use the one you evaluated earlier in this chapter. Use the story and your imagination to create a scene for a play.

"The All American Slurp"
"All Summer in a Day"
"A Secret for Two"
"Becky and the Wheels-and-Brake Boys"

There are two ways you can create your scene. You can change an event in the story into a scene, or you can imagine another event that might happen to one of the characters in the story. Either way, you should limit your scene to two characters. You'll probably have to use your imagination to make up some dialogue (the conversation) between the characters. You'll also have to make some notes about stage directions to describe the setting and what the characters are doing.

Writing, Evaluating, and Revising. Begin with the setting and stage directions. Then, write dialogue and directions to tell how the character looks and sounds. When you've finished writing, exchange scenes with a classmate. Using your classmate's suggestions and your own ideas, revise your scene.

Proofreading and Publishing. First, make sure that your punctuation and capitalization help to show who's speaking and what is happening. Next, find some other students to act out the parts in your scene. Be sure to give them suggestions about where to stand and how to speak. Finally, have your play performed in front of the whole class.

If you include this scene in your **portfolio,** date the paper and attach responses to these questions: How did writing a scene make you think more about the story? How did it help you to understand the story?

MAKING CONNECTIONS

Responding to Poetry

Here's a poem about two friends, one leaving another behind. As you read, think about your own personal response.

Poem
by Langston Hughes

I loved my friend.
He went away from me.
There's nothing more to say.
The poem ends,
Soft as it began—
I loved my friend.

How does this poem make you feel? Think about some times when you felt the same way.

Here are some ways to respond to this poem. Try one.

- What would Jenny (in "Boar Out There") say? Write a note she might send to the poem's speaker.

- Find a song that gives you the same feeling as "Poem," by Langston Hughes. Or, if you play an instrument, make up a rhythm and a melody for the poem.

- Convey your feelings through art. What pictures, colors, or designs express your response to the poem? Make a collage using your own drawings or photographs and pictures from magazines and newspapers. Or use paints or colored pencils to create an abstract design.

WRITING ACROSS THE CURRICULUM

Health: Evaluating School Lunches

Get together with a few classmates and evaluate what students at your school eat for lunch. First, make a list of standards for a healthful lunch. You can find information in a textbook. Or you can use this list.

1. A healthful lunch has fruit, bread or a roll, and some kind of protein (such as milk, fish, eggs, red beans and rice, or peanut butter).
2. It doesn't have much fat or sugar.
3. It has milk or juice, not a carbonated drink.

Then, ask several of your classmates what they had for lunch yesterday. You can use a chart like the one that follows and check off the columns as your classmates answer your question. Have one row for each student.

This chart shows that one student had a somewhat healthful lunch. Another student had a lunch that wasn't very healthful.

Fruit	Bread or roll	Protein	Low in fat and sugar	Milk or juice
✓		✓		✓
		✓		

Once you've filled out your own chart, look to see what you've learned. You can tally up how many students ate fruit, how many ate protein, and so on. (You can even change your tallies into percentages: What percentage of the students you surveyed ate fruit? ate protein? and so on.) Did most students have a lunch that was healthful? Can you write a sentence or two that presents your evaluation of what students at your school eat for lunch?

WRITING ABOUT CHARACTERS AND PLOT

Have you ever thought about how the plot—what happens in a story—might be different if one of the characters were different? If Scar hadn't been so bad, how might the movie *The Lion King* have been different? How would "Boar Out There" have been different if the boar hadn't been frightened?

Reread one of your favorite stories and think about these questions:

1. What is the character like? What does he or she enjoy? dislike? believe? care about? want?
2. How does this character affect what happens in the story?

Now write a paragraph explaining what you've discovered. You and your classmates might enjoy comparing your ideas.

9 WRITING A REPORT: EXPOSITION

Exploring Your World

Through research—looking for information—you can find out almost anything you want to know. You can **explore** the deepest underground caves. You can decipher ancient Egyptian hieroglyphics. You can discover how a music video is made.

Writing and You. Reports are summaries of information, and they're everywhere. On TV, journalists report happenings all over the world. In books, historians write reports about the American Civil War. And in magazines, sports writers report the most exciting moments of a champion's life. Have you read an interesting report recently?

As You Read. As you read this science report, you'll learn a surprising fact: one insect does the impossible— walks on water. How does the first paragraph grab your attention?

Detail of *Book of the Dead of the Scribe Ani,* circa 1250 B.C., Egyptian 19th dynasty. Collection of British Museum, London. Bridgeman Art Library/Superstock, Inc.

HOW CAN

Water Striders Walk on Water?

by Joanne Settel and Nancy Baggett

If you could step off a stream bank and skate on the water's surface, you'd be a candidate for *The Guinness Book of World Records*! Amazingly, however, this feat is so easy for the insects known as water striders that they spend most of their lives gliding around on ponds and streams.

Water striders, which look sort of like floating daddy longlegs, not only catch their insect prey and eat it on the water, they also meet mates and carry out their courtship there as well. In addition, once a pair of striders has mated, the female even deposits her eggs on a floating leaf, piece of bark, feather, or other object. Clearly, water striders haven't much need to go on land. As a matter of fact, they don't go unless rain or strong wind stirs up the water surface or the water drops below 32 degrees Fahrenheit.

One reason water striders can so easily "walk" on their liquid environment is that they have specially designed bodies and legs. Their bodies are covered with water-repellent scales so they won't get heavy with water and sink. Also, their middle and back legs, which are the ones striders use for rowing and steering, are long and widely

spaced. This arrangement spreads their weight over a larger area, so they don't push down hard enough in one spot to break through the water surface. In addition, the parts that actually touch the water, the feet and lower legs, are covered with unwettable hairs. These tiny hairs trap bubbles of air and work like mini-life preservers to buoy the striders up.

"If you could step off a stream bank and skate on the water's surface, you'd be a candidate for *The Guinness Book of World Records!*"

Another important reason striders can walk on water is that the water surface has a thin, strong, elastic film. Normally you don't see this film, but it's still there, helping to keep the striders afloat. The film forms because the very tiny parts, or molecules, that make up water tend to stick together when they contact the air.

from *How Do Ants Know When You're Having a Picnic?*

READER'S RESPONSE

1. What new facts did you learn? Which facts surprised or interested you most?
2. Name another animal you're curious about. If "animals" isn't your favorite topic, what would you rather read about?

WRITER'S CRAFT

3. Where do the writers begin to answer the question of the title? Where does the answer end?
4. Some reports, like this one, don't tell where the writer found the information. Yet, in school reports, you'll be asked to list your sources. What are some sources the writers of this report might have used?

Ways to Develop a Report

Every day, you can learn new facts from reports. You can rent a videotape to learn about kayaking. You can use a CD-ROM to learn about what it would be like to journey across the Australian outback. And you can get the latest news by reading reports in newspapers and magazines and on the Internet, or by watching and listening to TV and radio news broadcasts.

The report on water striders was developed with descriptions. Here are some other examples of the many different ways you can develop a report.

- in a biographical report, telling a story about a football player's teenage years
- in a history report, describing the order of events during the battle of the Alamo
- in a report for an art class, describing the history of African sculpture
- in a workplace report, explaining how your job duties differ from your co-worker's duties
- in a report for hikers, explaining how to tell which snakes are poisonous and which aren't
- in a report for off-road bicyclists, listing some of the advantages and disadvantages of several different models of mountain bikes

LOOKING AHEAD

In the main assignment in this chapter, you'll start by choosing a topic and gathering information about it. Then, you'll write a short, informative report. The report that you write will

- give factual information about a topic
- use both print and nonprint sources
- list the sources of information

Writing a Report

 *Prewriting*

Choosing and Narrowing a Subject

Who invented basketball? How does a telephone work? Where did our number system come from? Maybe you don't know the answers to these questions, but you can find out. Then you can tell other people about the information in a report.

Choosing a Subject. Think about your hobbies and what you like to read about. Would you enjoy an article about secret codes? Do bald eagles fascinate you? Do you wonder how ancient sailors navigated across the seas? A good report topic should be something that really interests you.

But "my pet turkey, Gobbler"—no matter how fascinating to you—isn't a good report topic. You will do research for this report, and you won't find anything about your pet in the library.

In the library's nonfiction books and magazines, though, you may find topic ideas. For example, a book about the things young people can do to save the earth may give you an idea for a report on "recycling." Or, a magazine article on wildlife in rain forests may give you an idea for a report on iguanas.

Narrowing a Subject. Suppose you've decided on a subject that interests you—perhaps "baseball" or "volcanoes." These subjects are too broad for a short report. In fact, entire books have been written about each subject! You need to narrow your subject to a topic that can be covered in a report of five or six paragraphs.

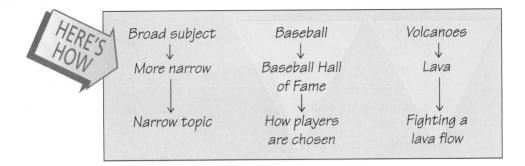

Broad subject	Baseball	Volcanoes
↓	↓	↓
More narrow	Baseball Hall of Fame	Lava
↓	↓	↓
Narrow topic	How players are chosen	Fighting a lava flow

EXERCISE 1 ▶ **Narrowing Subjects for a Report**

Practice thinking smaller and smaller and smaller. Narrow each of the following ten general subjects to a topic for a five-paragraph report. Try using an upside-down pyramid chart like the one in the Here's How above. You might want to get together with one or two classmates and compare your work. Was any subject particularly easy to narrow down? Was any really hard to narrow down? Why do you think so?

1. teenagers
2. exercising

3. computer games
4. Native Americans
5. the future
6. athletes
7. the moon
8. seeing-eye dogs
9. music
10. transportation

WRITING
ASSIGNMENT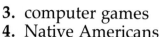

PART 1:
Choosing and Narrowing a Subject

What general subject are you interested in? If you don't have one in mind, skim through some books and magazines in your library. Then narrow your subject to a specific topic. Remember, you'll spend several days with your topic, so pick one you'll have fun exploring. Don't forget: It can't be personal, and it can't be too big.

WRITING
NOTE

Writing a report takes time. Don't start late and try to finish in a day or two. Make yourself a schedule, and stick to it. You'll need time for six activities:

1. finding information
2. taking notes
3. organizing your notes
4. writing your first draft

5. evaluating and revising the draft
6. proofreading and publishing your final report

 *Prewriting*

Planning Your Report

You can't build a treehouse until you gather the wood, nails, and tools. And before you start building, you need to figure out how to put it together. Just where will the doorway be? You need to do the same kind of planning for your report.

Thinking About Purpose and Audience. Your *purpose* in writing a report is to share interesting facts about your topic. You might include the opinion of an expert, but your own opinions do not belong in a factual report. Remember this difference:

- A *fact* is a piece of information that experts have checked and believe is true.
- An *opinion* is a belief or a feeling that cannot be proven.

The main *audience* for your report will probably be your teacher and classmates. To prepare for your audience, ask yourself these questions:

1. What do my readers already know about my topic?
2. What basic information do they need to know?
3. What information will they find most interesting?

Remember that your readers will enjoy your report more if they learn something new when they read it.

☞ REFERENCE NOTE: See pages 210–211 for more about facts and opinions.

Asking Questions. What do you want to find out about your topic? Plan your research by writing some questions you'd like to answer in your report. The

5W-How? questions—questions that begin with *Who, What, Where, When, Why,* or *How*—work well.

If you don't know much about your topic, you might get ideas for questions by looking at an encyclopedia article or by doing a keyword search on the World Wide Web. Here are some questions one writer prepared on the topic of "karate."

<u>Who</u> invented karate?

<u>What</u> was the original purpose of karate?

<u>Where</u> and <u>when</u> did karate start?

<u>How</u> is karate different from other kinds of martial arts?

<u>Why</u> is karate studied today?

EXERCISE 2 ▶ **Speaking and Listening: Asking Questions About a Topic**

Practice your questioning skills by exploring this topic. One morning a Russian tank on display in Prague, Czechoslovakia, had turned a shocking pink. If you were a newspaper reporter, what questions would you ask to find out what happened? With a classmate, take turns pretending you are newspaper reporters. Give your partner your topic as a newspaper story "assignment." Your partner (the reporter) has to come up with *5W-How?* questions to ask you. After you answer the questions, it's your turn to be the reporter. Think of several *5W-How?* questions to ask your partner about his or her topic.

Finding Sources. When you research, look for at least three good sources of information. You'll find *print sources* (books, encyclopedias, magazines) in your library. *Nonprint sources,* such as TV and radio programs, videotapes, interviews, CD-ROMs, and online sources, may also give you new facts.

 REFERENCE NOTE: See pages 716–724 for more about using library resources (including online catalogs, online databases, and the Internet) for research.

 CRITICAL THINKING

Evaluating Sources

When you *evaluate* a source, you decide how useful it is. Use these questions to evaluate possible sources for your report.

1. **Is the source nonfiction?** Don't use short stories or novels when you're looking for facts.
2. **Is the information up to date?** Check the copyright page of a book and the date of a magazine. For a current topic, such as "protective gear for Little Leaguers," use a source that's recently published.
3. **Can you trust the source?** Don't believe everything you read. Avoid gossipy magazines and newspapers and sources that present only one side of an issue. Encyclopedias, almanacs, and books written by experts can usually be trusted.

CRITICAL THINKING EXERCISE:
Evaluating Sources

You are writing a report on the most recent research into humans communicating with dolphins. Which of the following sources would you use? Explain your answers.

1. "Dolphin," by Daniel K. Odell, in the 1995 edition of *The World Book Encyclopedia*.
2. *A Ring of Endless Light* (1980), by Madeleine L'Engle, a novel about a girl who can communicate with dolphins.
3. An interview with your aunt, who once swam with a dolphin on the Florida Keys.
4. *Dolphins & Porpoises: A Worldwide Guide*, by Jean-Pierre Sylvestre, translated by Catherine Berthier, published by Sterling Publishing Company in New York in 1993.
5. "If You Need Me, Whistle," by Peter Tyac, an article about dolphin communication, in *Natural History Magazine*, August 1991.

Listing Sources. You'll need to keep track of where your information comes from by giving each source a number. You can write the *source number* and the following information on a note card or a sheet of paper:

INFORMATION ON SOURCES
1. **Books:** author, title, city of publication, publisher, copyright year.
2. **Magazine articles:** author, title of article, magazine, date, page numbers.
3. **Encyclopedia articles:** author (if given), title of article, encyclopedia, edition (year).
4. **Videotapes:** title, director or writer (if given), publisher, year.
5. **Electronic materials:** author (if given), title, electronic posting date (online), type of source (*CD-ROM* or *Online*), location of source (*Internet*, online service name, or, for CD-ROMs, city, if given), date of publication (CD-ROMs) or access date, Internet address (if any).

Taking Notes. Follow the guidelines below to take notes on sources that provide answers to your research questions. On the next page, you'll find an excerpt from a source, along with a sample note card.

1. Use 4″ × 6″ note cards, separate sheets of paper, or computer files.
2. Write the source number at the top of each note.
3. Write a *label* (a word or phrase) that tells what the note is about.
4. Write notes in your own words. If you copy someone's exact words, put quotation marks around the quote. (Plagiarism—using someone else's words without quotation marks—is wrong.)
5. If the information is from a print source, write at the end of each note the page numbers where you found the information.

LAVA AND MAGMA. Molten, or hot lique-
fied, rock located deep below the Earth's surface is
called magma. When a volcano erupts or a deep
crack occurs in the Earth, the magma rises and
overflows. When it flows out of the volcano or
crack, usually mixed with steam and gas, it is
called lava. Fresh lava ranges from 1,300° to
2,200° F (700° to 1,200° C) in temperature and
glows red hot to white hot as it flows.

Compton's Interactive Encyclopedia, 1996 ed.

What Lava Is	2
magma = hot liquid rock deep in earth	
lava = magma when it erupts from volcano—	
mixed with gas & steam	
1,300°–2,200° F. Glows red to white.	

label/source number

note written in your own words

no page numbers for nonprint sources

EXERCISE 3 ▶ **Taking Notes**

You're writing a report on how the Native Americans
helped the Pilgrims. Read the following encyclopedia
article, and write two note cards that answer these
questions: **(1.)** Who was Massasoit? **(2.)** How did he
help the Pilgrims? Be sure to use your own words.

Massasoit, *MAS uh* SOYT (1580?–1661), was a chief
of the Wampanoag tribe of Indians who lived in what
is now southern Massachusetts and Rhode Island. He
made a treaty with Governor John Carver of Plymouth

Colony in the spring of 1621, shortly
after the Pilgrims landed in America.
   Massasoit agreed that his people would
not harm the Pilgrims as long as he lived.
In turn, the Pilgrims guaranteed to protect
the Indians and their rights. Massasoit
kept the peace all his life.

> James Axtell, from
> *The World Book*
> *Encyclopedia*, 1996 ed.

When you're gathering information
for your report

- keep in mind what your audience
  wants and needs to know about
  your topic
- look for both print and nonprint
  sources
- give publishing information and
  assign a number for each source
- use your research questions to
  take notes

PART 2:
Taking Notes for Your Report

Researching facts is like hunting for treasure. First,
make up *5W-How?* questions on your topic. Next,
search through books, magazines, encyclopedias,
videotapes, CD-ROMs, and World Wide Web sites.
You might also talk to an expert. Find at least three
sources. Then, take notes for your report.

 *Prewriting*

Organizing and Outlining Your Information

Before you start writing, you'll need to sort through your notes and organize them. You'll group notes together and then decide on an order for the groups.

Grouping Notes. First, you'll group the notes into sets that have the same or a similar label. For a report on "the beginning of basketball," you might have one set that tells about basketball's inventor. Another set might be about the game's first rules. (Some notes may not fit into sets. You can leave them out at first, but you may need them later.)

Each of your note sets should be about one main idea (for example, "the inventor of basketball"). Each main idea can become one paragraph in your report.

Outlining. Next, you can make a plan, or outline, for your report. You'll create the main headings in your outline by writing down the main idea of each of your sets of notes. You can then take these steps:

1. Decide how to order your main headings and then write them down on a sheet of paper.
2. Go through the notes in each set, and put them in an order that makes sense. The main facts in each set are the outline's subheadings. Write the subheadings under the main headings.

 COMPUTER NOTE: Try making your outline on a computer. Many word-processing programs have built-in outliners.

Once you've created your plan, or *informal outline,* you can use it as a guide as you write your report. But remember, you may change your mind about some things as you write and revise. Maybe you'll decide to add some information or leave something out. Just jot down the change on your planning outline. Later, your teacher may ask you to make a *formal outline.* Here's a formal outline one writer created for a report on lava.

Controlling Lava Flow
I. Using bombs
    A. 1935--lava threatening Hilo, Hawaii
    B. Bombs dropped on lava source
    C. Lava stopped in 30 hours
II. Using sea water
    A. 1973--lava threatening harbor at Heimaey, Iceland
    B. Sea water sprayed from pipes for three weeks
    C. Lava flow cooled and stopped
III. Using barricades
    A. 1983--lava threatening ski resort at Mount Etna, Sicily
    B. Walls of volcanic ash and stone built at diagonal to lava flow
    C. Lava flow dynamited
    D. Lava flow changed direction

 REFERENCE NOTE: For more help with outlining, see page 761.

WRITING ASSIGNMENT

PART 3:
Organizing Your Notes and Making an Outline

You've collected many facts. Do they seem like a jumble? Read through your notes, and sort them into sets that have the same main idea. Then, outline the main ideas and supporting facts.

Writing Your First Draft

Understanding the Parts of a Report

Like every composition, a report has three main parts. It also has a fourth part, a list of sources.

The *introduction* is the beginning of your report. It tells what the report is about. To grab the reader's attention, you can use a question, a brief story, an interesting quotation, or a surprising fact.

The *body* presents the report's main ideas and specific details. Each paragraph develops one main idea.

The *conclusion* is the last paragraph. A strong conclusion ties together the ideas in the report. It also brings the report to a clear, definite ending.

The *list of sources* is a separate page at the end of your report. It tells where you found your information. Your readers might be interested in your topic and might want to read more about it. They can use your list of sources to find the sources you used in your report.

You'll start with the list you made before you took your notes. (See page 283.) Alphabetize the sources by the author's last name. If there's no author, alphabetize by the title. You can follow the form in the sample list on page 292 or another that your teacher shows you.

Writing Your Report

As you draft your report, you'll use your notes and outline as guides. Remember, however, that you can always change the order of ideas and drop or add information.

You might want to use the following report as a model for your own report. Notice how each paragraph in the body has a topic sentence that states the paragraph's main idea.

A WRITER'S MODEL

Controlling Lava

INTRODUCTION

Lava is the red-hot, boiling, melted rock that comes out of an erupting volcano. What would you do if a fiery stream of lava--at least 1,100 degrees F--was aimed at your doorstep? You would probably run fast. People have always done that. But scientists have been fighting back. They have tried different ways to stop lava flows or turn them.

BODY
Main topic:
Using bombs

At first, scientists bombed a volcano. In 1935 Mauna Loa erupted in Hawaii. A wide stream of lava was near the city of Hilo and came a mile closer every day. An American scientist, Thomas Jaggar, had a daring plan. Ten U.S. Army planes dropped powerful bombs on the lava flow high up on the side of Mauna Loa. A little more than a day later, the lava stopped, just twelve miles from Hilo.

Main topic:
Using sea water

Another plan used sea water to cool a lava flow. In Heimaey, Iceland, in 1973, a volcano erupted. The eruption went on for more than

five months. Lava and ash covered almost four hundred homes and threatened to fill up the city's harbor. Workers used forty-seven giant pumps and nineteen miles of pipes to dump four thousand tons of sea water a day on the lava flow. After three weeks, the wall of lava cooled from 1,800 degrees F to 215 degrees. The lava changed from a liquid to a solid—and it stopped.

**Main topic:
Using barricades**

Scientists have also changed a lava flow's direction. They have built barriers at a diagonal to the lava flow. In Sicily in 1983, for example, lava from Mount Etna destroyed parts of a ski resort. Workers built huge walls of volcanic ash and stone. They also dynamited the lava flow. The lava flow turned away from the ski resort.

CONCLUSION

Trying to control lava is difficult and dangerous work. Yet as long as people live in the shadows of volcanoes, scientists will look for new ways to control lava. Bombs, sea water, and barriers are the first attempts. Maybe someone like you will think of a better way.

List of Sources

Cashman, Katharine V. "Volcano." <u>The World
    Book Encyclopedia</u>. 1995 ed.
"Lava and Magma." <u>Compton's Interactive
    Encyclopedia</u>. 1996 ed. CD-ROM. Compton's
    NewMedia, 1995.
McPhee, John. "The Control of Nature: Cooling the
    Lava--I." <u>New Yorker</u> 22 Feb. 1988: 43-77.
Walker, Sally M. <u>Volcanoes: Earth's Inner Fire</u>.
    Minneapolis: Carolrhoda Books, 1994.

| WRITING ASSIGNMENT | PART 4: **Writing Your First Draft** |

Now you're ready to sit down and write! When
you've finished your draft, write a list of sources. Follow the style in the Writer's Model.

Evaluating and Revising

If you've followed your schedule, you should have time to put your draft away for a while. Then you can look at it with a fresh eye. This will help you recognize the strengths and weaknesses of your draft.

You can *evaluate* by asking yourself the questions on the left side of the chart on page 294. You can also ask a partner to read your report and make suggestions. You may find that you need to go back and look for additional information or reorganize some of your ideas. The chart on page 294 will also give you help with revising.

E X E R C I S E 4 ▶ **Analyzing a Writer's Revisions**

Study the changes the writer made when she revised the second paragraph of "Controlling Lava."

> *At first, scientists bombed a volcano.*
> ₍ᴧ₎In 1935 Mauna Loa erupted in — **add**
>
> Hawaii. An American scientist, — **reorder**
> Thomas Jaggar, had a daring plan. A
> wide stream of lava was near the city
> of Hilo and came a mile closer every
> ~Ten~
> day. U.S. Army planes dropped power- — **add**
> *high up on the side of Mauna Loa*
> ful bombs on the lava flow. A little — **add**
> more than a day later, the lava
> stopped, just twelve miles from Hilo.

1. Why did the writer add a new first sentence?
2. Why did she move the second sentence?
3. Where did the writer add facts? How do they make the report better?

EVALUATING AND REVISING REPORTS

EVALUATION GUIDE	REVISION TECHNIQUE
1 Does the introduction grab the reader's interest? Does it tell what the report is about?	**Add** an attention-getting question, brief story, or fact. **Add** a sentence that tells the report topic.
2 Does the body present the main ideas and supporting facts?	**Add** topic sentences to paragraphs. **Add** facts to support main ideas.
3 Is the information in the report clearly organized?	**Reorder** sentences or paragraphs until the organization of your ideas is clear.
4 Does the report have a conclusion?	**Add** a paragraph that ties together the main ideas and brings the report to a definite end.
5 Is the list of sources on a separate sheet at the end?	**Add** a list of your sources in the correct form (see page 292).

WRITING ASSIGNMENT

PART 5:
Evaluating and Revising Your Report

Two heads—or three or four—are usually better than one. Share your first draft with a small group of classmates. Ask for their suggestions, and consider them carefully. Then evaluate your draft yourself. Make changes based on all these evaluations.

Proofreading and Publishing

Proofreading. When you proofread, slow your reading down. Check every word and every sentence. Look for mistakes in spelling, punctuation, capitalization, and usage—and fix them.

MECHANICS HINT

Underlining and Quotation Marks

Underline the title of each book, magazine, encyclopedia, or videotape in your list of sources. Use quotation marks for the titles of articles in magazines or encyclopedias.

EXAMPLES   Book:
> Bray, Rosemary L. <u>Martin Luther King</u>. New York: Greenwillow Books, 1995.

Magazine:
> "New American Indian Museum Opens." <u>Junior Scholastic</u> 9 Dec. 1994: 19-20.

 REFERENCE NOTE: For more information on underlining and quotation marks, see pages 613–614 and 622.

Publishing. Now's the time to think of a good title for your report. You'll need to make a clean copy to share with some readers. Here are three suggestions for publishing your report:

- Give your class a one-page list of the highlights of your report. Leave a copy of the full report in the classroom or school library for students who want to read more.

- Get together with other students whose reports are in the same general area as yours (biography, science, sports, and so on). Each group can create a display with reports, drawings, photographs, and objects.
- Give an oral report based on your report. Don't just read your report, but *tell* your audience what you've learned. Volunteer to give your talk to a class or club that would be interested in your topic.

WRITING ASSIGNMENT

PART 6:
Proofreading and Publishing Your Report

You're almost finished! Copy your report on clean paper, and proofread it. Then share your report, using one of the ideas above or an idea of your own.

 Reflecting on Your Writing

Do you plan to add your report to your **portfolio**? If you do, date the report and attach written responses to the following questions.

- How did you choose a subject for your report? How did you narrow your subject down to a topic?
- How did your notes help you to write your report? How did your outline help you?

A STUDENT MODEL

The following excerpts are from a report by Kristen Kirdahy, a student in Cape Coral, Florida. Notice how she has clearly organized the facts from her sources.

Covered Wagons
by Kristen Kirdahy

Covered wagons were large ox- or horse-drawn wooden wagons that were used in the United States during the 1800s. A special group of people called the Pennsylvania Dutch created the first covered wagons used in America. These people had come from Germany and were living in the Conestoga Valley in Pennsylvania. The wagon they designed and built became known as the "Conestoga wagon."

The Conestoga wagon had a design that was different from other wagons in history. The bed of the wagon was deeper and longer than the older wagon beds. To keep goods from shifting as the wagon went up and down hills, the bed was scoop-shaped. It curved upward on both ends. A big, white canvas hood covered the wagon bed and protected the goods from rain.

When the pioneers began moving out west, many of them started to use lighter wagons. These lighter wagons became known as "prairie schooners," maybe because they had a boatlike shape and because their canvas covers looked a little like sails.

Some prairie schooners were light enough that they could be pulled by just two horses or oxen. Conestoga wagons, on the other hand, were so heavy that they usually had to be pulled by teams of six horses. For traveling over steep mountain roads, prairie schooners were probably better than Conestoga wagons.

WRITING WORKSHOP

A Book Report

You've probably read dozens of books. You've liked some and disliked others. When you write a **book report,** you tell what the book is about and what you think of it. You say exactly what you like or dislike about it.

A **biography** tells the life story of a real person. Here are some questions about biographies. They will help you give good reasons why you like or dislike a biography you have read.

1. Does the book tell about the most important events in the person's life?
2. Does the book include interesting details about the person's life and personality?
3. Does the book give a clear picture of the person's character? Does it make you care about the person?

As you read the following sample book report, look for information about events in the life of Martin Luther King, Jr.

Martin Luther King, Jr., a Man of Dreams

Have you ever dreamed of righting some wrong in the world? Martin Luther King, Jr., was a courageous leader who did just that. Margaret Davidson's biography I Have a Dream: The Story of Martin Luther King helps readers share in King's dream.

Davidson's biography describes King's childhood in Georgia, his many years of education, and his career as a minister and civil rights leader. King believed in nonviolent resistance. He tried to change unfair laws by

peacefully disobeying them. To protest the unequal treatment of African Americans, he led boycotts and marches.

King was arrested, his life was threatened, and his home was bombed, yet he never stopped believing in peaceful methods. King received the Nobel Peace Prize in 1964 for his work in the civil rights movement. But in 1968, he was shot and killed in Memphis, Tennessee. He was thirty-nine years old when he died.

Davidson's book helps readers come to know and admire Martin Luther King, Jr. Through many details and incidents, Davidson shows King's courage and strength. This biography will inspire you. It will help you understand what a great man Martin Luther King, Jr., was.

Thinking It Over

1. What do you learn from the first paragraph?
2. What purpose does the body of the report serve?
3. What does the writer think of the book? What reasons does the writer give for the opinion?

Writing a Book Report of a Biography

Prewriting. Think of a person you'd like to learn more about—perhaps a sports star or someone from history. Look through the biography shelves of your library for other ideas. As you read the book you have chosen, take notes to help you summarize it.

Writing, Evaluating, and Revising. Begin your introduction with an interesting fact or question. Tell whom the biography is about and why that person is important. The introduction should also give the title and the author. In the body, summarize some important events in the person's life. Then, write a conclusion that tells what you think of the biography. Be sure to give specific reasons why you did or didn't like the book.

Reread your report several times. Ask a classmate to read it, too. Think about what your classmate says. Then, add your own ideas and make changes.

Proofreading and Publishing. Make a clean copy of your book report, and proofread it carefully. Remember to underline the title of the book. Make a "Heroes and Heroines" display of class reports. Let other students sign a list to check out and read your report.

If you decide to include this book report in your **portfolio,** date the report and attach your responses to these questions: How did you choose an interesting fact or question to use in your introduction? What changes did you make after rereading your report?

MAKING CONNECTIONS

SPEAKING AND LISTENING

Giving a Television News Report

Turn on your television early in the morning or around dinner time, and you're bound to see a news program. If you were a TV reporter, you'd give reports all the time. Why not see how you'd like it?

Form a TV news team with two other classmates. Choose a local event to give an oral report on. For example, you might choose a holiday parade, a school basketball game, or a parent-teacher organization meeting. Remember to choose an event that your classmates will want to know about. Then, follow these steps:

1. Before the event, watch several TV news reports. Notice the kinds of information reporters present. Then work with your team to prepare a list of *5W-How?* questions about your local event.
2. Each person on the team should attend the event and take notes. Remember that you're trying to answer your *5W-How?* questions.
3. After the event, compare notes and agree on the information for your report. Then, prepare final note cards and put them in a clear order. Come up with an interesting way to begin and end.
4. Choose one member of your team to present the report. If you're the presenter, practice the report in front of your teammates.
5. Give your report to the entire class as though you were a reporter on a TV news program. If your school has videotaping equipment, you can also tape your report and present it to other classes.

RESEARCH ACROSS THE CURRICULUM

Mathematics

Do you know how mathematics began? Use your research skills to find out about the history of mathematics. Choose a topic from the following questions, or decide on a topic of your own.

1. Where did the idea of zero come from? If we had no zero, how would our number system change?
2. What kind of number system did the ancient Mayas use? How did they record numbers?
3. How did the ancient Romans record numbers?
4. What is an abacus? How does it work?

To find sources that answer the questions, check your school library or ask your math teacher for suggestions. Take notes on the sources you find, and then prepare a report to share with your math class.

10 WRITING EFFECTIVE SENTENCES

LOOKING
AHEAD

Have you ever polished a car or a tabletop until it gleamed? You can add "polish" to your sentence style, too, whether you are writing in school or in the workplace. That's what you will learn to do in this chapter. You will practice

- writing clear sentences
- combining sentences for smoothness and variety

Writing Clear Sentences

A clear sentence gives your reader just enough information. It doesn't leave out any important pieces, and it doesn't run together or string together too many ideas at once. You can learn how to spot three enemies of clear writing: *sentence fragments, run-on sentences,* and *stringy sentences.*

Sentence Fragments

What kind of sentence could you write about this picture?

You might write something like this:

> The fearless climber crawls inch by inch up the steep cliff.
>
> *or*
>
> Look at the size of that rock!
>
> *or*
>
> How does she know where the handholds are?

These groups of words say different things, but they have something in common. Each is a complete sentence. A *complete sentence* is a group of words that expresses a complete thought.

A part of each thought is expressed by the verb: *crawls, look, does know.* Another part is expressed by the subject: *climber, you, she.* [The *you* is understood in the second sentence even though it isn't expressed: (You) Look at the size of that rock!]

A *sentence fragment* is a part of a sentence that is punctuated as if it were a complete sentence. A fragment is confusing because it doesn't express a complete thought. The following word groups are the example sentences you just read—with some important words left out. Notice how unclear the word groups are when written as fragments.

Crawls inch by inch up the steep cliff. [The subject is missing. *Who* or *what* crawls?]
At the size of that rock. [The verb and the understood subject are missing. *What about* the size of the rock?]
Where the handholds are. [This word group has a subject and a verb, but it doesn't express a complete thought. *What about* the location of the handholds?]

Use this simple three-part test to help you decide whether a word group is a sentence fragment or a complete sentence.

1. Does the group of words have a subject?
2. Does the word group have a verb?
3. Does the word group express a complete thought?

WRITING NOTE Sometimes a fragment is really a part of the sentence that comes before or after it. You can correct the fragment by attaching it to the sentence it belongs with.

FRAGMENT   Mark is practicing his hook shot. **Because he wants to try out for the basketball team.**

CORRECT   Mark is practicing his hook shot because he wants to try out for the basketball team.

When you attach a fragment to a sentence, be sure to check your new sentence for correct punctuation.

EXERCISE 1▶   **Recognizing Fragments**

Decide which of the following word groups are sentence fragments and which are complete sentences. Write *S* for a complete sentence; write *F* for a fragment.

1. We visited the pet shop in the mall.
2. A bright-eyed hamster chewing on pieces of carrot.
3. Named him Mustard.

4. Has pouches inside each fat cheek.
5. The pouches are for carrying food.
6. Newspaper in lots of little shreds.
7. Making his cage quite comfortable.
8. He is plump and has white and tan fur.
9. A diet of mostly fruit, vegetables, and grain.
10. If you decide to raise hamsters.

EXERCISE 2 ▶ **Revising Fragments**

Some of the following groups of words are sentence fragments. First, identify the fragments. Then, revise each fragment by (1) adding a subject, (2) adding a verb, or (3) attaching the fragment to a complete sentence. You may need to change the punctuation and capitalization, too. If the word group is already a complete sentence, write *S*.

1. Was watching TV Wednesday night.
2. A movie about aliens invading from space.
3. Suddenly, the lights went out on the whole block.
4. Because the batteries in the flashlight were dead.
5. A strange noise in the back yard.
6. After our dog started to bark.
7. Crept slowly to the door and looked out.
8. Two small, glowing eyes in the dark.
9. When I saw it was just the cat from next door.
10. Maybe I should stop watching scary movies.

 COMPUTER NOTE: Use your word-processing program when you revise your draft for sentence fragments, run-ons, and style. By using the Cut and Paste commands, you can find the best place for words or phrases within a sentence and for sentences within your draft.

Run-on Sentences

A ***run-on sentence*** is actually two or more sentences run together into one sentence. It's often hard to tell where one idea in a run-on ends and the next one begins.

Like sentence fragments, run-on sentences usually appear in your writing because you are in a hurry to get your thoughts down on paper. You may leave out the correct end punctuation (period, question mark, or exclamation point) or use just a comma to separate the sentences.

There are two good ways to revise run-on sentences. You can break the run-on into two complete sentences, or you can link the two ideas with a comma and a coordinating conjunction (*and, but, or*).

RUN-ON
Sally Ride's mission began on June 18, 1983 she had to train for many months before then.

CORRECT
Sally Ride's mission began on June 18, 1983. She had to train for many months before then.
or
Sally Ride's mission began on June 18, 1983, **but** she had to train for many months before then.

MECHANICS HINT

Using Commas Correctly

A comma alone is not enough to link two complete ideas in a sentence. If you use just a comma between two complete ideas, you create a run-on sentence.

RUN-ON Sally Ride was the first American woman in space, she was a member of a shuttle crew.

CORRECT Sally Ride was the first American woman in space. She was a member of a shuttle crew.

☞ REFERENCE NOTE: For more about using a comma between two complete ideas, see page 597.

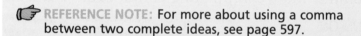

EXERCISE 3 ▶ **Identifying and Revising Run-on Sentences**

Decide which of the following groups of words are run-ons. Then revise each run-on by (1) making it into two separate sentences or (2) using a comma and a coordinating conjunction. You may have to change the punctuation and capitalization, too. If the group of words is already correct, write *C*.

1. Someday you may not live on Earth you may live in a space colony.
2. Space colonies will be important. They will be sources of raw materials and energy.
3. Space colonies will be enclosed otherwise people couldn't live in the alien climate.
4. If materials for the colony come from the moon and asteroids, construction will be difficult.
5. Electricity could come from solar cells, the cells would collect energy from the sun's rays.

6. The space station's orbiting platform could be covered with millions of solar cells.
7. The energy collected could be beamed to Earth then it could be used here for electricity.
8. Some people will build platforms, some will grow food.
9. Computer chips could even be manufactured in a space station.
10. A space colony is still many years away it is fun to imagine the future.

Stringy Sentences

For variety, you'll sometimes want to join sentences and sentence parts with *and*. But if you string many ideas together with *and*, you create a ***stringy sentence.*** Stringy sentences ramble on and on. They don't give the reader a chance to pause between ideas.

STRINGY   The ostrich is the largest living bird, and it stands nearly eight feet tall, and it weighs over three hundred pounds when it is fully grown, and this speedy bird can run up to forty miles an hour!

BETTER   The ostrich is the largest living bird. It stands nearly eight feet tall, and it weighs over three hundred pounds when it is fully grown. This speedy bird can run up to forty miles an hour!

In the revised version, only two ideas are linked by *and*. These ideas can be joined in one sentence because they are closely related. However, notice that a comma was added before the *and*. The comma is necessary to show a slight pause between the two complete ideas.

EXERCISE 4 ▶ **Identifying and Revising Stringy Sentences**

Some of the following sentences are stringy. Revise each stringy sentence by breaking it into two or more sentences. If an item is already correct, write *C*.

1. Thomas and José were playing softball at school, and Thomas hit the ball very hard, and then he saw it roll under the steps of the library.
2. Thomas peered under the dark steps to recover his ball, and when he reached for it he saw a giant raccoon, and Thomas wasn't sure what to do next!
3. José told Thomas that raccoons are fierce fighters, and then José warned him not to anger the raccoon, and by this time, other softball players had gathered to offer advice.
4. Thomas finally rolled the ball out from under the steps with a baseball bat. The raccoon stayed completely still, and it hissed and looked fiercely at the group. Then Thomas saw why the raccoon was behaving so strangely.
5. Five baby raccoons were hiding behind the mother, and they were too small to protect themselves, and that's why the mother raccoon was trying to frighten the softball players away!

R E V I E W **A**	**Revising Fragments, Run-on Sentences, and Stringy Sentences**

Decide which of the following word groups are fragments, run-ons, or stringy sentences. Then revise each of these word groups to make it clear and complete. Remember to add correct capitalization and punctuation. If a word group is already clear and complete, just write C.

1. An ordinary person goes into a dressing room a clown comes out.
2. Creates a special face.
3. Clown makeup starts with white greasepaint, and the greasepaint looks like a mask, and a special cream must be used to remove it.
4. After painting bright colors above the eyes, the clown adds eyebrows high on the forehead.

5. A lot of red is used around the mouth, and the mouth is very important, and it determines the personality of the clown.
6. Some clowns wear a large, red nose, it is fitted over the person's own nose.
7. A tight-fitting cap can make a clown look bald on each side the cap sometimes has funny, wild-looking hair.
8. Since a funny costume adds to the effect.
9. Baggy pants and a big shirt with a ruffled collar come next.
10. Floppy shoes the outfit.

Combining Sentences

Good writers usually use some short sentences, but they don't use them all the time. An entire paragraph of short sentences makes writing sound choppy. For example, notice how dull and choppy the following paragraph sounds.

Quicksand is really just sand. The sand is wet. The sand is loose. You can sink in quicksand. It won't actually suck you down. You might get caught in quicksand. You can lie on your back. You can float. Then you can roll or wriggle. Your movements must be slow. You can get to solid ground this way.

Now, see how the writer has revised the paragraph by combining some of the short sentences. Notice how sentence combining has helped to eliminate some repeated words and ideas. The result is a smoother paragraph with much more variety.

> Quicksand is really just wet, loose sand. You can sink in quicksand, but it won't actually suck you down. If you're caught in quicksand, you can lie on your back and float. Then you can slowly roll or wriggle to solid ground.

You can combine sentences in several different ways. Sometimes you can insert a word or a group of words from one sentence into another sentence. Other times you can combine two related sentences by using a connecting word.

Inserting Words

One way to combine two sentences is to pull a key word from one sentence and insert it into the other sentence. Sometimes you can just add the key word to the first sentence and drop the rest of the second sentence. Other times you'll need to change the form of the key word before you can insert it.

USING THE SAME FORM	
ORIGINAL	Martin Luther King, Jr., was a civil rights leader. He was an American.
COMBINED	Martin Luther King, Jr., was an **American** civil rights leader.
CHANGING THE FORM	
ORIGINAL	He was famous for his brilliant speeches. His fame was international.
COMBINED	He was **internationally** famous for his brilliant speeches.

WRITING NOTE When you change the forms of the key words, you often add endings such as *–ed, –ing, –ful,* and *–ly* to make adjectives and adverbs.

EXAMPLES

skill	⟹	skilled
crash	⟹	crashing
use	⟹	useful
quiet	⟹	quietly

EXERCISE 5 ▶ **Combining Sentences by Inserting Words**

Each of the following items contains two sentences. Combine the two sentences by taking the italicized key word from the second sentence and inserting it into the first sentence. The directions in parentheses will tell you how to change the form of the key word if you need to do so.

EXAMPLE
1. Chief Joseph was a Nez Perce Indian chief who fought for his people. He was a *brave* fighter. (Add –*ly*.)
1. *Chief Joseph was a Nez Perce Indian chief who fought bravely for his people.*

1. The name *Joseph* was given to him by missionaries. The missionaries were *white*.
2. His name means "thunder traveling over the mountains." That is his *Nez Perce* name.
3. Chief Joseph fought the United States Army to defend his people's homeland. The fighting was *fierce*. (Add *–ly*.)
4. When he realized he could not win, he led the Nez Perce band more than one thousand miles. The band was in *retreat*. (Add *–ing*.)
5. Chief Joseph's surrender speech is famous. It is *moving*.

Inserting Groups of Words

Often, you can combine two related sentences by taking an entire group of words from one sentence and adding it to the other sentence. When the group of words is inserted, it adds detail to the information in the first sentence.

ORIGINAL   The sailboats raced. They raced in the bay.
COMBINED   The sailboats raced **in the bay.**

ORIGINAL   The sailboats were beautiful. The sailboats were docked in the marina.
COMBINED   The sailboats **docked in the marina** were beautiful.

ORIGINAL   The boats are all built alike. These are boats in one-design sailboat races.
COMBINED   The boats **in one-design sailboat races** are all built alike.

Sometimes you'll need to put commas around the group of words you are inserting. Ask yourself whether the group of words renames or explains a noun or pronoun in the sentence. If it does, use a comma or commas to set off the word group from the rest of the sentence.

ORIGINAL   We'll watch the race from the marina. The marina is the best spot to see the race.

COMBINED   We'll watch the race from the marina**, the best spot to see the race.**

ORIGINAL   The catboat has only one sail. It is a popular racing boat.

COMBINED   The catboat**, a popular racing boat,** has only one sail.

☞ REFERENCE NOTE: For more about using commas in sentences, see pages 594–603.

After you combine two sentences, be sure to read your new sentence carefully. Then ask yourself the following questions:

- Is my new sentence clear?
- Does it make sense?
- Does it sound better than the two shorter sentences?

EXERCISE 6 ▶ **Combining Sentences by Inserting Word Groups**

Combine each of the following pairs of sentences by taking the italicized word group from the second sentence and inserting it into the first sentence. Be sure to add commas if they are needed.

EXAMPLE   **1.** Martha read *Island of the Blue Dolphins* for her book report. Martha is *a girl in my English class.*

   1. *Martha, a girl in my English class, read* Island of the Blue Dolphins *for her book report.*

1. *Island of the Blue Dolphins* is an exciting adventure story. It is *by Scott O'Dell.*

2. It is about Karana, a girl who lived alone. She lived alone *on an island.*

3. Karana built a shelter and found food. Karana was *a self-sufficient girl.*

4. She waited for a ship to rescue her. She waited *many years*.
5. Your library probably has a copy of *Island of the Blue Dolphins*. It is *an award-winning novel*.

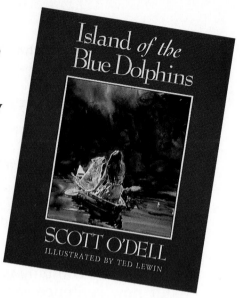

Illustration from *Island of the Blue Dolphins* by Scott O'Dell. Illustrated by Ted Lewin. Illustrations © 1996 by Ted Lewin. Reprinted by permission of Houghton Mifflin Company. All rights reserved.

Using Connecting Words

Another way you can combine sentences is by using connecting words called *conjunctions*. Conjunctions allow you to join closely related sentences and sentence parts.

Joining Subjects and Verbs

Sometimes two sentences are so closely related that they have the same subjects or verbs. If two sentences have the same subject, you can combine them by making a **compound verb.** If the sentences have the same verb, you can combine them by making a **compound subject.**

The conjunction you use is important. It tells your reader how the two subjects or verbs are related to one another.

Use *and* to join similar ideas.

ORIGINAL   Drawing is fun. Painting is fun.
COMBINED   **Drawing and painting** are fun. [compound subject]

Use *but* to join contrasting ideas.

ORIGINAL   Mike will cook the main course. Mike will buy the dessert.

COMBINED   Mike will **cook** the main course **but buy** the dessert. [compound verb]

Use *or* to show a choice between ideas.

ORIGINAL   Sara Tallchief may be elected president of the Student Council. Frances O'Connor may be elected president of the Student Council.

COMBINED   **Sara Tallchief or Frances O'Connor** may be elected president of the Student Council. [compound subject]

EXERCISE 7▶   **Combining Sentences by Joining Subjects and Verbs**

Use *and, but,* or *or* to combine each of the following pairs of sentences. If the sentences have the same verb, make one sentence by joining the two subjects. If the sentences have the same subject, make one sentence by joining the two verbs. The hints in parentheses will help you.

EXAMPLE   **1.** Beans are grown on that farm. Tomatoes are grown on that farm. (Join with *and.*)
1. *Beans and tomatoes are grown on that farm.*

1. Florida produces many citrus products. Florida exports many citrus products. (Join with *and.*)
2. Oranges are grown in Florida. Grapefruits are grown in Florida. (Join with *and.*)
3. Grapefruit looks sweet. It tastes sour. (Join with *but.*)
4. The orange will be chosen the Citrus Fruit of the Year. The grapefruit will be chosen the Citrus Fruit of the Year. (Join with *or.*)
5. The orange could win the contest. The grapefruit could win the contest. (Join with *or.*)

Joining Sentences

Sometimes you may want to combine two related sentences that express equally important ideas. You can connect the two sentences by using a comma and *and, but,* or *or.* The result is a ***compound sentence.***

ORIGINAL   Dad's favorite dog is a cocker spaniel. Mom's favorite dog is a collie.

COMBINED   Dad's favorite dog is a cocker spaniel**, but** Mom's favorite dog is a collie.

Other times you may want to combine two sentences that are related in a special way. One sentence helps explain the other sentence by telling *how, where, why,* or *when.* A good way to combine these sentences is to add a connecting word that shows the special relationship. In this kind of sentence combining, you create a ***complex sentence.***

ORIGINAL   The drawbridge was pulled up. The enemy knights could not get into the castle.

COMBINED   **When** the drawbridge was pulled up, the enemy knights could not get into the castle.

Some connecting words that you can use are *after, although, as, because, before, if, since, so that, until, when, whether,* and *while.* The word that you choose will depend on what you want your sentence to say.

EXERCISE 8 ▶ **Combining Complete Sentences**

Following are five sets of short, choppy sentences that need improving. Make each pair into one sentence by using the connecting word given in parentheses. Be sure to change the capitalization and the punctuation where necessary.

EXAMPLE   **1.** Planets move. Stars stay in their places. (but)
              1. *Planets move, but stars stay in their places.*

1. I would like to learn more about stars. They are interesting and beautiful. (because)

2. Planets do not give off light of their own. Stars do. (but)
3. Some stars are fainter than our sun. Some are many times brighter. (and)
4. Our sun will change. The change will be slow. (but)
5. We must continue to study the stars and planets. We will understand how we fit into our vast universe. (so that)

| R E V I E W **B** | **Revising a Paragraph by Combining Sentences** |

The following paragraph sounds choppy because it has too many short sentences. Use the methods you've learned in this section to combine some of the sentences. You'll notice how much better the paragraph sounds after you've revised it.

Many lizards defend themselves by playing tricks on their attackers. For example, the horned lizard frightens off its enemies by squirting a thin stream of blood. The lizard squirts the blood from its eyes. Another kind of lizard fools attackers with its long, brittle tail. This kind of lizard is the glass snake. Sometimes an enemy grabs the glass snake's tail. The lizard just breaks off the tail. The lizard crawls away. The tail keeps wriggling. The attacker doesn't see the lizard escape. The attacker keeps struggling with the tail.

320

MAKING CONNECTIONS

Reconstruct a Message

You have been shipwrecked on a tiny, uncharted island. You've built a sturdy shelter and have plenty of fish, coconuts, and sea vegetables to eat. But after being stranded for a month, you're eager to be rescued. You scratch a message on a piece of tree bark telling where your ship was lost. Then you stuff the bark into a bottle and send it out to sea.

A week later, you see the bottle bobbing in the water close to shore. The current has carried back a message! Excited, you bring the bottle to shore, pull out the cork, and find this message written in berry juice:

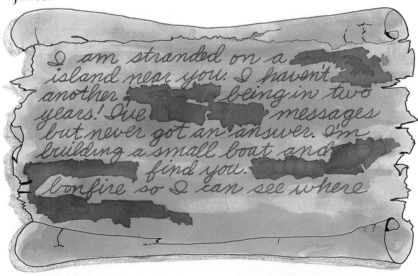

Oh, no! A few drops of water leaked into the bottle and washed away some of the writing! Try to piece together the original, complete sentences from the blurred fragments. What is the message? What does the person want you to do?

11 ENGLISH: ORIGINS AND USES

LOOKING
AHEAD

You know more words and word combinations than you could ever list. With its huge vocabulary (over 600,000 words!), English offers you many different ways to express your thoughts, observations, and feelings. How did English become such a rich, expressive language? How can you choose the best words for saying what you mean? This chapter will give you some answers to these and other questions about your language. You will learn

- where English comes from
- how English has grown and changed
- what the varieties of English are
- how to choose appropriate words for different situations

The Growth of English

No one knows exactly when or how English got started. We do know that English and many other languages come from an early language spoken thousands of years ago. The related languages still resemble that parent language, just as you resemble your parents. For example, notice how similar the words for "mother" are in the following modern-day languages.

ENGLISH	mother	ITALIAN	madre
FRENCH	mère	SWEDISH	moder
SPANISH	madre		

About 1,500 years ago, a few small tribes of people settled in the area that is now England. These tribes, called the Angles and Saxons, spoke the earliest known form of English. Their English was very different from ours. For example, look at the following passage from *Beowulf*, a poem that was probably written more than 1,100 years ago.

English has changed in many ways since it was first spoken and written. But some of our most basic words have been around in one form or another since the beginnings of the language.

PRESENT-DAY FORM	hand	daughter	answer	leap
EARLY FORM	hand	dohtor	andswaru	hleapan

Changes in Pronunciation and Spelling

If you traveled back in time a few hundred years, you'd probably have a hard time understanding the English being spoken. English words used to be pronounced differently from the way they're pronounced today. For example, in the 1200s, people pronounced *bite* like *beet* and *feet* like *fate*. They also pronounced the vowel sound in the word *load* like our word *awe*.

You've probably wondered why English words aren't always spelled as they sound. Changes in pronunciation help account for many strange spellings in English. For example, the *w* that starts the word *write* wasn't always silent. The *w* sound was gradually dropped, but the spelling lagged behind. The *g* in *gnat* and the *k* in *knee* were once part of the pronunciations of the words, too.

However, the spellings of many words have changed over time. Some changes in spelling have been accidental. For example, *apron* used to be spelled *napron*. People mistakenly attached the *n* to the article *a*, and *a napron* became *an apron*. Here are some more examples of everyday English words and their early forms.

PRESENT-DAY FORM	jail	look	sleep	time
EARLY FORM	jaile	locian	slæp	tima

Pronunciations and spellings still vary today. For instance, the English used in Great Britain differs from the English used in the United States. In Great Britain, people pronounce *bath* with the vowel sound of *father* instead of the vowel sound of *cat*. The British also tend to drop the *r* sound at the end of words like *copper*. In addition, the British spell some words differently from the way people in the United States do.

AMERICAN	theater	pajamas	labor
BRITISH	theatre	pyjamas	labour

Changes in Meaning

It may be hard to believe that the word *bead* once meant "prayer." Many English words have changed meaning over time. Some of these changes have been slight. Others have been more obvious, as with *bead*. Here are a few more examples of words that have changed meanings:

naughty—Back in the 1300s, *naughty* meant "poor or needy." It wasn't until around the 1600s that *naughty* was used to mean "poorly behaved."

lunch—In the 1500s, a *lunch* was a large chunk of something, such as bread or meat.

corn—The word *corn* was being used as long ago as the 800s. Originally it meant "a grain," as in a grain of sand or salt.

caboose—*Caboose* first entered English in the late 1700s. Back then, the word had nothing to do with trains. It meant "the kitchen of a ship."

Today, the meanings of words may vary from one place to another. For instance, some words mean different things in Great Britain than they do in the United States. A British person might ride the *tube* (subway) to work or put her suitcase in the *boot* (trunk) of the car.

How New Words Enter English

English grows and changes along with the people who use it. Four hundred years ago, words like *telescope* and *bicycle* didn't exist in English. The objects these words name hadn't been invented yet.

Over the centuries, people have invented thousands of English words to name new objects, places, ideas, and experiences. They've also borrowed many useful words from other languages.

Borrowed Words

Word borrowings first occurred as English-speaking people came into contact with people from other cultures and lands. Eventually, English speakers began to learn words from the languages of these peoples. Many of these foreign words became part of the English language.

English has borrowed hundreds of thousands of words from French, Hindi, Spanish, African languages, and many other languages spoken around the world. In many cases, the borrowed words have taken new forms.

FRENCH	ange	HINDI	chāmpo
ENGLISH	angel	ENGLISH	shampoo
AFRICAN	banjo	SPANISH	patata
ENGLISH	banjo	ENGLISH	potato

Words from Names

Many things get their names from the names of places or people. The word *Frisbee* is a good example. In the 1920s, someone in Bridgeport, Connecticut, discovered a new use for the pie plates from the Frisbie Bakery. He turned one upside down and sent it floating through the air. Flipping the pie plates soon became a popular game with local college students. The game sparked the idea for the plastic Frisbees of today.

Matching Words with Their Original Spellings and Meanings

The words in the left-hand column are English words that came from other languages. See if you can match each word with its original language, spelling, and meaning. [Hint: Use the process of elimination.]

1. pupil

2. tote

3. raccoon

4. tortilla

5. balloon

a. Kongo, *tota*, "to pick up"

b. Italian, *pallone*, "a large ball"

c. Spanish, *torta*, "a cake"

d. Latin, *pupillus*, "orphan"

e. Algonquian Indian, *aroughcun*, "one who scratches"

EXERCISE 2 ▶ **Researching Word Origins**

Use a dictionary to look up the origin of each of the following words. What language or name does each word come from?

1. kayak

2. prairie

3. cheddar

4. denim

5. lasso

6. macaroni

7. pretzel

8. jumbo

9. bloomers

10. skunk

Choosing Your Words

The variety and flexibility of English allow you to say the same thing in many different ways. Variety keeps the language interesting, but it also makes choosing the right words difficult sometimes. Choosing your words will be easier if you know the different uses and meanings words may have.

Dialects of American English

You probably know some people who speak English differently than you do. Maybe they pronounce some words differently or use them to mean different things. They may even use words you've never heard of before.

Different groups of people use different varieties of English. The kind of English we speak sounds most normal to us even though it may sound "funny" to someone else. The form of English a particular group of people speaks is called a ***dialect.*** Everyone uses a dialect, and no dialect is better or worse than another.

Regional Dialects

Do you *make* the bed or *make up* the bed? Would you order a *sub* with "the woiks" or a *hero* with "the werks"? In the evening, do you eat *supper* or *dinner*? How you answer these questions will probably depend on what part of the country you come from.

A dialect shared by people from the same area is called a *regional dialect.* Your regional dialect helps determine what words you use, how you pronounce words, and even how you put words together.

STYLE NOTE   You can use dialect in short stories to help your reader hear a character's language. As you read the following paragraph, notice how the use of dialect makes the character come alive. Can you tell what part of the country this character comes from?

> I traveled back home acrost the ridge just a-grinning myself. I had a full belly but I was light on my feet as everly. I don't need no light to show me where I'm going, nor a body to lead me the way. I know all the ways there is on Hurricane Mountain.
>
> Lee Smith, *Oral History*

When you write dialogue for a character, think about how your character would really talk. Try to capture the sound as well as the sense of the person's language.

Ethnic Dialects

Your cultural background can also determine the way you speak. A dialect shared by people from the same cultural group is called an *ethnic dialect.* Because Americans come from many cultures, American English includes many ethnic dialects. One of the largest ethnic dialects is the Black English spoken by many African Americans. Another is the Hispanic English of many people whose families come from Mexico, Central America, Cuba, and Puerto Rico.

Not everyone from a particular group speaks that group's dialect. Also, an ethnic or regional dialect may vary depending on the speakers' individual backgrounds and places of origin.

| EXERCISE 3 ▶ | **Reading a Dialect** |

In the following passage, a young African American boy is telling about his experience at a cafe with his mother. Read the passage aloud, pronouncing the words as the writer has spelled them. Does this character's dialect sound different from yours? If it does, tell how you would describe the same scene using your own dialect.

> She take a quarter out the hankercher and tie the hankercher up again. She look over her shoulder at the people, but she still don't move. I hope she don't spend the money. I don't want her spend it on me. I'm hungry, I'm almost starving I'm so hungry, but I don't want her spending the money on me.
>
> She flip the quarter over like she thinking. She must be thinking 'bout us walking back home. Lord, I sure don't want walk home. If I thought it done any good to say something, I say it. But my mama make up her own mind.
>
> Ernest J. Gaines, "The Sky Is Gray"

Standard American English

Every dialect is useful and helps keep the English language colorful and interesting. But sometimes it's confusing to try to communicate using two different dialects. That's why it's important to be familiar with *standard American English.*

Standard English is the most commonly understood variety of English. It allows English-speaking people from different regions and cultures to communicate with one another clearly. It is the most widely used form of American English.

You can find some of the rules and guidelines for using standard English in the **Handbook** in this textbook. Language that doesn't follow these rules and guidelines is called *nonstandard English.*

| NONSTANDARD | I don't want no more spinach. |
| STANDARD | I don't want **any** more spinach. |

| NONSTANDARD | Jimmy would of gone hiking with us. |
| STANDARD | Jimmy **would have** gone hiking with us. |

☞ REFERENCE NOTE: For more information about the kinds of nonstandard usage shown in the examples, see pages 538–539 and pages 549–557.

Formal and Informal English

Read the following sentences.

Many of my friends are excited about the game.
A bunch of my friends are psyched about the game.

Both sentences mean the same thing, but they have different effects. The first sentence is an example of *formal English.* The second sentence is an example of *informal English.*

Formal and informal English are each appropriate for different situations. For instance, you'd probably use the first, more formal example sentence if you were talking to a teacher about the game. But you'd probably choose the informal wording of the second example if you were talking to a classmate. Other situations in which formal English is used include television news programs and many workplace activities.

Colloquialisms

Informal English includes many words and expressions that are inappropriate in more formal situations. The most widely used informal expressions are *colloquialisms.* **Colloquialisms** are the colorful words and phrases of everyday conversation. They give our speaking and writing a casual, friendly tone. Many colloquialisms have meanings that are different from the basic meanings of the words.

EXAMPLES   I wish Gerald would **get off my case.**
Don't get **all bent out of shape** about it.
We were about to **bust** with laughter.

Slang

Slang words are made-up words or old words used in new ways. Slang is highly informal language. It is usually created by a particular group of people, such as students or artists. Often, slang is familiar only to the groups that invent it. You and your friends may have a slang vocabulary that your parents and teachers don't always understand.

Sometimes slang words become a lasting part of the English language. Usually, though, slang falls out of style quickly. The slang words in the following sentences will probably seem out of date to you.

That was a really **far-out flick.**
Those are some **groovy duds** you're wearing.
I don't have enough **dough** to buy a movie ticket.

STYLE NOTE   Colloquialisms and slang can add zest to language. However, they are acceptable only in the most informal speaking and writing. Don't use colloquialisms or slang in essays, test answers, or reports.

| EXERCISE 4 | **Using Formal and Informal English** |

You're thinking about starting a coin collection, but you'd like to find out more about coin collecting first. You've already written a formal letter to the woman who is in charge of the coin collection at a local museum. You also want to write to your cousin Dan, who has his own coin collection. Rewrite the formal letter using more informal language, so that it will be more appropriate to send to Dan.

Dear Mrs. Domingo,

I am interested in coin collecting, and I am writing to ask for your assistance. I have not actually started a collection yet. However, I am considering starting one as a hobby, and I would greatly appreciate any information about coin collecting that you could send me.

Sincerely,
[your name]

Denotation and Connotation

Would you rather be described as a *curious* person or a *nosy* person? Both words have the same basic meaning, or **denotation.** But they have different *connotations.* A **connotation** is the kind of meaning that affects people emotionally.

You probably wouldn't mind if someone described you as *curious.* For most people, the word suggests someone who is interested and eager to learn. But you probably wouldn't like to be described as *nosy.* That word suggests someone who is a busybody—who is *too* interested in other people's business.

It's important to think about the connotations of the words you use. Connotations can have a strong effect on your reader or listener. If you use a word without knowing its connotation, you may send the wrong message to your audience.

STYLE
NOTE

Sometimes you will need to choose between *synonyms*—words that have similar meanings. Thinking about the connotations of the words will help you choose the word that says what you really mean. For example, suppose you need to choose a word to fit the following sentence.

> I admire Coach Carlson because her rules are _____ and fair. (*firm, strict*)

Firm and *strict* have similar meanings. But *strict* carries the negative connotation of harshness or rigidness. You'd probably choose *firm* instead, because it has a more positive connotation.

COMPUTER NOTE: Most word-processing programs have a thesaurus tool. When you highlight a word in your draft, the thesaurus will list several synonyms for that word. Before you choose a synonym, think about possible connotations that would affect your readers.

EXERCISE 5 ▶ Recognizing Connotations

Read each of the following words. What kind of reaction do you have to each word—positive, negative, or neither? Compare your reactions with those of your classmates.

1. fancy
2. bold
3. shy
4. cheap
5. snowstorm
6. coward
7. kind
8. friendly
9. pity
10. flower

Name a Newly Discovered Animal

Throughout history, people have made up names for things that were new to them. For example, when English colonists arrived in the New World, they invented English names for many of the plants and animals they found there. Their language grew along with their knowledge of their new surroundings.

Now it's your turn to give names to some amazing discoveries. The year is 2520. You are on a team of Earthlings sent to explore Magdon, a newly discovered planet in a nearby solar system. After you land on the planet, you notice many strange-looking animals. They are different from any animals you've seen on Earth. As part of the exploration team, you have the honor of giving names to the creatures you find.

I
Write an interstellar postcard to a friend telling about one of the animals you've seen. First, draw a picture of the animal. Then, describe what the animal looks like, how it moves, and what noises it makes. Does it

live on land, in the water, or somewhere else? Finally, tell your friend the name you've decided to give to the creature.

Here's a sample postcard written by another member of the exploration team.

Dear Melanie,
I saw the most incredible animal yesterday. It's almost completely round and flat, and it doesn't have any legs. It hovers over the sand and coasts along at an amazing speed. It's mostly light brown, but it has these glowing orange eyes all around the edge. It makes a whirring noise like spinning wheels. I call it a sand-coaster.
Your friend,
Isabel

Ms. Melanie Jones
705 Maple Lane
Chicago,
IL 60614
USA
EARTH

II

You've returned to Earth after several months on Magdon. The Council for Understanding Magdonian Creatures asks you to give a formal report on the animal you described in your postcard. Using your drawing as a guide, write the report you will present to the council. Make sure your description is clear and precise.

PART TWO

HANDBOOK

12 THE SENTENCE

Subject and Predicate, Kinds of Sentences

Diagnostic Test

A. Identifying Sentences

Some of the following groups of words are sentences; others are not. If a group of words is a sentence, add a capital letter at the beginning and an appropriate punctuation mark at the end. If a group of words is not a sentence, write *sentence fragment*.

EXAMPLES
1. the big tree lost some limbs
1. *The big tree lost some limbs.*

2. after the storm yesterday
2. *sentence fragment*

1. leaves all over the front lawn and path
2. what is a black hole
3. every day this week Felipe practiced the piano
4. our best score in a basketball game this year
5. mail this letter on your way to school

B. Identifying Simple Subjects and Simple Predicates

Identify the *simple subject* and the *simple predicate* in each of the following sentences. Be on the alert for compound subjects, compound verbs, and verb phrases.

EXAMPLE   **1.** He removed the tire and patched it.
           1. *He—simple subject; removed, patched— simple predicate*

  6. The program about the Great Wall of China will be shown tonight.
  7. On the piano was a bowl of fresh flowers.
  8. After a test I check my answers carefully.
  9. At the beach my brother and my cousins built a sand castle.
10. Lucky ran to the door and barked loudly at the mail carrier.

C. Identifying Simple Sentences and Compound Sentences

Identify each of the following sentences as *simple* or *compound*.

EXAMPLE   **1.** The ship sank, but the crew was saved.
           1. *compound*

11. Lucia hunted carefully along the dry riverbed and found a rare fossil.
12. I rang the doorbell several times, but nobody was home.
13. The plane finally landed in Bombay at noon, and the passengers looked for their friends and family members.
14. The storm slowed cars and halted trains.
15. Aretha won the first two games, but Lisa won the match.

D. Classifying and Punctuating Sentences by Purpose

For each of the following sentences, add the correct end mark of punctuation. Then label each sentence *declarative, interrogative, imperative,* or *exclamatory.*

EXAMPLE   **1.** Are you ready

           1. *Are you ready?—interrogative*

16. Look at this picture of a Navajo hogan
17. What a fantastic display of fireworks this is
18. Who is studying Spanish
19. I always enjoy Independence Day
20. What is your favorite holiday

Sentence or Sentence Fragment?

12a.   A *sentence* is a group of words that expresses a complete thought.

A sentence begins with a capital letter and ends with a period, a question mark, or an exclamation point.

EXAMPLES   Octavio Paz won a Nobel Prize in literature.
               Walk in single file.
               Do you collect coins?
               Imagine me riding on an elephant!

When a group of words looks like a sentence but does not express a complete thought, it is a *sentence fragment.*

SENTENCE FRAGMENT   Alonzo's sisters and brothers. [This is not a complete thought. What about Alonzo's sisters and brothers?]

SENTENCE   Alonzo's sisters and brothers planned a surprise party for his birthday.

SENTENCE FRAGMENT	Visited an old Spanish mission in San Diego. [This is not a complete thought. Who visited the mission?]
SENTENCE	On our vacation last summer, we visited an old Spanish mission in San Diego.

SENTENCE FRAGMENT	On the way to school yesterday morning. [This thought is not complete. What happened on the way to school yesterday morning?]
SENTENCE	On the way to school yesterday morning, I saw Mr. Saunders walking his dog.

NOTE: In speech, people frequently use sentence fragments. Such fragments usually aren't confusing because the speaker's tone of voice and facial expressions help to complete the meaning. Professional writers, too, may use sentence fragments to create specific effects in their writing. However, in your writing at school, you will find it best to use complete sentences.

▶ EXERCISE 1 **Identifying Sentences**

Tell whether each of the following groups of words is a *sentence* or a *sentence fragment*. If a group of words is a sentence, use a capital letter at the beginning and add an end mark of punctuation.

EXAMPLES   **1.** my aunt and uncle raise shar-pei dogs
　　　　　　 1. *sentence—My aunt and uncle raise shar-pei dogs.*
　　　　　　 2. Queenie, my favorite of all their dogs
　　　　　　 2. *sentence fragment*

 1. my aunt, my uncle, and my cousins at their house last weekend
 2. after dinner Aunt Marie told me about the history of the shar-pei
 3. bred these dogs in China

4. just look at all that loose, wrinkled skin
5. protected them from injury during a fight
6. gentle and a lot of fun with children
7. playing catch with Queenie
8. on the porch were Queenie's new puppies
9. have you ever seen such a sight as these puppies
10. what a good time we had

Subject and Predicate

Every sentence has two main parts: a *subject* and a *predicate*.

The Subject

12b. The *subject* tells whom or what the sentence is about.

EXAMPLES **Lois Lenski** wrote *Strawberry Girl.*
The tooth with a point is a canine.

To find the subject, ask yourself *who* or *what* is doing something or *about whom* or *what* something is being said.

EXAMPLES **My best friend** sits next to me in science class.
[*Who* sits next to me? My best friend.]
Science class is very interesting this year. [*What* is interesting? Science class.]

The Position of the Subject

The subject may come at the beginning, in the middle, or even at the end of a sentence.

EXAMPLES After school, **Theresa** went to judo practice.
Under our house was **a tiny kitten**.
Who is **she?**

EXERCISE 2 **Identifying Subjects**

Identify the subject in each of these sentences.

EXAMPLE **1.** The final score was tied.
1. *The final score*

1. Many games use rackets or paddles.
2. Tennis can be an exhausting sport.
3. Badminton rackets don't weigh very much.
4. Table-tennis paddles are covered with rubber.
5. Racquetball uses special rackets.
6. In Florida, citrus trees grow an important crop.
7. After three to five years, fruit grows on the new trees.
8. Does Florida grow all of the citrus fruit in the United States?
9. California also grows oranges and other citrus fruit.
10. From Texas comes the Star Ruby grapefruit.

REVIEW A **Writing Complete Sentences**

Some of the following groups of words are sentences. Write these sentences, adding capital letters and punctuation. If a group of words is not a sentence, add a subject or a verb to make it a sentence.

EXAMPLES **1.** we brought costumes from home
1. *We brought costumes from home.*

2. wrote a play
2. *Our language arts class wrote a play.*

1. sent us a postcard from the Philippines
2. it was cold at the skating rink
3. helped me with my science project
4. a surfer on a huge wave
5. how hungry I am at lunch time
6. it is too late for a game of checkers
7. is that Niagara Falls or Horseshoe Falls
8. the Cuban family next-door
9. what time is your mom picking us up
10. the governor of my state

Complete Subject and Simple Subject

The *complete subject* consists of all the words needed to tell *whom* or *what* the sentence is about. The *simple subject* is part of the complete subject.

12c. The *simple subject* is the main word in the complete subject.

EXAMPLE **A bright-red cardinal** sat on the windowsill.
Complete subject A bright-red cardinal
Simple subject cardinal

EXAMPLE **The Korean market** is closed today.
Complete subject The Korean market
Simple subject market

If you leave out the simple subject, a sentence does not make sense.

A bright-red . . . sat on the windowsill.
The Korean . . . is closed today.

Sometimes the same word or words make up both the simple subject and the complete subject.

EXAMPLES   Above the canyon, **hawks** circled. [*Hawks* is both the complete subject and the simple subject.]
Little Rascal is the story of a boy and his pet raccoon. [The title *Little Rascal* is both the complete subject and the simple subject.]

NOTE: In this book, the term *subject* refers to the simple subject unless otherwise indicated.

▶ EXERCISE 3   **Identifying Complete Subjects and Simple Subjects**

Identify the complete subject of each sentence. Then underline the simple subject.

EXAMPLE   **1.** From the chimney came a thick cloud of smoke.
       1. *a thick <u>cloud</u> of smoke*

1. Tents were set up in the park.
2. Have you heard the new CD by Gloria Estefan?
3. News travels fast in our town.
4. Above the fort, the flag was still flying.
5. Beyond those mountains lies an ancient Native American village.
6. Those reporters have been interviewing the mayor all morning.
7. On the shelf was a copy of *Jonah's Gourd Vine.*
8. According to folklore, Johnny Kaw invented the catfish.
9. The blue candles burned all night long.
10. In the drawer were some chopsticks.

The Predicate

12d. The *predicate* of a sentence is the part that says something about the subject.

EXAMPLES   The best program **was about the Amazon River.**
              The students **took turns on the new computer.**

> EXERCISE 4   **Identifying Predicates**

Identify the predicate in each of these sentences.

EXAMPLE   **1.** Many people would like to have a robot.
              1. *would like to have a robot*

1. Robots are machines with "brains."
2. The robot's brain is a computer.
3. A robot does not always look like a person.
4. Pacemakers are little robots.
5. Pacemakers help control a faulty heartbeat.
6. Many companies use robots.
7. Cars of the future may be guided by robots.
8. Some household jobs can be done by robots.
9. A robot could clean your room.
10. You might like to have a robot to help with your chores.

The Position of the Predicate

The predicate usually comes after the subject. Sometimes, however, part or all of the predicate comes before the subject.

EXAMPLES   **Quickly** we **learned the layout of the small Hopi village.**
              At the entrance to the science fair were maps of the exhibits.

> EXERCISE 5   **Identifying Predicates**

Identify the predicate in each of the following sentences.

EXAMPLE   **1.** At noon we went to a Mexican restaurant.
              1. *At noon—went to a Mexican restaurant*

1. Our family likes different kinds of food.
2. Last night Dad prepared spaghetti and a salad for supper.
3. Sometimes Mom makes chow mein.

4. With chow mein she serves egg rolls.
5. At the Greek bakery we buy fresh pita bread.
6. Tomorrow Erica will make German potato salad.
7. Lately, tacos have become my favorite food.
8. Carefully, I spoon grated lettuce and cheese into a corn shell.
9. After that come the other ingredients.
10. In the United States people enjoy a wide variety of foods.

▶ EXERCISE 6   **Writing Predicates**

Make a sentence out of each of the following groups of words by adding a predicate to fill the blank or blanks.

EXAMPLE   **1.** ____ the people in this photograph ____
           1. *With a spirit of adventure, the people in this photograph are rafting down one of the fastest rivers in the state.*

1. Foamy white water ____
2. The hot summer air ____
3. A strong current ____
4. ____ the eyes of every person on board ____

5. The lightweight paddles ____
6. ____ dangerous rocks and swirls____
7. Quick action by everyone ____
8. A sleek, blue rubber raft ____
9. The man in the white helmet and blue life jacket ____
10. ____ everyone ____

Complete Predicate and Simple Predicate

The *complete predicate* consists of all the words that are not part of the complete subject.

12e. The *simple predicate,* or *verb,* is the main word or group of words in the complete predicate.

EXAMPLE   The nurse **lifted the patient carefully.**
　　　　　　Complete predicate   lifted the patient carefully
　　　　　　Simple predicate (verb)   lifted

EXAMPLE   I **saw a picture of a Siberian tiger.**
　　　　　　Complete predicate   saw a picture of a Siberian tiger
　　　　　　Simple predicate (verb)   saw

NOTE: In this book, the simple predicate is usually called the *verb.*

▶ EXERCISE 7   **Identifying Complete Predicates and Verbs**

Identify the complete predicate of each of the following sentences. Then underline the verb.

EXAMPLE   **1.** For several reasons, space travel fascinates me.
　　　　　　1. *For several reasons—fascinates me*

1. My class traveled by train to Houston, Texas.
2. In Houston we visited the Lyndon B. Johnson Space Center.

3. The center displays moon rocks.
4. At the center, astronauts train for their flights.
5. In one room we saw several unusual computers.
6. On the way home, we stopped at the Astro-dome for a tour.
7. The stadium in the Astrodome covers nine-and-a-half acres of land.
8. Several teams play there.
9. Every year the Astrodome attracts thousands of tourists.
10. Actually, I had more fun at the space center.

The Verb Phrase

A verb that is made up of more than one word is called a *verb phrase.*

EXAMPLES   Yoshi **will go** to Japan this summer.
The park **is located** near a lake.
We **should have planned** a picnic.

NOTE: The words *not* and *never* and the contraction *–n't* are not verbs. They are never part of a verb or verb phrase.

EXAMPLE   Kendra **should**n't **have added** another chile to the sauce.

EXERCISE 8   **Identifying Predicates, Verbs, and Verb Phrases**

Identify the complete predicate in each of the following sentences. Then underline the verb or the verb phrase.

EXAMPLE   **1.** The Liberty Bell was cast in London.
      1. *was cast* in London

1. I am writing a report on the Liberty Bell.
2. The Liberty Bell was ordered by the Philadelphia Assembly.

3. It was made by Thomas Lester in London.
4. In 1752, the bell was cracked by its own clapper.
5. American patriots hid the bell from the British Army.
6. The bell was not brought back to Philadelphia until 1778.
7. The Liberty Bell cracked again in 1835.
8. This famous bell has been rung on a number of historic occasions.
9. The bell is exhibited in the Liberty Bell Pavilion.
10. We will be seeing the bell during our class trip to Philadelphia.

Finding the Subject

Sometimes it may be difficult to find the subject of a sentence. In such cases, find the verb first. Then ask yourself *whom* or *what* the verb is referring to.

EXAMPLES **Next semester you may take art or music.** [The verb is *may take. Who* may take? *You* may take. *You* is the subject of the sentence.]
Can your sister drive us to the park? [The verb is *can drive. Who* can drive? The answer is *sister. Sister* is the subject of the sentence.]

PICTURE THIS

You are a writer for a travel magazine. The magazine has sent you to Brazil to cover the carnival in Rio de Janeiro. Surrounded by the crowd shown on the next page, you catch the excitement of carnival fever. As a dutiful reporter, you jot down some notes to help you prepare your article. In your notes, describe the people, things, and events you see. Explain how it feels to be part of this festive celebration. For each sentence in your notes, underline the simple subject and circle the verb.

Subject: the carnival in Rio
Audience: readers of a travel magazine
Purpose: to inform and entertain with description

Compound Subjects and Compound Verbs

Compound Subjects

12f. A *compound subject* consists of two or more connected subjects that have the same verb. The parts of the compound subject are most often connected by *and* and *or*.

EXAMPLES **Minneapolis** and **St. Paul** are called the "Twin Cities." [The two parts of the compound subject have the same verb, *are called.*]

Mrs. Jones or **Ms. Lopez** will chaperone our field trip. [The two parts of the compound subject have the same verb, *will chaperone.*]

Flutes, clarinets, and **oboes** are woodwind instruments. [The three parts of the compound subject have the same verb, *are.*]

☞ **REFERENCE NOTE:** Notice that commas are used to separate three or more parts of a compound subject. For more about this use of commas, see pages 594–595.

▶ EXERCISE 9 **Identifying Compound Subjects**

Identify the compound subjects in each of the following sentences.

EXAMPLE **1.** October and June are my favorite months.
    1. *October, June*

1. Wild ducks and geese migrate south from Canada each year.
2. Stars and planets form a galaxy.
3. In the Tower of London are famous jewels and crowns.
4. Baseball and soccer are the two most popular sports at my school.
5. Eggs and flour are two necessary ingredients for pancakes.
6. Every year bugs and rabbits raid our vegetable garden.
7. Pizza or ravioli will be served.
8. At a party, balloons or horns always make the best noisemakers.
9. Dachshunds, Chihuahuas, and Pekingese are small dogs.
10. Someday dolphins and people may be able to talk to each other.

Compound Verbs

12g. A *compound verb* is made up of two or more connected verbs that have the same subject. A connecting word such as *and* or *but* is used to join the verbs.

EXAMPLES   Ben **overslept** but **caught** his bus anyway.
Conchita **sings** or **listens** to the radio all day long.
My father **bought** a Chinese wok and **cooked** vegetables in it.

EXERCISE 10   **Identifying Compound Verbs**

Identify the compound verbs and verb phrases in the following sentences.

EXAMPLE   **1.** I proofread my paper and made a final copy.
1. *proofread, made*

1. Mai and her parents left Vietnam and arrived in California.
2. The Greek restaurant has closed but will reopen soon.
3. Every week our band practices together and writes songs.
4. Before supper I usually set the table or peel the vegetables.
5. Floyd asked for a watch but received a bike instead.
6. We gathered firewood and headed back to camp.
7. Last week everyone gave a speech or recited a poem.
8. The referee will call a rain delay or postpone the game.
9. I remembered the bread but forgot the milk.
10. Julie received good grades and made the honor roll.

▶ EXERCISE 11 **Writing Compound Subjects and Compound Verbs**

Make sentences by adding compound subjects or compound verbs to fill in the blanks in the following groups of words.

EXAMPLES **1.** ___ are coming to the party.
1. *Fran and Terry are coming to the party.*

2. At the mall, we ___.
2. *At the mall, we ate lunch and went to a movie.*

1. ___ are beginning a stamp collection.
2. ___ were my favorite teachers last year.
3. The creature from outer space ___.
4. At the end of the play, the cast ___.
5. Last week ___ were interviewed on a television talk show.
6. In the garage are ___.
7. During the storm, we ___.
8. At the front door were ___.
9. After school, my friends ___.
10. Before the birthday party, he ___.

▶ REVIEW B **Identifying Subjects and Verbs**

Identify the subjects and verbs in each of the following sentences. [Note: Some of the subjects and verbs are compound.]

EXAMPLE **1.** In the history of African American music are many unforgettable names.
1. *names—subject; are—verb*

1. You probably recognize the man in the picture on the next page.
2. Most people immediately think of his deep, raspy voice.
3. Ray Charles is called the father of soul music.
4. He lost his sight at the age of seven and became an orphan at fifteen.
5. However, misfortune and trouble did not stop Ray Charles.

6. His musical genius turned his troubles into songs.
7. Today, the songs of Ray Charles are heard the world over.
8. Do his songs contain different musical styles?
9. Gospel, jazz, blues, and even pop are all part of his sound.
10. His special style and powerful performances have drawn fans to Ray Charles for nearly fifty years.

A sentence may have both a compound subject and a compound verb.

EXAMPLES **Zina** and **I brought** corn and **fed** the ducks.

Carrots and **celery are** crunchy and **satisfy** your appetite.

EXERCISE 12   **Identifying Compound Subjects and Compound Verbs**

Identify the compound subject and the compound verb in each of the following sentences.

EXAMPLE **1.** Tina and Julia washed the dog and dried it with a towel.
1. *Tina, Julia—subject; washed, dried—verb*

1. Alice and Reiko sang and played the piano.
2. Either Dwayne or I will find the coach and ask his advice.
3. Patrick and she read the same biography of Dr. Martin Luther King, Jr., and reported on it.
4. Roses and lilacs look pretty and smell good.
5. The dentist or her assistant cleans and polishes my teeth.

▶ REVIEW C **Identifying Subjects and Predicates**

Identify the complete subject and the complete predicate in each of the following sentences. Then underline the simple subject and the verb. [Note: Some of the subjects and verbs are compound.]

EXAMPLE [1] Reports and legends of huge apelike creatures fascinate many people.
1. *subject—Reports and legends of huge apelike creatures; predicate—fascinate many people*

[1] These creatures are known as *Yeti* in the Himalayas and as *Rakshas* in Katmandu. [2] Native Americans of the Northwest call them *Mammoth*. [3] *Sasquatch* and *Bigfoot* are other common names for these creatures. [4] Since 1818, they have been seen and described by people in the United States and Canada. [5] According to most accounts, Bigfoot adults are very strong and large and smell very bad. [6] Their huge footprints have been measured and cast in plaster by eager searchers. [7] However, these reports and bits of evidence do not convince scientists. [8] Not one live Bigfoot has ever been seen by either scientists or the general public. [9] As a result, the Bigfoot is simply a fantasy to most people. [10] Yet in pockets of deep wilderness across the country may live whole families of these shy creatures.

Simple Sentences and Compound Sentences

12h. A *simple sentence* has one subject and one verb.

Although a compound subject has two or more parts, it is still considered one subject. In the same way, a compound verb or verb phrase is considered one verb.

EXAMPLES
$\qquad$ S $\qquad$ V
My **mother belongs** to the Friends of the Library. [single subject and verb]

$\qquad$ S $\qquad$ S $\quad$ V
Argentina and **Chile are** in South America. [compound subject]

$\qquad$ S $\qquad$ V $\qquad$ V
Jeannette read *Stuart Little* and **reported** on it. [compound verb]

$\qquad$ S $\qquad$ S $\quad$ V
The **acrobats** and **jugglers did** tricks and

$\qquad$ V
were rewarded with a standing ovation. [compound subject and compound verb]

12i. A *compound sentence* consists of two or more simple sentences, usually joined by a connecting word.

In a compound sentence, the word *and, but, or, nor, for, so,* or *yet* connects the simple sentences. A comma usually comes before the connecting word in a compound sentence.

EXAMPLES
I forgot my lunch**, but** Dad ran to the bus with it.
She likes sweets**, yet** she seldom buys them.

Notice in the second example above that a sentence is compound if the subject is repeated.

▶ EXERCISE 13 **Identifying Simple Sentences and Compound Sentences**

Identify each of the following sentences as *simple* or *compound*.

EXAMPLE **1.** That story by Lensey Namioka is good, and you should read it.
  1. *compound*

1. My dad and I like enchiladas, but my mother prefers fajitas.
2. Some trees and shrubs live thousands of years.
3. It rained, but we marched in the parade anyway.
4. Mr. Edwards will lead the singing, for Ms. Cruz is ill.
5. My aunts, uncles, and cousins from Costa Rica visited us last summer.
6. I had worked hard all morning, yet I had not finished the job by lunch time.
7. Abe peeled and chopped all of the onions and dumped them into a huge pot.
8. We made a doghouse for Reggie, but he will not use it.
9. Chippewa and Ojibwa are two names for the same American Indian people.
10. All ravens are crows, but not all crows are ravens.

▶ REVIEW D **Identifying Simple Sentences and Compound Sentences**

Identify each of the following sentences as *simple* or *compound*.

EXAMPLE **1.** Have you seen the movie *The Bridge on the River Kwai*?
  1. *simple*

1. My stepbrother is eight, and he is fascinated by bridges.
2. We buy postcards with pictures of bridges, for he collects them.

3. He has several cards of stone bridges.
4. Stone bridges are strong, but they are costly.
5. Many bridges are beautiful, but they must also be sturdy.
6. The Central American rope bridge on the right is one kind of suspension bridge.
7. The modern bridge below is another kind of suspension bridge.

8. Suspension bridges may look dangerous, yet they are safe.
9. Bridges must be inspected regularly.
10. My stepbrother collects postcards of bridges, and I collect postcards of towers.

Kinds of Sentences

12j. A *declarative sentence* makes a statement. It is always followed by a period.

EXAMPLES   Our media center has several computers.
Patrick Henry lived in Virginia.

12k. An *imperative sentence* gives a command or makes a request. It may be followed by a period or by an exclamation point.

EXAMPLES   Stop shouting! [command]
Please pass the potatoes. [request]

The subject of a command or a request is always *you*, even if *you* never appears in the sentence. In such cases, *you* is called the **understood subject.**

EXAMPLES   **(You)** Stop shouting!
(You) Please pass the potatoes.

12l. An *interrogative sentence* asks a question. It is followed by a question mark.

EXAMPLES   Did the spacecraft *Apollo* land on the moon?
How old are you?

12m. An *exclamatory sentence* shows excitement or expresses strong feeling. It is followed by an exclamation point.

EXAMPLES   What a difficult assignment that was!
I got her autograph!

▶ EXERCISE 14   **Classifying Sentences by Purpose**

Write each of the following sentences and the punctuation mark that should follow it. Label the sentence *declarative, interrogative, imperative,* or *exclamatory.*

EXAMPLE **1.** What a funny show that was
          1. *What a funny show that was!—exclamatory*

1. Please help me find my umbrella
2. How happy I am
3. Have you been to the new video store
4. Go east for three blocks, and look for a mailbox
5. My father and I are cleaning the attic
6. What a delicious salad this is
7. We toured the garment district in New York City
8. Do you like barbecued chicken
9. My surprise visit pleased my grandmother
10. When is your next piano lesson

WRITING APPLICATION

Using End Punctuation in a Comic Strip

In any kind of writing, correct end punctuation is important. However, it's especially important in written conversations. The punctuation helps a reader hear how a speaker says something. A sentence can mean very different things when its end punctuation is changed. Try reading the following sentences aloud to hear the difference.

    DECLARATIVE   He's my hero.
  INTERROGATIVE He's my hero?
   EXCLAMATORY He's my hero!

▶ WRITING ACTIVITY

As a special project, your social studies class is creating a comic book. Each class member will contribute a comic strip about a particular historical event or historical person. Each strip should be at least one page long. You can draw your own illustrations, cut out pictures from magazines, or make photocopies of pictures you would like to use. In your comic strip, include at least one of each of the four kinds of sentences—declarative, imperative, interrogative, and exclamatory.

Prewriting   First, jot down some ideas for the characters and story line of your comic strip. You may want to look through your social studies book for ideas. Then, plan the frames of your comic strip. Think about how you could include the four types of sentences in your characters' conversation. For example, what request or command could a character make? What could a character ask a question about or express amazement about?

Writing   Use your prewriting notes to help you write a draft of your comic strip. As you write, you may decide to add details. Keep in mind that you'll be able to add details in the pictures that go with the words.

Evaluating and Revising   Ask a friend to read your cartoon. Are your characters' conversations clear? Can your friend follow the story line? If not, you may need to add, revise, or rearrange sentences. Make sure you've used only complete sentences in your dialogue. Prepare a final version of your comic strip. Use word balloons to add the dialogue to the pictures.

Proofreading and Publishing   Check your comic strip for errors in grammar, spelling, or punctuation. Be sure that you have spelled and capitalized all proper names correctly. Take extra care with end punctuation. Make sure you've used periods, question marks, and exclamation points correctly for each kind of sentence. You and your classmates may wish to make a historical comic book. Photocopy all the comic strips and gather them in a folder for each member of the class.

▶ REVIEW E   **Classifying Sentences by Purpose**

For each of the following sentences, add the appropriate end mark of punctuation. Then label each sentence as *declarative, imperative, interrogative,* or *exclamatory.*

EXAMPLE **1.** Have you ever seen the Grand Canyon
        1. *Have you ever seen the Grand Canyon?—interrogative*

1. We enjoyed our vacation in the Southwest
2. Dad took these photographs when we visited the Grand Canyon
3. Our guide spoke Spanish and English
4. How pretty the sunset is
5. Don't stand so close to the edge
6. Did you buy any turquoise-and-silver jewelry
7. It was quite chilly at night
8. What a great movie we saw about the canyon
9. Did you take the short hike or the long one
10. Look at us riding on mules in this canyon

Review: Posttest 1

A. Identifying Sentences

If a group of words is a sentence, add a capital letter at the beginning and an end mark of punctuation. If a group of words is not a sentence, label it a *sentence fragment*.

EXAMPLES **1.** followed the trail on the map
1. *sentence fragment*

2. the López twins come from Nuevo Laredo, Mexico
2. *The López twins come from Nuevo Laredo, Mexico.*

1. we put up the postcards from our Asian pen pals
2. our neighborhood has a homework hotline
3. mailed the invitations yesterday
4. practice my guitar before dinner
5. the Washington Monument

B. Identifying Simple Subjects and Simple Predicates

Identify the simple subject and the verb in each of the following sentences. [Note: A subject or a verb may be compound.]

EXAMPLE **1.** Last year my family traveled to Mecca, Saudi Arabia.
1. *family—simple subject; traveled—verb*

6. My grandmother plays mah-jongg with my friends and me.
7. The farmers have plowed the fields and will plant potatoes.
8. At night you can rent roller skates at the rink near my house.

9. On the sand lay a beautiful seashell.
10. On Saturday, Amy, Theo, and I walked through Chinatown and took pictures.

C. Identifying Simple Sentences and Compound Sentences

Identify each of the following sentences as simple or compound.

EXAMPLE   **1.** Mom is late, but she will be here soon.
              1. *compound*

11. Jaleel learned several African folk tales and presented them to the class.
12. The dance committee has chosen a Hawaiian theme and will decorate the gym with flowers and greenery.
13. The school bus stopped suddenly, but no one was hurt.
14. Raccoons and opossums steal our garbage.
15. Luis Gonzalez stepped up to the plate, and the crowd roared.

D. Classifying and Punctuating Sentences by Purpose

For each sentence, add the appropriate end mark of punctuation. Then, label each sentence *declarative, interrogative, imperative,* or *exclamatory.*

EXAMPLE   **1.** Have you read this poem by José Garcia Villa
              1. *Have you read this poem by José Garcia Villa?—interrogative*

16. Please answer the phone
17. What a good time we had
18. Has anyone seen the cat
19. They sat on a bench and played checkers
20. Whose book is this

Review: Posttest 2

Writing Sentences

Identify each of the following sentence parts as a *subject* or a *predicate*. Then use each sentence part in a sentence. Begin each sentence with a capital letter, and end it with the correct mark of punctuation. Use a variety of subjects and verbs in your sentences.

EXAMPLE **1.** will drive us home
          1. *predicate —Will your mother drive us home?*

1. my favorite book
2. watched a good mystery
3. the flying saucer
4. the oldest house in town
5. prepares delicious Korean food
6. growled and bared its teeth
7. the shiny red car
8. caught a huge fish
9. can borrow your skates
10. the best tacos in town

13 THE PARTS OF SPEECH

Noun, Pronoun, Adjective

Diagnostic Test

Identifying Nouns, Pronouns, and Adjectives

Identify each italicized word in the following sentences as a *noun,* a *pronoun,* or an *adjective.* Each sentence contains two italicized words.

EXAMPLE   **1.** *Dad* tinkered with the *rusty* lock.
          1. *Dad—noun; rusty—adjective*

1. My *best* friend plays *soccer.*
2. *We* went to *Boston* last summer.
3. Help *yourself* to some *Chinese* food.
4. Juana invited *us* to *her* fiesta.
5. What a *beautiful* garden *Mrs. Murakami* has!
6. *My* directions were *accurate.*
7. The jacket on the *chair* is *yours.*
8. A *sharp* knife is *necessary* for making a wood carving.

9. Almost *everyone* in the band takes private music *lessons.*
10. This story, short and *funny,* is my *favorite.*

The Eight Parts of Speech

noun	adjective	adverb	conjunction
pronoun	verb	preposition	interjection

The Noun

13a. A *noun* is a word that names a person, place, thing, or idea.

PERSONS	parents, Scott, teacher, Ms. Vargas, sister, linebacker, baby sitter
PLACES	White House, state, Nairobi, school
THINGS	rocket, desk, ocean, hamster, computer, Newbery Medal, Golden Gate Bridge
IDEAS	anger, freedom, kindness, fear, dream

NOTE: Nouns that are made up of more than one word, like *Rita Rodriguez, Empire State Building,* and *family room,* are counted as one noun.

▶ EXERCISE 1 **Identifying Nouns**

Identify each of the twenty nouns in the following paragraph.

EXAMPLE   [1] Clara Barton had two brothers and two sisters.

1. *Clara Barton, brothers, sisters*

[1] Clara Barton was born in Massachusetts. [2] She was educated in a rural school and grew up with a love of books. [3] She began her career as a teacher. [4] During the Civil War, however, she distributed medicine and other supplies. [5] Later she helped find soldiers who were missing in action. [6] She organized the American Red Cross and was its president for many years. [7] She raised money for the Red Cross and worked with victims of floods and other disasters.

Proper Nouns and Common Nouns

A *proper noun* names a particular person, place, thing, or idea. It always begins with a capital letter. A *common noun* names any one of a group of persons, places, things, or ideas. It is generally not capitalized.

COMMON NOUNS	PROPER NOUNS
woman	Aunt Josie
teacher	Jaime Escalante
basketball player	Michael Jordan
city	Los Angeles
country	Morocco
continent	Asia
monument	Lincoln Memorial
team	Detroit Tigers
book	*Barrio Boy*
holiday	Chinese New Year
religion	Islam
language	Swahili

Notice that each noun listed above names a person, a place, a thing, or an idea.

☞ REFERENCE NOTE: For more about capitalizing proper nouns, see pages 565–573.

GRAMMAR

EXERCISE 2   **Identifying Common and Proper Nouns**

Identify each of the nouns in the following sentences as *common* or *proper*.

EXAMPLE   **1.** The people in Japan celebrate many holidays.
        1. *people—common; Japan—proper; holidays—common*

1. This picture is of the Snow Festival in Sapporo.
2. Many groups work together to build these giant sculptures.
3. Do you recognize any of the statues or buildings?
4. Is that the Statue of Liberty made out of snow?

5. In the city of Kyoto each June, you can see a parade of spears.
6. A popular fair in Tokyo offers pickled radishes.
7. Villages are colorfully decorated for the Feast of the Lanterns.
8. Toshiro said his town enjoys the Star Festival in the summer.
9. Several flowers, among them the iris and the lily, have their own special days.
10. The birthday of Buddha is observed in April.

▶ EXERCISE 3 **Substituting Proper Nouns for Common Nouns**

In the following sentences, substitute a proper noun for each italicized common noun. You may need to change some other words in each sentence. You may also make up proper names to use.

EXAMPLE **1.** The *principal* awarded the *student* the prize.
1. *Ms. Chen awarded Paula Perez the prize.*

1. The *student* is from a *city*.
2. Usually, my *uncle* looks through the *newspaper* after dinner.
3. The *child* watched a *movie*.
4. A *teacher* asked a *student* to tell the class about growing up in Mexico.
5. My *cousin* read that *book*.
6. Surrounded by reporters, the *mayor* stood outside the *building*.
7. Does the *girl* go to this *school*?
8. That *singer* wrote the *song*.
9. My *neighbor* bought a *car*.
10. When he was a college student, the *coach* played for that *team*.

▶ EXERCISE 4 **Using Proper Nouns**

Developers are planning to build a new shopping mall in your neighborhood. They are trying to find out what kinds of stores and other attractions the community would like at the mall. The developers have prepared the following survey. Answer each question with a complete sentence. Underline each proper noun that you use.

New Mall Questionnaire

1. What stores would you most like to see at the mall?
2. What would you be most likely to buy at the mall?

3. What types of movies would you like to see at the mall theater?
4. What restaurants would you like to have in the mall's Food Court?
5. Would you go to a mall arcade? If so, what games would you play?

▶ REVIEW A   **Identifying and Classifying Nouns**

Identify each of the twenty-five nouns in the following sentences as *common* or *proper*.

EXAMPLE   **1.** President George Bush gave General Colin Powell a big job.
           1. *President George Bush—proper; General Colin Powell—proper; job—common*

1. He appointed Powell to lead the Joint Chiefs of Staff.
2. Powell became one of the top military officers in the United States.
3. Here he's shown talking with soldiers during the Persian Gulf Conflict.
4. Do you think the troops were excited to meet the general?
5. Powell grew up in the Bronx, a neighborhood of New York City.

6. His parents came to the United States from Jamaica.
7. Powell graduated from the City College of New York.
8. It was there he joined the Reserve Officers Training Corps.
9. Did you know that Powell was awarded the Purple Heart during the Vietnam War?
10. In his speeches, he encourages students to graduate from high school.

The Pronoun

13b. A *pronoun* is a word used in place of one noun or more than one noun.

In each of the following examples, an arrow is drawn from a pronoun to the noun or nouns it stands for.

EXAMPLES   When Cindy Davis came to the bus stop, **she** was wearing a cast.

The trees and bushes are dry; **they** should be watered.

This stable is large. **It** has stalls for thirty horses.

The word that a pronoun stands for is called its *antecedent.*

EXAMPLES
antecedent pronoun
My **aunt** sold **her** car.

antecedent   pronoun
Anthony, call **your** mother.

Sometimes the antecedent is not stated.

EXAMPLES
pronoun
Call **your** mother.

pronoun
Has **it** been raining?

Personal Pronouns

A *personal pronoun* refers to the one speaking (*first person*), the one spoken to (*second person*), or the one spoken about (*third person*). Personal pronouns have singular and plural forms.

PERSONAL PRONOUNS		
	SINGULAR	PLURAL
First person	I, me, my, mine	we, us, our, ours
Second person	you, your, yours	you, your, yours
Third person	he, him, his, she, her, hers, it, its	they, them, their, theirs

NOTE: Some teachers prefer to call possessive forms of pronouns (such as *my, your,* and *our*) adjectives. Follow your teacher's instructions regarding possessive forms.

Reflexive Pronouns

A *reflexive pronoun* refers to the subject and directs the action of the verb back to the subject.

REFLEXIVE PRONOUNS	
First person	myself, ourselves
Second person	yourself, yourselves
Third person	himself, herself, itself, themselves

EXAMPLES We enjoyed **ourselves** at the party.
She prides **herself** on speaking Spanish well.

▶ EXERCISE 5   **Identifying Pronouns**

Identify all of the pronouns in each of the following sentences.

EXAMPLE   **1.** I lent her my camera.
       1. *I, her, my*

1. The dentist asked me three questions before examining my teeth.
2. Dad told the mechanics to call him about his bill.
3. Our aunt and uncle have decided that they will visit Guatemala.
4. I asked myself where I could have put my book.
5. He washed the mats and put them in the sun to dry.
6. Here is a postcard from Egypt for you and me.
7. We helped ourselves to tacos and refried beans.
8. You gave us your support when we needed it.
9. He did his math homework before playing soccer with us.
10. I found the weak battery and replaced it.

▶ EXERCISE 6   **Using Pronouns**

What a mess! Dolly told Jeffy to say *when*. But she didn't say *when* to say *when*! Write five sentences describing this scene. You can write what has happened or what you think will happen next. In each sentence, use a pronoun. Try to use a variety of pronouns in your sentences. Draw an arrow from the pronoun to its antecedent.

"Say when."   "When."

EXAMPLE   **1.** *Jeffy wanted some juice, but he didn't say how much.*

EXERCISE 7 **Substituting Pronouns for Nouns**

In each of the following sentences, replace the repeated nouns with pronouns.

EXAMPLE **1.** Viviana set up Viviana's game on the table.
         1. *Viviana set up her game on the table.*

1. The passengers waved to the passengers' friends on shore.
2. The test was so long that I almost didn't finish the test.
3. Rachel's neighbors asked Rachel to baby-sit.
4. Carlos said that Carlos had already cleaned Carlos's room.
5. The directions were long, but the directions were clear.

Possessive Pronouns

Possessive pronouns are personal pronouns that are used to show ownership. Like personal pronouns, possessive pronouns have singular and plural forms.

POSSESSIVE PRONOUNS		
	SINGULAR	PLURAL
First person	my, mine	our, ours
Second person	your, yours	your, yours
Third person	her, hers, his, its	their, theirs

EXAMPLES Nina stored **her** suitcase under **her** bed.
          Is that paper **yours** or **mine**?

☞ REFERENCE NOTE: Don't confuse the pronoun *its* with the contraction *it's*. The pronoun *its* means "belonging to it." The contraction *it's* means "it is" or "it has." The apostrophe stands for the missing letters in *it is* or *it has*. For more information about *it's* and *its* and other words often confused, see pages 552, 630, and 652.

Demonstrative Pronouns

A *demonstrative pronoun* points out a specific person, place, thing, or idea.

<table>
<tr><td colspan="4">Demonstrative Pronouns</td></tr>
<tr><td>this</td><td>that</td><td>these</td><td>those</td></tr>
</table>

EXAMPLES What is **that?**
This is the uniform once worn by Satchel Paige.
These are the shoes he used to wear.

NOTE: Demonstrative pronouns can also be used as adjectives. When these words tell *which one(s)* about a noun, they are called *demonstrative adjectives.*

PRONOUN   **This** is a delicious papaya.
ADJECTIVE   **This** papaya is delicious.

☞ REFERENCE NOTE: For more about demonstrative adjectives, see pages 384–385.

Indefinite Pronouns

An *indefinite pronoun* does not refer to a definite person, place, thing, or idea.

Common Indefinite Pronouns			
all	each	more	one
any	either	much	other
anybody	everybody	neither	several
anyone	everyone	nobody	some
anything	few	none	somebody
both	many	no one	something

EXAMPLES   **Everyone** in the class was invited to the party.
None of the boys knew **much** about camping.

▶ EXERCISE 8   **Identifying Pronouns**

Identify the pronoun or pronouns in each of the following sentences.

EXAMPLE   **1.** Their car is newer than ours.
          1. *Their, ours*

1. Is your puppy losing its baby teeth?
2. This jacket is mine; that one must be yours.
3. Something is different about your hair.
4. Carlota reminded herself to send Luís a card.
5. This is good, but her report is better.
6. Your locker is next to hers.
7. The videotapes on the TV are theirs.
8. They treated themselves to a bucket of popcorn.
9. My sister made her own dress for the Cinco de Mayo celebration.
10. Everyone knows the answer to that.

▶ REVIEW B   **Identifying Pronouns**

Identify the pronoun or pronouns in each of the following sentences.

EXAMPLE   **1.** Everyone in my class likes going on field trips.
          1. *Everyone; my*

1. Last week, we really enjoyed ourselves at the National Museum of African Art.
2. It has been part of the Smithsonian Institution in Washington, D.C., since 1979.
3. In 1987, the museum's collection was moved to its present underground facility.
4. Our teacher, Ms. Martínez, told us about the museum before we went there.
5. She said the entrance is made of pink granite.
6. I was surprised by the six domes on top.
7. Everyone had at least one question to ask our museum guide.
8. We enjoyed hearing her lively explanations of the artwork.

9. This is a photograph of one of my favorite objects at the museum.
10. What is your opinion of it?

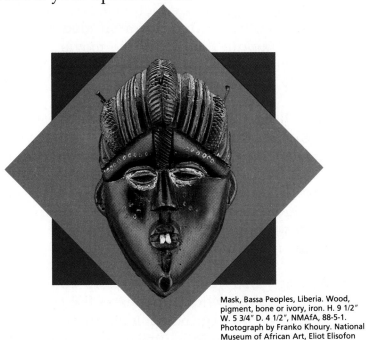

Mask, Bassa Peoples, Liberia. Wood, pigment, bone or ivory, iron. H. 9 1/2″ W. 5 3/4″ D. 4 1/2″, NMAfA, 88-5-1. Photograph by Franko Khoury. National Museum of African Art, Eliot Elisofon Archives, Smithsonian Institution.

WRITING APPLICATION

Using Pronouns Clearly

Pronouns are some of the handiest words in English. Sometimes, though, personal pronouns can be confusing. To avoid confusion, make sure each pronoun you use refers clearly to its antecedent.

CONFUSING   The monster snarled at Reggie as he stepped forward. [Who stepped forward, the monster or Reggie?]

CLEAR   As the **monster** stepped forward, **he** snarled at Reggie.

or

CLEAR   As **Reggie** stepped forward, the monster snarled at **him**.

▶ WRITING ACTIVITY

Your cousin is taking a filmmaking class at the community center and needs ideas for a project. The theme of the project is "Science Fiction Movie Spoofs." Help your cousin out by writing down an idea for a short movie script. Explain the plot of the movie and describe the characters. Be sure that the pronouns you use refer clearly to their antecedents.

Prewriting   In a *spoof*, a writer imitates and makes fun of another work. Imagine several science fiction movie spoofs—for example, *There's an Alien in My Soup* or *Nerds from Neptune*. Choose the idea that you like the best. Then brainstorm some ideas for a simple plot. (For more about developing plots, see pages 153–154.) Jot down brief descriptions of the setting and the characters in the movie.

Writing   Use your notes to help you write your first draft. Explain what happens in the movie from beginning to end. Describe each character as you introduce him or her. Keep the props and costumes simple—your cousin is working on a low budget.

Evaluating and Revising   Ask a friend to read your movie idea. Is the plot interesting? Is it funny? Can your friend tell which character is performing each action? If not, you may need to revise some details. As you revise, you may think of more suggestions for the script. Add any details that you think will make the movie better or more humorous.

Proofreading   Read your script one more time to catch other errors in spelling, grammar, and punctuation. Check to make sure each pronoun refers clearly to its antecedent. Also be sure you've used the pronoun *its* and the contraction *it's* correctly.

The Adjective

13c. An *adjective* is a word that modifies a noun or a pronoun.

To *modify* a word means to describe the word or to make its meaning more definite. An adjective modifies a noun or pronoun by telling *what kind, which one, how many,* or *how much.*

WHAT KIND?	WHICH ONE OR ONES?	HOW MANY OR HOW MUCH?
gentle dog	**sixth** grade	**two** tickets
foggy day	**these** books	**full** pitcher
scary movie	**other** people	**most** players
purple shoes	**any** CD	**no** work

Adjectives usually come before the words they modify. Sometimes, however, an adjective comes after the word it modifies.

EXAMPLES The dog is **gentle.** [The adjective *gentle* modifies *dog.*]
The tent, **warm** and **dry,** was under the tree. [The adjectives *warm* and *dry* modify *tent.*]

NOTE: The adjectives *a, an,* and *the* are called **articles.**

▶ EXERCISE 9 **Identifying Adjectives**

Identify the adjective or adjectives in each of the following sentences. Do not include *a, an,* or *the.*

EXAMPLE **1.** The sky was clear, and the night was cold.
1. *clear, cold*

1. A silvery moon rode down the western sky.
2. It shed a pale light on the quiet countryside.
3. Long meadows spread out between two hills.

4. The smell of the wild grass was strong.
5. The only sound we heard was the sharp crackle of the fire.
6. Suddenly, several stars came out.
7. I watched until the entire sky was glowing with bright stars.
8. I was lonely and happy at the same time.
9. I finally became sleepy and longed for my comfortable bed.
10. Soon I went indoors and fell into a deep sleep.

> EXERCISE 10 **Identifying Adjectives and the Words They Modify**

Identify the adjectives and the words they modify in the following sentences. Do not include *a, an,* or *the*.

EXAMPLE **1. It costs five dollars to go to that movie.**
         1. *five—dollars; that—movie*

1. I have a free ticket for the last game.
2. In New Orleans we ate spicy crawfish, and they were delicious.
3. The new neighbor is helpful and nice.
4. The bear, angry and hungry, surprised the campers.
5. Many students compete in the regional Special Olympics.

> EXERCISE 11 **Writing Adjectives for a Story**

The following story is about a cave exploration. Complete the story by adding an appropriate adjective for each blank. Underline the adjectives.

EXAMPLE **Exploring caves is [1] ____ on [2] ____ days.**
         Exploring caves is <u>fun</u> on <u>hot</u> days.

Have you ever been in a [1] ____ cave like the one shown on the next page? Would you say it looks [2] ____ and [3] ____? My father and I explored this

[4] ___ cave once. It was [5] ___ but [6] ___, too. We found some [7] ___ rock formations. We also heard [8] ___ sounds. We looked up, and [9] ___ bats flew above our heads. After exploring for about [10] ___ hours, we were ready to see the sky again.

Proper Adjectives

A ***proper adjective*** is formed from a proper noun and begins with a capital letter.

PROPER NOUNS	PROPER ADJECTIVES
Japan	**Japanese** islands
Christianity	**Christian** beliefs
Maya	**Mayan** art

☞ REFERENCE NOTE: For more about capitalizing proper adjectives, see page 576.

▶ EXERCISE 12 **Finding Common and Proper Adjectives**

Identify all of the adjectives in the following sentences. Then label each adjective as *common* or *proper*. Do not include *a, an,* or *the.*

EXAMPLE　**1.** The Navajo weaver made a blanket on a wooden loom.
　　　　　1. *Navajo—proper; wooden—common*

1. Music can express sad or happy feelings.
2. The quartet sang several Irish songs.
3. The gold watch with the fancy chain was made by a Swiss watchmaker.
4. She is a fine Balinese dancer.
5. On vacation, Mom enjoys long, quiet breakfasts.
6. Many Australian people are of British origin.
7. The Egyptian mummies are on display on the first floor.
8. We are proud of our heritage.
9. The movie is based on a popular Russian novel.
10. In Canadian football, a team is made up of twelve players.

> EXERCISE 13　**Changing Proper Nouns into Proper Adjectives**

Think of ten proper nouns. Change each proper noun into a proper adjective. Then use each proper adjective in a sentence. Here are some *types* of proper nouns that you might use. [Note: Some proper nouns, such as *Hopi* and *New England,* do not change spelling when they are used as proper adjectives.]

countries	cities
states	neighborhood names
regions	people's first or last names

EXAMPLES　**1.** *France—French*
　　　　　　We bought French bread at the bakery.
　　　　　2. *Jones—Jonesian*
　　　　　　My dad says I have a Jonesian nose like his.

Demonstrative Adjectives

This, that, these, and *those* can be used both as adjectives and as pronouns. When they modify a noun, they are called ***demonstrative adjectives.*** When they are used alone, they are called *demonstrative pronouns.*

ADJECTIVE   What are **these** skates doing in the living room?
PRONOUN   What are **these** doing in the living room?

ADJECTIVE   I prefer **that** brand of frozen yogurt.
PRONOUN   I prefer **that**.

👉 REFERENCE NOTE: For more information about demonstrative pronouns, see page 377.

PICTURE THIS

Yesterday, you won first prize in a kayaking race. A photographer from a sports magazine was able to capture the most incredible moment of the race on film. Now the editor of the magazine would like you to describe how you felt during this daring plunge down a waterfall. Write a description of this exciting moment for the magazine. In your description, use words that will help your readers see, hear, and feel what you experienced. Include at least five adjectives that appeal to the senses.

Subject: kayaking down a waterfall
Audience: readers of a sports magazine
Purpose: to describe your experience

▶ REVIEW C **Identifying Adjectives**

Identify the adjectives in the following sentences. Do not include *a*, *an*, or *the*.

EXAMPLE **1.** I enjoy visiting the large railroad museum in our city.
       1. *large, railroad*

1. Museums can be interesting.
2. Large cities have different kinds of museums.
3. Some museums display sculpture and paintings.
4. These museums may focus on one special kind of art.
5. For example, they might specialize in Chinese art or Mexican art.
6. Other museums feature birds, sea creatures, dinosaurs, and other animals.
7. A curator holds an important job in a museum.
8. A curator needs to know many facts about a particular display.
9. Some valuable objects must be displayed in a stable environment.
10. Some people prefer displays of modern art, while others enjoy exhibits of folk art.

▶ REVIEW D **Identifying Nouns, Pronouns, and Adjectives**

Identify all of the nouns, pronouns, and adjectives in the following sentences. Do not include the articles *a*, *an*, and *the*.

EXAMPLE **1.** Models make a great hobby.
       1. *Models—noun; great—adjective; hobby—noun*

1. Do you have a favorite hobby?
2. Models are enjoyable and educational.
3. They require little space.
4. I keep mine on my bookshelf my dad built in my room.

5. Models are packaged in kits.
6. My favorite models are historic ships and antique planes.
7. On my last birthday, my parents gave me two kits of biplanes.
8. They came with directions in several languages.
9. The tiny parts are designed for an exact fit.
10. Bright decals add a realistic look.

REVIEW E **Identifying Nouns, Pronouns, and Adjectives**

Identify all of the nouns, pronouns, and adjectives in each of the following sentences. Do not include *a, an,* or *the.*

EXAMPLE   **1.** Pueblos are practical housing for people in hot, dry regions.
      1. *Pueblos—noun; practical—adjective; housing—noun; people—noun; hot—adjective; dry—adjective; regions—noun*

1. The brown building in this photograph contains several individual homes.
2. *Pueblo* is a Spanish word for a structure like this and for a town.

3. This building is located at the Taos Pueblo in New Mexico.
4. Can you tell how pueblos are made?

5. They are built of adobe.
6. People make adobe by mixing mud with grass or straw.
7. They shape the mixture into bricks and dry them in the sun.
8. Buildings made with this material stay cool during the summer months.
9. Anyone on a visit to the Southwest can find many pueblos similar to this one.
10. Old pueblos built by the Hopi and the Zuni fascinate me.

Review: Posttest 1

Identifying Nouns, Pronouns, and Adjectives

Identify each italicized word in the following sentences as a *noun*, a *pronoun*, or an *adjective*.

EXAMPLE   **1.** Her older *brother* has an *important* test today.
           1. *brother*—noun; *important*—adjective

1. The *Roman* emperors built a huge system of aqueducts, *some* of which are still standing.
2. Last summer we visited *Alaska*, which is our *largest* state.
3. Put *yourself* in *my* position.
4. The *Hawaiian* dancers wore *colorful* costumes.
5. The volcano, *inactive* for years, is a popular tourist *attraction*.
6. *Everyone* watched the sun set behind the *mountains*.
7. "*That* notebook is *mine*," Angela said.
8. *They* made a touchdown just before the final *whistle*.
9. *Colombo* is the capital *city* of Sri Lanka.
10. The pen with the *blue* ink is *hers*.

Review: Posttest 2

Writing Sentences Using Nouns, Pronouns, and Adjectives

Write ten original sentences using the parts of speech given below. In each sentence, underline the word that is the listed part of speech.

EXAMPLE **1.** an adjective that comes after the word it describes
1. *Our guide was very <u>helpful</u>.*

1. a proper noun
2. a possessive pronoun
3. an adjective that tells *how many*
4. a reflexive pronoun
5. a proper adjective
6. a noun that names an idea
7. a third-person pronoun
8. a demonstrative adjective
9. an indefinite pronoun
10. an article

14 THE PARTS OF SPEECH

Verb, Adverb, Preposition, Conjunction, Interjection

Diagnostic Test

Identifying Verbs, Adverbs, Prepositions, Conjunctions, and Interjections

Identify each italicized word or word group in the following sentences as a *verb*, an *adverb*, a *preposition*, a *conjunction*, or an *interjection*.

EXAMPLE **1.** We *visited* a great new water park *on* Saturday.
   1. *visited—verb; on—preposition*

1. I *always* have fun *at* a water park.
2. You *should get* to the park *early* if you can.
3. If you don't, the parking lot *may be* full, and the park itself *uncomfortably* crowded.

4. You *can slide* as fast as a bullet *down* the huge water slide.
5. *Wow!* What a *truly* exciting ride that is!
6. People land in the water *and* splash everyone *around* them.
7. Some parks *rent* inner tubes *inexpensively.*
8. You climb on one and *whirl* around *in* the water.
9. You *may get* tired, *but* you won't be bored.
10. People *of* all ages *enjoy* water parks.

The Verb

14a. A **verb** is a word that expresses an action or a state of being.

EXAMPLES   We **went** to Boston last April.
Is a firefly a beetle?

Every sentence must have a verb. The verb says something about the subject.

☞ REFERENCE NOTE: For more information about subjects and verbs, see pages 342–357.

Action Verbs

(1) An **action verb** is a verb that expresses physical or mental action.

EXAMPLES   I **use** a computer in math class.
Please **cook** dinner, Jerome.
Fran **understands** the science assignment.

▶ EXERCISE 1   **Identifying Action Verbs**

Identify each action verb in the following sentences.

EXAMPLE [1] The Maricopa people live in Arizona.
1. *live*

[1] The Maricopa make unusual pottery. [2] For this pottery they need two kinds of clay. [3] One kind of clay forms the bowl or platter itself. [4] The other kind of clay colors the pottery. [5] First, the potters mold the clay by hand. [6] Then, they shape it into beautiful bowls and vases like the ones below. [7] With the second type of clay, they paint designs on the pottery. [8] In some cases they make designs with a toothpick. [9] Each family of potters has its own special designs. [10] These designs preserve Maricopa traditions from generation to generation.

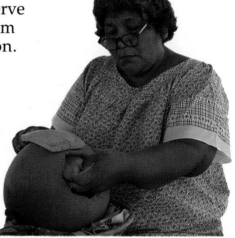

Transitive and Intransitive Verbs

A *transitive verb* is an action verb that expresses an action directed toward a person, place, or thing.

EXAMPLES Tamisha **entertained** the child. [The action of *entertained* is directed toward *child.*]
Felipe **visited** San Juan. [The action of *visited* is directed toward *San Juan.*]

Transitive verbs show an action that passes from the doer—the *subject*—to the receiver—the *object*.

☞ REFERENCE NOTE: For more information about subjects and objects in sentences, see pages 342–345 and 438–442.

An *intransitive verb* does not pass action to a receiver or an object. It simply expresses an action or tells something about the subject.

EXAMPLES   The children **smiled.**
The horses **galloped** across the prairie.

Some verbs may be either transitive or intransitive, depending on how they are used in a sentence.

EXAMPLES   My cousin Julio **plays** baseball on a Caribbean League team. [transitive]
My cousin Julio **plays** every week. [intransitive]

Katchina **studies** Chinese each day after school. [transitive]
Katchina **studies** hard. [intransitive]

EXERCISE 2 **Identifying Transitive and Intransitive Verbs**

In each of the following sentences, identify the italicized action verb as *transitive* or *intransitive*.

EXAMPLE   **1.** Computers *affect* our lives every day.
1. *transitive*

1. Computers *make* calculations incredibly fast.
2. They *perform* many tasks that people find boring and difficult.
3. Many businesses *benefit* from these machines.
4. Home computers *work* in similar ways.
5. They *do* word processing, a useful operation.
6. They also *run* programs for thousands of games.
7. Handy pocket computers *fit* easily into a wallet.
8. My mother *bought* a tiny computer no larger than a credit card.
9. The information in its memory *appears* on the screen at the touch of a button.
10. Addresses, phone numbers, notes, and other information on the screen *help* my mother with her work.

EXERCISE 3 **Writing Sentences with Transitive and Intransitive Verbs**

It's a busy day on the playground! Some children are playing ball and jumping rope. Others are enjoying hand-held computer games and checkers. Write ten sentences describing these children and their activities. In your sentences, include five of the following verbs. Use each one as a transitive verb and an intransitive verb. Be prepared to identify each verb as transitive or intransitive.

play	stop	win	jump
climb	throw	move	lose
practice	begin	learn	tell

EXAMPLE *1. Some boys and girls play different kinds of ballgames.*
2. They play every day.

Linking Verbs

(2) A *linking verb* is a verb that expresses a state of being. A linking verb connects the subject of a sentence with a word in the predicate that explains or describes the subject.

Not all verbs express mental or physical action. Some verbs help make a statement by linking the subject of a sentence with a word in the predicate.

EXAMPLES   Sandra Cisneros **is** a writer. [The verb *is* connects *writer* with the subject *Sandra Cisneros.*]
The firefighters **appeared** victorious. [The verb *appeared* connects *victorious* with the subject *firefighters.*]

Linking Verbs Formed From The Verb *Be*

am	has been	may be
is	have been	might be
are	had been	can be
was	will be	should be
were	shall be	would have been

Other Linking Verbs

appear	grow	seem	stay
become	look	smell	taste
feel	remain	sound	turn

Some verbs may be either action verbs or linking verbs, depending on how they are used.

ACTION   They **sounded** the bell for a fire drill.
LINKING   Mom **sounded** happy about her new job. [The verb *sounded* links *happy* with the subject *Mom.*]

ACTION   The judge **will look** at my science project.
LINKING   Sally Ann **will look** beautiful in her ballerina costume. [The verb *will look* links *beautiful* with the subject *Sally Ann.*]

▶ EXERCISE 4   **Identifying Linking Verbs**

List the ten linking verbs in the following sentences.

EXAMPLE **1.** Peanut soup, a favorite in Guyana, tastes good.
1. *tastes*

1. Peanuts remain an important crop in many parts of the world.
2. A high-protein food, the peanut is native to South America.
3. Peanuts grow ripe underground.
4. The seeds are the edible part of the plant.
5. Thanks to George Washington Carver, the peanut became one of the major crops of the South.
6. Carver, a scientist who experimented with peanuts and other plants, had been a slave.
7. It may seem strange, but Carver once prepared an entire dinner out of peanuts.
8. The peanut has become an ingredient in over three hundred different products, including wood stains, shampoo, printer's ink, and soap.
9. Of course, roasting peanuts smell wonderful.
10. Peanut butter was the invention of a St. Louis doctor in 1890.

▶ EXERCISE 5 **Identifying Action Verbs and Linking Verbs**

Identify the verb in each of the following sentences as an *action verb* or a *linking verb*.

EXAMPLES **1.** One of the most successful business leaders in the United States is John Johnson.
1. *is—linking verb*

2. Johnson publishes *Ebony, Jet,* and many other magazines.
2. *publishes—action verb*

1. The photograph on the next page shows John Johnson at his most successful.
2. Johnson's life was not always easy.
3. The small Arkansas town of his childhood had no high school.

4. Therefore, Johnson's mother moved to Chicago.
5. In Chicago, Johnson attended an all-black high school, with classmates Redd Foxx and Nat King Cole.
6. During the Depression, Johnson's family grew even poorer.
7. However, Johnson studied hard.
8. He soon became an honor student, the class president, and the editor of the high school newspaper.
9. Johnson started his first magazine with borrowed money.
10. Now he is the owner of a publishing empire worth $200 million per year.

Helping Verbs

(3) A **helping verb** (**auxiliary verb**) helps the main verb to express an action or a state of being.

EXAMPLES   **can** speak
           will learn
           should have been fed

Together, the main verb and its helping verb or verbs are called a *verb phrase.*

EXAMPLES   Many students **can speak** Spanish.
           I **will learn** all the state capitals tonight.
           The dog **should have been fed** by now.

GRAMMAR

Helping Verbs					
am	were	have	did	can	will
is	be	had	may	could	would
are	been	do	might	shall	
was	has	does	must	should	

Sometimes a verb phrase is interrupted by another part of speech.

EXAMPLES Suzanne **should** not **call** so late at night. [The verb phrase *should call* is interrupted by the adverb *not.*]

Did you **watch** Whitney Houston's new video? [The verb phrase *Did watch* is interrupted by the subject *you.*]

 EXERCISE 6 **Identifying Verb Phrases and Helping Verbs**

Identify the verb phrase in each of the following sentences. Then underline the helping verb or verbs.

EXAMPLE **1.** We are going to Arizona this summer.

       1. *are going*

1. The Petrified Forest has always attracted many tourists.
2. Their imaginations have been captured by its spectacular beauty.
3. Visitors to the forest can see the Painted Desert at the same time.
4. The colors of the desert do not remain the same for long.
5. Specimens of petrified wood are exhibited at the Visitors' Center.
6. Have you ever seen a piece of petrified wood?
7. A guide will gladly explain the process of petrification to you.
8. Visitors can purchase the wood as a souvenir.

9. Walking tours of the Petrified Forest are not recommended for amateur hikers.
10. Hikes must be arranged with park rangers.

EXERCISE 7 **Using Helping Verbs in Original Sentences**

Use each of the following word groups as the subject of a sentence with a verb phrase. Make some of your sentences questions. Underline the helping verb in each sentence.

EXAMPLE **1.** your neighbor's dog
1. _Can your neighbor's dog do tricks?_

1. my bicycle
2. the astronauts
3. a tiny kitten
4. the hard assignment
5. a famous singer
6. some strange footprints
7. my grandmother
8. the subway
9. a funny costume
10. the refreshments

REVIEW A **Identifying Verbs**

Identify the verb in each of the following sentences. Be sure to include helping verbs.

EXAMPLE **1.** Can you form the letters of the sign language alphabet?
1. _Can form_

1. The alphabet chart on the next page will help you.
2. Perhaps you and a friend could practice together.
3. At first, it may be a challenge.
4. Many people with hearing disabilities communicate with these letters and thousands of other signs.
5. Different forms of sign language are used by many people in many ways.
6. For example, football signals are sometimes given with sign language.
7. Some stroke victims must learn sign language during their recovery period.

8. Scientists have taught very simple signs to gorillas and chimpanzees.
9. These animals have been talking to each other and to people in sign language.
10. In this picture, the gorilla on the left and the woman are having a conversation in sign language.

REVIEW B **Identifying Verbs**

Identify the verbs in the following paragraph. Be sure to include helping verbs.

EXAMPLE [1] Fairy tales are sometimes called "folk tales."
   1. *are called*

[1] Long ago, many people could not read. [2] Instead, they would memorize stories. [3] Then, they would tell the stories to their families and friends.

[4] In this way, the people, or "folk," passed the tales on from generation to generation. [5] Finally, some people wrote the stories down. [6] Two German brothers, Jakob and Wilhelm Grimm, made a famous collection of German folk tales. [7] The brothers had heard many of their tales from older relatives. [8] Their collection of stories became extremely popular all over the world. [9] "Sleeping Beauty," "Cinderella," and "Rumpelstiltskin" were all preserved by the brothers Grimm. [10] In your library, you can find these tales and many others, too.

WRITING APPLICATION

Using *Be* as a Helping Verb and a Linking Verb

Can you tell the difference between the helping verb *be* and the linking verb *be*? As a helping verb, a form of *be* is always followed by a main verb. As a linking verb, a form of *be* is the main verb.

HELPING VERB   I **am** going to practice my trumpet every day.
LINKING VERB   I **am** nicer to my little brother this year.

▶ **WRITING ACTIVITY**

You and your classmates have decided to list some goals for the coming year. The theme for your lists is "How I Can Make the World a Better Place." Write a list of ten or more goals or resolutions for yourself. Make each of your resolutions a complete sentence. In your list, use the verb *be* at least two times as a helping verb and three times as a linking verb.

Prewriting   First, think of some realistic goals you can set for yourself. Could you be more careful about recycling? join a volunteer group? help clean up trash around your neighborhood? List as many goals as you can. Some goals may be very simple. For example, you might resolve to do little things like smile at people more or to help out more around the house.

Writing From your list, choose the resolutions that seem the most important and the most manageable. Write each of them as a complete sentence. (For more about complete sentences, see pages 340–355.)

Evaluating and Revising Read through your list. Are your resolutions clear and specific? Will you really be able to keep them? If not, revise or replace some of the resolutions. You may think of some good resolutions that didn't occur to you earlier. Add as many items as you wish. Be sure that you've used a form of the verb *be* as both a helping verb and a linking verb.

Proofreading Make sure that all of your sentences are complete. Do all subjects agree with their verbs? (For more about subject-verb agreement, see pages 456–470.) Identify each helping verb and linking verb. Make sure you've used the verb *be* correctly. Do a final check for errors in grammar, spelling, or punctuation.

The Adverb

14b. An *adverb* is a word that modifies a verb, an adjective, or another adverb.

EXAMPLES   Reporters **quickly** gather the news. [The adverb *quickly* modifies the verb *gather.*]
The route is **too** long. [The adverb *too* modifies the adjective *long.*]
Our newspaper carrier delivers the paper **very** early. [The adverb *very* modifies another adverb, *early.* The adverb *early* modifies the verb *delivers.*]

An adverb answers the following questions:

Where?	How often?	To what extent?
When?	*or*	*or*
How?	How long?	How much?

EXAMPLES   Please put the package **there.** [*There* modifies the verb *put* and tells *where.*]
I will call you **later.** [*Later* modifies the verb phrase *will call* and tells *when.*]
Softly I shut my door. [*Softly* modifies the verb *shut* and tells *how.*]
She **always** reads science fiction novels. [*Always* modifies the verb *reads* and tells *how often.*]
Would you please **briefly** explain what you mean? [*Briefly* modifies the verb phrase *would explain* and tells *how long.*]
An owl hooted **very** late last night. [The adverb *very* modifies the adverb *late* and tells *to what extent.*]
The lemonade was **too** sour. [*Too* modifies the adjective *sour* and tells *how much.*]

WORDS OFTEN USED AS ADVERBS	
Where?	here there away up outside
When?	now then later soon ago
How?	clearly easily quietly slowly
How often? or How long?	never always often seldom frequently usually forever
To what extent? or How much?	very too almost so really most nearly quite less only

NOTE: The word *not* is an adverb. When *not* is part of a contraction like *hadn't,* the *–n't* is an adverb.

The Position of Adverbs

Adverbs may appear at various places in a sentence. Adverbs may come before, after, or between the words they modify.

EXAMPLES **Quietly,** she will tiptoe from the room. [*Quietly* comes at the beginning of the sentence. *Quietly* modifies the verb phrase *will tiptoe.*]

She will **quietly** tiptoe from the room. [*Quietly* comes between *will* and *tiptoe,* the words it modifies.]

She will tiptoe **quietly** from the room. [*Quietly* comes after *will tiptoe,* the verb phrase it modifies.]

She will tiptoe from the room **quietly.** [*Quietly* comes at the end of the sentence.]

EXERCISE 8   **Identifying Adverbs and the Words They Modify**

Each of the following sentences contains at least one adverb. Identify the adverb or adverbs. Then give the word each adverb modifies. Be prepared to tell whether the word modified is a verb, an adjective, or an adverb.

EXAMPLE   **1.** If you look closely at a world map, you can quite easily find Brazil.

1. *closely—look; quite—easily; easily—can find*

1. Actually, Brazil is the largest country in South America.
2. A large portion of the Amazon rain forest grows there.
3. Many people have become more active in the preservation of the rain forest.
4. The loss of the forest may seriously affect the earth's climate.
5. Very early in the sixteenth century, Brazil was colonized by the Portuguese.

6. The country later became an independent republic.
7. Brazilians often say *Bom día*, which means "good day" in Portuguese.
8. In Brazil, sports fans can almost always find a soccer game in progress.
9. My aunt travels frequently, but she hasn't been to Brasília.
10. Brasília, the capital of Brazil, is an extremely modern city.

REVIEW C   **Finding Adverbs in a Paragraph**

Identify the ten adverbs in the following paragraph. Then give the word or words each adverb modifies.

EXAMPLE   [1] Williamsburg is a very interesting place.
       1. *very—interesting*

[1] Visitors to Williamsburg can truly imagine what life must have been like in the 1700s. [2] As you can see, Williamsburg was carefully built to resemble a small town of the past. [3] On one street a wigmaker carefully makes old-fashioned powdered wigs. [4] Nearby, a silversmith designs beautiful candlesticks, platters, and jewelry. [5] Down the block the bookbinder skillfully crafts book covers out of leather. [6] His neighbor, the blacksmith, was certainly important because he made shoes for horses. [7] In colonial times people could seldom afford new shoes for

themselves. [8] Nowadays, people enjoy watching this bootmaker at work. [9] Another very popular craftsman makes musical instruments. [10] Williamsburg definitely gives tourists the feeling that they have visited the past.

> EXERCISE 9 **Writing Appropriate Adverbs**

Write the following sentences. Fill each blank with an appropriate adverb. Use a different adverb in each sentence.

EXAMPLE **1.** ____ I learned some Spanish words.
         1. *Quickly I learned some Spanish words.*

1. I ____ watch TV after school.
2. You will ____ bait a hook yourself.
3. My little sister crept down the stairs ____.
4. Do you think that you can ____ find the answer to the problem?
5. She is ____ eager for lunch.

The Preposition

14c. A *preposition* is a word that shows the relationship between a noun or a pronoun and some other word in the sentence.

EXAMPLES Your math book is **underneath** your coat. [The preposition *underneath* shows the relationship of *book* to *coat.*]
The one **behind** us honked his horn. [The preposition *behind* shows the relationship of *one* to *us.*]

Notice how changing the preposition in the following sentences changes the relationship between *ball* and *net*.

I hit the ball **over** the net.
I hit the ball **into** the net.
I hit the ball **under** the net.

Commonly Used Prepositions				
aboard	at	down	off	under
about	before	during	on	underneath
above	behind	except	over	until
across	below	for	past	up
after	beneath	from	since	upon
against	beside	in	through	with
along	between	into	throughout	within
among	beyond	like	to	without
around	by	of	toward	

NOTE: Some prepositions are made up of more than one word. These are called *compound prepositions.*

Some Compound Prepositions		
according to	in addition to	next to
aside from	in place of	on account of
because of	in spite of	out of

▶ EXERCISE 10 **Writing Appropriate Prepositions**

While looking in an old trunk, you found the treasure map shown on the next page. Now, you want to go looking for the buried treasure. Make some notes to help you to plan your route. Think about any special supplies or equipment you'll need. In your notes, use at least ten different prepositions and underline each preposition you use.

EXAMPLE *I'll land the rowboat <u>on</u> Mournful Beach and pull it <u>under</u> the cliff, safe <u>from</u> the high tide.*

The Prepositional Phrase

A preposition is usually followed by at least one noun or pronoun. This noun or pronoun is called the *object of the preposition.* The preposition, its object, and the object's modifiers make up a *prepositional phrase.*

EXAMPLES **He poured sauce over the pizza.** [The preposition *over* relates its object, *pizza*, to *poured*. The article *the* modifies *pizza*.]
The pile of dry leaves had grown larger. [The preposition *of* relates its object, *leaves*, to *pile*. The adjective *dry* modifies *leaves*.]

A preposition may have more than one object.

EXAMPLE   The flea collar is **for cats and dogs.** [The
preposition *for* has the two objects *cats* and
dogs.]

👉 REFERENCE NOTE: For more about prepositional phrases, see
Chapter 15.

▶ EXERCISE 11   **Identifying Prepositions and Their
Objects**

Identify the prepositional phrase in each of the following sentences. Underline the preposition and circle its object. There may be more than one object.

EXAMPLE   **1.** Otters are related to weasels and minks.
1. *to* (weasels) *and* (minks)

1. Yesterday afternoon, we planted a sapling
   behind the garage.
2. I bought a pattern for a sari.
3. They live near the airport.
4. My brother wants a guitar for his birthday.
5. The pictures won't be developed until Friday
   or Saturday.
6. I received a letter from my aunt and uncle.
7. The arctic falcon is the largest of all falcons.
8. Did you have the correct answer to the third
   question?
9. There are many uses for peanuts.
10. I think that you might need a calculator for that
    problem.

Prepositions and Adverbs

Some words may be used as prepositions or as
adverbs. Remember that a preposition always has an
object. An adverb never does. If you can't tell
whether a word is used as an adverb or a preposition,
look for an object.

PREPOSITION	Meet me **outside** the gym. [*Gym* is the object of the preposition *outside.*]
ADVERB	Meet me **outside**. [no object]

PREPOSITION	Clouds gathered **above** us. [*Us* is the object of the preposition *above.*]
ADVERB	Clouds gathered **above**. [no object]

EXERCISE 12   **Writing Sentences with Prepositions and Adverbs**

Your family is on vacation, and you've just spent the whole day exploring this medieval castle. At the castle gift shop, you bought this cutaway drawing to send to your best friend. Write a brief letter to mail along with the drawing. In your letter, use five words as both prepositions and adverbs. Underline these words and be prepared to identify each as a preposition or an adverb.

EXAMPLES   *First, I walked completely <u>around</u> the wall.*
Then, I stood on the marshal's tower for a while and looked <u>around</u>.

The Conjunction

14d. A *conjunction* is a word that joins words or groups of words.

The most common conjunctions are the coordinating conjunctions.

Coordinating Conjunctions						
and	but	for	nor	or	so	yet

CONJUNCTIONS JOINING WORDS
beans **and** rice   movies **or** television
sad **but** true   Egypt, Italy, **and** Spain

☞ REFERENCE NOTE: For information on using commas in a series of words, see pages 594–595.

CONJUNCTIONS JOINING PHRASES
go for a walk **or** read a book
after breakfast **but** before lunch
cooking dinner **and** fixing breakfast

CONJUNCTIONS JOINING SENTENCES
I wanted to call, **but** it was late.
The deer ran toward the wide river, **for** they smelled smoke from the forest fire.
We knocked on the door, **and** they answered.

☞ REFERENCE NOTE: For information on using commas to join sentences, see pages 307–308.

▶ EXERCISE 13 **Identifying Conjunctions**

Identify the conjunction in each of the following sentences.

EXAMPLE **1.** Lena or I will pitch batting practice.
1. *or*

1. Julio and Roger joined the soccer team.
2. It may rain, but we will be there.

3. I have enough money for popcorn or juice.
4. You warm the tortillas, and I'll melt the cheese.
5. Did Nancy finish her book report, or is she still working on it?
6. He dove for the ball but missed it.
7. For breakfast I usually like to eat pancakes or a bran muffin.
8. The Boys Choir of Harlem sang for their friends and families.
9. I have already addressed the envelope but have not mailed it yet.
10. Many Chinese plays include dancing and acrobatics.

The Interjection

14e. An *interjection* is a word used to express emotion.

An interjection has no grammatical relationship to the rest of the sentence. Usually an interjection is followed by an exclamation point.

EXAMPLES **Aha!** I knew you were hiding there.
Oops! I punched in the wrong numbers.

Sometimes an interjection is set off by a comma.

EXAMPLES **Oh,** let's just stay home.
Well, what do you think?

Common Interjections			
aha	hey	ouch	whew
alas	hooray	ow	wow
aw	oh	ugh	yikes
goodness	oops	well	yippee

▶ EXERCISE 14 **Writing Interjections**

Have you ever heard the expression "an accident waiting to happen"? How many accidents are waiting to happen in the picture below? Write interjections to complete five sentences that the people in the picture might use.

EXAMPLE **1.** ____, Vince, have you seen my other skate?
    1. *Oh, Vince, have you seen my other skate?*

1. ____! I almost sat on the cat.
2. ____! Watch out for that book!
3. ____! Something on the stove is burning.
4. ____, Lila! Be careful with that milk!
5. ____, we'll have to get a new cord for our lamp.

Determining Parts of Speech

Remember that you can't tell what part of speech a word is until you know how it is used in a particular sentence. A word may be used in different ways.

  VERB Can you **test** the switch?
  NOUN Mr. Sanchez assigned a **test** for tomorrow.

GRAMMAR

ADVERB	The cat climbed **up.**
PREPOSITION	The cat climbed **up** the tree.

NOUN	We threw pennies in the wishing **well.**
ADJECTIVE	Janice isn't feeling **well.**
INTERJECTION	**Well,** what did he say?

REVIEW D   **Identifying Parts of Speech**

For each of the following sentences, label the italicized word as a *noun*, a *pronoun*, an *adjective*, a *verb*, an *adverb*, a *preposition*, a *conjunction*, or an *interjection*. Be prepared to give reasons for your answers.

EXAMPLE   **1.** Some scientists *study* bones.
1. *study—verb*

1. The fans lined up *outside* the stadium.
2. My mother *drives* to work.
3. Those *plants* grow best in sandy soil.
4. Rhea bought *paper* cups for the party.
5. *Their* parents own a card store.
6. N. Scott Momaday has written several books, *but* I have read only one of them.
7. *Oops!* I dropped my backpack.
8. We play *outdoors* every day until dinner time.
9. This videotape looks *new.*
10. You don't sound *too* happy.

PICTURE THIS

Wow! What a ride! You are a member of the National Roller Coaster Club. You are trying out the new roller coaster shown on the next page and are rating it for the club. Write a brief report for the club newsletter, describing the ride. Tell what you liked best about the coaster, and compare it to others you've heard about or ridden. In your report, use at least three conjunctions and two interjections.

Subject: a roller coaster ride
Audience: members of a roller coaster club
Purpose: to describe and rate the ride; to inform

Review: Posttest 1

Identifying Verbs, Adverbs, Prepositions, Conjunctions, and Interjections

For the following sentences, label each italicized word or word group as a *verb*, an *adverb*, a *preposition*, a *conjunction*, or an *interjection*.

EXAMPLE **1.** A tornado *is* a terrible *and* violent storm.
1. *is—verb; and—conjunction*

1. The tornado *struck* our neighborhood *without* warning.
2. *Unfortunately,* we do *not* have a basement.
3. I grabbed my dog Muffin *and* ran *into* the bathroom, the safest room in the house.
4. Muffin and I were *tightly* wedged *between* the sink and the tub.
5. The house *was shaking,* and the air *became* cold.
6. *Suddenly* the roof blew *off.*
7. The sky *was* full *of* loose boards.
8. Then everything suddenly *grew* calm—it seemed almost *too* calm.
9. I *was* frightened, *but* I was not hurt.
10. *Goodness!* Let's build a basement *soon.*

Review: Posttest 2

Writing Sentences Using Words as Different Parts of Speech

Write ten sentences of your own using the following words as directed. Underline the word and give its part of speech after each sentence. Use a variety of subjects and verbs in your sentences.

EXAMPLE **1.** Use *down* as an adverb and a preposition.
1. *We looked down.—adverb*
We looked down the hole.—preposition

1. Use *over* as an adverb and as a preposition.
2. Use *for* as a preposition and as a conjunction.
3. Use *yet* as a conjunction and as an adverb.
4. Use *well* as an interjection and as an adverb.
5. Use *through* as an adverb and as a preposition.

SUMMARY OF PARTS OF SPEECH

Rule	Part of Speech	Use	Example
13a	noun	names	His **report** is about **Medgar Evers**.
13b	pronoun	takes the place of a noun	I read quietly to **myself**.
13c	adjective	modifies a noun or pronoun	We found **three old Russian** coins in **that yellow** envelope.
14a	verb	shows action or a state of being	She **missed** the test because she **was** ill.
14b	adverb	modifies a verb, an adjective, or another adverb	He **seldom** gets **so** tired, but **today** he practiced **really hard**.
14c	preposition	relates a noun or pronoun to another word	The students **in** the play went **to** the auditorium.
14d	conjunction	joins words or groups of words	Tina **and** Shannon are invited, **but** they can't go.
14e	interjection	shows strong feeling	**Wow!** What great fireworks!

15 THE PREPOSITIONAL PHRASE

Adjective Phrases and Adverb Phrases

Diagnostic Test

Identifying Prepositional Phrases

Identify the prepositional phrase in each of the following sentences and tell whether the phrase is used as an *adjective phrase* or an *adverb phrase*. Then list the word that the phrase modifies.

EXAMPLE **1.** We hiked through the woods.
      1. *through the woods; adverb phrase—hiked*

1. The crowd waved banners during the game.
2. That book about the Underground Railroad is interesting.
3. A clown handed balloons to the children.
4. We always visit my grandparents in San Juan, Puerto Rico.

5. Uncle Eduardo carefully knocked the snow off his boots.
6. Someone left a package on the front porch.
7. Do you have the new CD by Whitney Houston?
8. Have you seen the pictures of the Yamatos' new house?
9. The swings in the park are a bit rusty.
10. Help yourself to some strawberries.

Phrases

15a. A *phrase* is a group of related words that is used as a single part of speech. A phrase does not contain both a subject and a verb.

Phrases cannot stand alone. They must always be used with other words as part of a sentence.

PHRASE **in the box**
SENTENCE **We put the tapes in the box.**

EXERCISE 1   **Identifying Phrases and Sentences**

Identify each of the following groups of words as a *phrase* or a *sentence*.

EXAMPLES **1.** in the winter, some people enjoy cross-country skiing
1. *sentence*

2. for many reasons
2. *phrase*

1. ski lifts are used for Alpine skiing
2. down the snowy hills
3. slalom skiers race through gates
4. during the race
5. before the other skiers

Prepositional Phrases

15b. A *prepositional phrase* includes a preposition, a noun or a pronoun called the *object of the preposition,* and any modifiers of that object.

Prepositions show the relationship of a noun or pronoun to another word in the sentence. The noun or pronoun that follows a preposition is called the *object of the preposition.* A preposition, its object, and any modifiers of the object are all part of the prepositional phrase.

EXAMPLES I met them **at the corner.** [The noun *corner* is the object of the preposition *at.*]
Did you bring these flowers **for me**? [The pronoun *me* is the object of the preposition *for.*]
We store carrots and potatoes **in our cool, dark basement.** [The noun *basement* is the object of the preposition *in.* The words *our, cool,* and *dark* modify *basement.*]

A preposition may have more than one object.

EXAMPLES Aaron showed his arrowhead collection **to Tranh and her.** [two objects]
The dinner of **baked chicken, salad, and two vegetables** also included dessert. [three objects]

☞ REFERENCE NOTE: For a list of commonly used prepositions, see page 407.

▶ EXERCISE 2   **Identifying Prepositional Phrases**

Identify the prepositional phrase in each of the following sentences. Underline each preposition and circle its object. A preposition may have more than one object.

EXAMPLE   **1.** The package was for my brother and me.
1. *for* my brother and me

1. The Sahara is a huge desert that lies south of the Mediterranean Sea.
2. We waited until lunch time.
3. The house across the street has green shutters.
4. Do not make repairs on the brakes yourself.
5. The word *lasso* comes from a Spanish word that means "snare."
6. May I sit between you and him?
7. The woman with the blue uniform is my aunt.
8. The *Cherokee Phoenix* was the first newspaper printed in an American Indian language.
9. He is saving money for a stereo and a guitar.
10. The messenger slipped the note under the door.

▶ EXERCISE 3 **Identifying Prepositional Phrases and Their Objects**

For each of the following sentences, identify the prepositional phrase and circle the object or objects of the preposition.

EXAMPLE **1.** Dinosaurs and other giant reptiles roamed across the earth sixty-five million years ago.
1. *across the (earth)*

1. Although some of the dinosaurs were enormous, others were quite small.
2. The drawings on the next page show a triceratops, thirty feet long, and a saltopus, less than three feet long.
3. Many dinosaurs fed on plants and vegetables.
4. Dinosaurs with sharp teeth ate flesh.
5. Can you imagine seeing this flying reptile, the pterodactyl, above you?
6. It once lived in Europe and Africa.
7. Until a few years ago, scientists believed that all dinosaurs were coldblooded.
8. According to recent studies, however, some dinosaurs may have been warmblooded.

9. Many scientists say that birds and crocodiles may be related to dinosaurs.
10. Some people even claim that birds are, in fact, living dinosaurs.

▶ EXERCISE 4   **Writing Appropriate Prepositional Phrases**

Write the following sentences, filling in each blank with an appropriate prepositional phrase.

EXAMPLE   **1.** We saw Jason ____.
          1. *We saw Jason at the mall.*

1. My favorite comedian will appear ____.
2. That bus always arrives ____.
3. The fans ____ cheered every score.
4. The children ran ____.
5. The light ____ is broken.

Adjective Phrases

A prepositional phrase used as an adjective is called an *adjective phrase.*

ADJECTIVE   **Icy** chunks fell from the skyscraper.
ADJECTIVE PHRASE   Chunks **of ice** fell from the skyscraper.

👉 REFERENCE NOTE: For more about adjectives, see pages 381–385.

15c.   An *adjective phrase* modifies a noun or a pronoun.

Adjective phrases answer the same questions that single-word adjectives answer.

> *What kind?   Which one?*
> *How many?   How much?*

EXAMPLES   Mr. Arnaud ordered a dinner **of boiled crawfish.**
[The adjective phrase modifies the noun *dinner.* The phrase answers the question *What kind?*]

The one **with the big pockets** costs more. [The adjective phrase modifies the pronoun *one.* The phrase answers the question *Which one?*]

There was enough room **for only three people.**
[The prepositional phrase modifies the noun *room.* The phrase answers the question *How much?*]

Notice in these examples that an adjective phrase always follows the word it modifies.

▶ EXERCISE 5   **Identifying Adjective Phrases**

Identify the adjective phrase in each of the following sentences. Then give the word that the phrase modifies.

EXAMPLE   **1.** Diego Rivera was a famous painter from Mexico.
           1. *from Mexico—painter*

1. People throughout the world enjoy Rivera's art.
2. The photograph below shows one of his murals.

Diego Rivera, *The Making of a Fresco Showing the*
Photo © 1992 Dirk Bakker

3. Rivera painted many murals, which are huge paintings on buildings.
4. His murals are beautiful examples of popular twentieth-century art.
5. Rivera's artworks often include symbols of Mexican culture.
6. His work with other Mexican artists was also very important.
7. Rivera was a major influence on another mural artist, Juan O'Gorman.
8. This mural by O'Gorman is in a university library.

9. O'Gorman does not paint his murals; instead, he uses tiny pieces of colored tile.
10. The complicated pattern upon the library walls fascinates everyone who sees it.

More than one adjective phrase may modify the same noun or pronoun.

EXAMPLE   That painting **of New England by Edward Bannister** is famous. [The two adjective phrases, *of New England* and *by Edward Bannister*, both modify the noun *painting.*]

An adjective phrase may also modify the object of another adjective phrase.

EXAMPLE   A number **of the paintings by that artist** are landscapes. [The adjective phrase *of the paintings* modifies the noun *number.* The adjective phrase *by that artist* modifies *paintings*, the object of the preposition in the first phrase.]

PICTURE THIS

You're the restaurant reviewer for a local newspaper. The Japanese restaurant shown on the next page has recently opened in town, and your job is to report on the food and service there. The server has just brought these colorful, tasty-looking dishes to your table. As you taste each food, write down some notes for your review. Describe how the food looks, tastes, and smells. Also describe the quality of the service. Mention any features of the restaurant that you find particularly interesting. [Note: You can use your imagination to describe features not shown in the photograph.] Decide whether you will or will not recommend this restaurant to your readers. In your notes, use at least five adjective phrases. Be prepared to identify the word or words that each phrase modifies.

Subject: a new Japanese restaurant
Audience: newspaper readers
Purpose: to inform by describing the food and
              service; to persuade

 EXERCISE 6   **Identifying Adjective Phrases**

In the following sentences, identify each adjective phrase. Then give the noun or pronoun the phrase modifies. [Note: Some sentences contain more than one adjective phrase.]

EXAMPLE **1.** This book about birds of North America has won many awards for photography.
         1. *about birds—book; of North America—birds; for photography—awards*

1. This book explains the importance of flight in the survival of the bird population.
2. The key to successful flight is the structure of the feather.

3. As you can see below, the shaft and the vane are the two main parts of a feather.
4. The area inside the quill of a feather is hollow.
5. Small barbs on the shaft form a feather's vane.
6. The curves in the vane and notches of the feather permit easy, quick movement.
7. Keratin, the same type of protein that gives strength to hair and nails, makes feathers strong.
8. Feathers on the wings and tails of birds often are quite showy.
9. Fast-flying birds like swifts usually have pointed wings.
10. Have you ever seen any of the birds that have these kinds of feathers?

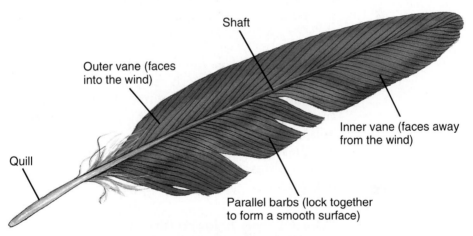

Shaft

Outer vane (faces into the wind)

Inner vane (faces away from the wind)

Quill

Parallel barbs (lock together to form a smooth surface)

▶ EXERCISE 7 **Writing Adjective Phrases**

Fill in the blank in each of the following sentences with an appropriate adjective phrase.

EXAMPLE **1.** That storm ____ might be dangerous.
 1. *That storm from the east might be dangerous.*

1. The shelf ____ is too high to reach.
2. My mariachi costume should win a prize ____.
3. The girl ____ is one of my best friends.
4. The argument ____ really wasn't very important.
5. My favorite birthday present was the one ____.

Adverb Phrases

A prepositional phrase used as an adverb is called an *adverb phrase.*

ADVERB We walk **there** every Saturday.
ADVERB PHRASE We walk **along the lake** every Saturday.

15d. An *adverb phrase* modifies a verb, an adjective, or an adverb.

Adverb phrases answer the same questions that single-word adverbs answer.

When?	*Why?*
Where?	*How often?*
How?	*How long?*

EXAMPLES The chorus sang **at the hospital.** [The adverb phrase modifies the verb *sang* and tells *where.*]
Will the rolls be ready **by dinner time?** [The adverb phrase modifies the adjective *ready* and tells *when.*]
Are these jeans long enough **for you?** [The adverb phrase modifies the adverb *enough* and tells *how.*]

EXERCISE 8 **Identifying Adverb Phrases**

Identify the adverb phrase used in each of the following sentences. Then write the word or words the phrase modifies.

EXAMPLE **1.** My hamster disappeared for three days.
1. *for three days—disappeared*

1. Dad hung a mirror in the front hall.
2. The cat is afraid of thunderstorms.
3. The acrobat plunged into the net but did not hurt herself.
4. Edward James Olmos will speak at our school.

5. Mom discovered several field mice in the cellar.
6. With great courage, Rosa Parks disobeyed the bus driver.
7. He plays well for a beginner.
8. We have planted day lilies along the fence.
9. Soon my shoes were full of sand.
10. Every morning she jogs around the reservoir.

Like adjective phrases, more than one adverb phrase may modify the same word.

EXAMPLE   My teacher said that César Chávez worked with the United Farm Workers for many years. [Both adverb phrases, *with the United Farm Workers* and *for many years,* modify the verb *worked.*]

An adverb phrase may be followed by an adjective phrase that modifies the object of the preposition in the adverb phrase.

EXAMPLE   We went **to an exhibit of rare coins.** [The adverb phrase *to an exhibit* modifies the verb *went.* The adjective phrase of *rare coins* modifies *exhibit,* the object of the preposition in the adverb phrase.]

▶ EXERCISE 9   **Identifying Adverb Phrases**

Identify the adverb phrase used in each of the following sentences. After each phrase, give the word or words the phrase modifies.

EXAMPLES   1. On Passover evening, we prepare a Seder, which is a Jewish holiday meal and ceremony.
   1. *On Passover evening—prepare*
   2. The Passover holiday celebrates a time long ago when Jewish slaves freed themselves from their masters.
   2. *from their masters—freed*

1. On Passover, our relatives visit our home.
2. We always invite them for the Seder.
3. Our whole family helps with the preparations.

GRAMMAR

4. Soon, everything is ready for the Seder.
5. In this photograph you can see how beautiful our holiday table is.

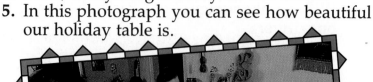

6. Holding all the special Passover foods, the Seder plate is displayed in the center of the table.
7. On the plate is a roasted egg representing new life.
8. Horseradish, which represents slavery's bitterness, is placed near the egg.
9. The other carefully arranged foods are also used during the Passover ceremony.
10. Throughout the entire meal, everyone enjoys a variety of delicious foods.

▶ EXERCISE 10   **Writing Sentences with Adverb Phrases**

Write five sentences using the following word groups as adverb phrases. Underline each phrase. Then draw an arrow from the phrase to the word or words it modifies.

EXAMPLE   **1.** for the airport

　　　　　2. *My grandparents have left already for the airport.*

1. down the hall
2. by them
3. in the mall

4. under the car
5. on the diving board

GRAMMAR

Identifying Adjective and Adverb Phrases

Each of the following sentences contains a preposi-tional phrase. Identify each phrase, and label it as an *adjective phrase* or an *adverb phrase.*

EXAMPLE **1.** Wilma Rudolph won three gold medals in the 1960 Olympic games.
1. *in the 1960 Olympic games—adverb phrase*

1. Wilma Rudolph did not have the childhood you might expect of a future Olympic athlete.
2. She and her twenty-one sisters and brothers were raised in a needy family.
3. Rudolph suffered from polio and scarlet fever.
4. Back then, illnesses like these were often deadly.
5. For many years afterward, Rudolph used a leg brace when she walked.
6. Yet, she never lost sight of her dreams.
7. She battled the odds against her.
8. With her family's help, she exercised hard every day.
9. All of her hard work made her strong.
10. Years later, she gained fame as a world-class athlete.

Identifying Adjective and Adverb Phrases

Each of the following sentences contains at least one prepositional phrase. Identify the phrase or phrases used in each sentence. Label each phrase as an *adjec-tive phrase* or an *adverb phrase.*

EXAMPLE **1.** In China, farmers are considered the backbone of the country.
1. *In China—adverb phrase; of the country— adjective phrase*

1. Most of the Chinese people are farmers.
2. They generally work their farms by hand.

3. Chinese farmers usually use hand tools instead of large machines.
4. Farmland throughout China is carefully prepared, planted, and weeded.
5. Farmers also harvest their crops with great care.
6. In the hills, the Chinese make flat terraces.
7. As you can see below, water from high terraces can flow to lower terraces.
8. Farmers build ridges around them so that they can be flooded during the growing season.
9. In flat sections, water is pumped out of the ground.
10. Other Chinese methods of irrigation are shown in the pictures below.

GRAMMAR

> **REVIEW C**   **Writing Sentences with Adjective and Adverb Phrases**

Use each of the following phrases in two separate sentences. In the first sentence, use the phrase as an adjective. In the second sentence, use the phrase as an adverb.

EXAMPLE   **1.** in Indiana
  1. *The people in Indiana are called "Hoosiers."*
    We once lived in Indiana.

1. from California
2. in my class
3. along the path

4. under the bridge
5. behind you

WRITING APPLICATION

Using Prepositional Phrases to Add Detail

Like one-word adjectives and adverbs, prepositional phrases add information to sentences. Adjective phrases tell *what kind, how many, how much,* and *which one.* Adverb phrases tell *when, where, why, how, how often, how long,* and *to what extent.*

WITHOUT PHRASES   I walked my dog.
  WITH PHRASES   On Saturday I walked my dog on the trail along the river.

> **WRITING ACTIVITY**
The Friends of Animals Society is having a contest for the best true-life pet story. The winner of the contest will have his or her story published in the local newspaper and will receive a fifty-dollar U.S. savings bond. Write a story to enter in the contest. In your story, tell

GRAMMAR

about an unusual pet that you've known or heard about. Use at least five adjective phrases and five adverb phrases in your story.

Prewriting First, you'll need to choose a pet to write about. Maybe you know of a cat that does clever tricks or a hamster that has a quirky personality. Perhaps you've read about a dog that's especially loyal or brave. Decide which story you want to write. Then jot down details about how the animal looks and how it acts. In your notes, focus on a specific time when the animal did something funny or amazing.

Writing Begin your draft with an attention-grabbing paragraph. Introduce and describe your main character. Be sure that you've included any human characters that play a part in the story. Also, describe the story's setting—for example, your kitchen, your neighbor's backyard, or the woods.

Evaluating and Revising Ask a friend to read your draft. Then ask him or her the following questions:

- Is the story interesting?
- Does it clearly show the animal's personality?
- Are events in the story logically connected?

If the answer to any of these questions is no, you may need to add, cut, or rearrange details. Make sure you've used at least five adjective phrases and five adverb phrases.

Proofreading and Publishing Check your story carefully for errors in grammar, spelling, and punctuation. Use a dictionary or another reference source to make certain that all proper names are spelled and capitalized correctly. You and your classmates may want to collect your stories into a booklet. Along with your stories, you might include pictures or drawings of the pets you've written about.

Review: Posttest 1

Identifying Adjective and Adverb Phrases

Identify the prepositional phrase in each of the following sentences, and tell whether the phrase is used as an *adjective phrase* or an *adverb phrase*. Then give the word or words that the phrase modifies.

EXAMPLE **1.** This newspaper article on weather patterns is interesting.
    1. *on weather patterns; adjective phrase—article*

1. The hikers are ready for a break.
2. Yesterday we rode our bikes through the park.
3. I always wear heavy woolen socks under my hiking boots.
4. The Rev. Jesse Jackson spoke at the convention.
5. Most children like books with colorful pictures.
6. Students from both South America and North America attended the meet.
7. That store has something for everyone.
8. Joel and Tina are participating in the Special Olympics this year.
9. I sent it to him this morning.
10. The road to town is flooded.
11. The camel is an important animal throughout the Middle East.
12. I will rake the leaves after lunch.
13. The plant by the kitchen window is a begonia.
14. We always camp close to a lake.
15. The stars of that movie are Rita Moreno and Joan Chen.
16. She rowed the boat across the lake.
17. Grandma Moses became an artist during her late seventies.
18. We covered the hot ashes with sand and rocks.
19. The actors quietly took their places on the stage.
20. Have you read the book about Sojourner Truth?

Review: Posttest 2

Writing Sentences with Prepositional Phrases

Use each of the following prepositional phrases in a sentence. After each sentence, write the word that the prepositional phrase modifies.

EXAMPLE **1.** across the street
1. *They live across the street.—live*

1. among the papers
2. about computers
3. under the surface
4. in the afternoon
5. for yourself

6. through the puddles
7. over the treetops
8. before dinner
9. along the fence
10. toward us

16 COMPLEMENTS

Direct and Indirect Objects, Subject Complements

Identifying Complements

Identify the complement or complements in each of the following sentences. Then label each complement as a *direct object*, an *indirect object*, a *predicate nominative*, or a *predicate adjective*.

EXAMPLE **1.** My grandparents sent me some old Moroccan coins.
1. *me—indirect object; coins—direct object*

1. A park ranger told us the history of Forest Park.
2. Tuesday is the last day for soccer tryouts.
3. She made her mother a sari for her birthday.
4. These peaches taste sweet and juicy.
5. James Baldwin wrote stories, novels, and essays.
6. He handed Amy and me an ad for the concert.
7. Two common desert creatures are the lizard and the snake.

8. My cousin Tena has become an excellent weaver of Navajo blankets.
9. Tropical forests give us many helpful plants.
10. The soil in that pot feels dry to me.

Recognizing Complements

16a. A *complement* is a word or group of words that completes the meaning of a verb.

Every sentence has a subject and a verb. Sometimes the subject and the verb can express a complete thought all by themselves.

                S   V
EXAMPLES   Adriana swam.

                   S   V
            The baby was sleeping.

Often a verb needs a complement to complete its meaning.

                         S   V
INCOMPLETE   My aunt found [*what?*]

                          S   V   C
    COMPLETE   My aunt found a **wallet.** [The noun *wallet* completes the meaning of the verb *found.*]

                          S   V
INCOMPLETE   The coach chose [*whom?*]

                          S   V   C
    COMPLETE   The coach chose **her.** [The pronoun *her* completes the meaning of the verb *chose.*]

                       S   V
INCOMPLETE   Raymond seemed [*what?*]

                        S   V   C
    COMPLETE   Raymond seemed **tired.** [The adjective *tired* completes the meaning of the verb *seemed.*]

Direct Objects

The *direct object* is one type of complement. It completes the meaning of a transitive verb.

☞ REFERENCE NOTE: Transitive verbs are discussed on pages 392–393.

16b. A *direct object* is a noun or a pronoun that receives the action of the verb or shows the result of that action. A direct object answers the question *What*? or *Whom*? after a transitive verb.

EXAMPLES My brother bought a **model.** [Bought *what?* Bought a model. The noun *model* receives the action of the verb *bought.*]
He built **it.** [Built *what*? Built it. The pronoun *it* is the result of the action of the verb *built.*]

A transitive verb may be followed by a compound direct object.

EXAMPLE He needed **glue, paint,** and **decals** for his model. [The compound direct object of the verb *needed* is *glue, paint,* and *decals.*]

A direct object can never follow a linking verb because a linking verb does not express action. Also, a direct object is never included in a prepositional phrase.

LINKING VERB Julia Morgan was an architect. [The verb *was* does not express action; therefore, it has no direct object.]

PREPOSITIONAL PHRASE She studied in Paris. [*Paris* cannot be the direct object of the verb *studied* because it is the object in the prepositional phrase *in Paris.*]

☞ REFERENCE NOTE: For more about linking verbs, see pages 394–395. For more about prepositional phrases, see Chapter 15.

▌▶ EXERCISE 1 **Identifying Direct Objects**

Identify the direct object or objects in each of the following sentences. Remember that a direct object may be compound.

EXAMPLE **1.** Do you enjoy books and movies about horses?
1. *books, movies*

1. Then you probably know some of the stories by Marguerite Henry.
2. Her books about horses have thrilled readers for more than forty years.
3. Henry's most popular books include *Misty of Chincoteague* and *King of the Wind*.
4. Her book *King of the Wind* won the Newbery Medal in 1949.
5. The book tells the adventures of the boy Agba and this beautiful Arabian horse.

6. Agba fed milk and honey to the newborn colt.
7. Sometimes the playful colt bit Agba's fingers.
8. The head of the stables often mistreated Agba and the colt.
9. Later, they both left their home and traveled to England.
10. To find out how the story ends, read *King of the Wind.*

Indirect Objects

The ***indirect object*** is another type of complement. Like the direct object, the indirect object helps to complete the meaning of a transitive verb. If a sentence has an indirect object, it also has a direct object.

16c. The ***indirect object*** is a noun or a pronoun that comes between the verb and the direct object. It tells *to whom* or *to what,* or *for whom* or *for what,* the action of the verb is done.

EXAMPLES   I gave that **problem** some thought. [The noun *problem* is the indirect object of the verb *gave* and answers the question "*To what* did I give some thought?"]
Dad bought **himself** some peanuts. [The pronoun *himself* is the indirect object of the verb *bought* and answers the question "*For whom* did Dad buy peanuts?"]

Do not mistake the object of a preposition for an indirect object.

OBJECT OF A   We sent the sombrero to **her.** [*Her* is the object
PREPOSITION   of the preposition *to.*]
INDIRECT   We sent **her** the sombrero. [*Her* is the indirect
OBJECT   object of the verb *sent.*]

Like a direct object, an indirect object can be compound.

EXAMPLE   She gave **Ed** and **me** the list of summer activities. [*Ed* and *me* are the indirect objects of the verb *gave*. They answer the question "*To whom* did she give the list?"]

EXERCISE 2   **Identifying Direct and Indirect Objects**

Identify the *direct object* and *indirect object* in each of the following sentences. Remember not to confuse objects of prepositions with direct objects and indirect objects. [Note: Some sentences do not have an indirect object.]

EXAMPLE   **1.** Gabriel sent me a postcard from Ecuador.
   1. me—indirect object; postcard—direct object

1. In Ecuador, Gabriel visited many of his relatives.
2. His aunt and uncle showed him the railroad in San Lorenzo.
3. They also visited the port in Esmeraldas.
4. Ecuador exports bananas and coffee.
5. Gabriel's cousin showed him some other sights.
6. She told Gabriel stories about Ecuadoran heroes.

7. Gabriel and his relatives rode a train into the mountains.
8. They took photos from the train four thousand feet up the Andes Mountains.
9. Gabriel enjoyed his visit to Ecuador.
10. He brought us some unusual souvenirs.

EXERCISE 3 **Writing Sentences with Direct and Indirect Objects**

You and a friend see the advertisement below for a clothing sale at the neighborhood thrift store. Each of you has saved twenty dollars, so you decide to purchase a few items for yourselves and your families. Using information in the ad and five of the verbs listed below, write five sentences about what you and your friend will buy. Include a direct object and an indirect object in each sentence. Underline the indirect object once and the direct object twice. Be sure to stay within your twenty-dollar budget!

buy	find	pay	show
give	sell	owe	ask

EXAMPLE **1.** *Sue will buy her <u>mother</u> a <u>purse.</u>*

GRAMMAR

WRITING APPLICATION

Using Direct and Indirect Objects

Many sentences contain action verbs. Often, more information is needed to complete the meaning of these verbs. Direct objects answer the questions *What?* or *Whom?* after transitive verbs. Indirect objects tell *to whom* or *to what*, or *for whom* or *for what*.

INCOMPLETE   I collect. [I collect *what*?]
    COMPLETE   I collect **stamps** from all over the world.
                  [direct object]

INCOMPLETE   My pen pal sends many unusual stamps.
                  [My pen pal sends stamps *to whom*?]
    COMPLETE   My pen pal sends **me** many unusual stamps.
                  [indirect object]

▶ WRITING ACTIVITY

For National Hobby Month, students in your class are making posters about their hobbies. Each poster will include drawings or pictures and a written description of the hobby. Write a short paragraph to go on the poster about your hobby. Use at least three direct objects and two indirect objects in your paragraph.

Prewriting   Choose a topic for your poster project. You could write about any collection, sport, craft, or activity that you enjoy in your free time. You could also write about a hobby that you're interested in starting. Freewrite about the hobby. Be sure to tell why you enjoy it or why you think you would enjoy it. If the hobby is new to you, find out more about it from another hobbyist or from the library.

Writing   Begin your paragraph with a main-idea sentence that clearly identifies the hobby or special interest. (For more about main-idea sentences, see pages

61–63.) Check your prewriting notes often to find details you can use in describing the hobby.

Evaluating and Revising Read your paragraph aloud. Does it give enough information about your hobby? Would someone unfamiliar with the hobby find it interesting? Add, cut, or rearrange details to make your paragraph easier to understand. Identify the transitive verbs in your paragraph. Have you used at least three direct objects and two indirect objects? You may need to revise some sentences.

Proofreading and Publishing Read over your paragraph for spelling, grammar, and punctuation errors. Check carefully for sentence fragments and run-on sentences. (For more about writing complete sentences, see pages 304–305 and 340–341.) You and your classmates may want to make posters using your paragraphs and some pictures. Cut pictures out of magazines and brochures or draw your own. Then attach your writing and art to a piece of poster board.

▶ REVIEW A **Identifying Direct and Indirect Objects**

Identify the *direct object* and *indirect object* in each of the following sentences. [Note: Some sentences do not have indirect objects.]

EXAMPLE **1.** Have you ever given board games much thought?
       1. *thought—direct object; games—indirect object*

1. For centuries, people have enjoyed war games.
2. This interest in war games has given us chess and checkers.
3. My brother showed me a book about different kinds of board games.

GRAMMAR

4. Board games reflect many different interests, such as earning money, buying property, and collecting things.
5. Some games may teach players lessons for careers and sports.
6. Of course, word games can give people hours of fun.
7. During the more difficult word games, Mrs. Hampton sometimes helps Chen and me.
8. Do you like quiz or trivia games?
9. Sharon's uncle bought Ronnie and her one of the new quiz games.
10. A popular television show inspired the game.

Subject Complements

16d. A *subject complement* completes the meaning of a linking verb and identifies or describes the subject.

EXAMPLES Mrs. Suarez is a helpful **neighbor.** [The subject complement *neighbor* identifies the subject *Mrs. Suarez.*]
The airport in Atlanta is very **busy.** [The subject complement *busy* describes the subject *airport.*]

Subject complements always follow linking verbs, not action verbs.

Common Linking Verbs					
appear	become	grow	remain	smell	stay
be	feel	look	seem	sound	taste

There are two kinds of subject complements—the *predicate nominative* and the *predicate adjective.*

Predicate Nominatives

16e. A *predicate nominative* is a noun or a pronoun that identifies or explains the subject of the sentence.

EXAMPLES   Seaweed is **algae.** [The noun *algae* is a predicate nominative following the linking verb *is. Algae* identifies the subject *seaweed.*]
My secret pal was really **he**! [The pronoun *he* is a predicate nominative following the linking verb *was. He* identifies the subject *pal.*]

Be careful not to mistake a direct object or the object of a preposition for a predicate nominative.

DIRECT OBJECT   My brother admired the **acrobat.**
OBJECT OF A   My brother spoke to the **acrobat.**
PREPOSITION

PREDICATE   My brother became an **acrobat.**
NOMINATIVE

A predicate nominative may be compound.

EXAMPLE   Maya Angelou is a great **poet** and **storyteller.**
[*Poet* and *storyteller* are predicate nominatives. They identify the subject and follow the linking verb *is.*]

NOTE: Expressions such as *It's I* and *That was she* sound awkward even though they are correct. In conversation, many people say *It's me* and *That was her.* Such expressions may one day become acceptable in writing, also. For now, however, it is best to follow the rules of standard English in your writing.

▶ EXERCISE 4   **Identifying Predicate Nominatives**

Identify the predicate nominative in each of the following sentences. [Note: A sentence may have a compound predicate nominative.]

EXAMPLE **1.** Mount Rushmore is a national memorial.
1. *memorial*

1. Was the author Chaim Potok or Amy Tan?
2. Her mother will remain president of the P.T.A.
3. Athens, Greece, has long been a center of art
   and drama.
4. The platypus and the anteater are mammals.
5. San Juan is the capital of Puerto Rico.
6. The peace pipe, or calumet, was a symbol of
   honor and power among Native Americans.
7. Quebec is the largest province in Canada.
8. In 1959, Hawaii became our fiftieth state.
9. That bird must be an eagle.
10. The fourth planet from the sun is Mars.

Predicate Adjectives

16f. A *predicate adjective* is an adjective that follows
a linking verb and describes the subject of the
sentence.

EXAMPLES **By 9:30 P.M., I was very tired.** [The adjective *tired*
describes the subject *I*.]
The baseball field looks too wet. [The adjective
wet describes the subject *field*.]

Like a predicate nominative, a predicate adjective
may be compound.

EXAMPLE **The blanket felt soft and fuzzy.** [Both *soft* and
fuzzy describe the subject *blanket*.]

EXERCISE 5 **Identifying Predicate Adjectives**

Identify the predicate adjective in each of the following sentences. [Note: A sentence may have a compound predicate adjective.]

EXAMPLE **1.** The porpoise seemed friendly.
1. *friendly*

1. Everyone felt ready for the test.
2. Those fresh strawberries smell delicious.
3. The front tire looks flat to me.
4. Everyone appeared interested in the debate.
5. That scratch may become worse.
6. She is talented in music.
7. During the movie, I became restless and bored.
8. Van looks upset about his grades.
9. Queen Liliuokalani was quite popular with the Hawaiian people.
10. The computer program does not seem difficult.

EXERCISE 6 **Writing Sentences with Predicate Adjectives**

You've been asked to write a movie review for your class newspaper. Think about a movie you've seen recently. Then write a review that tells why you think other students should or should not go to see the movie. In your review, include at least five sentences that contain predicate adjectives. Underline each predicate adjective.

EXAMPLE **1.** *Keanu Reeves is <u>believable</u> as the young attorney.*

PICTURE THIS

As you step outside one night, you are greeted by the fantastic starry night shown on the next page. You are amazed by the swirling light of the stars and moon, and you're surprised by the feeling the scene gives you. You want to remember exactly what you see and feel, so you decide to write about the night in your journal. Write a paragraph describing the night and your feelings about it. In your paragraph, use at least five predicate adjectives. (You may want to refer to the list of Common Linking Verbs on page 446.)

Subject: the night sky
Audience: yourself
Purpose: to remember this scene and your feelings

Vincent van Gogh. *The Starry Night* (1889). Oil on canvas, 29 x 36 1/4". Collection, The Museum of Modern Art, New York. Acquired through the Lillie P. Bliss Bequest.

▶ REVIEW B   **Identifying Subject Complements**

Identify each subject complement in the following sentences as a *predicate nominative* or a *predicate adjective*. [Note: A sentence may have more than one subject complement.]

EXAMPLE   **1.** The character Jahdu is a magical trickster.
          1. *trickster—predicate nominative*

1. A trickster is a character who plays tricks on others.
2. Tricksters have been popular in many folk tales throughout the world.

3. Jahdu, however, is the creation of Virginia Hamilton.
4. Her collections of folk tales, such as *The Dark Way* and *In the Beginning*, are very enjoyable.
5. Jahdu may be her most unusual hero.
6. He certainly seems clever and playful.
7. Even Jahdu's home, a forest on the Mountain of Paths, sounds mysterious.
8. Jahdu can stay invisible by using special dust.
9. He can become any object, from a boy to a taxicab.
10. Why are tricksters like Jahdu always such entertaining characters?

▶ REVIEW C   **Identifying Complements**

Identify each complement in the following sentences as a *direct object*, an *indirect object*, a *predicate nominative*, or a *predicate adjective*.

EXAMPLE   **1. One pet of President Theodore Roosevelt's family was Algonquin, a pony.**
     1. *Algonquin—predicate nominative*

1. Some presidents' pets have become famous.
2. Someone may have shown you the book by President George Bush's pet, Millie.
3. Millie, a spaniel, became an author.
4. With the help of Mrs. Bush, Millie told us a great deal about her days at the White House.
5. President Richard Nixon's best-known pet was Checkers, a cocker spaniel.
6. Some presidential pets looked quite strange at the White House.
7. President William Howard Taft kept a pet cow.
8. Herbert Hoover's family had two alligators.
9. A pet mockingbird was a favorite companion of Thomas Jefferson.
10. Calvin Coolidge's raccoon, Rebecca, appeared comfortable at the White House.

REVIEW D   **Identifying Complements**

Identify each complement in the following sentences as a *direct object*, an *indirect object*, a *predicate nominative*, or a *predicate adjective*. [Note: A sentence may have more than one complement.]

EXAMPLE   [1] Have you ever seen a sari or a bindi?
   1. *sari, bindi—direct objects*

[1] Many women from India wear these items. [2] A sari is a traditional Indian garment of cotton or silk. [3] Women wrap the sari's long, brightly printed cloth around their bodies. [4] As you can see, the softly draped sari is graceful and charming. [5] Some women buy themselves cloth woven with golden threads for an elegant look. [6] In cold climates, sari wearers can become quite chilly. [7] Consequently, Indian women wear their beautiful, lightweight garments under sturdy winter coats. [8] Another traditional item worn by many Indian women is the colored dot in the middle of their foreheads. [9] The Indian word for the dot is *bindi.* [10] The bindi gives the wearer a look of beauty and refinement.

Review: Posttest 1

Identifying Complements

Identify each complement in each of the following sentences as a *direct object,* an *indirect object,* a *predicate nominative,* or a *predicate adjective.* [Note: A sentence may have more than one complement.]

EXAMPLE **1.** Many forests are cold and snowy.
   1. *cold—predicate adjective; snowy—predicate adjective*

1. The home of the former president is now a library and museum.
2. The sun disappeared, and the wind suddenly grew cold.
3. We made our parents a family tree for their anniversary.
4. The newspaper published an article and an editorial about ex-Mayor Sharon Pratt Dixon.
5. My uncle gave my sister and me ice skates.
6. After the long hike, all of the scouts felt sore and sleepy.
7. Leaders of the Ojibwa people held a meeting last summer.
8. I wrote my name and address in my book.
9. Your dog certainly appears healthy.
10. They always send us grapefruit and oranges from Florida.
11. Most stars in our galaxy are invisible to the human eye.
12. Did the workers really capture an alligator in the sewer system?
13. Our trip on the Staten Island ferry soon became an adventure.
14. The air show featured balloons and parachutes.
15. The maples in the park are becoming gold and red.

GRAMMAR

16. My parents bought themselves several Celia Cruz CDs.
17. Aunt Kathleen gave Ricardo and me tickets for the show.
18. The two most popular sports at my school are football and baseball.
19. The water in the pool looked clean and fresh.
20. My mother's homemade Sabbath bread tastes delicious.

Review: Posttest 2

Writing Sentences with Complements

Write a sentence using each of the following kinds of complements. Underline the complement or complements in each sentence. Use a variety of subjects and verbs in your sentences.

EXAMPLE **1.** a compound predicate nominative
1. *My aunt is a swimmer and a jogger.*

1. a predicate adjective
2. an indirect object
3. a direct object
4. a predicate nominative
5. a compound predicate adjective

17 AGREEMENT

Subject and Verb

Diagnostic Test

Choosing Verbs That Agree in Number with Their Subjects

For each of the following sentences, identify the subject. Then choose the form of the verb in parentheses that agrees with the subject.

EXAMPLE 1. Here (*are, is*) the tickets for the game.
1. *tickets—are*

1. The flowers in that garden (*need, needs*) water.
2. She and her cousin (*play, plays*) tennis every weekend.
3. Either Paulette or Lily (*attend, attends*) all the local performances of the Alvin Ailey dancers.
4. There (*was, were*) several teachers at the game.
5. My brother and his dog (*has, have*) gone hunting.
6. (*Was, Were*) Liang and his sister born in Taiwan?

7. It (*doesn't, don't*) really matter to me.
8. My best friend at school (*doesn't, don't*) live in our neighborhood.
9. (*Was, Were*) you heating some burritos in the microwave?
10. Here (*come, comes*) Elena and James.

Number

Number is the form of a word that shows whether the word is singular or plural.

17a. When a word refers to one person, place, thing, or idea, it is *singular* in number. When a word refers to more than one person, place, thing, or idea, it is *plural* in number.

SINGULAR	tepee	I	baby	mouse
PLURAL	tepees	we	babies	mice

☞ **REFERENCE NOTE:** Most nouns ending in *–s* are plural (*igloos, sisters*). However, most verbs that end in *–s* are singular (*sings, tries*). For more about spelling the plural forms of nouns, see pages 644–646.

▶ EXERCISE 1 **Identifying Singular and Plural Words**

Identify each of the following words as *singular* or *plural*.

EXAMPLE **1.** activities
           1. *plural*

1. peach
2. libraries
3. highway
4. knife
5. shelves
6. children
7. they
8. enchiladas
9. women
10. America

Agreement of Subject and Verb

17b. A verb agrees with its subject in number.

A subject and verb *agree* when they have the same number.

(1) Singular subjects take singular verbs.

EXAMPLES The **ocean roars** in the distance. [The singular verb *roars* agrees with the singular subject *ocean.*]
Marla plays the violin well. [The singular verb *plays* agrees with the singular subject *Marla.*]

(2) Plural subjects take plural verbs.

EXAMPLES **Squirrels eat** the seeds from the bird feeder. [The plural verb *eat* agrees with the plural subject *squirrels.*]
The **dancers practice** after school. [The plural verb *practice* agrees with the plural subject *dancers.*]

NOTE: The singular pronouns *I* and *you* take plural verbs.

EXAMPLES **You look** puzzled, but **I understand.**

When a sentence has a verb phrase, the first helping verb in the phrase agrees with the subject.

EXAMPLES The **movie is** starting.
The **movies are** starting.

Has Latrice been studying Arabic?
Have they been studying Arabic?

EXERCISE 2   **Identifying the Number of Subjects and Verbs**

Identify each of the following subjects and verbs as either *singular* or *plural*. [Note: All verbs agree with their subjects.]

USAGE

EXAMPLE   **1. flag waves**
         1. *singular*

1. socks match
2. lightning crackles
3. leaves rustle
4. mosquitoes buzz
5. Lyle baby-sits

6. bands march
7. Richelle knits
8. they listen
9. singer practices
10. horses whinny

> **EXERCISE 3**

Changing the Number of Subjects and Verbs

All of the subjects and verbs in the following sentences agree in number. Rewrite each sentence, changing the subject and verb to the opposite number.

EXAMPLE   **1.** Lions roar across the plains of Kenya.
         1. *A lion roars across the plains of Kenya.*

1. Maps show the shape of a country.
2. What countries are highlighted on this map?

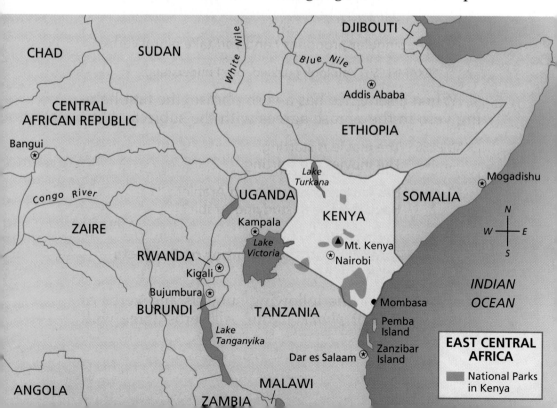

3. Does an ocean form Kenya's eastern border?
4. Visitors enjoy Kenya's beautiful scenery.
5. Mount Kenya's peaks are covered with snow.
6. Wildlife parks have been created in Kenya.
7. In the picture below, rangers patrol a park to protect the animals.
8. They certainly have unusual transportation.
9. Many industries are located in Kenya's capital, Nairobi.
10. Kenyan farmers grow such crops as wheat, corn, and rice.

▷ EXERCISE 4 **Choosing Verbs That Agree in Number with Their Subjects**

In each of the following sentences, choose the form of the verb in parentheses that agrees with the subject.

EXAMPLE **1.** The kitten (*pounces, pounce*) on the ball.
         1. *pounces*

1. Firefighters (*risks, risk*) their lives to save others.
2. The snowplow (*clears, clear*) the road quickly.
3. Some dancers (*like, likes*) reggae music best.
4. St. Augustine, Florida, (*has, have*) many old Spanish buildings.
5. Some students (*chooses, choose*) to play volleyball.
6. At the science fair, the winner (*receives, receive*) a savings bond.

7. Strong winds (*whistles, whistle*) through the old house.
8. Each Saturday, club members (*picks, pick*) up the litter in the park.
9. The principal (*makes, make*) announcements over the loudspeaker each day.
10. Doctors (*says, say*) that listening to loud music can harm people's hearing.

USAGE

PICTURE THIS

You saved up your money for months to order these products from an electronics catalog. Now that your order has arrived, you are dismayed to find that none of these gadgets work! You decide to write to the mail-order company and ask for a refund. Write a letter explaining what's wrong with each product and asking for your money back. Check your writing carefully for any errors in subject-verb agreement.

Subject: faulty products
Audience: a customer relations representative at a mail-order company
Purpose: to explain why you should get a refund

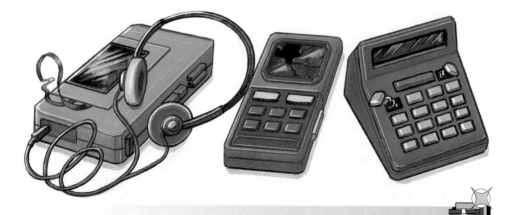

Problems in Agreement

Phrases Between Subject and Verb

17c. The number of a subject is not changed by a phrase following the subject.

EXAMPLES   These **shades** of blue **are** my favorite colors.
The smallest **puppy** of the three **is** sleeping in the basket.
The **ballerina** with long black braids **has** been my sister's ballet teacher for two years.

☞ REFERENCE NOTE: For more information about phrases, see Chapter 15.

▶ EXERCISE 5   **Choosing Verbs That Agree in Number with Their Subjects**

Choose the form of the verb in parentheses that agrees with the subject in each of the following sentences.

EXAMPLE   **1.** Islands off the coast (*has, have*) a life of their own.
1. *have*

1. The second-largest island in the United States (*is, are*) located in the Gulf of Alaska.
2. The thirteen thousand people on Kodiak Island (*is, are*) mostly of Native Arctic, Russian, or Scandinavian descent.
3. Sacks of mail (*is, are*) flown to the island from the mainland.
4. The citizens of Kodiak (*calls, call*) Alaska the mainland.
5. Industries in the community (*has, have*) suffered in recent years.
6. One cannery on the island (*cans, can*) salmon eggs, or roe.
7. Many residents on the mainland (*considers, consider*) roe a delicacy.

8. Bears like this one (*catch, catches*) fresh salmon.
9. However, their search for leftovers (*create, creates*) problems for Kodiak.
10. The officials of one town (*has, have*) had to put a special bear-proof fence around the garbage dump.

Indefinite Pronouns

Personal pronouns refer to specific people, places, things, or ideas. A pronoun that does not refer to a definite person, place, thing, or idea is known as an *indefinite pronoun.*

PERSONAL PRONOUNS	she	you	we	them
INDEFINITE PRONOUNS	each	many	anyone	all

17d. The following indefinite pronouns are singular: *each, either, neither, one, everyone, everybody, no one, nobody, anyone, anybody, someone, somebody.*

EXAMPLES **One** of the stars **is** Gloria Estefan.
Each of the tourists **was** given a souvenir.
Does everybody in the restaurant like pita bread?

> **EXERCISE 6**   **Choosing Verbs That Agree in Number with Their Subjects**

In the following sentences, choose the form of the verb in parentheses that agrees with the subject. Remember that the subject is never part of a prepositional phrase.

EXAMPLE   **1.** Neither of the teams (*is, are*) on the field.
         1. *is*

1. Nearly everybody in Lee's family (*enjoy, enjoys*) bird's nest soup.
2. Neither of them (*was, were*) wearing a helmet.
3. Somebody in the class (*speaks, speak*) French.
4. Nobody in the first two rows (*wants, want*) to volunteer.
5. Each of these tapes (*is, are*) by Natalie Cole.
6. Someone in the crowd (*is, are*) waving a pennant.
7. Everyone in those exercise classes (*has, have*) lost weight.
8. One of the band members (*plays, play*) lead guitar.
9. Either of those salads (*tastes, taste*) delicious.
10. No one (*was, were*) listening to the speaker.

17e.   The following indefinite pronouns are plural: *both, few, many, several.*

EXAMPLES   **Few** of the guests **are** wearing formal clothes.
Many of the newer houses **have** built-in smoke detectors.

17f.   The indefinite pronouns *all, any, most, none,* and *some* may be either singular or plural.

The number of the pronouns *all, any, most, none,* and *some* is determined by the number of the object in the prepositional phrase following the subject. If the pronoun refers to a singular object, the pronoun is singular. If the pronoun refers to a plural object, the pronoun is plural.

EXAMPLES **All** of the snow **has** melted. [*All* is singular because it refers to one thing—*snow.* The helping verb *has* is singular to agree with *snow*.]
All of the snowflakes **have** melted. [*All* is plural because it refers to more than one thing— *snowflakes.* The helping verb *have* is plural to agree with *snowflakes*.]

Some of the team **has** left the field. [*Some* is singular because it means "one part" of the team. The helping verb *has* is singular to agree with "one part."]
Some of the players **are** getting on the bus. [*Some* is plural because it refers to more than one player. The helping verb *are* is plural to agree with *players.*]

▶ REVIEW A **Choosing Verbs That Agree in Number with Their Subjects**

In the following sentences, choose the correct form of the verb in parentheses.

EXAMPLE **1.** One of these puppies (*needs, need*) a good home.
1. *needs*

1. Most of the balloons (*has, have*) long strings.
2. Everyone in the purple uniforms (*plays, play*) on the softball team.
3. Both of the sneakers (*gives, give*) me blisters.
4. Each of these recipes (*requires, require*) ricotta cheese.
5. Some of the artists (*paint, paints*) landscapes.
6. Neither of those songs (*was, were*) composed by Duke Ellington.
7. None of the apartments (*has, have*) been painted.
8. All of the jewels (*is, are*) in the safe.
9. Many of those designs (*is, are*) found on Navajo rugs.
10. All of the writing (*is, are*) upside down.

Compound Subjects

A compound subject is made up of two or more subjects that are connected by *and, or,* or *nor*. These connected subjects share the same verb.

17g. Subjects joined by *and* take a plural verb.

EXAMPLES   **Red** and **blue are** the school's colors.
New **uniforms** and **instruments were** ordered for the marching band.
Mr. Lewis, Mrs. Kirk, and **Ms. Jefferson have** applied for new jobs.

▶ EXERCISE 7   **Choosing Verbs That Agree in Number with Their Subjects**

Identify the compound subject in each of the following sentences. Then choose the form of the verb in parentheses that agrees with the compound subject.

EXAMPLE   **1.** Volcanoes and earthquakes (*is, are*) common in that area.
1. *Volcanoes, earthquakes—are*

1. The blanket and the robe (*has, have*) Navajo designs.
2. Wind, hail, and freezing rain (*is, are*) predicted for Thursday.
3. A desk and a bookcase (*was, were*) moved into Ella's room.
4. Savannas and velds (*is, are*) two kinds of grasslands found in Africa.
5. A truck and a car with a trailer (*was, were*) stalled on the highway.
6. A raccoon and a squirrel (*raid, raids*) our garden every night.
7. Mandy and her aunt (*goes, go*) to the Chinese market every Saturday.
8. Eric and Jarvis (*was, were*) asked to introduce the guest speaker.

USAGE

9. Mosquitoes and earwigs (*has, have*) invaded our backyard.
10. Ketchup, onions, and mustard (*goes, go*) well on many kinds of sandwiches.

17h. When compound subjects are joined by *or* or *nor*, the verb agrees with the subject nearer the verb.

> A new **statue** or a **fountain has** been planned for the park. [The singular verb *has* agrees with the nearer subject, *fountain.*]
> A soft **blanket** or warm **booties make** a baby comfortable. [The plural verb *make* agrees with the nearer subject, *booties.*]
> Neither the **coach,** the **fans,** nor the **players were** happy with the decision. [The plural verb *were* agrees with the nearest subject, *players.*]

ORAL PRACTICE 1 **Using Correct Verbs with Compound Subjects Joined by *Or* or *Nor***

Read each of the following sentences aloud, stressing the italicized words.

1. Either a *desert* or a *jungle is* the setting for the play.
2. The *table* or the *bookshelves need* dusting first.
3. Neither the *bus* nor the *train stops* in our town.
4. Neither *jokes* nor funny *stories make* Gordon laugh.
5. *Flowers* or a colorful *picture makes* a room cheerful.
6. Either the *story* or the *poems are* by Langston Hughes.
7. *Rice* or *potatoes come* with the tandoori chicken.
8. Neither the *Carolinas* nor *Illinois borders* Texas.

REVIEW B **Choosing Verbs That Agree in Number with Their Subjects**

For each of the following sentences, choose the form of the verb in parentheses that agrees with the subject.

USAGE

EXAMPLE   **1.** Tara and Chen (*are, is*) reading the same book.
       1. *are*

1. Many vegetables (*grow, grows*) quite large during Alaska's long summer days.
2. His mother (*teach, teaches*) math.
3. All of the sailboats in the harbor (*belong, belongs*) to the village.
4. You and your cousins (*are, is*) invited to the party.
5. Either the wall clock or our watches (*are, is*) not accurate.
6. The magazines on the kitchen table (*are, is*) for the hospital.
7. My list of favorite singers (*include, includes*) Tracy Chapman and Bonnie Raitt.
8. Both my brother and my sister (*deliver, delivers*) the morning newspaper.
9. Neither pencils nor an eraser (*are, is*) permitted.
10. The clowns and jugglers (*has, have*) always been my favorite circus performers.

▶ REVIEW C   **Proofreading for Errors in Subject-Verb Agreement**

Most sentences in the following paragraph contain a verb that does not agree in number with its subject. If a sentence is incorrect, give the correct verb form. If a sentence is correct, write *C*.

EXAMPLE   [1] Holiday customs throughout the world is interesting to study.
       1. *are*

[1] In Sweden, adults and children celebrates St. Lucia's Day. [2] Everyone there know St. Lucia as the Queen of Light. [3] Many people eagerly look forward to the December 13 holiday. [4] Girls especially enjoys the day. [5] By tradition, the oldest girl in the family dress as St. Lucia. [6] The girl in the picture on the next page is ready to play her part. [7] You surely has noticed the girl's headdress. [8] A crown of lighted

candles are hard to miss! [9] Each of the young Lucias also wear a white robe. [10] Early in the morning, the costumed girls bring breakfast to the adults of the household.

Subject After the Verb

17i. When the subject follows the verb, find the subject. Then make sure that the verb agrees with it.

The subject usually follows the verb in sentences that begin with *there* and *here* and in questions.

EXAMPLES   There **are** fifty **runners** in the marathon.
There **is** the **winner**.

There **are** my overdue library **books**.
Here **is** the **book** about reptiles.

Are the **birds** in the nest?
Is the **nest** on a high branch?

NOTE: The contractions *there's* and *here's* contain the verb *is*. These contractions are singular and should be used only with singular subjects.

EXAMPLES   There**'s Uncle Max**.
Here**'s your allowance**.

☞ REFERENCE NOTE: For more information about contractions, see pages 629–630.

▶ EXERCISE 8   **Choosing Verbs That Agree in Number with Their Subjects**

Identify the subject of each sentence. Then choose the form of the verb in parentheses that agrees with the subject.

EXAMPLE   **1.** There (*was, were*) a baby rabbit hiding in the grass.
      1. *rabbit—was*

1. There (*is, are*) three foreign exchange students at the high school.
2. (*Was, Were*) the fans cheering for the other team?
3. (*Has, Have*) the Washingtons moved into their new home?
4. Here (*is, are*) the tacos and fajitas.
5. (*Has, Have*) the bees left the hive?
6. (*There's, There are*) several correct answers to that question.
7. How long (*has, have*) the Huangs owned this tai chi studio?
8. (*Here are, Here's*) the shells from Driftwood Beach.
9. (*There's, There are*) a pint of strawberries in the kitchen.
10. There (*is, are*) Amy and Wanda in the doorway.

The Contractions *Don't* and *Doesn't*

17j. The word *don't* is a contraction of *do not.* Use *don't* with all plural subjects and with the pronouns *I* and *you.*

EXAMPLES   **I don't** have my keys.   **Dogs don't** meow.
          You don't care.   **They don't** know.
          We don't agree.   The **boots don't** fit.

17k. The word *doesn't* is a contraction of *does not.* Use *doesn't* with all singular subjects except the pronouns *I* and *you.*

EXAMPLES **He doesn't** know you. **Don doesn't** like thunder.
She doesn't care. The **car doesn't** run.
It doesn't work. A **penguin doesn't** fly.

ORAL
PRACTICE 2 **Using *Don't* and *Doesn't* Correctly**

Read the following sentences aloud, stressing the italicized words.

1. *He doesn't* want us to give him a party.
2. *Margo* and *Jim don't* have any money left.
3. *Lynna doesn't* remember the capital of Jamaica.
4. The *bus doesn't* stop here.
5. *They don't* believe that old story.
6. *It doesn't* snow here in October.
7. *They don't* sing the blues anymore.
8. That Zuñi *vase doesn't* look very old.

EXERCISE 9 **Writing *Don't* and *Doesn't* with Subjects**

Identify the subject in each of the following sentences. Then choose the contraction, either *don't* or *doesn't*, that agrees with the subject.

EXAMPLE **1.** Our cats _____ like catnip.
1. *cats—don't*

1. My parents _____ listen to rap music.
2. It _____ seem possible that Leon grew an inch in one month.
3. I _____ have much homework tonight.
4. Jerome _____ play the guitar as well as Angela.
5. The pizza _____ have enough onions, cheese, or mushrooms.
6. They _____ permit diving in the pool.
7. This bedroom _____ look very neat.
8. My ski boots _____ fit me this year.
9. Matthew enjoys playing lacrosse, but he _____ like to play soccer.
10. They _____ live on this street anymore.

WRITING APPLICATION

Using Subject-Verb Agreement in Writing

Contractions like *there's, here's,* and *don't* can make it difficult to spot errors in subject-verb agreement. However, when you spell out these contractions in full, you can easily see whether the verb should be singular or plural.

EXAMPLE   **There's carrots in the refrigerator.** [Spelled out, *There's* becomes *There is.*]

The singular verb *is* doesn't agree with the plural subject *carrots*. The sentence should be revised.

REVISED   **There are carrots in the refrigerator.**

▶ WRITING ACTIVITY

Your family is going on a weekend trip. A neighbor has agreed to look after your pet. Write a note giving your neighbor complete instructions for tending the animal. To avoid confusing your reader, make sure the subjects and verbs in your sentences agree.

Prewriting   Think about a pet that you've had or that you know about. It might be a rabbit, a cat, a dog, a hamster, or several animals, such as fish or birds. If you've never cared for a pet, talk to someone who has. Take notes on caring for the pet. What does it eat? How much and how often should it be fed? How much water does it need? What other special care does it need?

Writing   Now, write a draft of your note. Explain the daily care of the pet step by step. The more specific your instructions are, the better. You can use informal standard English if you're writing to someone you know well. (For more about informal English, see pages 330–331 and 544.)

USAGE

Evaluating and Revising Read your note aloud. Can you follow each step of the instructions? Are all the steps in order? Have you included all the necessary information? If not, revise your note to make it clear and complete.

 Proofreading After you've revised your note, check each sentence for subject-verb agreement. Take special care with any verb that is part of a contraction. Check your note for any other errors in grammar, punctuation, or spelling.

USAGE

▶ REVIEW D   **Proofreading for Errors in Subject-Verb Agreement**

Most of the following sentences contain a verb that does not agree in number with its subject. Correct each incorrect verb. If a sentence is correct, write C.

EXAMPLE   **1.** Is the people in the picture on the next page worried?
  1. *Are*

1. There is sharks swimming all around them.
2. However, the people doesn't seem to care.
3. Has they lost their senses?
4. No, there aren't anything for them to worry about in this shark exhibit.
5. There's a tunnel right through the shark pool.
6. Everyone who visits the exhibit ride a moving walkway through the tunnel.
7. The sharks don't seem to mind the people.
8. Actually, sharks in the wild doesn't attack people very often.
9. Of course, sharks does eat almost anything.
10. Caution and respect, therefore, needs to be shown by people in shark-inhabited waters.

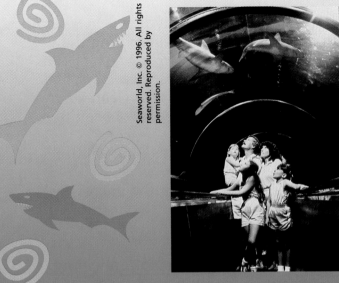

Review: Posttest

Choosing Verbs That Agree in Number with Their Subjects

For each of the following sentences, find the subject. Then choose the form of the verb in parentheses that agrees with the subject.

EXAMPLE   **1.** Janelle and Brad (*are, is*) in the drama club.
   1. *are*

1. Neither the passengers nor the pilot (*was, were*) injured.
2. There (*are, is*) two new rides at the amusement park.
3. That book of Spanish folk tales (*is, are*) selling out.
4. (*Here are, Here's*) some books about Hawaii.
5. Shel Silverstein and Ogden Nash (*appeal, appeals*) to both children and grown-ups.
6. Velma and her little sister (*was, were*) reading a story by Gyo Fujikawa.
7. (*Was, Were*) your parents happy with the results?

8. He (*doesn't, don't*) play chess anymore.
9. Why (*doesn't, don't*) she and Megan bring the lemonade?
10. Tickets for that concert (*are, is*) scarce.
11. The dishes on that shelf (*look, looks*) clean.
12. My mother and my brother (*has, have*) been in Florida since Sunday.
13. Either the cats or the dog (*has, have*) upset the plants.
14. Here (*are, is*) the instructions for the microwave.
15. There (*is, are*) ten provinces and two territories in Canada.
16. I (*am, is*) crocheting an afghan.
17. Why (*wasn't, weren't*) you at the scout meeting yesterday?
18. She (*doesn't, don't*) like spectator sports.
19. Several paintings by that artist (*are, is*) now on exhibit at the mall.
20. They (*doesn't, don't*) know how to get to the Juneteenth picnic.

18 USING VERBS CORRECTLY

Principal Parts, Regular and Irregular Verbs, Tense

Diagnostic Test

Using the Correct Forms of Verbs

For each of the following sentences, give the correct form of the verb in parentheses.

EXAMPLE **1.** Our family had (*drive*) three hundred miles.
1. *driven*

1. We had (*ride*) in the car for several hours.
2. Six inches of snow (*fall*) last night.
3. I never (*know*) snow was so beautiful.
4. The wind had (*blow*) some of it into high drifts.
5. As we (*go*) past them, they looked like white hills.
6. My brother Ernesto (*bring*) some comics to read on the trip.
7. I (*lie*) back and looked at the scenery.
8. Unfortunately, the car heater had (*break*).

9. We all (*wear*) our heavy coats and mittens.
10. However, my ears almost (*freeze*).
11. My favorite wool cap had (*shrink*) to a tiny size in the dryer.
12. During the long ride home, we (*sing*) some songs.
13. The clerk (*rise*) and asked if we would like some hot chocolate.
14. After lunch, Ernesto (*begin*) to feel sleepy.
15. We had (*come*) a long way.
16. I had never (*sit*) so long in a car before.
17. I should never have (*drink*) two cups of hot cocoa.
18. Mom and I (*run*) into the gas station.
19. At noon, we (*eat*) lunch at a roadside cafeteria.
20. All warmed up again, I (*sink*) into a deep sleep.

Principal Parts of Verbs

The four basic forms of a verb are called the ***principal parts*** of the verb.

18a. The four principal parts of a verb are the *base form*, the *present participle*, the *past*, and the *past participle.*

Notice that the present participle and the past participle are used with helping verbs (forms of *be* and *have*).

BASE FORM	PRESENT PARTICIPLE	PAST	PAST PARTICIPLE
start	(is) starting	started	(have) started
wear	(is) wearing	wore	(have) worn

NOTE: Some teachers refer to the base form as the infinitive. Follow your teacher's directions in labeling these words.

As you can see from their names, the principal parts of a verb are used to express time.

PRESENT TIME   She **wears** a blue uniform.
Ray **is wearing** a baseball cap.
PAST TIME   Yesterday, we **wore** sweaters.
I **had worn** braces for three months.
FUTURE TIME   Jessica **will wear** her new dress at the party.
By next spring Joey **will have worn** holes in those shoes.

Because *start* forms its past and past participle by adding *–ed*, it is called a *regular verb*. *Wear* forms its past and past participle differently, so it is called an *irregular verb*.

USAGE

Regular Verbs

18b. A *regular verb* forms its past and past participle by adding *–d* or *–ed* to the base form.

BASE FORM	PRESENT PARTICIPLE	PAST	PAST PARTICIPLE
wash	(is) washing	washed	(have) washed
hop	(is) hopping	hopped	(have) hopped
use	(is) using	used	(have) used

👉 REFERENCE NOTE: Most regular verbs that end in *–e* drop the *–e* before adding *–ing*. Some regular verbs double the final consonant before adding *–ing* or *–ed*. For a discussion of these spelling rules, see pages 640–642.

One common error in forming the past or past participle of a regular verb is to leave off the *–d* or *–ed* ending.

NONSTANDARD   Josh was suppose to meet us here.
STANDARD   Josh was **supposed** to meet us here.

👉 REFERENCE NOTE: For more about standard English, see pages 329–330.

▶ ORAL PRACTICE 1   **Using Regular Verbs**

Read the following sentences aloud, stressing the italicized verb.

1. We are *supposed* to practice sit-ups this morning.
2. With the help of his guide dog, the man *crossed* the street.
3. Carlos and Rita have *ordered* soup and salad.
4. Her family *moved* from Trinidad to Brooklyn.
5. Some Native Americans *used* to use shells for money.
6. They *called* shell money "wampum."
7. Larry has *saved* most of his allowance for the past two months.
8. My grandmother *worked* at the computer store.

▶ EXERCISE 1   **Forming the Principal Parts of Regular Verbs**

Give the principal parts for each of the following verbs. Remember that some verbs change their spelling when *–ing* or *–ed* is added.

EXAMPLE   **1.** work
          1. *work; (is) working; worked; (have) worked*

1. skate	**4.** move	**7.** enjoy	**9.** laugh
2. pick	**5.** talk	**8.** rob	**10.** love
3. live	**6.** stun		

▶ EXERCISE 2   **Using the Principal Parts of Regular Verbs**

For each of the following sentences, give the form of the italicized verb that will fit correctly in the blank.

EXAMPLE   **1.** *paint*   Henry Ossawa Tanner _____ many kinds of subjects.
          1. *painted*

1. *create* Tanner ____ images of people, nature, history, and religion.
2. *learn* What is the boy in this painting ____ to do?

3. *title* Not surprisingly, Tanner ____ this painting *The Banjo Lesson.*
4. *live* The artist, a native of Philadelphia, ____ from 1859 to 1937.
5. *move* At the age of thirty-two, Tanner ____ to Paris to study and work.
6. *visit* Other African American artists ____ Tanner in France.
7. *admire* For years, people have ____ Tanner's paintings.
8. *plan* Our teacher is ____ to show us more of Tanner's work.
9. *want* I have ____ to see Tanner's portrait of Booker T. Washington.
10. *praise* In his book *Up from Slavery,* Washington ____ Tanner's talent.

USAGE

Irregular Verbs

18c. An *irregular verb* forms its past and past participle in some other way than by adding *–d* or *–ed* to the base form.

An irregular verb forms its past and past participle by

■ changing vowels *or* consonants

BASE FORM	PAST	PAST PARTICIPLE
lend	lent	(have) lent
make	made	(have) made
win	won	(have) won

■ changing vowels *and* consonants

BASE FORM	PAST	PAST PARTICIPLE
catch	caught	(have) caught
draw	drew	(have) drawn
tear	tore	(have) torn

■ making no change

BASE FORM	PAST	PAST PARTICIPLE
burst	burst	(have) burst
cut	cut	(have) cut
hurt	hurt	(have) hurt

NOTE: If you are not sure about the principal parts of a verb, look in a dictionary. Entries for irregular verbs list the principal parts of the verb. If the principal parts are not listed, the verb is a regular verb.

COMMON IRREGULAR VERBS			
BASE FORM	**PRESENT PARTICIPLE**	**PAST**	**PAST PARTICIPLE**
begin	(is) beginning	began	(have) begun
blow	(is) blowing	blew	(have) blown
break	(is) breaking	broke	(have) broken
bring	(is) bringing	brought	(have) brought
choose	(is) choosing	chose	(have) chosen
come	(is) coming	came	(have) come
do	(is) doing	did	(have) done
drink	(is) drinking	drank	(have) drunk
drive	(is) driving	drove	(have) driven
eat	(is) eating	ate	(have) eaten
fall	(is) falling	fell	(have) fallen
freeze	(is) freezing	froze	(have) frozen
give	(is) giving	gave	(have) given
go	(is) going	went	(have) gone
know	(is) knowing	knew	(have) known

USAGE

▶ ORAL PRACTICE 2   **Using Irregular Verbs**

Read each of the following sentences aloud, stressing the italicized verb.

1. I have *begun* to learn karate.
2. We *chose* to stay indoors.
3. Earline has never *drunk* buttermilk before.
4. We *did* our homework after dinner.
5. Anna and Dee have almost *broken* the school record for the fifty-yard dash.
6. The wind has *blown* fiercely for three days.
7. Last Saturday, Isaac *brought* me a tape of reggae music.
8. The water pipes in the laundry room have *frozen* again.

EXERCISE 3 **Identifying the Correct Forms of Irregular Verbs**

For each of the following sentences, choose the correct verb form in parentheses.

1. We had (*began, begun*) our project when I got sick.
2. The Ruiz family (*drove, driven*) across the country.
3. Has anyone (*brung, brought*) extra batteries for the radio?
4. I have finally (*chose, chosen*) the orange kitten.
5. Last week the lake (*froze, frozen*) hard enough for skating.
6. My brother and I have (*gave, given*) away all my comic books to the children's hospital.
7. It is amazing that no one has ever (*fell, fallen*) off the old ladder.
8. Everyone (*went, gone*) back to the classroom to watch the videotape of the spelling bee.
9. David's whole family (*came, come*) for his bar mitzvah.
10. Have you (*ate, eaten*) at the new Philippine restaurant?

PICTURE THIS

Thrills! Chills! Death-defying feats! You are a newspaper reporter covering an air show. You and the rest of the audience are amazed at what the pilots can make their aircraft do. As you watch the aerial stunts shown on the next page, you take notes to use in your article. Jot down details about what you see, hear, and feel. Remember that your readers can share this experience only through your words. In your notes, use the past or past participle forms of at least five irregular verbs from the list on page 481.

Subject: air-show performance
Audience: yourself
Purpose: to record your impressions for use in a
                newspaper article

USAGE

MORE COMMON IRREGULAR VERBS			
BASE FORM	**PRESENT PARTICIPLE**	**PAST**	**PAST PARTICIPLE**
lead	(is) leading	led	(have) led
ride	(is) riding	rode	(have) ridden
ring	(is) ringing	rang	(have) rung
run	(is) running	ran	(have) run
see	(is) seeing	saw	(have) seen
shrink	(is) shrinking	shrank	(have) shrunk
sing	(is) singing	sang	(have) sung
sink	(is) sinking	sank	(have) sunk
speak	(is) speaking	spoke	(have) spoken
steal	(is) stealing	stole	(have) stolen
swim	(is) swimming	swam	(have) swum
take	(is) taking	took	(have) taken
throw	(is) throwing	threw	(have) thrown
wear	(is) wearing	wore	(have) worn
write	(is) writing	wrote	(have) written

USAGE

ORAL
PRACTICE 3   **Using Irregular Verbs**

Read each of the following sentences aloud, stressing
the italicized verb.

1. Despite the blinding snowstorm, the German shepherd had *led* the rescue party to the stranded hikers.
2. The school bell *rang* five minutes late every
   afternoon this week.
3. In New York, Julia *saw* the musical *Cats*.
4. How many sixth-graders have never *ridden* on
   the school bus?
5. What is the longest distance you have ever *swum*?
6. George *ran* to the corner to see the antique fire
   engine.
7. Gloria Estefan *sang* on the awards show.
8. Have you ever *written* haiku?

FAMILY CIRCUS

Copyright 1982
The Register and Tribune
Syndicate, Inc.

KEANE

"You don't say 'He taked my chair'
. . . it's 'My chair was tooken'."

EXERCISE 4 **Identifying the Correct Forms of Irregular Verbs**

For each of the following sentences, choose the correct verb form in parentheses.

1. Who (*ran, run*) faster, Jesse or Cindy?
2. That cute little puppy has (*stole, stolen*) a biscuit.
3. The Boys Choir of Harlem has never (*sang, sung*) more beautifully.
4. Jimmy's toy boat (*sank, sunk*) to the bottom of the lake.
5. Have you (*throwed, thrown*) away yesterday's paper?
6. Maria had (*wore, worn*) her new spring outfit to the party.
7. Until yesterday, no one had ever (*swam, swum*) across Crystal Lake.
8. In *Alice's Adventures in Wonderland*, Alice (*shrank, shrunk*) to a very small size!
9. The students have (*wrote, written*) a letter to the mayor.
10. I have never (*spoke, spoken*) to a large audience before.

REVIEW A **Proofreading for Errors in Irregular Verbs**

Most of the following sentences contain incorrect verb forms. Find each error and write the correct form of the verb. If a sentence is correct, write *C*.

EXAMPLE **1.** Many stories have been wrote about the American athlete Jesse Owens.
    1. *wrote—written*

1. Owens breaked several sports records during his career.
2. At the Olympic games of 1936, he winned four gold medals.

USAGE

3. A photographer took this picture of one of Owens's victories.
4. Owens's career begun in an unusual way.
5. As a little boy, Owens had been very sick, and later he run to strengthen his lungs.
6. In high school, the other boys on the track team did their practicing after school, but Owens had to work.
7. Owens's coach encouraged him to practice an hour before school and brung him breakfast every morning.
8. The coach knowed Owens's parents couldn't afford to send their son to college.
9. The coach seen that something had to be done, and he helped Owens's father find a job.
10. Later, Owens went to Ohio State University, where he became a track star.

> REVIEW B

Writing the Past and Past Participle Forms of Verbs

For each of the following sentences, give the past or past participle form of the verb that will fit correctly in the blank.

EXAMPLE   **1.** *take*   Gloria has ＿＿ the last game card.
          1. *taken*

1. *do*   Has everyone ＿＿ the assignment for today?
2. *burst*   Suddenly, the door ＿＿ open.
3. *drive*   We have ＿＿ on Oklahoma's Indian Nation Turnpike.
4. *eat*   Have you ＿＿ lunch yet?
5. *speak*   Who ＿＿ at this year's Hispanic Heritage awards ceremony?
6. *blow*   She ＿＿ out the candles on the cake.
7. *fall*   One of the hikers had ＿＿ into the river.
8. *give*   Mrs. Matsuo ＿＿ me a copy of the book *Origami: Japanese Paper-Folding*.
9. *freeze* The water in the birdbath has ＿＿ again.
10. *choose* Which play have they ＿＿ to perform?
11. *wear*   The Highland School Band has always ＿＿ Scottish kilts.
12. *know*   Noriko ＿＿ the way to Lynn's house.
13. *write* Ms. Brook has ＿＿ letters to all of us.
14. *shrink* My sweater ＿＿, so I gave it to my little sister.
15. *ring*   Who ＿＿ the doorbell a moment ago?
16. *drink* The puppy has ＿＿ all the water in the dish.
17. *steal* David ＿＿ third base in the ninth inning.
18. *swim*   Have you ＿＿ in the new pool at the park?
19. *see*   We had never ＿＿ a koala before.
20. *come*   Jerome ＿＿ early to help us with the decorations.

USAGE

▶ REVIEW C   **Revising Incorrect Verb Forms in Sentences**

Read each of the following sentences. If the form of a verb is wrong, write the correct form. If the sentence is correct, write *C*.

EXAMPLE   **1.** Dr. Seuss knowed how to please readers of all ages.
            1. *knew*

1. Have you ever saw either of the wacky characters shown below?
2. The imagination of Dr. Seuss brought both of them to life.
3. You may have bursted out laughing at the Cat in the Hat, Horton the elephant, the Grinch, or the Lorax.

4. In one story, the mean Grinch stoled Christmas.
5. In another, a bird gived Horton an egg to hatch.
6. The Lorax spoke out in support of the trees and the environment.

7. The Cat in the Hat has always wore his crazy hat.
8. During his lifetime, Dr. Seuss must have wrote about fifty books with unusual characters.
9. Many children have began reading with his books.
10. Dr. Seuss choosed *The Lorax* as his own favorite book.

Tense

18d. The *tense* of a verb indicates the time of the action or the state of being expressed by the verb.

Every verb has six tenses.

Present	Past	Future
Present Perfect	Past Perfect	Future Perfect

The following time line shows the relationships between tenses.

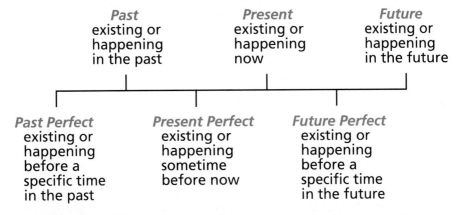

Past
existing or happening in the past

Present
existing or happening now

Future
existing or happening in the future

Past Perfect
existing or happening before a specific time in the past

Present Perfect
existing or happening sometime before now

Future Perfect
existing or happening before a specific time in the future

Listing all the forms of a verb is called *conjugating* the verb.

CONJUGATION OF THE VERB *WEAR*

PRESENT TENSE

SINGULAR	PLURAL
I wear	we wear
you wear	you wear
he, she, or it wears	they wear

PAST TENSE

SINGULAR	PLURAL
I wore	we wore
you wore	you wore
he, she, or it wore	they wore

FUTURE TENSE

SINGULAR	PLURAL
I will (shall) wear	we will (shall) wear
you will wear	you will wear
he, she, or it will wear	they will wear

PRESENT PERFECT TENSE

SINGULAR	PLURAL
I have worn	we have worn
you have worn	you have worn
he, she, or it has worn	they have worn

PAST PERFECT TENSE

SINGULAR	PLURAL
I had worn	we had worn
you had worn	you had worn
he, she, or it had worn	they had worn

FUTURE PERFECT TENSE

SINGULAR	PLURAL
I will (shall) have worn	we will (shall) have worn
you will have worn	you will have worn
he, she, or it will have worn	they will have worn

USAGE

> EXERCISE 5 **Writing Sentences with Different Tenses**

Do you ever make up stories about pictures or paintings? Look at this painting by Norman Rockwell. What is the story behind this scene? Write five sentences telling what you think is happening, has happened, and will happen in this winter scene. Use a different tense in each sentence. Be prepared to tell what tenses you've used. If you wish, give names to the man, the boy, and the dog.

EXAMPLE **1.** *The boy and his dog have hidden from the man.*

Six Confusing Verbs

Sit and *Set*

The verb *sit* means "to be seated" or "to rest." *Sit* seldom takes an object.

The verb *set* means "to place (something)" or "to put (something)." *Set* usually takes an object. Notice that *set* has the same form for the base form, past, and past participle.

BASE FORM	PRESENT PARTICIPLE	PAST	PAST PARTICIPLE
sit	(is) sitting	sat	(have) sat
set	(is) setting	set	(have) set

EXAMPLES   **I will sit** in the easy chair. [no object]
I will set the book on the counter. [I will set what? *Book* is the object.]

Shannon **has sat** there for an hour. [no object]
The workers **have set** their equipment aside. [The workers have set what? *Equipment* is the object.]

NOTE: If you don't know whether to use *sit* or *set* in a sentence, try substituting *put.* If the sentence makes sense with *put,* use *set.*

ORAL PRACTICE 4   **Using the Forms of *Sit* and *Set* Correctly**

Read each of the following sentences aloud, stressing the italicized verb.

1. Josie *set* two loaves of French bread on the kitchen table.
2. The clown *sat* on the broken chair.
3. Let's *sit* down and rest awhile.
4. Did you *set* your bracelet on the night stand?

5. The Clarks' car has *sat* in the driveway for a week.
6. My little brother *sits* still for only a few seconds at a time.
7. The teacher *sets* the best projects in the display case.
8. The librarian *set* the book about Michael Jordan on the table.

▶ EXERCISE 6   **Writing the Forms of *Sit* and *Set***

For the blank in each of the following sentences, give the correct form of *sit* or *set*.

EXAMPLE   **1.** The twins ___ together on the porch swing.
            1. *sat*

1. At the party yesterday, we ___ the birthday presents on the coffee table.
2. Then we ___ on the floor to play a game.
3. Alana always ___ next to Rosa.
4. The Jiménez twins never ___ together, even on their birthday.
5. Mrs. Jiménez ___ a large cake on the table in the dining room.
6. Mr. Jiménez had already ___ party hats and favors around the table.
7. One of the twins ___ on a hat by mistake.
8. Mr. Jiménez ___ out another plate.
9. At every party we always ___ quietly while the birthday person makes a wish.
10. Yesterday we ___ still twice as long for the Jiménez twins!

Rise and *Raise*

The verb *rise* means "to go upward" or "to get up." *Rise* never takes an object.

The verb *raise* means "to lift (something) up." *Raise* usually takes a direct object.

USAGE

BASE FORM	PRESENT PARTICIPLE	PAST	PAST PARTICIPLE
rise	(is) rising	rose	(have) risen
raise	(is) raising	raised	(have) raised

EXAMPLES   The full moon **is rising.** [no object]
The winner **is raising** her arms in triumph. [The winner is raising what? *Arms* is the object.]

The kite **rose** quickly in the wind. [no object]
Congress **raised** taxes again. [Congress raised what? *Taxes* is the object.]

ORAL **Using the Forms of *Rise* and *Raise***
PRACTICE 5 **Correctly**

Read each of the following sentences aloud, stressing the italicized verb.

1. The audience had *risen* from their seats to applaud Mariah Carey.
2. They *raised* the curtains for the play to start.
3. Dark smoke *rose* from the fire.
4. They always *rise* early on Saturday mornings.
5. The wind will *raise* the Chinese dragon kite high above the trees.
6. Has the sun *risen* yet?
7. The huge crane can *raise* the steel beams off the ground.
8. Bread dough *rises* very slowly in a cold room.

EXERCISE 7   **Writing the Forms of *Rise* and *Raise***

For the blank in each of the following sentences, supply the correct form of *rise* or *raise*.

EXAMPLE   **1.** If our team wins, we will ____ the victory flag.
         1. *raise*

1. Before the game the color guards ____ the flag.
2. The fans ____ for the national anthem.

3. The pitcher ___ his arm to throw the ball.
4. The baseball seemed to ___ above the batter's head.
5. Someone in front of me ___ and blocked my view.
6. I have ___ my voice to cheer a hundred times during one game.
7. If the sun ___ too high, the players can't see the high fly ball.
8. Whenever someone hits a home run, the fans ___ their mitts to catch the baseball.
9. Yesterday everyone ___ when Marcus Jackson hit a home run.
10. As soon as the ninth inning was over, we ___ to leave.

USAGE

Lie and *Lay*

The verb *lie* means "to recline," "to be in a place," or "to remain lying down." *Lie* never takes an object.

The verb *lay* means "to put (something) down" or "to place (something)." *Lay* usually takes an object.

BASE FORM	PRESENT PARTICIPLE	PAST	PAST PARTICIPLE
lie	(is) lying	lay	(have) lain
lay	(is) laying	laid	(have) laid

EXAMPLES   My new wristwatch **is lying** on the dresser. [no object]
The workers **are laying** the new carpet. [The workers are laying what? *Carpet* is the object.]

These clothes **have lain** in the corner for days. [no object]
They **have laid** the beach blanket under the umbrella. [They have laid what? *Blanket* is the object.]

ORAL
PRACTICE 6

**Using the Forms of *Lie* and *Lay*
Correctly**

Read each of the following sentences aloud, stressing
the italicized verb.

1. The corrected test paper *lay* on the desk.
2. My teddy bear has *lain* under my bed for a long
   time.
3. Before the sale, the clerk *laid* samples on the
   counter.
4. Have those toys *lain* outside too long?
5. The Inuit hunter *laid* his harpoon on the ice.
6. Last night, I was *lying* on the sofa and reading
   Sounder when the phone rang.
7. The hero has *laid* a trap for the villain.
8. Finally, the baby *lay* quietly in the crib.

EXERCISE 8   **Writing the Forms of *Lie* and *Lay***

For each blank in the following sentences, supply the
correct form of *lie* or *lay*.

EXAMPLE   **1.** Children often ____ their toys and other things
                 in the wrong places.
           1. *lay*

1. The remote control for the television is ____ under
   the chair.
2. How long has it ____ there?
3. My brother Ramón probably ____ it there last
   night.
4. He was ____ on the floor, watching television.
5. Julia, my younger sister, always ____ her toys in
   front of the television set.
6. She has ____ little parts from her games all over
   the house.
7. Whenever Mom and Dad find one of these
   parts, they usually ____ it on the bookcase.
8. Yesterday, Dad ____ down on some hard plastic
   pieces on the sofa.

USAGE

9. Now those broken bits of plastic ___ at the bottom of the wastebasket.
10. Today, Julia has ___ every single toy safely in the toy chest.

REVIEW D

Identifying the Correct Forms of *Sit* and *Set*, *Rise* and *Raise*, and *Lie* and *Lay*

For each of the following sentences, choose the correct verb in parentheses.

EXAMPLE **1.** Dad (*sat, set*) the pictures from our visit to the Hopi Reservation on the table.
1. *set*

1. Do you know what kind of doll is (*lying, laying*) in this Hopi girl's arms?

2. Someone had (*lain, laid*) down a kachina doll, and this girl picked it up.
3. A Hopi artist probably (*sat, set*) for hours working on this one doll.
4. At the reservation, everyone (*sat, set*) quietly during the Hopi Snake Dance.

5. One dancer (*rose, raised*) a snake above his head for the crowd to see.
6. The growing corn (*rises, raises*) high in the Hopi country of Arizona.
7. Hot and tired, I (*lay, laid*) on a bench at the Hopi trading post.
8. When we entered the pueblo, a Hopi woman (*rose, raised*) from her chair to greet us.
9. Dad had (*rose, raised*) his camera to take the woman's picture.
10. Smiling, the woman (*sat, set*) a beautiful coiled basket on the shelf behind her.

▶ REVIEW E   **Proofreading for Correct Verb Forms**

For each of the following sentences, identify the incorrect verb form. Then give the correct form.

EXAMPLE   **1.** Lately, everyone in our neighborhood has did a lot more to keep physically fit.
 1. *did—done*

1. No one is setting down anymore—except on stationary bicycles.
2. My mom has rode 150 miles so far.
3. In addition, I have never knew so many aerobic dancers.
4. Yesterday afternoon, I swum twelve laps in the pool myself.
5. Last month, a famous exercise instructor choosed our neighborhood for her new fitness center.
6. Many people seen her interviews on local talk shows.
7. All of a sudden, adults and children have began going to the center.
8. Each person is suppose to use different kinds of equipment.
9. Last night, I rose fifty pounds of weights.
10. So far, no one has broke a leg on the cross-country ski machine.

WRITING APPLICATION

Using Verb Forms Correctly to Make Writing Clear

A sentence without a verb is like a sailboat without a sail. Just as a sail moves a sailboat forward, a verb carries a sentence forward. If you use the wrong form or tense of a verb, your sentence won't go where you want it to go. Look at the two pairs of sentences below.

CONFUSING   In the future, people will have wore different clothes than they did now. The clothes are made of a shiny, dirt-resistant fabric.

CLEAR   In the future, people **will wear** different clothes than they **do** now. The clothes **will be made** of a shiny, dirt-resistant fabric.

USAGE

WRITING ACTIVITY

Many scientists and writers make predictions about the future. They base their predictions on past and present trends. You've decided to write a story set in the future. First, you need to imagine what the future will be like. Write a paragraph or two describing how an everyday item such as a car, a house, a home appliance, or a school might be different one hundred years from now. In your description, be sure to use the correct forms and tenses of verbs.

Prewriting   Choose a topic that interests you, such as "video games" or "skyscrapers." Based on what you already know about the topic, make some predictions about the future. Jot down as many details as you can think of. For example, if you're writing about cars of the future, tell what the cars will look like, how fast they will go, and what kind of fuel they will use.

Writing   Begin your draft by telling what time period your predictions are for. Then use your notes to write a clear, vivid description of something in that future time. You may want to compare a present-day example of the item with your prediction of what the item will be like in the future.

Evaluating and Revising Ask a friend to read your description. Is it clear and believable? Do the details help your reader picture the item you've described? If not, you'll need to add, cut, or revise details. Make sure you've used the correct tense for each of your verbs.

Proofreading Read your paragraph carefully to check for errors in grammar, spelling, or punctuation. Take special care with the forms of verbs. Use a dictionary to check the forms of any verbs you're not sure about.

Review: Posttest

Revising Incorrect Verb Forms in Sentences

Most of the following sentences contain an error in the use of a verb. If a verb is incorrect, give the correct verb form. If the sentence is correct, write C.

EXAMPLE   **1.** The last movie I seen was terrible.
          1. *saw*

1. My friends and I have set through several bad movies.
2. Has anyone ever wrote a letter to complain about how many bad movies there are?
3. Last Saturday they run two bad movies!
4. My friends J.D. and Conchita had went with me to our neighborhood theater.
5. We had hoped we would enjoy *Out of the Swamp.*

6. In the beginning of the movie, a huge swamp creature raised out of the muddy water.
7. It begun to crawl slowly toward a cow in a field.
8. The cow had been laying under a tree.
9. She never even seen the swamp monster.
10. I sunk back in my seat, expecting the monster to pounce.
11. Then the lights come back on.
12. What a disappointment—the film inside the projector had broke!
13. It taked a long time before the machine came back on.
14. Some children got bored and throwed popcorn up in the air.
15. Others drunk noisily through their straws.
16. I had sat my popcorn on the floor, and someone kicked it over.
17. Finally, the theater manager choosed another movie to show us, but it was only a silly cartoon about a penguin.
18. The penguin wore a fur coat it had stole from a sleeping polar bear.
19. The bear awoke, become angry, and chased the penguin.
20. Finally, the penguin gave back the coat and swum to Miami Beach to get warm.

19 USING PRONOUNS CORRECTLY

Subject and Object Forms

Diagnostic Test

Identifying Correct Pronoun Forms

For each of the following sentences, choose the correct form of the pronoun in parentheses.

EXAMPLE **1.** Our parents and (*they, them*) play tennis together.
1. *they*

1. Could it be (*she, her*) at the bus stop?
2. The guest speakers were Sandra Cisneros and (*he, him*).
3. Are you and (*they, them*) going to the basketball game?

4. You and (*I, me*) have been friends for a long time.
5. Sometimes, even our parents cannot tell (*we, us*) twins apart.
6. (*We, Us*) players surprised the coach with a victory party.
7. (*Who, Whom*) is bringing the holiday turkey?
8. Latisha lent my sister and (*I, me*) the new Celia Cruz CD.
9. Mr. Lee will divide the money between you and (*I, me*).
10. To (*who, whom*) is the envelope addressed?

The Forms of Personal Pronouns

The form of a personal pronoun shows its use in a sentence. Pronouns used as subjects and predicate nominatives are in the *subject form.*

EXAMPLES   **He** and **I** went to the post office. [subject]
The winner of the marathon is **she.** [predicate nominative]

Pronouns used as direct objects and indirect objects of verbs and as objects of prepositions are in the *object form.*

EXAMPLES   Mr. García helped **him** and **me** with yesterday's homework. [direct objects]
The clerk gave **us** the package. [indirect object]
When is Theo going to give the flowers to **her**? [object of a preposition]

The *possessive form* (*my, your, his, her, its, their, our*) is used to show ownership or relationship.

☞ REFERENCE NOTE: For more about possessive forms, see pages 376 and 624–628.

PERSONAL PRONOUNS			
SUBJECT FORM		**OBJECT FORM**	
Singular	**Plural**	**Singular**	**Plural**
I	we	me	us
you	you	you	you
he, she, it	they	him, her, it	them

Notice that the pronouns *you* and *it* are the same in the subject form and object form.

USAGE

▶ EXERCISE 1   **Classifying Pronouns**

Classify each of the following pronouns as the *subject form* or *object form*. If the pronoun can be either the subject form or the object form, write *either*.

EXAMPLE   **1.** they
        1. *subject form*

1. him	**3.** it	**5.** she	**7.** you	**9.** her
2. me	**4.** we	**6.** them	**8.** I	**10.** us

▶ EXERCISE 2   **Classifying Pronouns in Sentences**

In the following sentences, identify each pronoun in italics as either a *subject form* or an *object form*.

EXAMPLE   **1.** Ever since *he* could remember, Edward
        Bannister had wanted to be an artist.
        1. *subject form*

1. *He* had to work hard to reach his goal.
2. *We* consider Bannister an American artist, but he was born in Canada.
3. Bannister's parents died when *he* was young.
4. The little money *they* had was left to their son.
5. The young Bannister couldn't afford paper, so *he* drew on barn doors and fences.

6. Later, Bannister met Christiana Carteaux and married *her*.
7. *She* was from Rhode Island, where her people, the Narragansett, lived.
8. In 1876, a Philadelphia artistic society recognized Bannister by awarding *him* a gold medal for the painting shown below.
9. Bannister treasured his prize and regarded *it* as a great honor.
10. What do *you* think of the painting?

Edward Bannister, *Under the Oaks* (1876). Oil on canvas. National Museum of American Art, Smithsonian Institution. Gift of the Frank Family/Art Resource, New York.

Under the Oaks

USAGE

The Subject Form

19a. Use the subject form for a pronoun that is the subject of a verb.

EXAMPLES **I walked to school.** [*I* is the subject of the verb *walked.*]
He and she live on the Tigua reservation in El Paso, Texas. [*He* and *she* are the compound subject of the verb *live.*]

USAGE

▶ ORAL
PRACTICE 1 **Using Pronouns as Subjects**

Read the following sentences aloud, stressing the italicized pronouns.

1. *She* and Ahmed solve crossword puzzles.
2. *They* are very hard puzzles to solve.
3. Dad and *I* finished putting together a jigsaw puzzle last night.
4. *We* worked for three hours!
5. Finally, *you* and *he* found the missing pieces.
6. *He* and *I* liked the completed picture of flamenco dancers.
7. *They* are gypsies from Spain.
8. *We* would like to see a colorful gypsy dance.

To test if a pronoun is used correctly in a compound subject, try each form of the pronoun separately.

EXAMPLE: Tina and (*he, him*) always win.
He always wins.
Him always wins.
ANSWER: **Tina and he always win.**

EXAMPLE: (*She, Her*) and (*I, me*) practiced hard.
She practiced hard.
Her practiced hard.
I practiced hard.
Me practiced hard.
ANSWER: **She and I practiced hard.**

▶ EXERCISE 3 **Identifying the Correct Forms of Pronouns**

For each of the following sentences, choose the correct form of the pronoun in parentheses.

EXAMPLE **1.** Brad and (*me, I*) wrote a skit based on the myth about Pygmalion.
1. *I*

1. (*Him, He*) and I thought the myth was funny.
2. (*We, Us*) asked Angela to play a part in the skit.
3. Neither (*she, her*) nor Doreen wanted to play a statue that came to life.
4. Finally Brad and (*me, I*) convinced Doreen that it would be a funny version of the myth.
5. (*Him, He*) and I flipped a coin to see who would play the part of Pygmalion.
6. The next day (*we, us*) were ready to perform.
7. Doreen and (*me, I*) began giggling when Brad pretended to be the beautiful statue.
8. In the skit, when Pygmalion returned from the festival of Venus, (*him, he*) and the statue were supposed to hug.
9. Instead of hugging, (*they, them*) laughed too hard to say the lines correctly.
10. Doreen, Brad, and (*I, me*) finally took a bow, and the class applauded.

19b. Use the subject form for a pronoun that is a predicate nominative.

A *predicate nominative* follows a linking verb and explains or identifies the subject of the sentence. A pronoun used as a predicate nominative usually follows a form of the verb *be* (such as *am, are, is, was, were, be, been,* or *being*).

EXAMPLES   The next singer is **she.** [*She* follows the linking verb *is* and identifies the subject *singer.*]
The first speakers might be **he** and **I.** [*He* and *I* follow the linking verb *might be* and identify the subject *speakers.*]

NOTE: Expressions such as *It's me* or *That's him* are acceptable in everyday speaking. In writing, however, such expressions should be avoided.

☞ REFERENCE NOTE: For more information about predicate nominatives, see page 447.

USAGE

▶ ORAL
PRACTICE 2
Using Pronouns as Predicate Nominatives

Read the following sentences aloud, stressing the italicized pronouns.

1. The stars of *The Man from Snowy River* were *he* and *she*.
2. The actors from Australia must be *they*.
3. Of course, the mountain man is *he*.
4. Was the actress really *she*?
5. The director could have been *he*.
6. The villains are *he* and *they*.
7. The movie's biggest fans may be *you* and *I*.
8. The next ones to rent the film will be *we*.

▶ EXERCISE 4
Writing Sentences with Pronouns Used as Predicate Nominatives

For the following sentences, supply pronouns to fill in the blanks. Use a variety of pronouns, but do not use *you* or *it*.

EXAMPLE **1.** The people in the silliest costumes were ____.
          1. *she and they*

1. The person in the gorilla suit must be ____.
2. The next contestants will be ____ and ____.
3. The winners should have been ____.
4. Can that singer be ____?
5. It was ____ sitting in the back row.

▶ EXERCISE 5
Identifying Pronouns Used as Predicate Nominatives

For each of the following sentences, choose the correct form of the pronoun in parentheses.

1. Was that (*he, him*) at the door?
2. The winners are you and (*me, I*).
3. The cooks for the traditional Vietnamese meal were (*them, they*).

4. Could it have been (*we, us*)?
5. Every year the speaker has been (*her, she*).
6. That was Carl and (*they, them*) in the swimming pool.
7. The volleyball fans in our family are Dad and (*she, her*).
8. First on the Black History Month program will be (*us, we*).
9. It might have been (*he, him*).
10. Last year, the class treasurer was (*he, him*).

▶ REVIEW A **Identifying the Correct Use of Pronouns**

For each of the following sentences, choose the correct form of the pronoun in parentheses.

EXAMPLE **1.** Last summer Carl, Felicia, and (*we, us*) went to San Antonio.
1. *we*

1. Carl and (*she, her*) took these photographs.
2. Early one morning (*he, him*) and (*she, her*) visited the Alamo.

3. That could be (*he, him*) in the crowd outside the Alamo.
4. Felicia and (*I, me*) listened to a mariachi band on the Riverwalk.

USAGE

5. Of course, the guitar players in the picture below are (*they, them*).
6. Don't (*they, them*) look as though they're having a good time?
7. Carl and (*I, me*) enjoyed visiting the Spanish Governor's Palace.
8. Felicia, Carl, and (*we, us*) particularly liked this adobe building.
9. In fact, the first guests there that morning were (*us, we*).
10. Maybe you and (*they, them*) will get a chance to visit San Antonio someday.

Spanish Governor's Palace

Riverwalk

WRITING APPLICATION

Using Correct Pronoun Forms in Writing

When you write a story or a report, you want your writing to be its best. Read the following two sentences. Which would be better to use in a report for school?

> Luisa and me will dress up as giant toothbrushes for the skit.
>
> Luisa and I will dress up as giant toothbrushes for the skit.

You might hear the first sentence spoken in a casual conversation. However, the second sentence is better to use in a report. In school or in any other formal situation, your audience usually expects you to follow the rules and guidelines of formal English.

▶ WRITING ACTIVITY

Health Awareness Week is coming up soon. Your class has been chosen to perform a skit on a health-related topic for the rest of the school. Your teacher has asked each class member to write down an idea for an entertaining, informative skit. Write a paragraph or two describing a skit that your class could perform. Be sure to use correct pronoun forms in your description.

USAGE

Prewriting First, you'll need to decide on a topic for the skit. Think about the health concerns of people your age. For example, you might plan a skit about the dangers of smoking or the importance of regular dental check-ups. After you choose a topic, brainstorm some ideas for a simple, entertaining skit. Be sure to list any props or costumes your class will need.

Writing Use your notes to help you write your draft. First, tell what the skit is about and why it is appropriate for Health Awareness Week. Then, explain what happens in the skit from beginning to end. Be sure to tell in a general way what each character does and says. Describe the props and costumes that your class can make or bring from home.

Evaluating and Revising Ask a classmate to read your paragraph. Is the information given in the skit correct? Does the skit sound entertaining? Is it clear which character does and says what? If not, revise your paragraph. Add details that will make the skit more fun and interesting. Check your sentences to be sure you've used pronouns correctly and clearly.

Proofreading and Publishing Read through your description carefully to check for errors in grammar, spelling, or punctuation. Use this chapter to help you check for errors in pronoun forms. Your class may want to hold a contest for the best skit idea. Using the best idea, work together to develop the skit in more detail. Then, with your teacher's permission, give a performance of the skit for other classes.

The Object Form

19c. Use the object form for a pronoun that is the direct object of a verb.

A *direct object* follows an action verb and tells *who* or *what* receives the action of the verb.

EXAMPLES   The teacher thanked **me** for cleaning the chalkboard. [*Teacher* is the subject of the verb *thanked.* The teacher thanked whom? The direct object is *me.*]

The answer surprised **us.** [*Answer* is the subject of the verb *surprised.* The answer surprised whom? The direct object is *us.*]

Fred saw **them** and **me** last night. [*Fred* is the subject of the verb *saw.* Fred saw whom? The direct objects are *them* and *me.*]

To help you choose the correct pronoun in a compound object, try each pronoun separately in the sentence.

EXAMPLE: Ms. Stone praised Alonzo and (*we, us*).
             Ms. Stone praised *we.*
             Ms. Stone praised *us.*
ANSWER: Ms. Stone praised Alonzo and **us.**

👉 REFERENCE NOTE: For more about direct objects, see
     page 439.

🔲▶ ORAL
     PRACTICE 3   **Using Pronouns as Direct Objects**

Read the following sentences aloud, stressing the italicized pronouns.

1. Kathy found *them* and *me* by the fountain.
2. Mr. Winters took *us* to the rodeo.
3. Did you see *her* and *him* at the Cajun restaurant?
4. Tyrone frightened *us* with his rubber spider.
5. Ellis invited Luis, Jiro, and *me* to his party.
6. The mayor met *them* at Howard University.
7. Uncle Ken thanked *her* for the gift.
8. The fans cheered Anthony and *her.*

🔲▶ EXERCISE 6   **Identifying Pronouns Used as
                  Direct Objects**

For each of the following sentences, choose the correct form of the pronoun in parentheses.

1. Mrs. Freeman invited Leroy and (*I, me*) to a
    Kwanzaa party.
2. The spectators watched (*we, us*) and (*they, them*).
3. The shoes don't fit either (*her, she*) or (*I, me*).
4. Sean called Marco and (*he, him*) on the telephone.
5. Our new neighbors asked (*we, us*) for directions
    to the synagogue.
6. The new neighbors hired Tía and (*us, we*) to
    rake their yard.
7. The puppy followed Louis and (*he, him*) all the
    way home.

USAGE

8. Last week, friends from Panama visited (*us, we*).
9. Odessa thanked (*her, she*) and (*me, I*) for helping.
10. The usher showed Greg and (*them, they*) to their seats.

19d. Use the object form for a pronoun that is the indirect object of a verb.

An ***indirect object*** comes between an action verb and a direct object. The indirect object tells *to whom* or *to what* or *for whom* or *for what* something is done.

EXAMPLES **Scott handed me a note.** [Scott handed what? *Note* is the direct object. To whom did he hand a note? The indirect object is *me.*]

Coretta baked them some muffins. [*Coretta* baked what? *Muffins* is the direct object. For whom did Coretta bake muffins? The indirect object is *them.*]

Elizabeth sent him and me some oranges from Florida. [Elizabeth sent what? *Oranges* is the direct object. To whom did Elizabeth send oranges? The indirect objects are *him* and *me.*]

ORAL
PRACTICE 4   **Using Pronouns as Indirect Objects**

Read the following sentences aloud, stressing the italicized pronouns.

1. Mr. Krebs showed Bill and *them* the rock collection.
2. Paco told *me* the answer to the riddle.
3. Mr. Thibaut gives *us* lacrosse lessons.
4. We bought *her* and *him* a present.
5. The artists drew *us* and *them* some pictures.
6. The server brought *me* a bagel with cream cheese.
7. A pen pal in Hawaii sent *her* some shells.
8. My uncle Shannon told *us* a funny story about leprechauns.

USAGE

> ▶ EXERCISE 7

Identifying the Correct Forms of Pronouns Used as Indirect Objects

For each of the following sentences, choose the correct form of the pronoun in each set of parentheses.

EXAMPLE   **1.** At the start of class, Mr. Chou assigned (*we, us*) new seats.
   1. *us*

1. The store clerk gave (*they, them*) a discount.
2. For lunch, Anthony fixed (*he, him*) and (*she, her*) bean burritos.
3. Would you please show (*her, she*) and (*me, I*) that Navajo dream catcher?
4. Those green apples gave both Earl and (*he, him*) stomachaches.
5. The waiter brought (*us, we*) some ice water.
6. Why don't you sing (*she, her*) a lullaby?
7. Have they made (*we, us*) the costumes for the play?
8. An usher handed (*me, I*) a program of the recital.
9. The Red Cross volunteers showed (*we, us*) and (*they, them*) a movie about first aid.
10. Please send (*I, me*) your new address.

> ▶ REVIEW B

Revising Incorrect Pronoun Forms in Paragraphs

In most of the sentences in the following paragraphs, at least one pronoun has been used incorrectly. Identify each incorrect pronoun and give the correct form. If all of the pronouns in a sentence are correct, write *C*.

EXAMPLE   [1] Ms. Fisher took several of my friends and I to the museum.
   1. *I—me*

[1] At the Museum of Natural History, Luisa and me wanted to see the American Indian exhibit. [2] The

museum guide showed she and I the displays of Hopi pottery and baskets. [3] Both she and I were especially interested in the kachina dolls. [4] After half an hour, Ms. Fisher found us. [5] Then Luisa, her, and I joined the rest of the group. [6] Another guide had been giving Ms. Fisher and them information about the Masai people in Africa. [7] Them and us decided to see the ancient Egyptian exhibit next.

[8] A group of little children passed Ms. Fisher and we on the stairway, going to the exhibit. [9] It was them who reached the exhibit first. [10] Jeff, the jokester, said that they wanted to find their "mummies." [11] Ms. Fisher and us laughed at the terrible pun. [12] She gave him a pat on the back. [13] We asked her not to encourage him. [14] The museum guide led the children and we to the back of the room. [15] There, he showed us and they a model of a pyramid. [16] Then Ms. Fisher and him explained how the Egyptians prepared mummies. [17] It must have been her who asked about King Tutankhamen. [18] Of course, Luisa and I recognized this golden mask right away. [19] As we were leaving, the guide gave the children and we some booklets about King Tut and other famous ancient Egyptians. [20] The ones he handed Luisa and I were about the builders of the pyramids.

19e. Use the object form for a pronoun that is the object of a preposition.

The *object of a preposition* is a noun or a pronoun that follows a preposition. Together, the preposition, its object, and any modifiers of that object make a *prepositional phrase*.

EXAMPLES   above **me**   beside **us**   with **them**
               for **him**   toward **you** next to **her**

☞ REFERENCE NOTE: For a list of prepositions, see page 407.

When a preposition is followed by two or more pronouns, try each pronoun alone to be sure that you have used the correct form.

EXAMPLE: The puppy walked behind Tom and (*I, me*).
             The puppy walked behind I.
             The puppy walked behind me.
ANSWER: The puppy walked behind Tom and **me.**

EXAMPLE: Carrie divided the chores between (*they, them*) and (*we, us*).
             Carrie divided the chores between they.
             Carrie divided the chores between them.
             Carrie divided the chores between we.
             Carrie divided the chores between us.
ANSWER: Carrie divided the chores between **them** and **us.**

ORAL
PRACTICE 5

Using Pronouns as Objects of Prepositions

Read the following sentences aloud, stressing the italicized pronouns.

1. The lemonade stand was built by Chuck and *me.*
2. The younger children rode in front of *us.*
3. Just between *you* and *me,* that game wasn't much fun.
4. Everyone has gone except the Taylors and *them.*
5. Give the message to *him* or *her.*
6. Why don't you sit here beside *me?*

7. Were those pictures of Amish farmhouses taken by *him*?
8. Donna went to the Cinco de Mayo parade with *them*.

 EXERCISE 8

Identifying the Correct Forms of Pronouns Used as Objects of Prepositions

For each of the following sentences, choose the correct form of the pronoun in parentheses.

EXAMPLE   **1.** Someone should have sent an invitation to (*they, them*).
                 1. *them*

1. In the first round, Michael Chang played against (*he, him*).
2. Did you sit with Martha or (*her, she*) at the game?
3. Peggy sent homemade birthday cards to you and (*them, they*).
4. There is a bee flying around (*he, him*) and you.
5. If you have a complaint, tell it to Mr. Ramis or (*she, her*).
6. Ms. Young divided the projects among (*us, we*).
7. This secret is strictly between you and (*me, I*).
8. Can you believe the weather balloon dropped in front of (*we, us*)?
9. Please don't ride the Alaskan ferry without Jim and (*I, me*).
10. One of the clowns threw confetti at us and (*they, them*).

Special Pronoun Problems

Who and *Whom*

The pronoun *who* has two different forms. *Who* is the subject form. *Whom* is the object form.

When you are choosing between *who* or *whom* in a question, follow these steps:

STEP 1: Rephrase the question as a statement.
STEP 2: Identify how the pronoun is used in the statement—as subject, predicate nominative, direct object, indirect object, or object of a preposition.
STEP 3: Determine whether the subject form or the object form is correct according to the rules of standard English.
STEP 4: Select the correct form—*who* or *whom.*

EXAMPLE: (*Who, Whom*) rang the bell?
STEP 1: The statement is (*Who, Whom*) *rang the bell.*
STEP 2: The pronoun is the subject, the verb is *rang,* and the direct object is *bell.*
STEP 3: As the subject, the pronoun should be in the subject form.
STEP 4: The subject form is *who.*
ANSWER: **Who** rang the bell?

EXAMPLE: (*Who, Whom*) do you see?
STEP 1: The statement is *You do see (who, whom).*
STEP 2: The subject is *you,* and the verb is *do see.* The pronoun is the direct object of the verb.
STEP 3: A direct object should be in the object form.
STEP 4: The object form is *whom.*
ANSWER: **Whom** *do you see?*

EXAMPLE: To (*who, whom*) did you give the gift?
STEP 1: The statement is *You did give the gift to (who, whom).*
STEP 2: The subject is *you,* the verb is *did give,* and the pronoun is the object of the preposition *to.*
STEP 3: The object of a preposition should be in the object form.
STEP 4: The object form is *whom.*
ANSWER: To **whom** did you give the gift?

NOTE: The use of *whom* is becoming less common in spoken English. When you are speaking, you may correctly begin any question with *who.* In written English, however, you should distinguish between

USAGE

who and *whom. Who* is used as a subject or a predicate nominative, and *whom* is used as an object.

▶ ORAL PRACTICE 6 **Using Pronouns Correctly in Sentences**

Read the following sentences aloud, stressing the italicized pronouns.

1. *Who* owns the boat?
2. To *whom* did you throw the ball?
3. *Whom* did Miguel marry?
4. *Who* was the stranger?
5. For *whom* did you knit that sweater?
6. *Who* is the author of *The Jackie Robinson Story*?
7. *Whom* did Josh choose as his subject?
8. By *whom* was this work painted?

Pronouns with Appositives

Sometimes a pronoun is followed directly by a noun that identifies the pronoun. Such a noun is called an *appositive.* To help you choose which pronoun to use before an appositive, omit the appositive and try each form of the pronoun separately.

EXAMPLE: **(We, Us)** boys swam in the lake. [*Boys* is the appositive identifying the pronoun.]
We swam in the lake.
Us swam in the lake.
ANSWER: **We** boys swam in the lake.

EXAMPLE: The director gave an award to (*we, us*) actors. [*Actors* is the appositive identifying the pronoun.]
The director gave an award to *we*.
The director gave an award to *us*.
ANSWER: The director gave an award to **us** actors.

☞ REFERENCE NOTE: For more information about appositives, see pages 599–600.

▶ EXERCISE 9 **Identifying the Correct Forms of Pronouns in Sentences**

For each of the following sentences, choose the correct form of the pronoun in parentheses.

EXAMPLE **1.** (*Who, Whom*) can do the most jumping jacks?
1. *Who*

1. (*We, Us*) baseball players always warm up before practice.
2. (*Who, Whom*) knows how to stretch properly?
3. Coach Anderson has special exercises for (*us, we*) pitchers.
4. To (*who, whom*) did the coach assign thirty sit-ups?
5. (*Who, Whom*) do you favor for tomorrow's game?

▶ REVIEW C **Revising Incorrect Pronoun Forms in Sentences**

Identify each incorrect pronoun in the following sentences. Then write the correct pronoun. If a sentence is correct, write C.

EXAMPLE **1.** At first Karen and me thought that Lucy was imagining things.
1. *me, I*

1. Lucy told Karen and I that space creatures had landed.
2. She was certain it was them at the park.
3. Whom would believe such a ridiculous story?
4. Us girls laughed and laughed.
5. Lucy looked at we two with tears in her eyes.
6. Karen and I agreed to go to the park to look around.
7. Lucy walked between Karen and me, showing the way.
8. In the park she and us hid behind some tall bushes.
9. Suddenly a strong wind almost blew we three down.

10. A green light shined on Karen and I, and a red one shined on Lucy.
11. Whom could it be?
12. One of the creatures spoke to us girls.
13. Very slowly, Karen, Lucy, and me stepped out from behind the bushes.
14. "You almost scared they and me silly!" shouted a creature, pointing at the others.
15. Neither Karen nor her could speak, and I could make only a squeaking noise.
16. Then the man inside the costume explained to we three girls that a movie company was filming in the park.
17. They and we could have been in an accident.
18. The fireworks hidden in the bushes might have hurt one of we girls.
19. Lucy told the director and he about being afraid of the space creatures in the park.
20. If you see the movie, the short purple creatures under the spaceship are us three girls.

PICTURE THIS

You and some friends are on your way to a weekend campsite. From the car you see the surprising sign shown on the next page. The sign gives you an idea for a tall tale—a humorous, highly unlikely story that stretches the facts. Using the sign to spark your imagination, write a tall tale to tell your friends around the campfire. In your tale, use at least five subject forms and five object forms of pronouns.

Subject: surprising road sign
Audience: friends gathered around a campfire
Purpose: to entertain

Review: Posttest

Revising Incorrect Pronoun Forms in Sentences

Most of the following sentences contain an incorrect pronoun form. If a pronoun is used incorrectly, write the incorrect form of the pronoun and give the correct form. If a sentence is correct, write *C*.

EXAMPLE **1.** The police officer complimented us and they on knowing the rules of bicycle safety.
1. *they—them*

1. The members of our bicycle club are Everett, Coral, Jackie, and me.
2. Us four call our club the Ramblers, named after a bicycle that was popular in the early 1900s.

3. Mrs. Wheeler gave an old three-speed bike to we four.
4. Whom explained the special safety course?
5. Our cousins gave Coral and I their old ten-speed bikes.
6. Each of we Ramblers rides after school.
7. Sometimes we ride with the members of the Derailers, a racing club.
8. On Saturday mornings, we and them meet at the school.
9. Who told us about the bike trail along the river?
10. Everett warned we three to be careful because sometimes the Derailers are reckless.
11. He saw other riders and they at an intersection.
12. A car almost ran over two of them!
13. When the Ramblers ride with the Derailers, it is us who obey all the safety rules.
14. Everett, Coral, Jackie, and I entered a contest.
15. Other clubs and us competed for a tandem bike.
16. Everett and her taught Jackie how to ride it and shift gears.
17. One by one, us riders went through the course.
18. Of all of we contestants, the most careless were the members of the Derailers.
19. Jackie and me were nervous as the judges were deciding.
20. Finally, the judges announced that the winners of the safety contest were us Ramblers.

20 USING MODIFIERS CORRECTLY

Comparison of Adjectives and Adverbs

Diagnostic Test

A. Identifying the Correct Forms of Modifiers

In each of the following sentences, choose the correct form of the modifier in parentheses.

EXAMPLE **1.** We felt (*sleepy, sleepily*) after lunch.
    1. *sleepy*

1. Cool water tastes (*good, well*) on a hot day.
2. The wind howled (*fierce, fiercely*) last night.
3. Who is (*taller, tallest*), Marcus or Jim?
4. *Forever Friends* is the (*bestest, best*) book I've read this year.
5. Sergio has always played (*good, well*) during an important match.
6. The roses in the vase smelled (*sweet, sweetly*).
7. They could view the eclipse (*more clear, more clearly*) than we could.
8. Which of the two winter coats is the (*better, best*) value?

9. Of all the days in the week, Friday goes by (*more slowly, most slowly*).
10. Ernesto felt (*good, well*) about volunteering to help collect money for the homeless.
11. Is this the (*darker, darkest*) copy of the three?
12. The (*faster, fastest*) runner is the captain of the track team.
13. Mr. Chen told them to be (*better, more better*) prepared tomorrow.
14. Joni's way of solving the math puzzle was much (*easier, more easier*) than Kadeem's.
15. Some people think that *Voyager* is the (*most amazing, amazingest*) space probe launched by the United States.

B. Correcting Double Negatives

Most of the following sentences contain errors in the use of negative words. If the sentence is incorrect, write it correctly. If the sentence is correct, write **C**. [Note: In some cases a double negative can be corrected in more than one way.]

EXAMPLE **1.** Mr. Gómez didn't give us no homework today.
1. *Mr. Gómez didn't give us any homework today.*

or

Mr. Gómez gave us no homework today.

16. None of us knows nothing about Halley's comet.
17. Willie can hardly wait to see Bobby McFerrin in concert.
18. Kristin hasn't never heard of the Navajo art of sand painting.
19. Last night we could not see no stars through our binoculars.
20. Whenever I want fresh strawberries, there are never none in the house.

USAGE

Comparison of Adjectives and Adverbs

A *modifier* is a word or a phrase that describes or limits the meaning of another word. The two kinds of modifiers—adjectives and adverbs—may be used to make comparisons. In making comparisons, adjectives and adverbs take special forms. The form that is used depends on how many things are being compared.

20a. The three degrees of comparison of modifiers are the *positive*, the *comparative*, and the *superlative*.

(1) The **positive degree** is used when only one thing is being described.

EXAMPLES *Felita* is a **good** book.
Shawn runs **quickly.**

(2) The **comparative degree** is used when two things are being compared.

EXAMPLES In my opinion, *Nilda* is a **better** book than *Felita.*
Juanita runs **more quickly** than Shawn.

(3) The **superlative degree** is used when three or more things are being compared.

EXAMPLES *Nilda* is one of the **best** books I've read.
Which member of the track team can run **most quickly?**

NOTE: In conversation you may hear such expressions as *Put your best foot forward.* This use of the superlative is acceptable in spoken English. In your writing, however, you should follow the rules above.

REFERENCE NOTE: For a discussion of standard usage, see pages 329–330.

Regular Comparison

Most one-syllable modifiers form the comparative degree by adding *–er* and the superlative degree by adding *–est*.

POSITIVE	COMPARATIVE	SUPERLATIVE
dark	dark**er**	dark**est**
sad	sad**der**	sad**dest**
cute	cut**er**	cut**est**
bright	bright**er**	bright**est**

Some two-syllable modifiers form the comparative degree by adding *–er* and the superlative degree by adding *–est*. Other two-syllable modifiers form the comparative degree by using *more* and the superlative degree by using *most*.

POSITIVE	COMPARATIVE	SUPERLATIVE
fancy	fanci**er**	fanci**est**
lonely	loneli**er**	loneli**est**
cheerful	**more** cheerful	**most** cheerful
quickly	**more** quickly	**most** quickly

Whenever you are unsure about which way a two-syllable modifier forms its degrees of comparison, look in a dictionary.

☞ REFERENCE NOTE: For guidelines on how to spell words when adding *–er* or *–est*, see pages 641–642.

Modifiers that have three or more syllables form their comparative and superlative degrees by using *more* and *most*.

POSITIVE	COMPARATIVE	SUPERLATIVE
difficult	**more** difficult	**most** difficult
interesting	**more** interesting	**most** interesting
clumsily	**more** clumsily	**most** clumsily
skillfully	**more** skillfully	**most** skillfully

EXERCISE 1 **Writing Comparative and Superlative Forms**

Give the comparative form and the superlative form for each of the following modifiers. Use a dictionary if necessary.

EXAMPLE **1.** calm
1. *calmer, calmest*

1. nervous   4. funny   7. poor   9. swiftly
2. great   5. noisy   8. young   10. intelligent
3. hot   6. easily

EXERCISE 2 **Using the Comparative and Superlative Forms Correctly in Sentences**

For each blank in the following sentences, give the correct form of the modifier in italics. Use a dictionary if necessary.

EXAMPLE **1.** *large*   As the illustration on the next page shows, the moon appears ____ during the full-moon phase.
1. *largest*

1. *near*   The moon is the earth's ____ neighbor in space.

2. *close*   At its ____ point to the earth, the moon is 221,456 miles away.

3. *bright*   Seen from the earth, the full moon is ____ than the new moon.

USAGE

4. *small*   The moon appears ___ during the crescent phase.

5. *difficult*   It is ___ to see the new moon than the crescent moon.

6. *common*   The word *crescent* is ___ than the word *gibbous,* which means "partly rounded."

7. *frequently*   We notice the moon ___ when it is full than when it is new.

8. *big*   Do you know why the moon appears ___ on some nights than on others?

9. *fast*   The changes in the moon's appearance take place because the moon travels ___ around the earth than the earth travels around the sun.

10. *slowly*   The moons of some other planets move ___ than our moon.

Phases of the Moon

waxing gibbous · first quarter · waxing crescent · full moon · new moon · waning gibbous · last quarter · waning crescent

Irregular Comparison

Some modifiers do not form their comparative and superlative degrees by using the regular methods.

POSITIVE	COMPARATIVE	SUPERLATIVE
good	better	best
well	better	best
bad	worse	worst
many	more	most
much	more	most

NOTE: You do not need to add anything to an irregular comparison. For example, *worse*, all by itself, is the comparative form of *bad*. *Worser* and *more worse* are nonstandard forms.

USAGE

▶ EXERCISE 3   **Using Irregular Comparative and Superlative Forms**

For each blank in the following sentences, give the correct form of the italicized modifier.

EXAMPLE   **1.** *many*   Let's see which team can wash the ___ cars.

1. *most*

1. *bad*   This is the ___ cold I've ever had.
2. *much*   We have ___ homework this year than we had last year.
3. *well*   Derrick feels ___ today than he did last night.
4. *good*   This peach has a ___ flavor than that one.
5. *well*   Of all the instruments he can play, Shen Li plays the banjo ___.
6. *much*   Catherine ate ___ enchilada casserole on Monday than she had on Sunday.
7. *many*   Doreen has collected the ___ donations for the animal shelter.
8. *bad*   Our team played the ___ game in history.
9. *good*   The judges will now award the prize for the ___ essay.
10. *many*   I have ___ baseball cards than John does.

Special Problems in Using Modifiers

20b. The modifiers *good* and *well* have different uses.

(1) Use *good* to modify a noun or a pronoun.

EXAMPLES   The farmers had a **good** crop this year. [The adjective *good* modifies the noun *crop.*]
The book was **better** than the movie. [The adjective *better* modifies the noun *book.*]
Of all the players, she is the **best** one. [The adjective *best* modifies the pronoun *one.*]

Good should not be used to modify a verb.

NONSTANDARD   N. Scott Momaday writes good.
STANDARD   N. Scott Momaday writes **well.**

(2) Use *well* to modify a verb.

EXAMPLES   The day started **well.** [The adverb *well* modifies the verb *started.*]
The team played **better** in the second half. [The adverb *better* modifies the verb *played.*]
Bill Russell played **best** in the final game. [The adverb *best* modifies the verb *played.*]

Well can also mean "in good health." When *well* has this meaning, it acts as an adjective.

EXAMPLE   Does Sherry feel **well** today? [The adjective *well* modifies the noun *Sherry.*]

▶ EXERCISE 4   **Writing Sentences with the Correct Forms of *Good* and *Well***

You are a famous chef and the host of the popular TV cooking show *Food, Food, Food.* You are preparing for next Friday's program. For this episode, you have decided to show viewers how to get more value for their dollar by shopping wisely. As you look at the grocery ad below, write five sentences you might use on your show. In each sentence, use one of the words in the following list.

EXAMPLE **1.** good
      1. *Thrifty shoppers look for good buys like this bargain on strawberries.*

1. good   **2.** best   **3.** well   **4.** better   **5.** well

USAGE

20c. Use adjectives, not adverbs, after linking verbs.

Linking verbs, such as *look, feel,* and *become,* are often followed by predicate adjectives. These adjectives describe, or modify, the subject.

EXAMPLES Jeanette looked **alert** (not *alertly*) during the game. [The predicate adjective *alert* modifies the subject *Jeanette.*]
    Mayor Rodríguez should feel **confident** (not *confidently*) about this election. [The predicate adjective *confident* modifies the subject *Mayor Rodríguez.*]

NOTE: Some linking verbs can also be used as action verbs. As action verbs, they may be modified by adverbs.

    EXAMPLE Jeanette looked **alertly** around the gym. [*Alertly* modifies the action verb *looked.*]

☞ REFERENCE NOTE: For a complete list of linking verbs, see page 395.

▶ EXERCISE 5   **Writing the Correct Modifiers After Linking Verbs and Action Verbs**

For each of the following sentences, give the correct modifier of the two in parentheses.

EXAMPLE   **1.** Murray's matzo ball soup tasted (*delicious, deliciously*).
1. *delicious*

1. The band became (*nervous, nervously*) before the show.
2. You will likely get a higher score if you can remain (*calm, calmly*) while taking the test.
3. We (*eager, eagerly*) tasted the potato pancakes.
4. Peg looked at her broken skate (*anxious, anxiously*).
5. The mariachi band appeared (*sudden, suddenly*) at our table.
6. Sylvia certainly looked (*pretty, prettily*) in her new outfit.
7. The plums tasted (*sour, sourly*).
8. Mr. Duncan was looking (*close, closely*) at my essay.
9. Erica was (*happy, happily*) to help us.
10. One by one, they felt the contents of the big mystery bag (*cautious, cautiously*).

20d.   Avoid double comparisons.

A *double comparison* is the use of both *–er* and *more* or *–est* and *most* to form a single comparison. When you make a comparison, use only one of these forms, not both.

NONSTANDARD   That was Raul Julia's most scariest role.
STANDARD   That was Raul Julia's **scariest** role.

NONSTANDARD   The kitten is more livelier than the puppy.
STANDARD   The kitten is **livelier** than the puppy.

PICTURE THIS

The people in your neighborhood are sick and tired of looking at this vacant lot. The lot has been a hazard and an eyesore for years. Now, you and your neighbors would like the city to clean up the lot to make it safer and more attractive. Write a letter to the city planning board, explaining why it should sponsor such a project. In your letter, use a total of at least five comparative and superlative forms of modifiers. Underline each comparative or superlative modifier that you use.

Subject: cleaning up a vacant lot
Audience: members of the city planning board
Purpose: to persuade

USAGE

REVIEW A | **Writing Comparative and Superlative Forms in Sentences**

For each blank in the following sentences, give the correct form of comparison for the italicized word.

EXAMPLE   **1.** *noisy*   This is the _____ class in school.
               1. *noisiest*

1. *bad*   Yesterday was the ___ day of my entire life.
2. *good*   Tomorrow should be ___ than today was.
3. *old*   The ___ American Indian tepee in the world can be seen at the Smithsonian Institution.
4. *soon*   Your party ended ___ than I would have liked.
5. *funny*   That is the ___ joke I've ever heard.
6. *rapidly*   Which can run ___, the cheetah or the lion?
7. *beautifully* This piñata is ___ decorated than the other one.
8. *well*   The test had three sections, and I did ___ on the essay questions.
9. *joyfully*   Of all the songbirds in our yard, the mockingbirds sing ___.
10. *strange*   This is the ___ book I have ever read!

▶ REVIEW B   **Proofreading for Correct Forms of Modifiers**

Most of the sentences in the following paragraph have errors in English usage. If a sentence contains an error, identify it and then write the correct usage. If a sentence is correct, write *C*.

EXAMPLE   [1] You may not recognize the man in the picture on the next page, but you probably know his more famous characters.
          1. *more famous—most famous*

[1] This man, Alexandre Dumas, wrote two of the most popularest books in history—*The Three Musketeers* and *The Count of Monte Cristo*. [2] Born in France, Dumas was poor but had a good education. [3] As a young playwright, he rose quick to fame. [4] In person, Dumas always seemed cheerfully. [5] Like their author, his historical novels are colorful and full of adventure. [6] Their fame grew rapid, and the

public demanded more of them. [7] In response to this demand, Dumas hired many assistants, who probably wrote most of his later books than he did. [8] Dumas's son, Alexandre, was also a writer and became famously with the publication of *Camille*. [9] At that time, the younger Dumas was often thought of as a more better writer than his father. [10] Today, however, the friendship of the three musketeers remains aliver than ever in film, print, and even comic books.

Double Negatives

Negative words are a common part of everyday speaking and writing. These words include *no, not, never,* and *hardly*. Notice how negative words change the meaning of the following sentences.

POSITIVE   We can count in Spanish.
NEGATIVE   We can**not** count in Spanish.

POSITIVE   They ride their bikes on the highway.
NEGATIVE   They **never** ride their bikes on the highway.

USAGE

20e. Avoid the use of double negatives.

A *double negative* is the use of two negative words to express one negative idea.

Common Negative Words			
barely	never	none	nothing
hardly	no	no one	nowhere
neither	nobody	not (−n't)	scarcely

NONSTANDARD   Sheila didn't tell no one her idea. [The two negative words are *−n't* and *no.*]

STANDARD   Sheila **didn't** tell anyone her idea.

STANDARD   Sheila told **no one** her idea.

NONSTANDARD   Rodney hardly said nothing. [The two negative words are *hardly* and *nothing.*]

STANDARD   Rodney **hardly** said anything.

STANDARD   Rodney said almost **nothing.**

 EXERCISE 6   **Revising Sentences by Eliminating Double Negatives**

Revise each of the following sentences to eliminate the double negative. [Note: Some double negatives may be corrected in more than one way.]

EXAMPLE   **1.** Those books don't have no pictures.

1. *Those books don't have any pictures.*

or

Those books have no pictures.

1. The Plains Indians did not waste no part of a bear, deer, or buffalo.

2. Ms. Wooster never tries nothing new to eat.

3. Movie and TV stars from Hollywood never visit nowhere near our town.

4. Until last summer, I didn't know nothing about Braille music notation.

5. By Thanksgiving, the store didn't have none of the silver jewelry left.
6. I'm so excited I can't hardly sit still.
7. No one brought nothing to eat on the hike.
8. Strangely enough, Freida hasn't never tasted our delicious Cuban bread.
9. There isn't no more pudding in the bowl.
10. Our dog never fights with neither one of our cats.

USAGE

WRITING APPLICATION

Using Negative Words in Writing

Negative words are powerful. Just one of them can change the whole meaning of a sentence. Two negative words can create confusion.

EXAMPLE   **I never see nobody in that store.** [What does the writer mean? Is the store always empty, or is it busy? The sentence needs to be revised to eliminate the confusion.]

REVISED   **I never see anybody in that store.**
                              or
          I always see someone in that store.

▶ **WRITING ACTIVITY**
Everyone has a bad day now and then. Yesterday, it was your turn. You were late for school because your alarm clock didn't go off. From then on, things just got worse. Write a letter to a friend giving a comical description of your unlucky day. Make sure that you use negative words correctly.

Prewriting   Jot down some notes about a real or imaginary bad day in your life. List at least five things that went wrong during the day. The events can be big or small. Tell how you felt when one thing after another went wrong.

 **Writing** Before beginning your first draft, you may want to look at pages 739–740 for tips on writing a friendly letter. In your letter, explain the events of your day in the order they happened. Describe each event in detail. Also describe your reactions to the events. You may want to exaggerate some details for a humorous effect.

Evaluating and Revising Ask a friend to read your letter. Have you described the events clearly? Do your descriptions give a vivid, humorous picture of your day? If not, add or revise details. Be sure that your letter follows the correct form for a friendly letter.

Proofreading Proofread your letter carefully for errors in grammar, spelling, or punctuation. Read through each sentence one more time to check that negative words are used correctly.

REVIEW C **Proofreading Sentences for Correct Use of Modifiers**

Most of the following sentences contain errors in the use of modifiers. If a sentence is incorrect, write it correctly. If a sentence is correct, write C. [Note: Some double negatives may be corrected in more than one way.]

EXAMPLE **1.** Haven't you never made a paper airplane or a paper hat?
1. *Haven't you ever made a paper airplane or a paper hat?*
or
Have you never made a paper airplane or a paper hat?

1. Making paper constructions requires some skill, but they are much more easier to make than Japanese origami figures.
2. Origami, the ancient Japanese art of paper folding, wasn't hardly known in the United States until the 1960s.
3. Now, many Americans know how to fold the most cleverest traditional origami animals.
4. In true origami, artists do not never cut or paste the paper.
5. A beginner doesn't need nothing but a sheet of paper to create an origami figure.
6. With a bit of patience, anyone can quick make a folded-paper figure.
7. Even kindergarteners can do a good job making the simple sailboat shown in this diagram.
8. Other origami figures require more greater time and patience than this sailboat.
9. Today, there probably isn't no one better at origami than Akira Yoshizawa.
10. Even the most difficult figure is not too hard for him, and he has invented many beautiful new figures.

Review: Posttest

Revising Sentences by Correcting Errors in the Use of Modifiers

Most of the following sentences contain errors in the use of modifiers or negative words. If a sentence has an error, rewrite the sentence correctly. If a sentence is correct, write *C*.

EXAMPLE   **1.** The weather looks more worse today.
   1. *The weather looks worse today.*

1. Of the students in class, Odelle writes better.
2. Can you type fastest on a word processor or on a typewriter?
3. Juan seemed glad that we had visited him.
4. No one knew nothing about the tornado.
5. Throughout history, many people have written regular in their diaries.
6. The people who moved in next door are the most friendliest neighbors who have ever lived there.
7. The bread smelled wonderfully when it came out of the oven.
8. Wynton Marsalis plays the trumpet good.
9. If you don't feel well today, you shouldn't go out.
10. Mai is one of the most persistent people I know.
11. I felt sadly at the end of *Old Yeller*.
12. Pedro, please look careful as I wrap this tamale.
13. It doesn't make no difference to Brian.
14. I'm not sure which I like best, CDs or tapes.
15. Arthurine's piano playing sounds very nicely.
16. The storm appeared so sudden that it surprised us.
17. Tanya is the youngest of my brothers and sisters.
18. Lena and Ivan are twins, but Lena is the oldest.
19. We couldn't hardly believe the news!
20. Miyoko looks well in her new kimono.

21 A GLOSSARY OF USAGE

Common Usage Problems

Diagnostic Test

Revising Sentences by Correcting Errors in Usage

In each of the following sets of sentences, choose the letter of the sentence that contains an error. Then write the sentence correctly, using standard English.

EXAMPLE **1. a.** Did you read this book?
      b. It's almost time for dinner.
      c. My sister learned me how to do that.
     1. *c. My sister taught me how to do that.*

  1. a. Everyone was at the meeting except Diego.
     b. Is that you're dog?
     c. Andy waited outside the dentist's office.
  2. a. The landfill smelled badly.
     b. No one knew whose knapsack that was.
     c. We could hardly wait for the rain to stop.
  3. a. How come Ginger can't go?
     b. I feel rather tired today.
     c. The team played well in the last game.

4. a. Nina can run faster than he can.
   b. Anna would have finished, but she was interrupted.
   c. Be sure to bring a extra pencil with you.
5. a. The cow and its calf stood in the meadow.
   b. The team members were proud of theirselves.
   c. What is the difference between these brands of basketball shoes?
6. a. We did as we were told.
   b. Everyone was already to go.
   c. I used to enjoy playing tennis.
7. a. Penny, bring this book when you go home.
   b. Ms. Mishima told us our plan was all right.
   c. Julie said that it's already time to go.
8. a. The team had fewer fouls in the last game.
   b. They looked everywhere for him.
   c. Do you know where he is at?
9. a. Water-skiing is more fun than I thought.
   b. We hiked a long way before we pitched camp.
   c. Try and get to the meeting on time, please.
10. a. Their team has never beaten your team.
   b. A pop fly is when a ball is batted high in the air into the infield.
   c. I finished my homework; then I called Duane.

This chapter contains an alphabetical list, or glossary, of common problems in English usage. You will notice throughout the chapter that some examples are labeled *standard* or *nonstandard*. **Standard English** is the most widely accepted form of English. It is used in *formal* situations, such as in speeches and compositions for school. It is also used in *informal* situations, such as in conversations and everyday writing.

   Nonstandard English is language that does not follow the rules and guidelines of standard English.

☞ REFERENCE NOTE: For more discussion of standard English, see pages 329–330.

a, an Use *a* before words beginning with a consonant sound. Use *an* before words beginning with a vowel sound. The first letter in a word does not always determine the sound that the word begins with. The first letter in the words *herb* and *honor* is the consonant *h*. However, both words begin with a vowel sound.

EXAMPLES The airplane was parked in **a** hangar.
She lives on **a** one-way street.
They arrived **an** hour early.
My father works in **an** office.

accept, except *Accept* is a verb. It means "to receive." *Except* may be either a verb or a preposition. As a verb, it means "to leave out." As a preposition, *except* means "excluding" or "but."

EXAMPLES The winners of the spelling bee proudly **accepted** their awards.
Because Josh had a sprained ankle, he was **excepted** from gym class. [verb]
All the food was ready **except** the won-ton soup. [preposition]

ain't Avoid this word in speaking and writing. It is nonstandard English.

"Beats me why I ain't gettin' no better marks in English."

all right *All right* can be used as an adjective that means "satisfactory" or "unhurt." As an adverb, *all right* means "well enough." *All right* should always be written as two words.

EXAMPLES   This tie looks **all right** with that blue shirt. [adjective]
The baby squirrel had fallen out of its nest, but it was **all right**. [adjective]
Lorenzo and I did **all right** on the pop quiz. [adverb]

a lot *A lot* should always be written as two words.

EXAMPLE   I can make **a lot** of my mom's recipes.

already, all ready *Already* means "previously." *All ready* means "completely prepared" or "in readiness."

EXAMPLES   We looked for Jay, but he had **already** left.
The players were **all ready** for the big game.
I had studied for two hours on Sunday night and was **all ready** for the test on Monday.

among See **between, among.**

anywheres, everywheres, nowheres, somewheres Use these words without the final –*s*.

EXAMPLE   They looked **everywhere** [not *everywheres*] for the missing puzzle piece.

at Do not use *at* after *where.*

NONSTANDARD   Where is the Chinese kite exhibit at?
STANDARD   Where is the Chinese kite exhibit?

bad, badly *Bad* is an adjective. It modifies nouns and pronouns. *Badly* is an adverb. It modifies verbs, adjectives, and adverbs.

EXAMPLES   The milk smelled **bad.** [The predicate adjective *bad* modifies *milk.*]
Before I took lessons, I played the piano **badly.** [The adverb *badly* modifies the verb *played.*]

NOTE: The expression *feel badly* has become acceptable in informal English.

INFORMAL   Beth felt badly about hurting José's feelings.
FORMAL   Beth felt **bad** about hurting José's feelings.

between, among Use *between* when you are referring to two things at a time. The two things may be part of a group consisting of more than two.

EXAMPLES   Kim got in line **between** Lee and Rene.
Be sure to weed **between** all ten rows of carrots. [Although there are ten rows of carrots, the weeding is done *between* any two of them.]
Alicia can't see much difference **between** the three pictures. [Although there are more than two pictures, each one is compared with each other one separately.]

Use *among* when you are referring to a group rather than to separate individuals.

EXAMPLE   The four winners divided the prize **among** themselves.

EXERCISE 1   **Identifying Correct Usage**

Choose the correct word or words in parentheses in each of the following sentences.

EXAMPLE   **1.** The picture on the next page is titled *After Supper, West Chester*, but the scene could be almost (*anywhere, anywheres*).
1. *anywhere*

1. This colorful work was painted by (*a, an*) artist named Horace Pippin, who lived from 1888 to 1946.
2. By the time Pippin was in elementary school, he was (*already, all ready*) a talented artist.
3. In fact, he had won a drawing contest and had eagerly (*accepted, excepted*) the prize, a box of crayons and watercolor paints.

USAGE

4. In World War I, Pippin was once caught (*among, between*) American troops and the enemy.

5. During this battle (*somewheres, somewhere*) in France, Pippin's right arm—the arm he painted with—was seriously wounded.

6. For a long time, Pippin felt (*bad, badly*) about his disability, but he was determined to paint again.

7. (*Among, Between*) the many ways of painting he tried, the most successful was to hold up his right hand with his left arm.

8. It (*ain't, isn't*) surprising that one of his first paintings after the war was a battle scene.

9. When Pippin painted *After Supper, West Chester*, in 1935, he was remembering the small town in Pennsylvania (*where he was born, where he was born at*).

10. I think that the painter of this peaceful scene must have felt (*all right, alright*) about his work and about himself.

Horace Pippin, *After Supper, West Chester* (1935). © 1991 Gridley/Graves. Collection Leon Hecht and Robert Pincus-Witten, New York City.

bring, take *Bring* means "to come carrying something." *Take* means "to go carrying something." Think of *bring* as related to *come*. Think of *take* as related to *go*.

EXAMPLES Make sure that you **bring** your book when you come to my house.
Take your coat when you go outside.

could of Do not write *of* with the helping verb *could*. Write *could have*. Also avoid *ought to of, should of, would of, might of,* and *must of*.

EXAMPLES Yvetta wished she could **have** [not *of*] gone to the movie.
We should **have** [not *of*] asked your mom for permission.

don't, doesn't See pages 469–470.

everywheres See **anywheres**, etc.

except, accept See **accept, except**.

fewer, less *Fewer* is used with plural words. *Less* is used with singular words. *Fewer* tells "how many." *Less* tells "how much."

EXAMPLES This road has **fewer** stoplights than any of the other roads.
This road has **less** traffic than any of the other roads.

good, well *Good* is always an adjective. Never use *good* to modify a verb. Use *well*, which is an adverb.

NONSTANDARD Heather sings good.
STANDARD Heather sings **well**.

Although it is usually an adverb, *well* may be used as an adjective to mean "healthy."

EXAMPLE Keiko went home today because she didn't feel **well**.

USAGE

Good is often used in conversation as an adverb but should not be used as an adverb in writing.

NOTE: *Feel good* and *feel well* mean different things. *Feel good* means "to feel happy or pleased." *Feel well* means "to feel healthy."

EXAMPLES I feel **good** when I'm with my friends.
Rashid had a cold, and he still doesn't feel **well**.

had of See **of**.

had ought, hadn't ought The verb *ought* should never be used with *had*.

NONSTANDARD They had ought to be more careful.
You hadn't ought to have said that.
STANDARD They **ought** to be more careful.
You **oughtn't** to have said that.
or
You **shouldn't** have said that.

hardly, scarcely The words *hardly* and *scarcely* are negative words. They should never be used with other negative words.

EXAMPLES Pedro **can** [not *can't*] **hardly** wait for the fiesta.
The sun **has** [not *hasn't*] **scarcely** shone today.

hisself, theirself, theirselves These words are nonstandard English. Use *himself* and *themselves*.

EXAMPLES Mr. Ogata said he would do the work **himself** [not *hisself*].
They congratulated **themselves** [not *theirselves*] on their victory.

how come In informal English, *how come* is often used instead of *why*. In formal English, *why* is always preferred.

INFORMAL How come she can leave early?
FORMAL **Why** can she leave early?

▶ EXERCISE 2   **Identifying Correct Usage**

Choose the correct word or words in parentheses in each of the following sentences.

EXAMPLE   **1.** There might be (*fewer, less*) accidents if people were more alert around small children.
   1. *fewer*

1. Everyone knows that children are not always as careful as they (*ought, had ought*) to be.
2. However, young children (*can hardly, can't hardly*) be blamed for being curious and adventurous.
3. Recently, I was involved in a situation that (*could of, could have*) led to a serious accident.
4. After I (*brought, took*) my little brother Gerald home from a walk, I called my friend Latoya.
5. Before I knew it, Gerald had wandered off by (*hisself, himself*).
6. I don't know (*how come, why*) he always disappears when I'm on the phone.
7. I found Gerald climbing on the stove, and in (*fewer, less*) than a second I lifted him down.
8. I (*might have, might of*) scolded him more, but he seemed sorry for what he had done.
9. He said he would be (*good, well*) from now on.
10. Although the experience was frightening, it turned out (*good, well*).

▶ REVIEW A   **Proofreading a Paragraph for Correct Usage**

Each of the sentences in the following paragraph has at least one error in English usage. Identify each error. Then write the correct usage.

EXAMPLE   [1] The game of soccer has proved to be more popular than the king of England hisself.
   1. *hisself—himself*

[1] Derby, England, may have been the town where soccer was first played at. [2] Sometime around the

third century, an early version of the game was played among two towns. [3] Anywheres from fifty to several hundred people played in a match. [4] Back then, soccer had less rules than it does today, and the participants probably didn't behave very good. [5] By the fifteenth century, the government had all ready outlawed the sport. [6] The king said that young people had ought to train theirselves in archery instead of playing soccer. [7] According to the king, archery practice was alright because bows and arrows could be used against a enemy. [8] Obviously, many people didn't hardly obey the king's rule, because soccer continued to grow in popularity. [9] Perhaps later kings felt badly about outlawing soccer. [10] Eventually the government had to except that soccer had become the most popular sport in England.

its, it's *Its* is the possessive form of the personal pronoun *it*. *Its* is used to show ownership. *It's* is a contraction of *it is* or *it has*.

EXAMPLES   The raccoon washed **its** face in the stream. [possessive pronoun]
My grandparents have a dog; **it's** a collie. [contraction of "it is"]
It's been sunny and warm all day. [contraction of "it has"]

kind of, sort of In informal English, *kind of* and *sort of* are often used to mean "somewhat" or "rather." In formal English, however, it is better to use *somewhat* or *rather*.

INFORMAL   That story is kind of funny.
FORMAL   That story is **rather** funny.

learn, teach *Learn* means "to gain knowledge." *Teach* means "to instruct" or "to show how."

EXAMPLES   The students from Vietnam are **learning** English.
Ms. Sanita is **teaching** them.

less See **fewer, less.**

lie, lay See page 495.

might of, must of See **could of.**

nowheres See **anywheres,** etc.

of Do not use *of* with prepositions such as *inside, off,* and *outside.*

EXAMPLES   Mrs. Cardona waited **outside** [not *outside of*] the office.
The child jumped **off** [not *off of*] the swing.
We heard a noise **inside** [not *inside of*] the engine.

Of is also unnecessary with *had.*

EXAMPLE   If we **had** [not *had of*] known it was the Purim holiday, we would have planned a costume party.

👉 REFERENCE NOTE: For more about using *of* with helping verbs, see *could of.*

ought to of See **could of.**

rise, raise See pages 493–494.

should of See **could of.**

sit, set See page 492.

somewheres See **anywheres,** etc.

sort of, kind of See **kind of, sort of.**

take, bring See **bring, take.**

than, then Do not confuse these words. *Than* is a conjunction. *Then* is an adverb.

EXAMPLES   This cheese is tastier **than** that one.
First the phone rang, and **then** someone knocked at the door.

that there See **this here, that there.**

USAGE

their, there, they're *Their* is the possessive form of *they*. It is used to show ownership. *There* is used to mean "at that place" or to begin a sentence. *They're* is a contraction of *they are*.

EXAMPLES   The children played with **their** toys.
We are going over **there**.
There are twelve members in our club.
They're going to have a Juneteenth picnic.

theirself, theirselves See **hisself,** etc.

them *Them* should not be used as an adjective. Use *these* or *those*.

EXAMPLE   How much do you want for **those** [not *them*] baseball cards?

PICTURE THIS

You are the health reporter for your classroom's monthly newsletter. While researching your story on dental care, you've discovered something that many people share. They are afraid of going to the dentist. To help these people overcome their fear, you decide to write about why they need not dread a visit to the dentist. In gathering information for your article, you have interviewed the young patient shown on the next page. Write your notes from this interview. Be sure to record both your questions and the patient's responses. In your notes, use at least five of the following terms correctly:

all right	ought
bad	less
badly	fewer
good	it's
well	who's

Subject: a visit to the dentist

Audience: yourself and readers of a classroom newsletter

Purpose: to record information

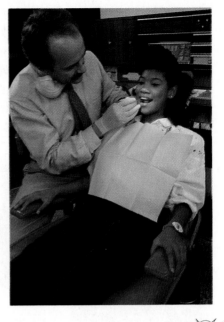

▶ EXERCISE 3 **Identifying Correct Usage**

Choose the correct word or words in parentheses in each of the following sentences.

EXAMPLE [1] For years, scientists have studied Mayan writing on temples and (*inside of, inside*) caves.

1. *inside*

[1] Some scientists are (*learning, teaching*) themselves how to understand this writing. [2] The Maya didn't use an alphabet to write (*there, their, they're*) language. [3] Instead, they drew symbols like (*them, these*) small pictures shown on the next page. [4] As you can see, the sign for *jaguar* looked (*rather, sort of*) like a jaguar. [5] At times, it could be (*kind of, rather*) difficult to tell what a picture stood for. [6] (*Its, It's*) meaning was made clear by the use of another small symbol.

[7] *(There, Their, They're)* is an example of this technique in the illustration below. [8] If a scarf symbol was added to the symbol for *man, (then, than)* the picture meant "lord." [9] Mayan writing contained other symbols that were more like syllables *(then, than)* entire words. [10] *(Its, It's)* clear we still have a great deal to learn about this beautiful, ancient language.

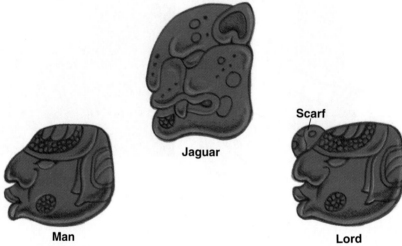

Jaguar

Scarf

Man

Lord

this here, that there The *here* and *there* are not necessary after *this* and *that*.

> EXAMPLE   Do you want **this** [not *this here*] book or **that** [not *that there*] one?

try and In informal English, *try and* is often used for *try to.* In formal English, *try to* is preferred.

> INFORMAL   Pat will try and explain the problem.
> FORMAL   Pat will **try to** explain the problem.

use to, used to Be sure to add the *–d* to *use. Used to* is in the past tense.

> EXAMPLE   Dr. Chang **used to** [not *use to*] live next door to us.

way, ways Use *way*, not *ways*, when referring to a distance.

> EXAMPLE   We traveled a long **way** [not *ways*] today.

well, good See **good, well.**

when, where Do not use *when* or *where* incorrectly in writing a definition.

NONSTANDARD	A *phrase* is when a group of words is used as a part of speech.
STANDARD	A *phrase* is a group of words that is used as a part of speech.

Do not use *where* for *that.*

EXAMPLE	I read **that** [not *where*] the concert has been canceled.

whose, who's *Whose* is the possessive form of *who.* It shows ownership. *Who's* is a contraction of *who is* or *who has.*

EXAMPLES	**Whose** dog is that? [possessive pronoun] **Who's** the bravest person you ever met? [contraction of *who is*] Sarah is the only student **who's** turned in a report. [contraction of *who has*]

would of See **could of.**

your, you're *Your* is the possessive form of *you.* *You're* is the contraction of *you are.*

EXAMPLES	Do you have **your** watch with you? [possessive pronoun] **You're** late today. [contraction of *you are*]

USAGE

▶ EXERCISE 4 **Identifying Correct Usage**

Choose the correct word or words in parentheses in each of the following sentences.

EXAMPLE	[1] For (*your, you're*) best camping trip ever, take along a trail map. **1.** *your*

[1] A trail map is (*when a map shows, a map that shows*) trails, campsites, and geographical features.

USAGE

[2] For a safe camping trip, a map like (*this here, this*) one can be very important. [3] Hikers who are not (*used to, use to*) an area often lose their way. [4] Every year, you can read reports (*where, that*) some campers were lost for several days. [5] If you don't want to be one of them, (*try and, try to*) get a good trail map. [6] In fact, every hiker in your group (*who's, whose*) able to read a map should have one. [7] With the map, you can choose a (*good, well*) location for your campsite. [8] When you begin your hike, mark where (*your, you're*) campsite is on the map. [9] If you go quite a (*way, ways*) from your campsite, note your path on the map, too. [10] As (*your, you're*) walking, your trail map can help you figure out exactly where you are.

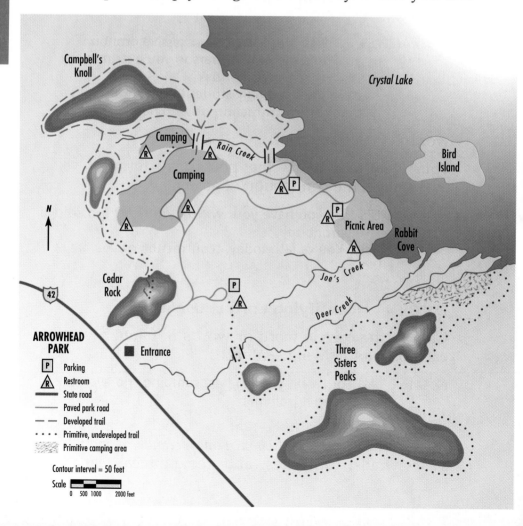

WRITING APPLICATION

Using Formal English in Writing

Standard, formal English isn't necessarily the "best" or the "right" form of English. It's simply the most appropriate kind of English to use in most formal situations. These situations include essays, speeches, reports, and business letters. This chapter gives you a number of guidelines for using formal, standard English.

INFORMAL   I feel badly about not being able to baby-sit tonight.

FORMAL   I feel **bad** about not being able to baby-sit tonight.

INFORMAL   How come this remote-control airplane won't fly?

FORMAL   **Why** won't this remote-control airplane fly?

WRITING ACTIVITY

You are an after-school helper at a day-care center. The teachers at the center plan to take the children on a field trip. One of the teachers has asked you to write a letter to send to the children's parents. The letter should tell where the children will visit and describe some of the things they will do there. The letter should also list any special items the children need to bring. Use this **Glossary of Usage** and other parts of the **Handbook** to help you write the letter in formal, standard English.

Prewriting   First, decide where the children will go on their field trip. They might go to a library, a park, a museum, or a fire station. Then, list the kinds of activities the children might participate in there. Note how the children will travel—for example, by bus or car. Also note any special clothing or other things they might need for the field trip. List all the details you can think of.

USAGE

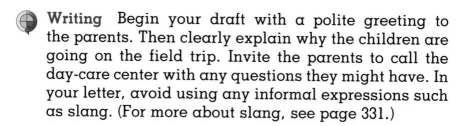

Writing Begin your draft with a polite greeting to the parents. Then clearly explain why the children are going on the field trip. Invite the parents to call the day-care center with any questions they might have. In your letter, avoid using any informal expressions such as slang. (For more about slang, see page 331.)

Evaluating and Revising Ask a friend or a classmate to read your letter. Does your reader understand the information in the letter? Does the letter follow the guidelines for a proper business letter? Revise any details that are not clear. Also, insert additional information where it is needed. (For more information about writing business letters, see pages 741–745.)

Proofreading Read your work carefully. Check for correct spelling, punctuation, and grammar. Pay extra attention to the punctuation of the greeting and closing of your letter.

▭▶ REVIEW B   **Proofreading a Paragraph for Correct Usage**

Most of the following sentences contain errors in usage. If a sentence is incorrect, write it correctly. If a sentence is correct, write *C*.

EXAMPLE   [1] Do you know someone who can learn you how to dance the Texas Two-Step?
    1. *Do you know someone who can teach you how to dance the Texas Two-Step?*

[1] Country music lovers like the ones shown on the next page enjoy the two-step because its fun to dance. [2] If you don't know anyone who can teach you the two-step, you can use this here diagram to

learn the basic steps. [3] So, grab you're partner and get ready. [4] First, listen closely to them musicians. [5] Try and catch the rhythm of the music with a small double shuffle step. [6] Remember, men, your always starting with the left foot; women, you do just the opposite. [7] The man steps to the left, touches his left shoe with his right foot, and then steps to the right and does the same thing. [8] Then, he takes two kind of quick steps forward followed by two slow shuffle steps. [9] You can dance the same steps for a ways, or you can try doing a sidestep or a turn. [10] Their you have one version of the Texas Two-Step.

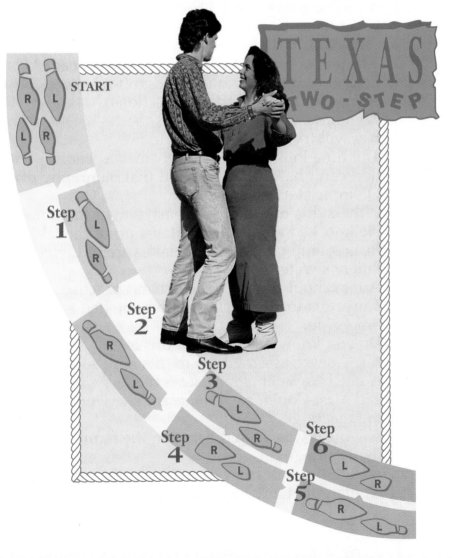

USAGE

Review: Posttest

Revising Sentences by Correcting Errors in Usage

Each of the following sentences contains an error in usage. Write each sentence correctly, using standard, formal English.

EXAMPLE **1.** I knew all the answers accept the last one.
1. *I knew all the answers except the last one.*

1. If you're going to the library, would you please bring these books back there for me?
2. The water tasted kind of salty.
3. Has Jamila finished the assignment all ready?
4. Leon took a nap because he didn't feel good.
5. They should of asked for directions.
6. We found nothing but a old shoe.
7. Bao will try and fix her bike today.
8. The tuna looked all right but smelled badly.
9. Bert can't hardly wait to read that biography of Olympic star Jesse Owens.
10. Why is this mitt more expensive then that one?
11. He knocked a bowl of plantains off of the table.
12. In Vietnam, children often take care of there family's water buffalo.
13. After school we use to have band practice.
14. Tanya made less mistakes after she had started practicing.
15. Do you know who's pencil this is?
16. Mr. Abeyto assigned me to this here seat.
17. A glitch is when a mistake is made by a computer.
18. Did Mrs. Cohen say how come she won't be at the meeting?
19. The meat was shared between the families of the Innupiat village.
20. At one time, Bessie Coleman was the only black woman pilot anywheres in the world.

22 CAPITAL LETTERS

Rules for Capitalization

Diagnostic Test

Proofreading Sentences for Correct Capitalization

For each of the following sentences, find each word that has an error in the use of capital letters. Write the word correctly.

EXAMPLE **1.** Did president Lincoln deliver his Gettysburg Address during The Civil War?
1. *President, the*

1. Shawn's dog, Ransom, is a german shepherd.
2. Our Spring break begins on march 26.
3. Write to me at 439 Walnut street.
4. Do you know why the *titanic* sank?
5. In 1991, aung san suu kyi of burma won the Nobel peace prize.
6. As soon as i finish my English homework, i'll call you.
7. I would like to go to College someday.
8. We watched a scene from *Romeo And Juliet*.

9. Eric's orthodontist is dr. Chun.
10. On saturday my aunt is taking us to jones beach.
11. Dad used the general Electric waffle iron to make breakfast.
12. have you seen my copy of *sports illustrated?*
13. The Peace corps volunteers helped build a bridge.
14. The capital of Peru is lima.
15. The age of Reason brought many changes to european society.
16. The *viking* space probes landed on mars.
17. Tranh's brother is a buddhist monk.
18. The storm is coming from the North.
19. Are you taking spanish or art this year?
20. The gulf of Mexico lies west of Florida.

22a. Capitalize the first word in every sentence.

EXAMPLES **My** sister has soccer practice after school. **Then** she has to do her homework.

The first word of a direct quotation should begin with a capital letter, whether or not the quotation starts the sentence.

EXAMPLE Reiko asked, "**Have** you finished your report?"

Usually, the first word of every line of poetry begins with a capital letter.

EXAMPLE **Let** the rain kiss you.
Let the rain beat upon your head with silver liquid drops.
Let the rain sing you a lullaby.

The rain makes still pools on the sidewalk.
The rain makes running pools in the gutter.
The rain plays a little sleep-song on our roof at night—

And I love the rain.

"April Rain Song," Langston Hughes

NOTE: Some poets do not follow this style. When you quote from a poem, use capital letters exactly as the poet uses them.

☞ REFERENCE NOTE: For more about using capital letters in quotations, see page 616.

22b. Capitalize the pronoun *I.*

EXAMPLES When I returned home, I walked the dog.

▶ EXERCISE 1 **Proofreading Sentences for Correct Capitalization**

If a sentence has an error in capitalization, write correctly the word or words that should be capitalized. If a sentence is correct, write C.

EXAMPLE **1.** What time should i call?
1. *I*

1. the library report for my English class is due at the end of next month.
2. My sister memorized the limerick that begins, "a tutor who tooted a flute."
3. Aren't you glad tomorrow is a holiday?
4. Mary Elizabeth said, "we need to buy some more shampoo."
5. My parents let me watch television only after i have finished all my chores.

22c. Capitalize proper nouns.

A *proper noun* names a particular person, place, thing, or idea. Proper nouns are always capitalized. A *common noun* names any one of a group of persons, places, things, or ideas. A common noun is not capitalized unless it begins a sentence or is part of a title.

☞ REFERENCE NOTE: For more information about proper nouns and common nouns, see page 369.

MECHANICS

PROPER NOUNS	COMMON NOUNS
Fairview School	middle school
November	month
Toni Morrison	woman
Red Sox	team
Kenya	country

(1) Capitalize the names of persons.

EXAMPLES   **Kazue Sawai, Harriet Tubman, Golda Meir, Heitor Villa-Lobos, Paul Bunyan**

(2) Capitalize geographical names.

TYPE OF NAME	EXAMPLES	
Continents	Asia Australia	North America Europe
Countries	Denmark Burkina Faso	Thailand Costa Rica
Cities, Towns	Minneapolis Havana	New Delhi San Diego
States	Maryland West Virginia	Mississippi Oregon
Islands	Hawaiian Islands Leyte	Block Island Key West
Bodies of Water	Yangtze River Hudson Bay	Lake Okeechobee Caribbean Sea
Streets, Highways	Front Street Chelmsford Road Fifth Avenue	Michigan Avenue Darryl Drive Interstate 55

NOTE: In a hyphenated street number, the second part of the number is not capitalized.

EXAMPLE   **Forty-ninth Street**

TYPE OF NAME	EXAMPLES	
Parks	Mammoth Cave San Antonio Missions	Yellowstone National Park
Mountains	Adirondacks Pine Mountain	Mount Kilimanjaro Andes
Sections of the Country	the South Corn Belt	the Northwest New England

NOTE: Words such as *east, west, northeast,* or *southwest* are not capitalized when the words indicate a direction.

EXAMPLES Turn **east** when you reach the river.
[direction]
My cousin goes to college in the **East.**
[section of the country]

EXERCISE 2   **Writing Proper Nouns**

For each common noun given below, write two proper nouns. You may use a dictionary and an atlas. Be sure to use capital letters correctly.

EXAMPLE **1.** lake
1. *Lake Louise, Lake Ontario*

1. river	**4.** park	**7.** island	**9.** country
2. street	**5.** friend	**8.** state	**10.** ocean
3. actor	**6.** singer		

EXERCISE 3   **Recognizing the Correct Use of Capital Letters**

If a sentence contains an error in capitalization, write correctly the word that should be capitalized. If the sentence is correct, write *C.*

EXAMPLE **1.** Huge rigs pump oil from beneath the North sea.
1. *Sea*

MECHANICS

1. María Ayala and eileen Barnes are going to Chicago.
2. Our neighbor Ken Oshige recently moved to canada.
3. Midway island is in the Pacific Ocean.
4. We could see mount Hood from the airplane window.
5. After you turn off the highway, head north for three miles.
6. During the sixteenth century, Spanish explorers brought the first horses to the west.
7. Several of us in the youth group went canoeing on blue River.
8. My closest friend just moved to ohio.
9. Hawaii Volcanoes National park is on the island of Hawaii.
10. The store is located on Maple street.

(3) Capitalize the names of organizations, teams, businesses, institutions, and government bodies.

TYPE OF NAME	EXAMPLES	
Organizations	Math Club Boy Scouts	Oakdale Chamber of Commerce
Teams	New York Mets Riverside Raiders	Los Angeles Lakers Pine Hill Jets
Businesses	J. and J. Construction, Inc. Uptown Shoe Store Grommet Manufacturing Company	
Institutions	University of Oklahoma Kennedy Middle School Mount Sinai Hospital	
Government Bodies	League of Arab States Department of Education Federal Bureau of Investigation	

MECHANICS

NOTE: Do *not* capitalize words such as *hotel, theater,* or *high school* unless they are part of a proper name.

EXAMPLES
Fremont Hotel	the hotel
Apollo Theater	a theater
Ames High School	that high school

☞ REFERENCE NOTE: The names of government bodies are often abbreviated. For information on abbreviations, see pages 589–591 and 602.

(4) Capitalize the names of special events, holidays, and calendar items.

TYPE OF NAME	EXAMPLES	
Special Events	**World Series** **New York Marathon**	**Parade of Roses** **Tulip Festival**
Holidays	**Thanksgiving** **Labor Day**	**Martin Luther** **King, Jr., Day**
Calendar Items	**Sunday** **Father's Day**	**December** **April Fools' Day**

NOTE: Do *not* capitalize the name of a season unless it is part of a proper name.

EXAMPLES   a **w**inter storm, the **W**inter **F**estival

(5) Capitalize the names of historical events and periods.

TYPE OF NAME	EXAMPLES	
Historical Events	**Boston Tea Party** **Battle of Hastings** **War of 1812**	**New Deal** **Fall of Rome** **Renaissance**
Historical Periods	**Bronze Age** **Reformation**	**Great Depression** **Mesozoic Era**

MECHANICS

▶ EXERCISE 4 **Correcting Errors in the Use of Capital Letters**

In each of the following sentences, find the word or words that should be capitalized but are not. Then write the word or words correctly.

EXAMPLE **1.** Hart middle school is having a book fair.
1. *Middle School*

1. Would you like to go to the movies on friday?
2. The special Olympics will be held in our town this year.
3. What plans have you made for easter?
4. My sister and I were born at memorial Hospital.
5. The Rotary club donated equipment for our school's new gym.
6. Did dinosaurs live during the stone Age?
7. My favorite baseball team is the Atlanta braves.
8. Lionel works at the Beattie box company.
9. Congress is made up of the senate and the house of representatives.
10. Did you see any fireworks on the fourth of July?

WRITING APPLICATION

Using Capital Letters Correctly

Using capital letters correctly helps your readers understand your meaning. For example, read these two sentences:

> I would like to go hiking in the rocky mountains.
> I would like to go hiking in the Rocky Mountains.

The capital letters in the second sentence make it clear that *Rocky Mountains* is the name of a particular mountain range, not just a description of mountains that are rocky.

▶ WRITING ACTIVITY

Would you like to visit Washington, D.C.? Cairo, Egypt? the Great Wall of China? Your social studies teacher has asked you to write about a vacation you'd like to take to a historical place. Write an essay telling where you'd like to go and why you'd like to go there. In your essay, use at least five proper nouns. Include at least two geographical names and two personal names. Be sure to capitalize each proper noun you use.

Prewriting First, brainstorm a list of historical places that interest you. (You might want to look in a social studies textbook, an atlas, or an encyclopedia for ideas.) Which of these places would you most like to visit? After you choose a place, think about what monuments and other historical sights you would see there. What events in history do these landmarks mark? Jot down notes about what you would do during your visit.

Writing Begin your rough draft by stating where you'd like to go and why. Explain what historical event(s) happened at that place. Then tell what particular areas or landmarks you would visit. Tell what you think you'd most enjoy about your vacation. Be sure to use at least five proper nouns naming places, events, and people.

Evaluating and Revising Use an encyclopedia or other reference source to check any names and facts you're not sure about. Then have a friend read your draft. Have you clearly identified the place you want to visit? Can your friend understand why you want to go there? If not, you'll probably need to give additional specific details.

Proofreading Proofread your essay carefully for any errors in grammar, spelling, or punctuation. Be sure that you have capitalized each proper noun correctly and have not misspelled any names.

MECHANICS

(6) Capitalize the names of nationalities, races, and peoples.

TYPE OF NAME	EXAMPLES	
Nationalities	Mexican	Swiss
Races	Micronesian	Caucasian
Peoples	Cherokee	Bantu

NOTE: The words *black* and *white* may or may not be capitalized when they refer to people.

EXAMPLE During the Civil War, many **B**lacks [*or* blacks] joined the Union forces.

(7) Capitalize the brand names of business products.

EXAMPLES **G**oodyear tire, **W**hirlpool washer, **F**ord truck [Notice that names of types of products are not capitalized.]

(8) Capitalize the names of ships, trains, airplanes, spacecraft, buildings and other structures, and monuments and awards.

TYPE OF NAME	EXAMPLES	
Ships	*Santa Maria*	*Monitor*
Trains	*Metroliner*	*City of Miami*
Airplanes	*Concorde*	*Spirit of St. Louis*
Spacecraft	*Columbia*	*Ranger 7*
Buildings and Other Structures	Flatiron Building World Trade Center	Hoover Dam Golden Gate Bridge Astrodome
Monuments and Awards	Lincoln Memorial Statue of Liberty	Pulitzer Prize Medal of Honor

MECHANICS

(9) Capitalize the names of religions and their followers, holy days, sacred writings, and specific deities.

TYPE OF NAME	EXAMPLES	
Religions and Followers	Buddhism Taoism	Christian Jew
Holy Days	Purim Christmas	Ramadan Potlatch
Sacred Writings	Dead Sea Scrolls Bible	Koran Talmud
Specific Deities	Allah God	Vishnu Jehovah

NOTE: The word *god* is not capitalized when it refers to a god of ancient mythology. The names of specific gods *are* capitalized.

EXAMPLE   The Roman god of the sea was Neptune.

(10) Capitalize the names of planets, stars, and other heavenly bodies.

EXAMPLES   Mars, Pluto, North Star, Betelgeuse, Milky Way, Big Dipper, Ursa Minor

NOTE: The word *earth* is not capitalized unless it is used along with the names of other heavenly bodies. The words *sun* and *moon* are never capitalized.

EXAMPLES   China is home to one fourth of the people on earth.
How far is Saturn from Earth?
The sun rose at 7:09 this morning.

EXERCISE 5   **Correcting Sentences by Using Capital Letters Correctly**

For each of the following sentences, write correctly the word or words that should be capitalized.

MECHANICS

EXAMPLE   **1.** We went to the leesburg library to learn more about african american history.
              1. *Leesburg Library, African American*

1. The methodist minister quoted a verse from the bible.
2. Bob has a chevrolet truck.
3. On a clear night, you can see venus from earth.
4. Last summer, my history teacher took a cruise on the *song of Norway.*
5. Meet me in front of the Woolworth building.
6. Pilar received the Junior Achievement award.
7. Otis made a detailed scale model of *gemini* for his science project.
8. Helga wrote a poem about the greek god zeus.
9. Some navajo artists make beautiful silver jewelry.
10. Who were the first europeans to settle in Mexico?

 REVIEW A   **Correcting Sentences by Capitalizing Proper Nouns**

For each of the following sentences, write correctly the word or words that should be capitalized.

EXAMPLE   **1.** In the late nineteenth century, henry morton stanley explored an area of africa occupied by ancestors of the bambuti.
              1. *Henry Morton Stanley, Africa, Bambuti*

1. The bambuti live in the ituri forest, which is in northeast zaire.
2. This forest is located almost exactly in the middle of africa.
3. It lies east and just north of kisangani, as shown in the boxed area on the map on the next page.
4. The bambuti, also known as twides, aka, or efe, have lived there for many thousands of years.
5. The earliest record of people like the Bambuti is found in the notes of explorers from egypt about 2500 B.C.

Garamba National Park

Bomokandi River — Ituri Forest

Isiro
Wamba
Mungbere
Avakubi
Mambasa
Bafwasende — Aruwimi River
Lindi River
Irumu

Congo River — Banalia
Mbandaka
Kisangani
Butembo
Lubero
Goma

Luilaka River
Tshuapa River
Lomela River
Salonga National Park
Lokoro River

Lake Mai-Ndombe

Kasai River
Sankuru River

ZAIRE

Lake Tanganyika

Kinshasa
Kenge
Kikwit
Lusambo
Kongolo
Kalemie
Kananga
Tshikapa

Lulua River

Upemba National Park
Marungu Mts.
Kamina
Lake Mweru
Kolwezi
Likasi
Lubumbashi

ZAIRE

MECHANICS

6. Other early reports of these people are found on colorful tiles in italy and in the records of explorers from portugal.
7. Stanley met the bambuti, but he didn't write much about them.
8. In the 1920s, paul schebesta went to africa to learn more about them.
9. He learned that the bambuti are very different from the bantu and their other neighbors.
10. In fact, the bambuti were likely the first people in the tropical rain forest that stretches across zaire from the atlantic ocean on the western coast to the eastern grasslands.

22d. Do *not* capitalize the names of school subjects, except languages and course names followed by a number.

EXAMPLES   social studies, science, health, art, Spanish, English, Woodworking I, Consumer Education I

22e. Capitalize proper adjectives.

A *proper adjective* is formed from a proper noun. Such adjectives are usually capitalized.

PROPER NOUN	PROPER ADJECTIVE
Mexico	Mexican carvings
King Arthur	Arthurian legend
Judaism	Judaic laws
Mars	Martian landscape

22f. Capitalize certain abbreviations.

Many abbreviations are capitalized.

EXAMPLES   M.D., Mr., Ms., Mrs., FBI, TV, UN, U.S., NAACP

However, some abbreviations, especially those for measurements, are not capitalized.

EXAMPLES   etc., e.g., vol., chap., in., yd, lb, cc, ml, mm

☞ REFERENCE NOTE: Some of the abbreviations in the two sets of examples above are followed by periods and some are not. For information on when to use periods with abbreviations, see rule 23e on pages 589–591.

Capitalize both letters in a two-letter abbreviation for a state name. Do not place a period after the abbreviation.

EXAMPLES   VA   NY   TX   RI

☞ REFERENCE NOTE: For more on using abbreviations for state names, see pages 590 and 602.

22g. Capitalize titles.

(1) Capitalize the title of a person when the title comes before a name.

EXAMPLES
    Judge O'Connor   **Principal Walsh**
    Mayor Santos   **Doctor Nakamura**
    Senator Topping   **President Truman**

(2) Capitalize a title used alone or following a person's name only when the title refers to someone holding a high office.

EXAMPLES
    The **Secretary** of **State** flew to Madrid.
    Judy Klein, club **p**resident, led the meeting.

A title used alone in direct address is usually capitalized.

EXAMPLES
    Can the cast come off today, **Doctor**?
    Good morning, **Ma**'am. [*or* ma'am]

(3) Capitalize a word showing a family relationship when the word is used before or in place of a person's name.

EXAMPLES
    Are **Uncle** Carlos and **Aunt** Rosa here yet?
    I wrote to **Grandpa** Wilson yesterday.
    Either **M**om or **D**ad will drive us to the show.

Do not capitalize a word showing a family relationship when a possessive comes before it.

EXAMPLES
    My **c**ousin Dena and her **n**iece Leotie made these baskets.

▶ EXERCISE 6   **Correcting Sentences by Capitalizing Words**

For each of the following sentences, write correctly the word that should be capitalized but is not. If a sentence is correct, write *C*.

MECHANICS

EXAMPLE **1.** I like french bread with onion soup.
1. *French*

1. Velma is taking biology 100 and typing.
2. Reuben's mother, mrs. Santos, owns the new restaurant.
3. Will your uncle be at the party?
4. Well, doctor Sakamoto, do I need braces?
5. Danish, Yiddish, Icelandic, and Flemish are all germanic languages.
6. The recipe calls for a few slices of swiss cheese.
7. I wonder why *lb* is the abbreviation for *pound.*
8. On Saturday afternoon, aunt Latisha will arrive from Savannah.
9. Does professor Jones teach American history?
10. I learned to swim at grandpa Brown's cottage on the lake.

REVIEW B **Correcting Sentences by Using Capital Letters Correctly**

For each of the following sentences, write correctly the word or words that should be capitalized but are not. If a sentence is correct, write C.

EXAMPLE **1.** The Civil war is sometimes called the war between the states.
1. *War, War Between the States*

1. There is a fountain in the middle of lake Eola.
2. dr. jones teaches at York high school.
3. Some of these folk songs are mexican.
4. the atlantic ocean borders all the states from maine to florida.
5. Someday i would like to bicycle through europe.
6. all of my friends came to the party.
7. Have you visited the Washington monument?
8. Our class wrote letters to president clinton.
9. There's a long detour on highway 50 just east of brooksville, dad.
10. Our first fall camping trip will be in october.

MECHANICS

PICTURE THIS

This white rabbit led Alice to Wonderland, but where will he lead you? Racing right behind this scatter-brained, watch-watching rabbit, you follow him to another fantastic place. Write a description of this other wonderland for a child that you know. You can follow the rabbit underground, above ground, or out of this world. Name the land itself, three of its inhabitants, and at least six different structures, geographical features, or other landmarks that you discover. Capitalize all geographical and personal names.

Subject: a fantastic, imaginary place
Audience: a child you know
Purpose: to entertain

MECHANICS

Illustration from *The Complete Alice and the Hunting of the Snark* by Lewis Carroll. Illustrated by Ralph Steadman. Illustrations © 1986 Ralph Steadman. Reprinted by permission of HarperCollins Publishers.

(4) Capitalize the first and last words and all important words in titles and subtitles of books, magazines, newspapers, poems, short stories, plays, movies, television programs, works of art, and musical works.

Unimportant words in a title include

- articles (*a, an, the*)
- coordinating conjunctions (*and, but, for, nor, or, so, yet*)
- prepositions of fewer than five letters (such as *by, for, into, with*)

☞ REFERENCE NOTE: For a list of prepositions, see page 407.

TYPE OF NAME	EXAMPLES
Books	*The Horse and His Boy* *Dust Tracks on a Road*
Magazines	*Essence* *Sports Illustrated* *Reader's Digest* *for Kids*
Newspapers	*Detroit Free Press* *Tulsa Tribune*
Poems	"The City Is So Big" "For a Poet"
Short Stories	"The Six Rows of Pompons" "The Day the Sun Came Out"
Plays	*Once on This Island* *A Chorus Line*
Movies	*In the Heat of the Night* *An American Tail: Fievel Goes West*
Television Programs	*A Different World* *Star Trek: The* *Step by Step* *Next Generation*
Works of Art	*Delfina and Dimas* *Forever Free*
Musical Works	"Oh, What a Beautiful Morning" *Peter and the Wolf*

☞ REFERENCE NOTE: For guidelines on using italics (underlining) and quotation marks with titles, see pages 613–614 and 622.

MECHANICS

NOTE: An article (*a, an,* or *the*) before a title is not capitalized unless it is the first word of the title.

EXAMPLES   Do you read the *Sacramento Bee?*
Grandmother showed me an article in *The Workbasket.*

▶ EXERCISE 7   **Writing Titles for Imaginary Works**

Create a title for each item described below. Be sure each title is capitalized correctly.

1. a movie about an American Indian detective who solves a murder mystery
2. a magazine for people interested in video games
3. a book about choosing the best breed of dog as a pet for your family
4. a song about saving the rain forests
5. a painting about life in the United States

▶ EXERCISE 8   **Correcting Sentences by Capitalizing Titles**

For each of the following sentences, correct any errors you find in the capitalization of a title. If a sentence is correct, write *C.*

EXAMPLE   **1.** Mom gave me an article called "The Importance Of Fitness."
1. *"The Importance of Fitness"*

1. "Heart And Soul" is the only piano duet we can play.
2. Do you read *National geographic World?*
3. My little sister loves *the Cat in the Hat.*
4. I saw *Around the World In Eighty Days* on television.
5. We enjoyed *The Cosby show* last night.

▶ REVIEW C   **Proofreading a Paragraph to Correct Errors in Capitalization**

Proofread the following paragraph, correcting any errors in capitalization.

MECHANICS

EXAMPLE   [1] what a huge ship the *titanic* was!
       1. *What, Titanic*

[1] This magnificent ocean liner sank on april 15, 1912. [2] For more than seventy years, the *Titanic* lay untouched in the icy waters of the atlantic ocean. [3] Then, on September 1, 1985, Dr. Robert Ballard of the woods hole oceanographic institution and his crew found the ship. [4] To view the ocean floor, the scientists used the remote-controlled vehicle *argo,* shown here being prepared for launching. [5] Once they discovered the ship, they attached a special underwater Sled to *Argo.* [6] The sled, with its lights and camera, provided dr. Ballard with more than twenty thousand photographs of the *Titanic.* [7] In 1986, Dr. Ballard and his team returned to explore the wreck of the british ocean liner once more. [8] Using a mini-submarine, the Team was able to explore the sunken ship. [9] after years of wondering about the *Titanic,* underwater explorers finally found the wreck and uncovered the truth about its fate. [10] In his book *The discovery of the Titanic,* Dr. Ballard tells about his underwater adventures.

THE DISCOVERY OF THE

Titanic

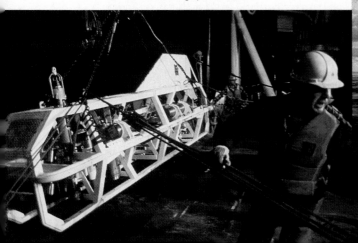

Woods Hole Oceanographic Institution

Painting from *The Discovery of the Titanic* by Dr. R. Ballard. Painting by Ken Marshall. Reprinted by permission of Warner-Madison Press.

Review: Posttest

Correcting Sentences by Capitalizing Words

For each of the following sentences, write correctly the word or words that should be capitalized but are not.

EXAMPLE   **1.** our guest speaker will be mayor Masella.
          1. *Our, Mayor*

1. Today i learned the song "simple gifts" from my friend amy, who is a quaker.
2. "Hansel and gretel" is a well-known fairy tale.
3. The kane county fall carnival will be held on saturday, october 19.
4. The trip to japan was led by dr. fujikawa.
5. Let's ask the club treasurer, ms. lee.
6. Have you met professor martínez, rondelle?
7. Luis valdez filmed *the shepherd's play*, a traditional mexican play, for tv.
8. The greek god of war was ares.
9. My mother wrote to senator smith about the closing of the base.
10. members of congress often debate issues.
11. Our class pictures will be taken on tuesday.
12. Have you seen any of Mary cassatt's paintings?
13. I didn't know that there are mummies in the american museum of natural history.
14. A venezuelan exchange student will live with our family for eight months.
15. The graduation ceremony at Newberry college was held last week.
16. When is the jewish holiday yom kippur this year?
17. Grandma asked me what i want for my birthday.
18. That movie is about World war II.
19. Next spring uncle William is going to take me on a hiking trip to mount Elbert.
20. Darnell took a raft trip on the Colorado river.

MECHANICS

SUMMARY STYLE SHEET

Names of Persons

Mae Jemison	an astronaut
Gary Soto	a writer
Maria Tallchief	a dancer

Geographical Names

Levittown	a town in New York
Fayette County	a county in Kentucky
Hawaiian Islands	islands in the Pacific Ocean
Israel	a country
in the West	heading west
Rhine River	a river in Germany
Twenty-first Street	a busy street
Everglades National Park	a park in Florida
the Green Mountains	camping in the mountains

Names of Organizations, Teams, Businesses, Institutions, Government Bodies

the Rotary Club	a service club
Texas Longhorns	a baseball team
General Mills	a large company
Largo High School	my dad's high school
Department of Agriculture	a department of the government

Names of Historical Events and Periods, Special Events, Holidays, Calendar Items

the Revolutionary War	a long war
the Stone Age	an age long ago
Fourth of July	a national holiday
the Super Bowl	a football game
March	a rainy month

Names of Nationalities, Races, Peoples, Religions

Vietnamese	a nationality
Mohawk	a Native American people
Caucasian	a race
Christianity	a religion
God	gods in Greek myths

(continued)

SUMMARY STYLE SHEET *(continued)*

Brand Names

Cheerios	a bowl of cereal
Schwinn	a ten-speed bicycle

Names of Ships, Airplanes and Spacecraft, Buildings, Monuments, and Awards

Queen Mary	a ship
Enola Gay	an airplane
Apollo	a spacecraft
Plaza Hotel	a hotel
Nobel Prize	a prize
Civil Rights Memorial	a monument

Names of Heavenly Bodies

Mars, Earth	from the earth to the sun
Ursa Major	a constellation
the Milky Way	our galaxy

Names of Languages, School Subjects

Art I	an art class
Spanish	a modern language
World History II	a history course

Titles

Governor Wilder	the governor of Virginia
the President of the United States	the president of the club
Aunt Janell	my favorite aunt
Julie of the Wolves	a novel
Time	a magazine
the *Nashville Banner*	a newspaper
"The Medicine Bag"	a short story
"Fire and Ice"	a poem
Places in the Heart	a movie
Get a Life	a television program
Young Woman with a Water Jug	a painting
"To a Wild Rose"	a song

MECHANICS

23 PUNCTUATION

End Marks, Commas, Semicolons, Colons

Diagnostic Test

Using End Marks, Commas, Semicolons, and Colons to Punctuate Sentences Correctly

Punctuation marks are missing in the following sentences. Write the word before each missing punctuation mark and add the correct mark.

EXAMPLE **1.** I read my library book studied my spelling words and finished my math homework
1. *book, words, homework.*

1. Flora please pass the salsa
2. Do you think it will rain tomorrow Fred
3. We are learning about meteorology the study of weather
4. The shirts come in the following colors blue, green brown and red

5. Yasunari Kawabata won the 1968 Nobel Prize in literature he was the first Japanese writer to win the prize
6. Watch out
7. I wish I could go to camp this summer but I have to stay home to watch my brother
8. The scouts will swim ride horses and play tennis
9. I taught Zachary how to swim
10. Mrs Sanchez is our substitute teacher for Mr Arico is on jury duty.
11. My youngest sister was born on April 12 1990
12. She is a bright lively child
13. His address is 2330 River Rd Sterling VA 22170
14. The Mandan and Hidatsa peoples in North Dakota harvested wild rice and they traded it for buffalo hides and dried meat
15. Have you ever been to San Francisco California
16. Well my favorite actress is Jasmine Guy
17. Connie Chung a national newscaster was born in Washington D C
18. I get up at 6 00 A M on school days
19. Yes a taco is a fried folded tortilla
20. The meeting will be held Sunday February 28 1993 at 2 00 P M

End Marks

An ***end mark*** is a punctuation mark placed at the end of a sentence. *Periods, question marks,* and *exclamation points* are end marks. Periods are also used after some abbreviations.

23a. Use a period at the end of a statement.

EXAMPLES　French is the official language of Haiti, but many people there also speak Haitian Creole.
I will write to you soon.

23b. Use a question mark at the end of a question.

EXAMPLES   **Have you heard Gloria Estefan's new song?**
Where should I meet you?

23c. Use an exclamation point at the end of an exclamation.

EXAMPLES   **What a cute kitten that is!**
This egg-drop soup is delicious!

23d. Use either a period or an exclamation point at the end of a request or a command.

EXAMPLES   **Please sit down.** [a request]
Sit down! [a command]

EXERCISE 1   **Correcting Sentences by Adding End Marks**

Write the last word of each sentence, and add a period, a question mark, or an exclamation point.

EXAMPLE   **1. What time is it**
     1. *it?*

1. When does the bus come
2. What a great game that was
3. Did you bring your lunch today
4. Hyo was born in Korea
5. I don't understand the assignment

EXERCISE 2   **Correcting Paragraphs by Adding Capital Letters and End Marks**

Decide where the sentences in the following paragraphs begin and end. Rewrite each paragraph, providing the needed capital letters and end marks.

EXAMPLE   what an ancient art weaving is
     What an ancient art weaving is!

MECHANICS

have you ever been to Hawaii the first Europeans who landed there found chiefs dressed in beautiful feather cloaks feathers for cloaks like the one on the left came from thousands of birds different colored feathers were arranged in royal designs then the feathers were attached to a base of woven fibers cloaks were worn into battle and ceremonies most of the islanders did not wear such fine garments

nowadays colorful prints like the ones on the right are worn by all kinds of people on the islands every Friday is Aloha Friday on that day many people wear Hawaiian prints and live flowers wouldn't it be fun if all the students in our school wore clothes to show their heritage once a week

Robert Dampier, *Kamehameha III* (1825). Oil on canvas, 24 1/8 × 20 1/16". Honolulu Academy of Arts, gift of Mrs. C. Montague Cooke, Jr., Charles M. Cooke III, and Mrs. Heston Wren, in memory of Dr. C. Montague Cooke, Jr.

MECHANICS

23e. Use a period after certain abbreviations.

TYPES OF ABBREVIATIONS	EXAMPLES	
Personal Names	I. M. Pei N. Scott Vicki L. Ruíz Momaday	
Titles Used with Names	Mr. Mrs. Ms. Jr. Dr.	
Organizations	Assn. Co. Corp. Inc.	

MECHANICS

NOTE: Abbreviations for government agencies and some widely used abbreviations are written without periods. Each letter of such abbreviations is capitalized.

EXAMPLES   ASPCA, CIA, CNN, GI, NAACP, PC, RFD, SOS, TV, YMHA

TYPES OF ABBREVIATIONS	EXAMPLES		
Addresses	Ave.	Blvd.	Ct.
	P.O. Box	Rd.	St.
Geographical Names	Ark.	Colo.	D.C.
	St. Paul	P.R.	U.S.

NOTE: A two-letter state abbreviation without periods is used only when it is followed by a ZIP Code. Both letters of the abbreviation are capitalized. No mark of punctuation is used between the abbreviation and the ZIP Code.

EXAMPLES   Washington, **DC** 20013
San Juan, **PR** 00904

TYPES OF ABBREVIATIONS	EXAMPLES		
Times	A.M.	B.C.	Aug.
	P.M.	A.D.	Sat.

NOTE: Abbreviations for units of measure are usually written without periods. However, you should use a period with the abbreviation *in.* (for *inch*) to prevent confusing it with the word *in.*

EXAMPLES   cc, kg, ml, m, ft, lb, qt

If you're not sure whether to use periods with an abbreviation, look in a dictionary, an encyclopedia, or another reliable reference source.

NOTE: When an abbreviation that has a period ends a sentence, another period is not needed. However, a question mark or an exclamation point is used in such situations if it is needed.

> EXAMPLES   The game lasted until 8:30 P.M.
> Did it start at 5:00 P.M.?

☞ **REFERENCE NOTE:** For more information on using capital letters for abbreviations, see page 576.

▶ EXERCISE 3   **Correcting Sentences by Adding Punctuation**

Write the following sentences, adding end marks where they are needed.

EXAMPLE   **1.** Some caterpillars become butterflies
           1. *Some caterpillars become butterflies.*

1. Will Mr Highwater be teaching the science course
2. Just after 3:00 P M the sun came out
3. The letter from Ms E J Hunter was dated Fri, Nov 12
4. How heavy the traffic was on First Avenue
5. Do your measuring cups show both ml and oz

WRITING APPLICATION

Using End Marks Correctly

End marks let your readers understand your purpose at a glance. Compare the following examples. Which end mark shows that the writer is pleased and excited?

> This is great news.
> This is great news!
> This is great news?

The period at the end of the first sentence tells the reader that the writer is simply making a statement. The question mark at the end of the third sentence indicates that the writer questions whether the news is "great." Only the exclamation mark at the end of the second sentence signals the writer's excitement and happiness.

▶ WRITING ACTIVITY

You are a scriptwriter for a popular TV show. You're writing a scene in which one of the characters wins one million dollars in a sweepstakes. Write down the character's response when he or she hears the good news. Use a variety of end marks to help express the character's feelings.

Prewriting First, you'll need to choose a character. You can either make up a character or use one from a TV show you've seen. Next, put yourself in the place of the character. How would that person feel if he or she won a million dollars? Jot down some notes on how you think your character would react. Would he or she give some or all of the money to charity? put it in a bank? buy a boat? fly around the world?

Writing Using your prewriting notes, write a draft of what your character will say. Make your draft at least one page long. Use end punctuation to help express the character's emotions.

Evaluating and Revising Read your character's response aloud. Does it sound realistic? If not, revise it to make it sound more like what a person would actually say. Check to make sure you've used a variety of end marks to express your character's feelings.

Proofreading Check your writing for any errors in grammar, spelling, or punctuation. Be sure that all proper names are correctly spelled and capitalized.

▶ REVIEW A **Using End Marks Correctly**

For each of the following sentences, write the word or words that should be followed by an end mark. Add the proper end mark after each word.

EXAMPLE **1.** My neighbor Mr Nhuong showed me this picture of people celebrating the Vietnamese holiday Tet
1. *Mr.; Tet.*

1. Unlike our New Year's Day, which is always on Jan 1, Tet can fall on any day late in January or early in February
2. Moreover, Tet isn't just one single day; the celebration lasts a whole week
3. Wouldn't you like a week-long holiday
4. Even here at 8420 Beaconcrest Ave, the Nhuong family still enjoy their traditions
5. According to Mr. Nhuong, the name of the first person to visit a house can bring good or bad luck to the family
6. Since my nickname is Lucky, the Nhuongs asked me to be their first visitor and to arrive by 7:00 A M
7. Please don't be late
8. One of the Nhuongs' relatives had flown in from Santa Barbara, Calif, just that morning
9. Mrs Nhuong prepared a huge breakfast, and we all sat down to enjoy it
10. What a great meal that was

MECHANICS

Commas

End marks separate complete thoughts. Commas separate words or groups of words *within* a complete thought.

Items in a Series

23f. Use commas to separate items in a series.

A *series* is three or more items written one after the other. The items may be single words or groups of words.

WORDS IN A SERIES
Sugar, bananas, and citrus are grown in Jamaica. [nouns]
Yesterday I dusted, vacuumed, and mopped. [verbs]
The day was wet, cold, and windy. [adjectives]
GROUPS OF WORDS IN A SERIES
At the beach we swam, built sand castles, and played volleyball. [predicates]
I searched for the lost contact lens in the sink, on the counter, and on the floor. [prepositional phrases]

NOTE: Some writers do not use the comma before *and* in a series. It's a good idea always to use that comma, however. Sometimes the comma is needed to make your meaning clear. Notice how using a comma before *and* changes the meaning in these examples.

EXAMPLES   Grandma, Mom, and Dad came to the game.
[Three people were at the game.]
Grandma, Mom and Dad came to the game.
[Grandma is being told who came to the game.]

Always be sure that there are at least three items in a series before you add commas. Two items do not need a comma between them.

INCORRECT   Today is sunny, and warm.
 CORRECT   Today is sunny and warm.

When all the items in a series are joined by *and* or *or,* do not use commas to separate them.

EXAMPLES   I've seen snakes **and** lizards **and** toads in our yard.
Shall we go bowling **or** rent a movie **or** listen to tapes?

EXERCISE 4   **Proofreading Sentences for the Correct Use of Commas**

Most of the following sentences need commas. If a sentence needs commas, write the word before each missing comma; then add the comma. If a sentence is correct, write *C.*

EXAMPLE   **1.** Cora Jack and Tomás all entered the contest.
1. *Cora, Jack,*

1. I finished my dinner brushed my teeth and ran out the door.
2. The nurse checked the patient's pulse took his temperature and gave him a glass of water.
3. For lunch we had milk a tuna sandwich and pears.
4. Camille Cosby Queen Latifah and Maxine Waters won Candace Awards in 1992.
5. Marcus plays the piano and the guitar and the drums.

23g. Use commas to separate two or more adjectives that come before a noun.

EXAMPLES   Pita is a round, flat bread of the Middle East.
James Earl Jones certainly has a deep, strong, commanding voice.

Do not place a comma between an adjective and the noun immediately following it.

INCORRECT   I found an old, rusty, bicycle.
   CORRECT   I found an old, rusty bicycle.

Sometimes the last adjective in a series is closely connected in meaning to the noun. In that case, do not use a comma before the last adjective.

EXAMPLES   The tall pine tree swayed in the wind. [not *tall, pine tree*]
   Kimchi is a spicy Korean dish made with pickled cabbage. [not *spicy, Korean dish*]

To see whether a comma is needed, add *and* between the adjectives (*tall and pine,* for example). If *and* sounds awkward, don't use a comma.

▶ EXERCISE 5   **Proofreading Sentences for the Correct Use of Commas**

For each of the following sentences, write the word that should be followed by a comma; then add the comma. If a sentence is correct, write C.

EXAMPLE   **1.** Mrs. Hirata taught us several beautiful old Japanese folk songs.
   1. *beautiful,*

1. His calm wrinkled face told a story.
2. François Toussaint L'Ouverture was a brilliant patriotic Haitian leader.
3. The huge lively kingfish wriggled off the hook.
4. There's a sleek shiny bicycle in the store window.
5. The sound of the soft steady rain put me to sleep.
6. We read Chief Black Hawk's moving farewell speech.
7. After our hike I washed in the cold clear spring water.
8. May I have some more of that cold delicious gazpacho soup?

9. The old diary had ragged yellowed pages.
10. The crowded dining room is filled with people celebrating my parents' anniversary.

23h. Use a comma before *and, but, for, or, nor, so,* and *yet* when they join the parts of a compound sentence.

EXAMPLES   Theo will bring the potato salad, and Sarah will bring the apple juice.
Congress passed the bill, but President Bush vetoed it.
I went to bed early, for I had a big day ahead of me.

☞ REFERENCE NOTE: If you're not sure that you can recognize a compound sentence, review pages 318 and 357.

In many cases, a very short compound sentence does not need a comma before *and, but,* or *or.*

EXAMPLE   I'm tired and I'm hungry.

NOTE: Don't confuse a compound sentence with a simple sentence containing a compound verb. No comma is needed between the parts of a compound verb.

COMPOUND SENTENCE   We ran relay races first, and then we ate lunch.
COMPOUND VERB   We **ran** relay races first and then **ate** lunch.

☞ REFERENCE NOTE: For more about compound verbs, see pages 353–355.

▷ EXERCISE 6   **Correcting Compound Sentences by Adding Commas**

Some of the following sentences are compound and need to have commas added. If a sentence needs a comma, write the word before the missing comma; then add the comma. If a sentence is correct, write C.

EXAMPLE **1.** The storm brought a lot of rain but a tornado did the most damage.

1. *rain,*

1. At the Native American Heritage Festival, Mary Johns wove baskets from sweet grass and Alice Billie made rings from beads.
2. The sailboat was almost hidden by the fog yet we could see part of the mast.
3. German Silva of Mexico was the fastest male runner in the 1994 and 1995 New York City Marathons and Tegla Loroupe of Kenya was the female winner in both races.
4. Would you like to play checkers or shall we go to the mall instead?
5. I called my friends and told them the news.
6. Jim practiced the piano piece for hours for he wanted to do well at the recital.
7. The African American festival Kwanzaa begins the day after Christmas yet the two holidays are celebrated in very different ways.
8. Neither the students nor their science teacher could make the experiment work.
9. The old oak tree shaded the house but the shade kept the grass from growing.
10. The lake contains large fish and it is also home to several alligators.

PICTURE THIS

The year is 1910. You are one of the immigrants shown on the next page. You are about to land on Ellis Island, and the Statue of Liberty stands majestically before you. Before the boat docks, record in your journal your first impressions of your new country. How does the statue make you feel? What are your hopes and dreams for your new life? In your journal entry, correctly use at least five commas.

Subject: the Statue of Liberty
Audience: yourself
Purpose: to record your impressions and feelings

Interrupters

23i. Use commas to set off an expression that interrupts a sentence.

Two commas are needed if the expression to be set off comes in the middle of the sentence. One comma is needed if the expression comes first or last.

EXAMPLES My favorite gospel singers, BeBe and CeCe
            Winans, were on TV last night.
          Yes, I'll call back later.
          How did you do in karate class today, Kami?

(1) Use commas to set off appositives and appositive phrases that are not needed to understand the meaning of a sentence.

An *appositive* is a noun or a pronoun that identifies or explains another noun or pronoun beside it. An *appositive phrase* is an appositive with its modifiers.

EXAMPLES   A gymnast, **Mrs. Shaw,** will coach us. [The appositive *Mrs. Shaw* identifies who the gymnast will be.]

This book is about geology, **the science of the earth and its rocks.** [*The science of the earth and its rocks* is an appositive phrase that explains the word *geology.*]

Do not use commas when an appositive is needed to understand the meaning of a sentence.

EXAMPLES   My cousin Roberto lives in Puerto Rico. [I have more than one cousin and am using his name to identify which cousin I mean.]

My cousin, Roberto, lives in Puerto Rico. [I have only one cousin and am using his name as extra information.]

MECHANICS

EXERCISE 7   **Writing Sentences with Appositives**

In the painting on the next page, young people are enjoying themselves at an outdoor party. Some of the people are dancing. Others are talking or having refreshments. Write five sentences about the people at the party. In your sentences, use five of the following groups of words as appositives. Insert commas wherever they are needed.

Eliza Wolcott
the best dancer
the sounds of people
    having fun
a quiet spot for
    conversation
a refreshing drink

the happiest couple on
    the dance floor
the girl in the striped
    dress
a beautiful place for a
    party

EXAMPLE   *You can hear the murmuring voices and bursts of laughter, the sounds of people having fun.*

Pierre-Auguste Renoir, *Ball at the Moulin de la Galette*. Giraudon/Art Resource, New York.

MECHANICS

(2) Use commas to set off words used in direct address.

Using the name of the person to whom you are speaking is using *direct address.* Commas are used to set off words used in direct address.

EXAMPLES   Ms. Jacobs, please explain the assignment.
Do you know who Santa Anna was, Beth?
You're right, Inés, he was a Mexican general.

(3) Use a comma after such words as *well, yes, no,* **and** *why* **when they begin a sentence.**

EXAMPLES   Well, I'll help you.
Yes, the table is set.
Why, there's Yoko!

▶ EXERCISE 8   **Correcting Sentences by Adding Commas**

For each of the following sentences, write each word that should be followed by a comma; then add the comma.

EXAMPLE **1.** Will Ruben her oldest brother meet us at the park tomorrow?
1. *Ruben, brother,*

1. Wood Buffalo National Park the world's largest national park is in Canada.
2. The park was named for the wood buffalo a species slightly smaller than the plains buffalo.
3. Michi will you read the haiku you wrote?
4. Why you and I were born on the same day!
5. If you mow the lawn Kelly I'll rake the clippings.
6. I read about whooping cranes in *Natural History* a magazine about nature.
7. Did you bring the tickets Jorge?
8. Yes I have them right here.
9. Well I'm glad you didn't forget them.
10. My cousin Velma my favorite relative wants to visit Ghana.

23j. Use commas in certain conventional situations.

(1) Use commas to separate items in dates and addresses.

EXAMPLES Bill Cosby was born on July 12, 1937, in Philadelphia, Pennsylvania.
Saturday, May 10, will be the day of the soccer playoff.
My aunt lives at 41 Jefferson Street, Northfield, Minnesota.

Notice that a comma separates the last item in a date or in an address from the words that follow it. However, a comma does *not* separate a month and a day (*July 12*) or a house number and a street name (*41 Jefferson Street*).

NOTE: Use the correct ZIP Code on every envelope you address. No punctuation is used between the state abbreviation and the ZIP Code.

EXAMPLE Cerritos, CA 90701

(2) Use a comma after the salutation of a friendly letter and after the closing of any letter.

EXAMPLES   **Dear Grandma and Grandpa,**   **Love,**
                 Dear Tyrone,   **Sincerely,**

EXERCISE 9   **Using Commas Correctly in Conventional Situations**

Write the following items and sentences, inserting commas where they are needed.

1. Yours truly
2. Shirley Chisholm was born on November 30 1924.
3. The first woman principal chief of the Cherokee Nation is Wilma Mankiller, who was born near Rocky Mountain Oklahoma.
4. Write to me at 327 Adams Way Darrouzett TX 79024.
5. The Harvest Carnival is on Friday October 29 1993.

REVIEW B   **Proofreading a Letter for the Correct Use of Commas**

The following letter contains ten errors in the use of commas. Rewrite the letter, adding or deleting commas as needed.

EXAMPLES   [1] July, 6, 1997
      1. *July 6, 1997*

      [2] Dear Tom
      2. *Dear Tom,*

[1] Well on July 4, 1997, Aunt Lil kept her promise and took me up in her airplane. [2] Wow! What a view of the canyons valleys, and plateaus we had! [3] We were lucky, and saw a small herd of mustangs on a hill. [4] Aunt Lil circled above the horses and the plane's shadow frightened the stallion. [5] The whole herd stampeded with tails, and manes and hooves flying in a storm of dust all the way down into the

valley. [6] One black colt trailed behind, but his mother quickly nudged him onward. [7] In a moment the swift sturdy mustangs, descendants of the fiery steeds of the Spanish conquistadors were galloping into the woods. [8] I wish you could have seen them Tom! [9] At least I remembered my camera so here is a picture of those beautiful horses.

[10] Yours truly

Sal

MECHANICS

Semicolons

A semicolon is part period and part comma. Like a period, it separates complete thoughts. Like a comma, it separates items within a sentence.

23k. Use a semicolon between parts of a compound sentence if they are not joined by *and, but, or, nor, for, so,* or *yet.*

EXAMPLES   Todd's report is on Arizona; mine is on Utah.
            The rain clouds are moving in quickly; let's head
            home.

NOTE: Don't overuse semicolons. Sometimes it is better to
       separate a compound sentence into two sentences
       rather than to use a semicolon.

    ACCEPTABLE   Parrots make interesting pets; some can
                  learn to repeat whole sentences or whistle
                  tunes.
    BETTER   Parrots make interesting pets. Some
                  can learn to repeat whole sentences or
                  whistle tunes.

EXERCISE 10   **Proofreading Sentences for the Correct
               Use of Semicolons**

Most of the following sentences have commas where
there should be semicolons. If a sentence needs a
semicolon, write the words before and after the missing semicolon; then insert the semicolon. If a sentence is correct, write C.

EXAMPLE   **1.** Mary Vaux Walcott treasured her box of
              watercolor paints, she took it with her
              everywhere she went.
           1. *paints; she*

1. As a young girl, she visited the Canadian
   Rockies each year, and there she began to
   paint wildflowers.
2. She loved mountain climbing, she often crossed
   rugged areas to find new wildflowers.
3. She painted her flowers from life, for she did
   not like to rely on pencil sketches.
4. You can see five of her paintings on the next page,
   aren't they beautiful?
5. Painting A shows a western red lily, it withers
   quickly when it is picked.
6. Painting B is of a bottle gentian, a fall flower, it
   grows in bogs and swamps.

7. American wisteria is a climbing plant, and you can see in Painting C that it has many showy flowers.

8. Painting D shows blossoms of the American waterlily opening in early morning, their aroma draws insects.

9. In Painting E is the vine of Carolina jessamine, it spreads its fragrant flowers through treetops.

10. Mary Vaux Walcott is known as the "Audubon of North American wildflowers," for she painted more than seven hundred species.

Mary Vaux Walcott/National Museum of American Art.

Colons

A colon usually signals that more information follows.

23l. Use a colon before a list of items, especially after expressions such as *the following* and *as follows.*

EXAMPLES   These are the winners of the poetry contest: Carmen Santiago, Justin Douglass, and Steven Yellowfeather.
Pack the following items for your overnight trip: a toothbrush, toothpaste, and your hairbrush.
The order of the colors seen through a prism is as follows: red, orange, yellow, green, blue, indigo, violet.

Never use a colon immediately after a preposition or a verb. Instead, either omit the colon or reword the sentence.

INCORRECT   My report includes: a table of contents, three chapters, illustrations, and a list of sources.
CORRECT   My report includes a table of contents, three chapters, illustrations, and a list of sources.
CORRECT   My report includes the following parts: a table of contents, three chapters, illustrations, and a list of sources.

23m. Use a colon between the hour and the minute when you write the time.

EXAMPLES   8:55 A.M., 9:15 P.M., 6:22 this morning

23n. Use a colon after the salutation of a business letter.

EXAMPLES   Dear Sir or Madam: Dear Mrs. Jordan:
Dear Sales Manager: To Whom It May Concern:

MECHANICS

EXERCISE 11 **Using Colons Correctly**

If one of the following items needs a colon, copy the word the colon should follow; then add the colon. For numbers, write the entire number and insert the colon. If a sentence is correct, write C.

EXAMPLE **1.** Bring the following items to class your
notebook, a pencil, and your textbook.
1. *class:*

1. We visited the following cities Bayamón, Ponce, and San Juan.
2. A good baby sitter should have the following qualities promptness, an interest in children, and common sense.
3. To stay healthy, you should not smoke or chew tobacco.
4. Add these items to your shopping list tissues, toothpaste, and shampoo.
5. A good friend must be loving, loyal, and honest.
6. The first bell rings at 8 10 A.M.
7. Your homework includes studying your spelling words, reading one chapter, and working on your composition.
8. The recipe for Brunswick stew called for these ingredients lamb, carrots, potatoes, and onions.
9. The next show begins at 6 00 P.M.
10. Dear Sir or Madam

REVIEW C **Proofreading a Letter for the Correct Use of End Marks, Commas, Semicolons, and Colons**

Proofread the following letter for errors in punctuation. Rewrite the letter, adding the necessary end marks, commas, semicolons, and colons.

EXAMPLE [1] 1200 E Halifax Avenue
Baltimore, MD 21213
1. *1200 E. Halifax Avenue*
Baltimore, MD 21213

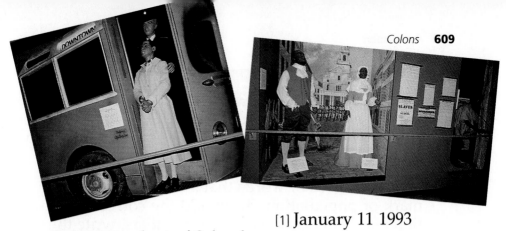

[1] January 11 1993

Superintendent of Schools
Baltimore City Board of Education
200 E. North Avenue
Baltimore, MD 21202

[2] Dear Superintendent

[3] Would your students be interested in visiting an African American wax museum [4] The only one of its kind is right here in Baltimore [5] The Great Blacks in Wax Museum features life-size wax models of famous African Americans [6] These wax images include leaders in education, civil rights and science [7] The museum displays statues of the following people Rosa Parks, Phillis Wheatley and Crispus Attucks (shown in the enclosed publicity photographs), Carter G Woodson, Dred Scott, Harriet Tubman, Booker T. Washington, Frederick Douglass, and many others.

[8] During Black History Month our company offers students and teachers discount tours of the museum tours of other historic attractions are also available [9] For more information, please call me between 8 30 AM and 5 30 PM

[10] Yours truly

Jane Lee Harper

Jane Lee Harper
President
Uhuru Guided Tours

Review: Posttest

Using End Marks, Commas, Semicolons, and Colons Correctly

Write the word or words that should be followed by a mark of punctuation. Then add the correct punctuation mark after each word. For numbers, write the entire number and insert the correct punctuation mark.

EXAMPLE **1.** Mr. Cotton my next-door neighbor asked me to pick up his mail while he is away
1. *Cotton, neighbor, away.*

1. The mangos and papayas and avocados will make a good fruit salad
2. Ms Jee gave a short clear history of Korea
3. Ray Charles the popular singer and musician became blind at the age of seven
4. I have registered for classes in photography ceramics and weaving
5. When will dinner be ready
6. Ted mowed the lawn cleaned the garage and painted the shed
7. Here comes a tornado
8. Cheryl will take gymnastics Eddie will take piano lessons
9. Would 6 30 P M be too early
10. This Zuni ring was made in Santa Fe NMex
11. I finished the letter but I haven't proofread it yet
12. Dear Senator Kay Bailey Hutchison
13. We will learn about the U S court system then we will visit the county courthouse.
14. Sara Eric and Manuel can speak both Spanish and English
15. Hurry, get me some ice
16. Yes I did clean my room
17. When you go cross-country skiing, bring the following items skis boots poles and ski wax

18. Shall we leave at 9 00 A M
19. Mr Pak when is the Chinese New Year
20. The Scouts' Annual Dinner will be held February 19 1993.

SUMMARY OF USES OF THE COMMA

23f Use commas to separate items in a series—words and groups of words.

23g Use commas to separate two or more adjectives that come before a noun.

23h Use a comma before *and, but, for, or, nor, so,* and *yet* when they join the parts of a compound sentence.

23i Use commas to set off an expression that interrupts a sentence.

(1) Use commas to set off appositives and appositive phrases that aren't needed to understand the meaning of a sentence.

(2) Use commas to set off words used in direct address.

(3) Use a comma after words such as *well, yes, no,* and *why* when they begin a sentence.

23j Use a comma in certain conventional situations.

(1) Use commas to separate items in dates and addresses.

(2) Use a comma after the salutation of a friendly letter and after the closing of any letter.

MECHANICS

24 PUNCTUATION

Underlining (Italics), Quotation Marks, Apostrophes, Hyphens

Diagnostic Test

Using Underlining (Italics), Quotation Marks, Apostrophes, and Hyphens

Each of the following sentences contains one error in the use of underlining (italics), quotation marks, apostrophes, or hyphens. Write each sentence correctly.

EXAMPLE **1.** "Its important for everyone to vote," Jesse Jackson said.

1. *"It's important for everyone to vote," Jesse Jackson said.*

1. I like to sing This Land Is Your Land."
2. Washingtons largest city is named for Chief Seattle.

3. Chapter 2 is called *The Siamese Cat*.
4. I haven't read the book Treasure Island yet.
5. "I remember making a barometer in the fourth grade. "I had to start over twice before it would work," I said.
6. "Deva, will you please show me how to make a weather vane"? asked Todd.
7. "It took me only forty five minutes to make a sundial," Carlos remarked.
8. We built a model airplane, but it crashed on it's test flight.
9. All student's projects are due next Friday.
10. "Everyones project must be in on time," Mrs. Tolliver said.

Underlining (Italics)

Italics are printed letters that lean to the right—*like this*. When you write or type, you show that a word should be *italicized* by underlining it. If your writing were printed, the typesetter would set the underlined words in italics. For example, if you typed

Zora Neale Hurston wrote <u>Mules and Men</u>.

the sentence would be printed like this:

Zora Neale Hurston wrote *Mules and Men*.

NOTE: If you use a personal computer, you can probably set words in italics yourself. Most word processing software and many printers can produce italic type.

24a. Use underlining (italics) for titles of books, plays, periodicals, films, television programs, works of art, long musical works, ships, aircraft, and spacecraft.

TYPE OF NAME	EXAMPLES
Books	*Number the Stars* *To Kill a Mockingbird* *House Made of Dawn*
Plays	*Song of Sheba* *The Sound of Music* *Life with Father*
Periodicals	the *Sioux City Journal* *Latin American Literary Review* *Highlights for Children*
Films	*Toy Story* *The Wizard of Oz* *Oliver & Company*
Television Programs	*Under the Umbrella Tree* *Fun with Watercolors* *Reading Rainbow*
Works of Art	*The Old Guitarist* *Gamin* *Confucius and Disciples*
Long Musical Works	*Chôros* *Treemonisha* *A Little Night Music*
Ships	*Flying Cloud*　　　USS *Lexington*
Aircraft	*Solar Challenger* *Spirit of St. Louis*
Spacecraft	*Pioneer 13*　　　*Discovery*

MECHANICS

NOTE: An article (*a, an,* or *the*) before the title of a magazine or a newspaper is not italicized or capitalized when it is part of a sentence rather than part of the title.

EXAMPLES　I deliver the *Evening Independent.* [*The* is part of the sentence, not part of the title.]
Is that the latest issue of *The New Yorker?* [*The* is part of the magazine's title.]

REFERENCE NOTE: For examples of titles that use quotation marks instead of italics, see page 622.

▶ EXERCISE 1   **Using Underlining (Italics) Correctly**

For each of the following sentences, write each word or item that should be printed in italics, and underline it.

EXAMPLE   **1.** We saw Rodin's famous work The Thinker.
            1. *The Thinker*

1. The magazine Popular Science reports news about science.
2. Have you ever seen the movie The Shaggy Dog?
3. My favorite painting is Morning of Red Bird by Romare Bearden.
4. We read a scene from the play The Piano Lesson.
5. How do you like the new fashions in the latest issue of Seventeen?
6. Tcheky Karyo starred in the 1988 movie The Bear.
7. Have you read today's Chicago Sun-Times or the Chicago Tribune?
8. My sister watches Sesame Street every day.
9. Apollo 11 landed on the moon on July 20, 1969.
10. The book The Path Between the Seas is about the Panama Canal.

Quotation Marks

24b.   Use quotation marks to enclose a **direct quotation**—a person's exact words.

EXAMPLES   Our team leader Lana says, "I always try to practice every day."
            "Let's go home," Jeanne suggested.

Do not use quotation marks for an **indirect quotation**—a rewording of a direct quotation.

DIRECT QUOTATION   Juan said, "The bus is late." [Juan's exact words]
INDIRECT QUOTATION   Juan said that the bus was late. [not Juan's exact words]

MECHANICS

MECHANICS

24c. A direct quotation begins with a capital letter.

EXAMPLES   Mrs. Talbott said, "Please get a pencil."
Kristina asked, "Is it my turn?"

24d. When a quoted sentence is divided into two parts by an expression that identifies the speaker, the second part of the quotation begins with a small letter.

EXAMPLE   "Will you take care of my lawn," asked Mr. Franklin, "while I'm on vacation next month?"

When the second part of a divided quotation is a new sentence, it begins with a capital letter.

EXAMPLE   "Yes, we will," I said. "We can certainly use the extra money."

24e. A direct quotation is set off from the rest of the sentence by a comma, a question mark, or an exclamation point, but not by a period.

Set off means "to separate." If a quotation comes at the beginning of a sentence, a comma follows it. If a quotation comes at the end of a sentence, a comma comes before it. If a quoted sentence is interrupted, a comma follows the first part and comes before the second part.

EXAMPLES   "I think that dogs make better pets than cats do," said Frank.
Maria asked, "What makes you say that?"
"Oh," Donna commented, "he's just saying that because he's never had a cat."

When a quotation ends with a question mark or an exclamation point, no comma is needed.

EXAMPLES   "Does Frank have a dog?" Todd asked.
"He has three of them!" Donna exclaimed.

EXERCISE 2   **Punctuating and Capitalizing Quotations**

For each of the following sentences, add commas, end marks, quotation marks, and capital letters where they are needed. If a sentence is correct, write C.

EXAMPLE   **1.** We're going tubing next Saturday said Carlos.
   1. *"We're going tubing next Saturday," said Carlos.*

1. May I go with you I asked.
2. We'd like to go, too added Barbara and Tranh.
3. Barbara asked who will bring tubes for everyone
4. Jim said I'll bring them
5. I offered to bring sandwiches and lemonade
6. My dad will drive Carlos said he has a van.
7. The river is fed by a glacier Tranh stated.
8. That means Barbara said that the water will be cold.
9. It should feel good I pointed out if Saturday is as hot as today is.
10. Carlos told all of us to meet him at his house at 8:30 A.M.

24f. A period or a comma should always be placed *inside* the closing quotation marks.

EXAMPLE   "I can't wait to see Shirley Caesar's new video," James said. "It's supposed to come out next week."

24g. A question mark or an exclamation point should be placed *inside* closing quotation marks when the quotation itself is a question or an exclamation. Otherwise, it should be placed *outside*.

EXAMPLES   "What time will you be home from work, Mom?" asked Michael. [The quotation is a question.]
   Who said, "All the world's a stage"? [The sentence, not the quotation, is a question.]

"Stop!" yelled the crossing guard. [The quotation is an exclamation.]

What a surprise to hear Susana say, "We're moving back to Puerto Rico in June"! [The sentence, not the quotation, is an exclamation.]

 EXERCISE 3 **Punctuating and Capitalizing Quotations**

Rewrite each of the following sentences correctly, inserting punctuation and adding capitalization where needed.

EXAMPLE **1.** Clementine Hunter was born in 1887 said María and she died in 1988.

1. *"Clementine Hunter was born in 1887," said María, "and she died in 1988."*

1. Staci said here is a photograph of this self-taught American artist.
2. Clementine Hunter was born in Natchitoches, Louisiana Staci remarked.
3. She started working on a plantation when she was only fourteen María added.
4. When she was fifty-three years old said Staci Hunter decided to do what she loved most—paint.
5. Staci continued she began painting on almost any surface that would hold the paint!

MECHANICS

6. Her early pieces were painted on brown paper bags and cardboard boxes María remarked and then on canvas, wood, and paper.

7. Hunter used bright colors Mike explained to paint everyday scenes like this one, called *Wash Day*.

Clementine Hunter, *Wash Day*. Courtesy of the Association for the Preservation of Historical Natchitoches, Melrose Plantation.

8. It may surprise you to learn added Mike that her paintings sold for as little as twenty-five cents fifty years ago!

9. Nowadays he continued her paintings are worth thousands of dollars.

10. Moreover Staci concluded Clementine Hunter's paintings have been exhibited throughout the United States.

EXERCISE 4 **Revising Indirect Quotations to Create Direct Quotations**

Revise each of the following sentences by changing the indirect quotation to a direct quotation. Be sure to use capital letters and punctuation marks where they are needed. [Note: Although the example gives two revisions, you need to write only one.]

MECHANICS

EXAMPLE   **1.** I asked the cashier for change for a dollar.
　　　　　1. *"May I please have change for a dollar?" I asked the cashier.*

or

I asked the cashier, "Would you please give me change for a dollar?"

1. The cashier replied that she wasn't allowed to make change unless a purchase was made.
2. I said that I needed a new pen.
3. The cashier told me that it cost seventy-nine cents.
4. I said that I would give her $1.79.
5. She told me that she could then give me change for a dollar.

24h. When you write dialogue (conversation), begin a new paragraph every time the speaker changes.

EXAMPLE　　In Khanabad, Mulla Nasrudin was sitting in a teahouse when a stranger walked in and sat down beside him.

The newcomer said:

"Why is that man over there sobbing his heart out?"

"Because I have just arrived from his home-town and told him that all his winter camel fodder was lost in a fire."

"It is terrible to be a bearer of such tidings," said the stranger.

"It is also interesting to be the man who will shortly tell him the good news," said Nasrudin. "You see, his camels have died of a plague, so he will not need the fodder after all."

Idries Shah, "Camel Fodder"

24i. When a quotation consists of several sentences, put quotation marks only at the beginning and the end of the whole quotation.

EXAMPLE　　"Will you help with the scenery for our play, Bao? Zachary and Pia have offered to make costumes," Aaron said.

24j. Use single quotation marks to enclose a quotation within a quotation.

EXAMPLES   "Read the chapter ʻComets and Asteroids,' "
            stated Mr. Mendoza.
            "Mrs. Engle distinctly said, ʻYour book reports
            are due Thursday,' " Krista told me.

PICTURE THIS

Your class is holding a contest to see who can write an unlikely story that stretches the facts. You get an idea for a great tall tale when you see this scene. Write a brief tall tale about cows waiting for a book-mobile. In your tale, include at least two titles of books that these cows might check out. Also include three or more lines of dialogue. Be sure to use italics and quotation marks correctly.

Subject: cows waiting for a bookmobile
Audience: your teacher and classmates
Purpose: to entertain

MECHANICS

24k. Use quotation marks to enclose the titles of short works such as short stories, poems, newspaper or magazine articles, songs, episodes of television programs, and chapters and other parts of books.

TYPE OF NAME	EXAMPLES
Short Stories	"Raymond's Run" "Two Kinds" "Amigo Brothers"
Poems	"Jetliner" "Mother to Son" "Song of the Sky Loom"
Articles	"Celebrating Our Heritage" "The Giants of Easter Island" "Pollen"
Songs	"Aloha Oe" "Georgia on My Mind" "America the Beautiful"
Episodes of Television Programs	"Kali the Lion" "Soul of Spain" "The Trouble with Tribbles"
Chapters and Other Parts of Books	"Energy from the Stars" "I Go to Sea" "Behind the Cotton Curtain"

REFERENCE NOTE: For examples of titles that use italics instead of quotation marks, see pages 613–614.

EXERCISE 5   **Punctuating Quotations**

Write each of the following sentences, adding single or double quotation marks where they are needed.

EXAMPLE   **1.** I just finished the chapter The Circulatory System in our health book, Dell told me.
   1. *"I just finished the chapter 'The Circulatory System' in our health book," Dell told me.*

1. Diane is learning the song Tarantella for her piano recital.
2. Angelo, can we meet after school tomorrow? We need to practice our presentation, Sam said.
3. I'm sure I heard the announcer say, Schools are closed because of the storm, I said.
4. I can pronounce all the words in Lewis Carroll's poem Jabberwocky Nina told Lou.
5. Ted said, My dad will pick us up on Saturday at 7:30 A.M. After the race, he is taking us to Lucy Ho's for lunch. Do you like Chinese food?

▶ REVIEW A   **Punctuating Paragraphs in a Dialogue**

Rewrite the following paragraphs, using capital letters, as well as quotation marks and other marks of punctuation, where they are needed. [Note: The punctuation marks already in the exercise are correct.]

EXAMPLE   [1] What are you writing my grandfather asked.
　　　　　1. *"What are you writing?" my grandfather asked.*

[1] Grandpa I said I'm writing a report about your hero Octaviano Larrazolo. Can you tell me how he helped Mexican Americans?

[2] Grandpa got out his scrapbook. Octaviano did many things for our people he began. In 1912, New Mexico became a state. Octaviano and other Hispanic leaders wanted to be sure that Mexican Americans could hold political office. They wanted to make certain that they would always be allowed to vote. When New Mexico's new constitution was written, Octaviano and the other leaders fought for these rights.

[3] How did Mr. Larrazolo know how to protect the rights of people?

[4] Grandpa replied he had studied law. His knowledge of the law helped him understand the constitution. It also helped him later when he became interested in politics.

[5] When did Mr. Larrazolo become involved in politics I asked.

[6] In 1916, he campaigned for Ezequiel Cabeza de Baca for governor said Grandpa. De Baca was elected, but he died a month later. Another election was held and Larrazolo became New Mexico's governor.

[7] I asked what are some things that Mr. Larrazolo felt strongly about?

[8] He answered Octaviano believed that public schools should teach children about Mexican American culture. He also was in favor of both English and Spanish being spoken in schools. Here is a picture of him with his daughters.

[9] What else should I know about Octaviano Larrazolo I asked.

[10] Octaviano was elected to the United States Senate in 1928 Grandpa said. He continued to work hard for the rights of Hispanic Americans until he died.

Wesley Bradfield/Courtesy Museum of New Mexico #47760.

Apostrophes

Possessive Case

The *possessive case* of a noun or a pronoun shows ownership or relationship.

OWNERSHIP	RELATIONSHIP
Heidi's comb **his** jacket **our** dog	**no one's** fault a **week's** vacation **my** stepbrother

241. To form the possessive case of a singular noun, add an apostrophe and an –*s*.

EXAMPLES   a student**'s** grant   Tanaka**'s** store
the child**'s** toy   Tess**'s** painting

NOTE: A proper noun ending in *s* may take only an apostrophe to form the possessive case if adding *'s* would make the name awkward to say.

EXAMPLES   Kansas**'** climate
Ms. Andrews**'** class

▶ EXERCISE 6   **Using Apostrophes for Singular Possessives**

For each of the following sentences, identify the word that needs an apostrophe. Then write the word correctly punctuated.

EXAMPLE   **1.** Kenyans celebrate 1963 as the year of their countrys independence.
1. *country's*

1. Soon the young nations athletes were setting records in international sports.
2. Leading Kenyas world-class distance runners was Kipchoge Keino, shown here with his Olympic medals.

3. Keino increased his endurance by running many miles in his homelands mountains.
4. In 1965, he burst into his sports top ranks by setting world records for both the 3,000-meter race and the 5,000-meter race.
5. His training in the mountains helped Keino win his first gold medal at Mexico Citys 1968 Olympics.
6. His record in that years 1,500-meter race stood until 1984.
7. In fact, the Kenyan teams runners took home a total of eight medals in 1968.
8. In the 1972 Olympics, Keinos performance won him a second gold medal, this time for the 3,000-meter steeplechase.
9. A silver medal in the 1,500-meter race marked his careers remarkable completion.
10. His victories not only won Keino the worlds praise but also set new standards for runners everywhere.

| **24m.** | To form the possessive case of a plural noun that does not end in *s*, add an apostrophe followed by an *s*. |

EXAMPLES   geese's feathers   men's clothing
              children's books   feet's bones

| **24n.** | To form the possessive case of a plural noun ending in *s*, add only the apostrophe. |

EXAMPLES   boxes' lids   ten minutes' time
              beetles' shells   the Ozawas' address

NOTE: Do not use an apostrophe to form the *plural* of a noun. Remember that the apostrophe shows ownership or relationship.

INCORRECT   Two boys' left their books here.
CORRECT   Two **boys** left their books here.

▶ EXERCISE 7   **Writing Possessives**

Rewrite each of the following expressions by using the possessive case. Be sure to add an apostrophe in the right place.

EXAMPLE   **1.** the speeches of the politicians
1. *the politicians' speeches*

1. the books of the children
2. the prize of the winner
3. the bed of the kittens
4. the home of my friend
5. the streets of the city

▶ EXERCISE 8   **Writing Plural Possessives**

For each sentence, identify the word that needs an apostrophe. Then write the word correctly punctuated.

EXAMPLE   **1.** Wild creatures survival depends on their ability to adapt.
1. *creatures'*

1. Animals ways of dealing with cold are fascinating.
2. At night, chickadees feathers are fluffed over the soft down next to their skin.
3. In addition, the birds breathing rates and heart-beats slow, and their body temperatures fall, saving energy.
4. Deers winter coats, with their hollow hairs filled with air, keep body heat from escaping.
5. Soft undercoats of fine hair are many animals thermal underwear.
6. In this picture, you can see how squirrels tails, flattened against their backs and necks, keep them warm when they leave their nests.

7. The picture above shows how red foxes tails are used as muffs curled around their heads while they sleep.
8. On grouses toes are comblike structures that make walking easier.
9. In cold weather, fur grows on the bottom of snowshoe hares feet for protection.
10. Traits like these make possible wild creatures survival during freezing temperatures and snow.

24o. Do not use an apostrophe with possessive personal pronouns.

EXAMPLES   Is this pencil **yours** or **mine**?
            Our apartment is smaller than **theirs**.
            Her enchiladas are spicier than **his**.

24p. To form the possessive case of some indefinite pronouns, add an apostrophe and an *–s*.

EXAMPLES   either**'s** topic
            everyone**'s** favorite
            somebody**'s** notebook

☞ REFERENCE NOTE: For more about possessive personal pronouns, see page 503. For more about indefinite pronouns, see page 377.

▶ EXERCISE 9 | **Writing the Possessive Case of Indefinite Pronouns**

Rewrite each of the following expressions by using the possessive case. Be sure to add an apostrophe in the correct place.

EXAMPLE **1.** the speeches of everybody
1. *everybody's speeches*

1. the wishes of everyone
2. the fault of nobody
3. the answer of no one
4. the album of someone
5. the guess of anybody

Contractions

24q. Use an apostrophe to show where letters, numerals, or words have been left out in a contraction.

A *contraction* is a shortened form of a word, a number, or a group of words. The apostrophe in a contraction shows where letters, numerals, or words have been left out.

Common Contractions			
I am	I'm	they have	they've
1994	'94	here is	here's
let us	let's	you are	you're
of the clock	o'clock	she is	she's
he would	he'd	you will	you'll

The word *not* can be shortened to *n't* and added to a verb. The spelling of the verb usually does not change.

MECHANICS

EXAMPLES 　is not . . . . **isn't** 　　has not . . . .**hasn't**
　　　　　　are not . . . . . **aren't** 　　have not . . . . . **haven't**
　　　　　　does not . . .**doesn't** 　　had not . . . . **hadn't**
　　　　　　do not . . . .**don't** 　　should not . .**shouldn't**
　　　　　　was not. . . . .**wasn't** 　　would not. . .**wouldn't**
　　　　　　were not. . **weren't** 　　could not . . . .**couldn't**

EXCEPTIONS 　will not. . . . . **won't** 　　cannot . . . .**can't**

Don't confuse contractions with possessive pronouns.

CONTRACTIONS	POSSESSIVE PRONOUNS
It's raining. [*It is*] **It's** been a long day. [*It has*]	**Its** tires are flat.
Who's your coach? [*Who is*] **Who's** been in my room? [*Who has*]	**Whose** watch is this?
You're welcome. [*You are*]	**Your** sister won.
They're late. [*They are*] **There's** the bell. [*There is*]	**Their** house is next door. That car is **theirs.**

▶ EXERCISE 10　**Using Apostrophes in Contractions**

For each of the following sentences, write the word requiring an apostrophe, and add the apostrophe. If a sentence is correct, write *C*.

EXAMPLE　**1.** Well be leaving soon.
　　　　　1. *We'll*

　1. Youve been a big help.
　2. Its time to leave for the party.
　3. Whose umbrella is this?
　4. Were having a fund-raiser for the homeless.
　5. I cant find my skate key.
　6. He promised hed wear his seat belt.
　7. Lets get tickets to see Los Lobos.
　8. Youd better hurry up.
　9. Its too late now.
10. Ill wash the car tomorrow morning.

EXERCISE 11 **Writing Contractions**

For each of the following sentences, write the contraction of the italicized word or words.

EXAMPLE **1.** *We will* see a performance of the puppet theater when we visit the Japan America Theatre in Los Angeles.
1. *We'll*

1. *Have not* you always wondered what goes on backstage at a puppet show?
2. *Here is* an illustration that takes you behind the scenes at a seventeenth-century puppet theater in Japan.
3. The audience *cannot* see all the backstage action because of the curtain.
4. The men *who are* handling the puppets are very highly trained.
5. They *do not* speak the characters' lines, though.
6. *It is* the man sitting on the right on the table who narrates the play.
7. As you can see, *he is* accompanied by a musician.
8. On the right are more puppets; *they have* been hung there for future use.
9. In the box at the top, *that is* the Japanese word that means "puppet."
10. As *you will* notice, the Japanese system of writing is very different from ours.

MECHANICS

Plurals

24r. Use an apostrophe and an *−s* to form the plurals of letters, numerals, and symbols, and of words referred to as words.

EXAMPLES   The word *Mississippi* has four *i*'s, four *s*'s, and two *p*'s.
Your *1*'s and *7*'s look alike.
You wrote +'s instead of *x*'s on all these math problems.
Try not to use so many *you know*'s when you talk.

WRITING APPLICATION

Using Apostrophes Correctly to Make Writing Clear

Important information can come in small packages. For instance, punctuation marks don't take up much room in your writing, yet they express a great deal in meaning. Compare the following sentences:

Well, go see what's going on.
We'll go see what's going on.

 WRITING ACTIVITY

You've been so busy at summer camp that you haven't had time to write to your best friend. Write a letter to your friend, telling about your first week at camp. Be sure to use apostrophes correctly to make your meaning clear.

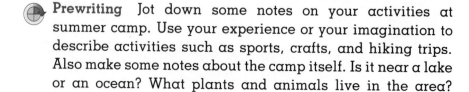 **Prewriting** Jot down some notes on your activities at summer camp. Use your experience or your imagination to describe activities such as sports, crafts, and hiking trips. Also make some notes about the camp itself. Is it near a lake or an ocean? What plants and animals live in the area?

MECHANICS

Where do you sleep? What do you eat? If you've never been to a summer camp, get information from a friend who has.

Writing Before beginning your first draft, you may want to look at page 739 for tips on writing a personal letter. Include specific details about the natural setting and special or daily activities at the camp. Tell your friend what you've enjoyed most. You may also want to mention new friends you've made and new things you've learned. Try to give your friend a clear, vivid picture of your first week.

Evaluating and Revising Ask a friend or a family member to read your letter. Can he or she imagine the activities you've described? If not, revise your letter to make it clearer and more descriptive. Be sure you've used the correct form for friendly letters.

Proofreading As you proofread your letter, take extra care with apostrophes. Check your use of contractions and pronouns like *its, it's, your, you're, their,* and *they're.* Also look for any other errors in grammar, spelling, and punctuation.

MECHANICS

Hyphens

24s. Use a hyphen to divide a word at the end of a line.

When you divide a word at the end of a line, remember the following rules:

(1) Divide a word only between syllables.

INCORRECT	Uncle Payat, Aunt Nina, and Ayita will jou-rney eighty miles to join us.
CORRECT	Uncle Payat, Aunt Nina, and Ayita will jour-ney eighty miles to join us.

(2) Do not divide a word of one syllable.

INCORRECT	They are bringing a salad, ham, and rye bre-ad.
CORRECT	They are bringing a salad, ham, and rye bread.

(3) Do not divide a word so that one letter stands alone.

INCORRECT	Is that your family's brand-new car parked a-cross the street?
CORRECT	Is that your family's brand-new car parked across the street?

24t. Use a hyphen with compound numbers from *twenty-one* to *ninety-nine*.

EXAMPLE   Until 1959, the United States had only forty-eight states.

▶ REVIEW B   **Using Apostrophes and Hyphens Correctly**

For each of the following sentences, write the word or term that needs an apostrophe or a hyphen. Add the missing punctuation mark.

EXAMPLE   **1.** Wheres my history book?
1. *Where's*

1. Do you know where the atlases and the diction aries are?
2. There are two *r*s in *tomorrow.*
3. He cant tie a square knot.
4. The tiger cubs arent on view yet.
5. Is that one of Issey Miyakes new designs?
6. I have several of Tish Hinojosas albums.
7. Forty nine students signed the get-well card.
8. The mens chorus gave a great performance.
9. Whos going to the fair this weekend?
10. Its almost time to leave.

Review: Posttest

Proofreading Sentences for the Correct Use of Underlining (Italics), Quotation Marks, Apostrophes, and Hyphens

Each of the following sentences contains at least one error in the use of underlining (italics), quotation marks, apostrophes, or hyphens. Write each sentence correctly.

EXAMPLE **1.** We havent finished dinner yet.
1. *We haven't finished dinner yet.*

1. Melba built a model of the Santa Maria for extra credit in social studies.
2. My teachers house is being painted.
3. Each classroom has thirty four desks.
4. This recipe calls for fresh greens, potatoes, car rots, and onions.
5. The pots boiling over!
6. Whos going to sample this dish?
7. Dont forget the soy sauce.
8. The three chefs recipes were prepared by the chefs themselves on television.
9. Jiro's last name has two *l*s.
10. Have you seen Faith Ringgolds story quilts?
11. We could hear the flapping of the geeses wings.
12. Isn't your favorite poem The Unicorn?
13. "Wasn't that a song? asked Carrie."
14. I think a folk singer wrote it, answered Tony.
15. Juanita said that "she would hum a bit of it."
16. Brad commented, "I think my parents have a copy of it".
17. "Can you bring it to class"? Elena asked.
18. "Who said, Time is money"? Gerald asked.
19. "Benjamin Franklin wrote it," answered Karen, "in a book called Advice to a Young Tradesman."
20. "I think, said Theo, that you're right."

MECHANICS

25 SPELLING

Improving Your Spelling

Good Spelling Habits

The following techniques can help you spell words correctly.

1. **To learn the spelling of a word, pronounce it, study it, and write it.** Pronounce words carefully. Mistakes in speaking can cause mistakes in spelling. For instance, if you say *ad•je•tive* instead of *ad•jec•tive,* you will probably spell the word wrong.

   - First, make sure that you know how to pronounce the word correctly, and then practice saying it.
   - Second, study the word. Notice any parts that might be hard to remember.
   - Third, write the word from memory. Check your spelling.
   - If you misspelled the word, repeat the three steps of this process.

2. **Use a dictionary.** If you are not absolutely sure about the spelling of a word, look it up in a dictionary. Don't guess about the correct spelling.

3. **Spell by syllables.** A *syllable* is a word part that can be pronounced by itself.

> EXAMPLES   ear•ly [two syllables]
>   av•er•age [three syllables]

Instead of trying to learn how to pronounce a whole word, break it into its syllables whenever possible. It's easier to learn a few letters at a time than to learn all of them at once.

4. **Keep a list of your spelling errors.** Whenever you misspell a word, add it (correctly spelled) to your list. Review your list often.

5. **Proofread for careless spelling errors.** Always proofread your written work carefully to correct misspellings.

Spelling Rules

ie and *ei*

25a. Write *ie* when the sound is long *e*, except after *c*.

> EXAMPLES   chief, believe, brief, receive, ceiling
> EXCEPTIONS   either, neither, weird, seize

Write *ei* when the sound is not long *e*, especially when the sound is long *a*.

> EXAMPLES   neighbor, weigh, reindeer, height, foreign
> EXCEPTIONS   friend, fierce, ancient, mischief

This verse may help you remember the *ie* rule:

> *I* before *e*
> Except after *c*,
> Or when sounded like *a*,
> As in *neighbor* and *weigh*.

MECHANICS

MECHANICS

▶ EXERCISE 1 **Writing Words with *ie* and *ei***

Complete the following letter by adding the *ie* or *ei* to each numbered word.

EXAMPLE I wrote Aunt Han a [1] br____f thank-you note.
1. *brief*

February 12, 1997

Dear Aunt Han,

Thank you very much for the [1] sl____gh you sent me. I [2] rec____ved it on the [3] ____ghth of this month, just in time for our first big snowstorm. Here's a picture to show you how much I am enjoying your gift. My new [4] fr____nds and I also have great fun pulling each other across the [5] f____lds in it. The [6] n____ghbor's dog races alongside us, barking [7] f____rcely all the way.

Thank you again for your thoughtfulness. So far, I like living here in Vermont, but I can't quite [8] bel____ve how different everything is from life in California.

Your loving [9] n____ce,

Mai

P.S. If only we had some [10] r____ndeer to pull us!

Prefixes and Suffixes

25b. When adding a prefix to a word, do not change the spelling of the word itself.

A *prefix* is a letter or a group of letters added to the beginning of a word to create a new word that has a different meaning.

EXAMPLES dis + satisfy = **dis**satisfy
mis + lead = **mis**lead
over + due = **over**due
pre + view = **pre**view

▶ EXERCISE 2 **Spelling Words with Prefixes**

Combine each of the following prefixes and words to create a new word.

EXAMPLE **1.** mis + place
1. *misplace*

1. fore + word   **5.** un + common **9.** dis + loyal
2. un + fair   **6.** im + patient **10.** over + coat
3. in + dependent **7.** pre + historic
4. mis + use   **8.** mis + spell

▶ EXERCISE 3 **Spelling Words with Prefixes**

Create five words by combining the prefixes given below with the words listed beside them. (You may use each prefix and each word more than once.) Check each of your new words in a dictionary. Then use each word in a sentence.

Prefixes			Words			
un–	mis–	dis–	able	do	judge	place
pre–	over–	re–	cover	trust	pay	informed

EXAMPLE **1.** *repay*—*I'll repay you when I get my allowance.*

25c. When adding the suffix *–ness* or *–ly* to a word, do not change the spelling of the word itself.

A *suffix* is a letter or a group of letters added at the end of a word to create a new word that has a different meaning.

EXAMPLES   kind + ness = kind**ness**
sincere + ly = sincere**ly**

EXCEPTIONS   For most words that end in *y,* change the *y* to *i* before *–ly* or *–ness.*

happy + ly = happ**ily**
friendly + ness = friendl**iness**

25d. Drop the final silent *e* before a suffix beginning with a vowel. *Vowels* are the letters *a, e, i, o, u,* and sometimes *y.* All other letters of the alphabet are *consonants.*

EXAMPLES   cause + ing = caus**ing**
reverse + ible = revers**ible**
strange + er = strang**er**

EXCEPTIONS   Keep the silent *e* in words ending in *–ce* and *–ge* before a suffix beginning with *a* or *o.*

change + able = change**able**
courage + ous = courage**ous**

25e. Keep the final silent e before a suffix beginning with a consonant.

EXAMPLES   hope + less = hope**less**
agree + ment = agree**ment**
force + ful = force**ful**

EXCEPTIONS   argue + ment = arg**ument**
judge + ment = judg**ment**
true + ly = tru**ly**

▶ EXERCISE 4   **Spelling Words with Suffixes**

Combine each of the following words and suffixes to create a new word.

EXAMPLE   **1.** sudden + ness
   1. *suddenness*

1. active + ity   **5.** gentle + er   **9.** decorate + ed
2. sure + ly   **6.** silly + ness   **10.** breathe + ing
3. state + ment **7.** suspense + ful
4. locate + ion **8.** little + est

25f. For words ending in a consonant plus *y*, change the *y* to *i* before any suffix that does not begin with *i*.

EXAMPLES   cry + ed = cr**ied**   lonely + est = lonel**iest**
pretty + er = prett**ier**   lazy + ness = laz**iness**

Keep the *y* if the suffix begins with an *i*.

EXAMPLE   carry + ing = carry**ing**

Keep the *y* if the word ends in a vowel plus *y*.

EXAMPLES   stay + ed = stay**ed**   key + ed = key**ed**

25g. Double the final consonant before adding *–ing,* *–ed, –er,* or *–est* to a one-syllable word that ends in a single vowel followed by a single consonant.

EXAMPLES   beg + ing = be**gging**   sad + er = sa**dder**
quiz + ed = qui**zzed**   big + est = bi**ggest**

When a one-syllable word ends in two vowels followed by a single consonant, do *not* double the consonant before adding *–ing, –ed, –er*, or *–est*.

EXAMPLES   sleep + ing = slee**ping**   cool + er = coo**ler**
              treat + ed = treat**ed**   fair + est = fair**est**

EXERCISE 5   **Spelling Words with Suffixes**

Combine each of the following words and suffixes to create a new word.

EXAMPLE   **1.** creep + er
            1. *creeper*

1. say + ing	**5.** steady + ness	**8.** easy + ly
2. slim + er	**6.** beat + ing	**9.** chop + ed
3. squeak + ing	**7.** rely + ing	**10.** step + ing
4. rainy + est		

REVIEW A   **Proofreading Sentences for Correct Spelling**

Most of the following sentences contain misspelled words. Write each misspelled word correctly. If a sentence is correct, write C.

EXAMPLE   **1.** My grandma often says, "Let slepping dogs lie."
            1. *sleeping*

1. It's unnusual weather for this time of year.
2. In 1991, Lithuania regainned its independence.
3. With Sacagawea's help, Lewis and Clark maped out the Northwest.
4. Now that Bao Duc is on the team, our hiting has gone up.
5. Serita and I can easyly make enough burritos for the entire class.
6. We visited my grandmother in the Dominican Republic during the rainyest month of the year.
7. Please resstate the question.

8. My sister has the loveliest voice I've ever heard.
9. Former astronaut Sally Ride earned recognition for her courage and steadyness.
10. The temperature has droped ten degrees in the last hour.

REVIEW B | **Proofreading a Paragraph for Correct Spelling**

For each sentence in the following paragraph, write correctly the word or words that are incorrectly spelled. If a sentence is correct, write C.

EXAMPLE [1] My cousin Chris was very couragous after she was baddly hurt in a car accident.
   1. *courageous; badly*

[1] After the accident, Chris found that she truely needed other people. [2] Her friends, family, and nieghbors gladly helped her. [3] However, Chris liked the idea of geting along on her own as much as possible, so she was disatisfied. [4] Fortunatly, she was able to join an exciting program called Helping Hands. [5] This program provides monkeys like this one as friends and helpers for people with disabilities. [6] Chris said that the baby monkeys are raised in lovving foster homes for four years, and then they go to Boston to recieve special training. [7] There, they

learn how to do tasks on command, such as opening and closeing doors, turning lights on and off, and puting tapes into a VCR or tape player. [8] Chris has been happyly working with her own monkey, Aldo, for six months now. [9] Aldo retreives anything that Chris has droped, works the TV remote control, and even scratches Chris's back when it itches! [10] Chris is always jokeing, "Pretty soon Aldo will be writting my book reports for me!"

Forming the Plural of Nouns

25h. Follow these rules for spelling the plural of nouns:

(1) To form the plural of most nouns, add –s.

SINGULAR   snack   oven   heap   valley   organization
PLURAL   snack**s**   oven**s**   heap**s**   valley**s**   organization**s**

(2) Form the plural of nouns ending in *s, x, z, ch,* or *sh* by adding –es.

SINGULAR   glass   fox   buzz   patch   bush
PLURAL   glass**es**   fox**es**   buzz**es**   patch**es**   bush**es**

NOTE: Proper nouns usually follow this rule, too.

EXAMPLES   the Cruz**es**   the Jones**es**

EXERCISE 6   **Spelling the Plural of Nouns**

Spell the plural form of each of the following nouns.

EXAMPLE   **1.** scratch
1. *scratches*

1. tax	**5.** box	**9.** waltz
2. dish	**6.** branch	**10.** radish
3. address	**7.** loss	
4. lens	**8.** peach	

(3) Form the plural of nouns ending in a consonant plus *y* by changing the *y* to *i* and adding *–es*.

SINGULAR	country	puppy	berry
PLURAL	countries	puppies	berries

EXCEPTION   With proper nouns, just add *–s*.
EXAMPLES   the Shelbys   the Mabrys

(4) Form the plural of nouns ending in a vowel plus *y* by adding *–s*.

SINGULAR	boy	turkey	holiday
PLURAL	boys	turkeys	holidays

(5) Form the plural of nouns ending in a vowel plus *o* by adding *–s*.

SINGULAR	rodeo	patio	stereo
PLURAL	rodeos	patios	stereos

(6) Form the plural of nouns ending in a consonant plus *o* by adding *–es*.

SINGULAR	tomato	echo	veto	torpedo
PLURAL	tomatoes	echoes	vetoes	torpedoes

EXCEPTIONS   auto—autos   Latino—Latinos   silo—silos

NOTE: Form the plural of musical terms ending in *o* by adding *–s*.

SINGULAR	piano	trio	soprano	cello
PLURAL	pianos	trios	sopranos	cellos

MECHANICS

EXERCISE 7   **Spelling the Plural of Nouns**

Spell the plural form of each of the following nouns.

EXAMPLE   **1.** story
          1. *stories*

1. cargo
2. apology
3. valley
4. laundry
5. piano
6. potato
7. emergency
8. chimney
9. radio
10. video

(7) The plural of a few nouns is formed in irregular ways.

SINGULAR	woman	mouse	foot	man	child
PLURAL	women	mice	feet	men	children

(8) Some nouns are the same in the singular and the plural.

SINGULAR AND PLURAL   salmon   Sioux   deer   fowl   sheep

(9) Form the plural of numerals, letters, symbols, and words referred to as words by adding an apostrophe and −s.

SINGULAR	1990	A	+	*and*
PLURAL	1990's	A's	+'s	*and*'s

NOTE: In your reading, you may notice that these plurals are sometimes written with no apostrophe, as in *1990s.* Leaving out the apostrophe can cause confusion in some cases. Therefore, it is a good idea for you always to use the apostrophe.

EXERCISE 8   **Spelling the Singular and Plural Forms of Nouns**

Spell the singular form and the plural form of each italicized word in the following sentences. [Note: A word may have more than one correct plural form.]

EXAMPLES   **1.** We use strong line to fish for *salmon.*
1. *salmon—singular; salmon—plural*

2. Field *mice* invaded the food supplies in the tent.
2. *mouse—singular; mice—plural*

1. Our guide Robert Tallchief, a *Sioux,* knows llamas.
2. Robert and his father use llamas like the ones shown on the next page to carry equipment people need for hiking and for catching *fish.*
3. The trips are very popular with both men and *women.*

4. *Children* especially are fascinated by the sure-footed llamas.
5. However, the llama has one very disagreeable habit—if upset, it bares its *teeth* and spits.
6. The Tallchiefs' llama trips have attracted tourists from all over the world, including many *Japanese.*
7. One highlight of these trips is viewing *moose* in their natural habitat.
8. *Deer* thrive in this area of the Northwest.
9. In addition, families of mountain *sheep* clamber up the steep cliffs.
10. Most people who go on the llama trips take many pictures of the wild *game.*

▶ REVIEW C   **Proofreading Sentences for Correct Spelling**

For each sentence in the following paragraph, write correctly the word or words that are incorrectly spelled. If a sentence is correct, write *C*.

EXAMPLE   **1.** Aunt Dorothy Kelly talks mostly in expressions from the 1930s and earlyer.
   1. *1930's; earlier*

1. When we want something because our friends have it, Aunt Dorothy says we're trying to keep up with the Jones'.
2. If we get into mischief, she exclaims, "You little monkies!"
3. When my brother's run through the house, she shakes her head and mutters, "Boys will be boys."
4. Every time she can't find her eyeglasses, Aunt Dorothy says, "I've beaten the bushes, looking for them."

5. Aunt Dorothy believes that there are only two things in life that are certain: death and taxs.
6. We've heard her say "There's no use crying over spilled milk" and "Wishs won't wash dishs" about a thousand times apiece.
7. Aunt Dorothy's old-time sayings are echos of her childhood.
8. Sometimes we get tired of hearing these little bits of folk wisdom, especially when Aunt Dorothy and all the little Kellies come over to visit for the holidays.
9. However, Aunt Dorothy is so lovable that we just smile and listen to her proverbs and storys.
10. Sometimes she says something really worthwhile, like "There are only two things that money can't buy—true love and home-grown tomatos."

Words Often Confused

People often confuse the words in each of the following groups. Some of these words are *homonyms.* They are pronounced the same, but they have different meanings and spellings. Others have the same or similar spellings.

already	*at an earlier time*
	The show has *already* begun.
all ready	*all prepared; completely prepared*
	The floats are *all ready* for the fiesta.
altar	[noun] *a table or stand used for religious ceremonies*
	My uncle Chee wove the cloth for the *altar.*
alter	[verb] *to change*
	A flood can *alter* a riverbed.

altogether	*entirely*
	I'm *altogether* lost.
all together	*everyone or everything in the same place*
	Let's sit *all together* at the movie.

brake	[noun] *a device to stop a machine*
	The front *brake* on my bike squeaks.
break	[verb] *to fracture; to shatter*
	Try not to *break* your promises.

 EXERCISE 9   **Choosing Between Words Often Confused**

From each pair in parentheses, choose the word or words that will make the sentence correct.

EXAMPLE   **1.** Can the artist (*altar, alter*) the design?
              1. *alter*

1. Did you help (*brake, break*) the piñata, Felipe?
2. Who arranged the flowers on the (*altar, alter*)?
3. I've (*all ready, already*) seen that movie.
4. My mom was (*all together, altogether*) pleased with my report card.
5. Don't forget to set the emergency (*brake, break*).

capital	*a city, the location of a government*
	Havana is the *capital* of Cuba.
capitol	*building; statehouse*
	Our state *capitol* is made of granite.

cloths	*pieces of cloth*
	My aunt brought these kente *cloths* home from Ghana.
clothes	*wearing apparel*
	Bob irons his own *clothes*.

MECHANICS

coarse	[adjective] *rough, crude, not fine*
	Some cities still use *coarse* salt to melt snow on streets and roads.
course	[noun] *path of action; series of studies* [also used in the expression *of course*]
	What *course* should we follow to accomplish our goal?
	The counselor suggested several *courses* for us to take.
	I can't, *of course*, tell you what to do.

desert	[noun] *a dry, sandy region; a wilderness*
[des′ert]	Plants and animals of the *desert* can survive on little water.
desert	[verb] *to abandon, to leave*
[de·sert′]	Don't *desert* your friends when they need you.
dessert	[noun] *the final course of a meal*
[de·sert′]	What's for *dessert* tonight?

EXERCISE 10 **Choosing Between Words Often Confused**

From each pair in parentheses, choose the word that will make the sentence correct.

EXAMPLE **1.** The sand on the beach is (*coarse, course*).
       1. *coarse*

1. The Mojave (*Desert, Dessert*) is located in southeastern California.
2. Juan packed lightweight (*clothes, cloths*) for his trip to Mexico.
3. The sailor set a (*coarse, course*) for the port of Pago Pago.
4. When was the (*capital, capitol*) built, and how long has the state legislature been meeting there?
5. For (*desert, dessert*) we had pears and cheese.

 REVIEW D **Proofreading Sentences to Correct Spelling Errors**

For each of the following sentences, write correctly the word or words that are misspelled.

EXAMPLE **1. The students are already for the Fall Festival.**
1. *all ready*

1. Throughout history, most societies and cultures from the hot dessert regions to the cold northern regions have celebrated the harvest.
2. The Jewish celebration of Sukkot marks the time when the harvest was gathered and the people were already for winter.
3. The most important tradition of Sukkot called for the family to live altogether in a temporary shelter called a sukkah.
4. Today, of coarse, Jews still celebrate Sukkot, but they simply eat a meal outdoors under a shelter like this one.

5. Native Americans believed that without the help of the gods there would be a brake in their good fortune.

MECHANICS

6. During their planting ceremonies, most Native Americans honored their gods by wearing special cloths.
7. To thank their harvest gods, the Chinese and Japanese placed wheat on alters.
8. Today, however, the Japanese do not altar this tradition much.
9. In most Japanese cities, including the capitol, the people hold parades to thank the ocean for the food it provides.

T. Harmon Parkhurst/Courtesy Museum of New Mexico #55189

10. Many families in the United States celebrate Thanksgiving by sharing a special holiday meal, often with pumpkin pie for desert.

hear	[verb] *to receive sounds through the ears* When did you *hear* the news?
here	[adverb] *in this place* The mail is *here*.

its	[possessive form of *it*] You cannot judge a book by *its* cover.
it's	[contraction of *it is* or *it has*] *It's* your turn, Theresa. *It's* been a long day.

MECHANICS

lead [verb, present tense, rhymes with *need*]
[lēd]   *to go first, to be a leader*
        Will you *lead* the singing, Rachel?
  led [verb, past tense of *lead*] *went first*
        The dog *led* its master to safety.
 lead [noun, rhymes with *red*] *a heavy metal;*
[lĕd]   *graphite used in pencils*
        Lead is no longer used in household
          paints.
        Use a pencil with a softer *lead* if you want
          to draw dark, heavy lines.

loose [adjective, rhymes with *moose*] *not tight*
        A *loose* wheel on a bike is dangerous.
  lose [verb] *to suffer loss*
        That sudden, loud noise made me *lose*
          my place.

MECHANICS

▶ EXERCISE 11   **Choosing Between Words Often Confused**

From each pair in parentheses, choose the word that will make the sentence correct.

EXAMPLE   **1.** Rabbi Epstein (*lead, led*) our group during our tour of Israel.
         1. *led*

1. We could (*hear, here*) the clanking of the heavy (*lead, led*) gates.
2. A kimono is a (*loose, lose*) Japanese garment with short, wide sleeves and a sash.
3. Mom said that (*its, it's*) your turn to wash the dishes tonight.
4. (*Hear, Here*) is a good article about Black History Month.
5. I hope the team doesn't (*loose, lose*) (*its, it's*) opening game.

passed	[verb, past tense of *pass*] *went by* We *passed* you on the way to school this morning.
past	[noun] *that which has gone by;* [preposition] *beyond;* [adjective] *ended* You can learn much from the *past*. The band marched *past* the school. The *past* week was a busy one.
peace	*quiet, order, and security* People all over the world long for *peace*.
piece	*a part of something* I had a delicious *piece* of spinach pie at the Greek festival.
plain	[adjective] *simple, common;* [noun] *a flat area of land* Raul's directions were *plain* and clear. The coastal *plain* was flat and barren.
plane	[noun] *a flat surface; a tool; an airplane* A rectangle is a four-sided *plane* with four right angles. Wood shavings curled from the *plane* to the workshop floor. The *plane* flew nonstop to Atlanta.
principal	[noun] *the head of a school;* [adjective] *chief, main* The middle-school *principal* visited the high school. The committee's *principal* task is preserving the park.
principle	[noun] *a rule of conduct; a general truth* Freedom of speech is one of the *principles* of democracy.

> **EXERCISE 12**

Choosing Between Words Often Confused

From each pair in parentheses, choose the word that will make the sentence correct.

EXAMPLE **1.** Florence Griffith-Joyner quickly (*passed, past*) the other runners.
   1. *passed*

1. The Old Order Amish wear (*plain, plane*) clothes.
2. Many Americans believe that the golden rule is a good (*principal, principle*) to live by.
3. The trees are just (*passed, past*) their most beautiful fall colors.
4. One (*peace, piece*) of the puzzle was missing.
5. Komako used a (*plain, plane*) to smooth the rough edge of the door.

> **REVIEW E**

Proofreading a Paragraph to Correct Spelling Errors

For each sentence in the following paragraph, write correctly the word or words that are misspelled.

EXAMPLE [1] Often, people don't know how precious something is until they loose it.
   1. *lose*

[1] Several months ago, my aunt had what we all thought was a plane old cold. [2] In the passed her doctor had said there was no cure for a cold, so my aunt didn't even seek treatment. [3] No one knew that she had an ear infection that would led to a hearing loss in one ear. [4] Soon, my aunt realized that she was hearing only peaces of conversations, and could no longer hear out of her left ear. [5] When she went to the doctor, he explained that an infection had caused her to loose hearing in that ear. [6] The doctor gave her a chart like the one on the next page, showing the principle types of hearing aids. [7] He suggested the in-the-canal hearing aid because its barely

MECHANICS

noticeable when in place. [8] It's small size really surprised me. [9] The doctor told my aunt, of coarse, that new advances in hearing technology are being made every day. [10] Some people who could not here at all before can now be helped.

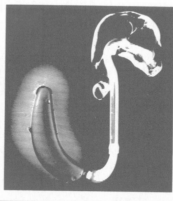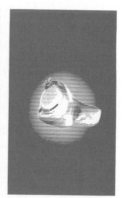

stationary	[adjective] *in a fixed position* The desks are *stationary*, but the chairs can be moved.
stationery	[noun] *writing paper* Sarah designs her own *stationery*.
their	[possessive form of *they*] *Their* pitcher struck out six players.
there	[adverb] *a place* [also used to begin a sentence] I'll see you *there*. *There* are more than two million books in the Harold Washington Library in Chicago.
they're	[contraction of *they are*] *They're* right behind you.
threw	[verb, past tense of *throw*] *tossed* Zack *threw* the ball to me.
through	[preposition] Let's walk *through* the park.

▶ EXERCISE 13 **Choosing Between Words Often Confused**

From each group in parentheses, choose the word that will make the sentence correct.

EXAMPLE **1.** (*Their, They're, There*) goes the space shuttle!
1. *There*

1. The 100-yard dash will begin over (*their, there, they're*).
2. The girls (*threw, through*) everything into (*their, there, they're*) lockers and ran onto the field.
3. Earth was once thought to be (*stationary, stationery*) in space.
4. (*Threw, Through*) the door bounded a large dog.
5. Are you sure (*their, there, they're*) not coming?

to	[preposition] We drove *to* Mexico City.
too	[adverb] *also; more than enough* Am I invited *too*? Your poem has *too* many syllables to be a haiku.
two	*one plus one* Ms. Red Cloud's last name is *two* words.
weak	[adjective] *feeble; not strong* People with *weak* ankles have difficulty ice-skating.
week	[noun] *seven days* The club meets once a *week*.
who's	[contraction of *who is* or *who has*] *Who's* wearing a watch? *Who's* seen Frida Kahlo's paintings?
whose	[possessive form of *who*] I wonder *whose* backpack this is.

MECHANICS

> **your** [possessive form of *you*]
> Rest *your* eyes now and then when you read.
> **you're** [contraction of *you are*]
> *You're* my best friend.

EXERCISE 14 **Choosing Between Words Often Confused**

From each group in parentheses, choose the word that will make the sentence correct.

EXAMPLE **1. I wonder (*who's, whose*) won the election.**
1. *who's*

1. (*Who's, Whose*) story did you like best?
2. Walking (*to, too, two*) the store, he began to feel (*weak, week*).
3. Does (*your, you're*) dad work there (*to, too, two*)?
4. It took me a (*weak, week*) to complete my project.
5. If (*your, you're*) not making that noise, (*who's, whose*) doing it?

REVIEW F **Choosing Between Words Often Confused**

From each group in parentheses, choose the word or words that will make the sentence correct.

EXAMPLE **1. Don't (*loose, lose*) your house key.**
1. *lose*

1. Which of these (*to, too, two*) boxes of (*stationary, stationery*) do you like better?
2. The Israelis and the Palestinians met in Madrid, the (*capital, capitol*) of Spain, for the (*peace, piece*) talks.
3. (*Principal, Principle*) Wong raised his hand for silence, and the students waited to (*hear, here*) what he would say.

4. These curtains will likely be hard to (*altar, alter*) because the fabric is so (*coarse, course*).
5. (*Its, It's*) (*all together, altogether*) too easy to confuse similar words.
6. Ruth vowed to (*lead, led*) the life of an exile rather than to (*desert, dessert*) Naomi.
7. Can that (*plain, plane*) (*brake, break*) the sound barrier?
8. We're (*all ready, already*) for the big game this (*weak, week*).
9. (*Your, You're*) next chore is to dust; the (*clothes, cloths*) are on the counter.
10. The (*to, too, two*) friends (*passed, past*) the time pleasantly reading (*there, their, they're*) books.

▶ REVIEW G **Proofreading a Paragraph to Correct Spelling Errors**

For each sentence in the following paragraph, write correctly the word or words that are misspelled. If a sentence is correct, write C.

EXAMPLE [1] Its time to test you're knowledge of South American history.
      1. *It's; your*

[1] Starting about A.D. 1200, people known as the Incas began too take over the western portion of South America. [2] Look at the map on the next page, and you'll see that thier territory included mountains, seacoasts, river valleys, and desserts. [3] The capitol of the Incan empire was Cuzco. [4] The Incas created an impressive road system that connected Cuzco with the rest of there empire. [5] These hard-working people also built storehouses and developped large irrigation projects. [6] To help them manage their huge empire, they used a device called a *quipu* as their principle method of keeping records. [7] The quipu (shown on the next page) is a series of knotted, colored cords. [8] With it, the Incas recorded such information as the number of people liveing in an

area, the movements of the planets, and the amount of goods in storage. [9] The Incan civilization lasted until the Spanish arrived in the mid-1500s. [10] In only a short time, Spanish conquistadors were able to defeat the Incas and brake up their empire.

SOUTH AMERICA

Chan Chan
Moche
Chavin
Machu Picchu
Cuzco
Pacific Ocean
Lake Titicaca
Amazon River
Andes
Mountains
Atacama Desert

Incan Civilization
A.D. 1200–1500

50 Commonly Misspelled Words

As you study the following words, pay special attention to the letters in italics. These letters usually cause the biggest problems in spelling the words correctly.

a*ch*e	co*l*or	fri*e*nd	pi*e*ce	tea*r*
a*gai*n	cou*gh*	g*u*ess	rea*d*y	th*ough*
a*l*ways	cou*l*d	ha*l*f	s*ai*d	thr*ough*
an*gle*	cou*n*try	h*ou*r	s*a*ys	toni*gh*t
ans*w*er	docto*r*	instea*d*	se*e*ms	trou*b*le
bri*e*f	do*e*s	*k*new	sho*e*s	wea*r*
b*u*ilt	don*'*t	lai*d*	sin*c*e	*wh*ere
bu*s*y	ea*r*ly	min*u*te	strai*gh*t	women
bu*y*	eas*y*	of*t*en	s*u*gar	won*'*t
can*'*t	ever*y*	on*c*e	s*u*re	*w*rite

100 Spelling Words

absence
achieve
adjective
advertisement
against
aisles
announce
apologize
arithmetic
assignment

autobiography
average
background
bacteria
ballad
benefit
brilliant
business
career
ceased

century
choice
communicate
conservation
constitution
courteous
criticism
curiosity
decimal
delicate

dinosaur
disguise
divide
ecology
eighth
embarrass
environment
equipment

especially
excellent

experience
explanation
fantasy
faucet
fourth
gasoline
gene
genuine
grammar
height

humorous
imitation
immediately
jewelry
legislature
liter
magazine
medicine
message
musician

myth
neighbor
nuclear
occurrence
ounce
passage
physical
poisonous
popularity
population

practice
preferred
prejudice
probably
pyramid
recipe

remainder
rescue
resources
review

rumor
seize
separate
shiny
similar
solar
solemn
species
surface
surprise

temporary
theme
tomorrow
tragedy
treasure
trial
valuable
vegetable
weapon
wrestle

MECHANICS

26 CORRECTING COMMON ERRORS

Key Language Skills Review

This chapter reviews key skills and concepts that pose special problems for writers.

- Sentence Fragments and Run-on Sentences
- Subject-Verb Agreement
- Verb Forms
- Pronoun Forms
- Comparison of Modifiers
- Capitalization
- Punctuation—Commas, End Marks, Colons, Semicolons, Quotation Marks, and Apostrophes
- Spelling
- Standard Usage

Most of the exercises in this chapter follow the same format as the exercises found throughout the grammar, usage, and mechanics sections. You will notice, however, that the two sets of review exercises are presented in standardized test formats. These exercises are designed to provide you with practice not only in solving usage and mechanics problems but also in dealing with these kinds of problems on such tests.

 EXERCISE 1 **Identifying Sentences and Sentence Fragments**

Tell whether each of the following groups of words is a *sentence* or a *sentence fragment*. If a group of words is a sentence, use a capital letter at the beginning and add an end mark of punctuation.

EXAMPLES **1.** the squirrel hopped across the branch
1. *sentence—The squirrel hopped across the branch.*

2. Jeremy's collection of comic books
2. *sentence fragment*

1. near the door of the classroom
2. all members of the safety patrol
3. sumo wrestling is popular in Japan
4. please pass me the fruit salad
5. will become a member of Junior Achievement
6. after school Sonya repaired her backpack
7. what an active puppy that is
8. lived in British Columbia for many years
9. do you like the sound of ocean waves
10. on the top shelf of the refrigerator

EXERCISE 2 **Correcting Sentence Fragments**

Some of the following groups of words are sentence fragments. First, identify the fragments. Then, make each fragment a complete sentence by adding (1) a subject, (2) a verb, or (3) both. You may need to change the punctuation and capitalization, too. If the word group is already a complete sentence, write *S.*

EXAMPLE **1.** Finished reading an exciting book by Jean Craighead George.
1. *I finished reading an exciting book by Jean Craighead George.*

1. Titled *The Case of the Missing Cutthroats.*
2. A book for young detectives who love nature.
3. In the book, a girl named Spinner goes fishing.

4. During the trip, she catches a giant cutthroat trout.
5. Thought cutthroat trout had died out where she was fishing in the Snake River.
6. Both she and her family are surprised by her catch.
7. Puzzled by the presence of a cutthroat trout.
8. What has happened to the cutthroat trout?
9. Spinner and her cousin Al on an adventure.
10. Hope to find clues that will help them solve the mystery.

▶ EXERCISE 3 **Revising Run-on Sentences**

Decide which of the following groups of words are run-on sentences. Then, revise each run-on sentence by (1) making two separate sentences or (2) using a comma and a coordinating conjunction. You may have to change the punctuation and capitalization, too. If the group of words is already a complete sentence, write *S*.

EXAMPLE　**1.** Both girls enjoy playing soccer one is usually the goalie.
　　　　　1. *Both girls enjoy playing soccer, and one is usually the goalie.*

1. Puffins are shorebirds, they have bright beaks and ducklike bodies.
2. Cement is a fine powder it is mixed with sand, water, and small rocks to make concrete.
3. Alicia collects birth dates, she has recorded the birthdays of all her friends and of her favorite movie stars.
4. We may go to the fair on Saturday we may wait until next weekend.
5. The band placed first in regional competitions, it did not win at the state contests.
6. I plan to go to the Florida Keys someday, I want to skin-dive for seashells.

7. Kerry is having a party tomorrow night, we are planning to go.
8. The school board could vote to remodel the old cafeteria, or they may decide to build a new one.
9. My brother would like to live on a space station someday I would, too.
10. These rocks are too heavy for me to lift, I asked Christy to help me move them.

EXERCISE 4 **Correcting Run-on Sentences and Sentence Fragments**

Decide which of the following word groups are run-on sentences and which are sentence fragments. Then, revise each word group to make one or more complete sentences. Remember to use correct capitalization and punctuation. If a word group is already a complete sentence, write *S*.

EXAMPLES **1.** Do you like brightly colored art you should see Faith Ringgold's paintings.
1. *Do you like brightly colored art? You should see Faith Ringgold's paintings.*

2. Uses color boldly and imaginatively.
2. *Ringgold uses color boldly and imaginatively.*

1. Ringgold was born in Harlem in 1930 at a young age, she knew she wanted to be an artist.
2. Today her artwork in museums around the world.
3. Paints on fabric and sometimes uses fabric to frame her paintings.
4. Her creativity led her to invent a whole new art form she decided to call it the "story quilt."
5. Story quilts blend storytelling with painting.
6. One of her series of story quilts about an African American woman in Paris.
7. Much of Ringgold's work represents her African American roots.
8. Ringgold's painting *Tar Beach* is based on her childhood experiences she completed the work in 1988.

9. Shows Ringgold's playground on the roof of an apartment building.
10. Behind the rooftop lies the George Washington Bridge, a bridge whose string of lights reminded Ringgold of a diamond necklace.

▶ EXERCISE 5 **Choosing Verbs That Agree in Number with Their Subjects**

In each of the following sentences, choose the form of the verb in parentheses that agrees with the subject.

EXAMPLE **1.** Everyone except my twin sisters (*want, wants*) to go to the beach.
1. *wants*

1. Here (*come, comes*) the marching bands in the parade!
2. Several of my friends (*have, has*) trail bikes.
3. I (*don't, doesn't*) like to swim when the water is so cold.
4. Neither the guinea pigs nor the hamster (*is, are*) awake yet.
5. (*Has, Have*) Mr. Baldwin and Sherry been talking long?
6. One of the scientists (*was, were*) Isaac Newton.
7. Thunderstorms usually (*don't, doesn't*) bother me.
8. (*Are, Is*) the swimsuits still on sale?
9. All of the movie (*was, were*) filmed in Vietnam.
10. The boy in the red shoes (*run, runs*) fast.

▶ EXERCISE 6 **Proofreading Sentences for Correct Subject-Verb Agreement**

Most of the following sentences contain a verb that does not agree in number with its subject. If a sentence is incorrect, give the correct verb form. If a sentence is already correct, write *C*.

EXAMPLE **1.** A carved slice of potato make a good stamp.
1. *makes*

1. Images from this type of stamp are called potato prints.
2. Both my cousins and my younger brother creates potato prints.
3. It don't cost much to make these prints.
4. A firm potato, a knife, paint, a paintbrush, and paper is the necessary supplies.
5. My friend James find unique shapes and patterns in magazines.
6. He then carves these designs on the flat surfaces of cut potatoes.
7. Next, each carved design on the potato slices are coated with paint.
8. Pieces of fabric or a sheet of paper offer a good surface for stamping.
9. Each of my cousins like to make greeting cards with stamped designs.
10. Other uses for a potato stamp includes making writing paper and wrapping paper.

▶ EXERCISE 7 **Using the Principal Parts of Regular Verbs**

For each of the following sentences, give the form of the italicized verb that will correctly fill in the blank.

EXAMPLE **1.** *help*   Regular exercise has ____ many people stay fit.

1. *helped*

1. *climb*   Yesterday the cat ____ the tree easily, but it could not get down.
2. *joke*   We can never tell when our uncle is ____ with us.
3. *shop*   My friend and I once ____ all day at Mall of America in Bloomington, Minnesota.
4. *fill*   Have the fans ____ the auditorium yet?
5. *enter*   Too many cars are ____ the parking lot.
6. *watch*   The class is ____ a film about the ancient Incan culture in Peru.
7. *call*   Who ____ my name a few seconds ago?

8. *measure*   My mother has ___ the space for the new bookcase.
9. *load*   Two men ___ our furniture in the truck last week.
10. *jump*   A deer has ___ over the fence.

▶ EXERCISE 8   **Using Irregular Verbs**

For each of the following sentences, give the past or the past participle form of the italicized verb that will correctly fill in the blank.

EXAMPLE   **1.** *drink* The guests ___ all of the raspberry tea.
1. *drank*

1. *blow*   The wind has ___ the kite out of the tree!
2. *shrink*   The boy in the movie ___ to the size of a squirrel.
3. *steal*   "I've never ___ anything in my life," Abe declared.
4. *drive*   Pat and Justin ___ go-carts at the park.
5. *freeze*   The water in the birdbath has ___.
6. *sink*   The toy boat ___ in the sudsy bath water.
7. *throw*   Each athlete has ___ the javelin twice.
8. *sing*   The choir ___ at the celebration last night.
9. *swim*   Have you ever ___ in warm mineral springs?
10. *burst*   The balloon ___ when the cat clawed it.

▶ EXERCISE 9   **Proofreading for Errors in the Use of Irregular Verbs**

Most of the following sentences contain incorrect verb forms. Find each error, and write the correct form of the verb. If the form of the verb is already correct, write *C*.

EXAMPLE   **1.** We have went to the ballpark two weekends in a row.
1. *gone*

1. Sarah done well at yesterday's track meet.

2. My stepfather brung me a stuffed animal when I was in the hospital.
3. Nickelodeon movie theaters begun to be quite popular in the United States around 1905.
4. Manuel's grandfather come to the United States forty years ago.
5. We seen the Rio Grande when we drove through New Mexico.
6. Chris knew that a basement was a good place to take shelter during a tornado.
7. Judy taked a few minutes to decide what to say.
8. Maria's team choosed the oak tree in her front yard as home base.
9. The poison ivy in the woods gived me a rash.
10. Dr. Seuss wrote the poem "The Sneetches."

▶ EXERCISE 10 **Using the Past and Past Participle Forms of Verbs**

For each of the following sentences, give the past or the past participle form of the italicized verb that will correctly fill in the blank.

EXAMPLE **1.** *establish* In the 1980s, Robert D. Ballard, a marine geologist, ____ the JASON Foundation for Education.

      1. *established*

1. *create* JASON, an underwater robot, was ____ for scientific research.
2. *build* JASON was ____ to dive much deeper than humans can dive.
3. *sink* More than 1,600 years ago, the Roman ship *Isis* ____ in the Mediterranean Sea.
4. *know* Ballard ____ that students would want to share in the exploration of the wrecked ship.
5. *make* A network of satellites ____ it possible for students to see JASON explore the wreck.
6. *see* Some 250,000 schoolchildren ____ JASON on giant video screens.

7. *ask*   While JASON searched the ship, students ____ questions of Ballard and his team.

8. *take*   Ballard has ____ students on some amazing electronic field trips by televising himself working aboard JASON.

9. *give*   He has ____ much of his time and energy to involving students in scientific discoveries.

10. *write*   Ballard has ____ about finding the *Isis* and about the 1985 discovery of the *Titanic*, which sank in 1912.

▶ EXERCISE 11 **Choosing Correct Pronoun Forms**

For each of the following sentences, choose the correct form of the pronoun in parentheses.

EXAMPLE   **1. The pitcher gave (*she, her*) the signal.**
            1. *her*

1. The winners may be you and (*her, she*).
2. Gregory asked (*her, she*) to the dance.
3. The ending of the movie really amazed Andrew and (*us, we*)!
4. Should Emily and (*they, them*) put up the tent?
5. The bus driver gave (*he, him*) a warning.
6. The competition is really between Mario and (*I, me*).
7. Who gave (*her, she*) that opal necklace?
8. The best player on our team is (*him, he*).
9. The next step for Michael and (*them, they*) is to check with the principal.
10. My cousin and (*me, I*) are learning to sew.

▶ EXERCISE 12 **Proofreading for Correct Pronoun Forms**

Most of the following sentences contain a pronoun that has been used incorrectly. Identify each incorrect pronoun. Then, write the correct form. If a sentence is already correct, write *C*.

EXAMPLE **1.** Carrie sat between Melissa and I at the concert.
1. *I—me*

1. Who did you meet at the skating rink last night?
2. You and them are the only ones who are going on the hike.
3. My pen pal in Vietnam will soon receive another letter from me.
4. Just between you and I, the other book was much easier to understand.
5. One of the actors in that play was her.
6. The pencils, paints, and colored paper belong to Kimiko and he.
7. Matthew has invited you and I to go camping next weekend.
8. Either her or I will make a poster for the school carnival.
9. Who is the fastest runner on the baseball team?
10. They and us went swimming in Lake Travis.

▶ EXERCISE 13 **Choosing Correct Regular and Irregular Modifiers**

Choose the correct form of the adjective or adverb in parentheses in each of the following sentences.

EXAMPLE **1.** The stars tonight look (*more bright, brighter*) than usual.
1. *brighter*

1. This puzzle book is (*difficulter, more difficult*) than the other one.
2. Kevin is the (*taller, tallest*) of the four Sutherland brothers.
3. The (*most exciting, excitingest*) day of our trip was still to come.
4. I like drawing, but I like painting (*best, better*).
5. If you blend strawberries, bananas, and yogurt really (*good, well*), you'll have a great drink.
6. Felicia had the (*worst, worse*) case of chicken pox of anyone in the sixth grade.

7. My two brothers and I were taught how to wash, iron, and mend clothes, and we are (*gladder, glad*) that we were.
8. Rachel can't decide which of the two wallpaper patterns would look (*prettier, prettiest*) in her room.
9. Our schoolyard has been (*cleanest, cleaner*) since the Ecology Club asked people not to litter.
10. I am going to practice American Sign Language until I sign (*good, well*) enough to communicate easily.

EXERCISE 14 Correcting Errors in the Use of Modifiers

Identify the incorrect modifier in each of the following sentences. Then, give the correct form of the modifier.

EXAMPLE   **1. Do you like Western boots or hiking boots most?**
1. *most—more*

1. Ernest runs very good, but William can run even better.
2. Katherine is the more curious of the four Matsuo children.
3. Which flavor of ice cream do you think would be worser, cheddar or carrot?
4. Did you do gooder on this week's spelling test than on last week's?
5. After carefully rehearsing several times, Toni felt confidently about giving her speech.
6. If you look close at the painting, you can see how tiny the brushstrokes are.
7. Gloria became more worriedly as the storm grew worse.
8. Of the Amazon, Nile, and Mississippi rivers, the Nile is the longer.
9. It was a good crop, and it grew quick, too.
10. Icarus foolishly flew more nearer to the sun than he should have.

▶ EXERCISE 15 **Correcting Double Comparisons and Double Negatives**

Revise each of the following sentences to correct the double comparison or double negative.

EXAMPLE   **1.** Grandma thought learning to swim would be more harder than it was.

　　　　　1. *Grandma thought learning to swim would be harder than it was.*

1. My sister gave me her soccer ball because she never plays soccer no more.
2. You can get a more clearer idea of what the trail is like by looking at this map.
3. We couldn't hardly believe our eyes when we saw what was under the rock!
4. You shouldn't stand nowhere around a tall tree during a thunderstorm.
5. Keisha's uncle just adopted the most strangest pet I've ever seen.
6. My little sister can't scarcely reach the doorknob without standing on tiptoe.
7. I'm not going to put off practicing my trumpet no more.
8. That was the most worst movie we've ever seen.
9. Didn't neither of the books have the information you needed?
10. I've read that potbellied pigs learn more faster than dogs do.

▶ EXERCISE 16 **Identifying Correct Usage**

Choose the correct word or words in parentheses in each of the following sentences.

EXAMPLE   **1.** My aunt was working in Athens, Greece, (*then, than*).

　　　　　1. *then*

1. Everyone on the committee is here (*accept, except*) Roseanne.

2. Steve said he thought the new batting line-up looked (*allright, all right*).
3. The two friends felt (*bad, badly*) after they had been arguing.
4. The children helped (*theirselves, themselves*) to the fruit juice.
5. Do you know (*whose, who's*) sunglasses and towel these are?
6. The boys will (*try to, try and*) finish painting the mural today.
7. Be sure to (*bring, take*) your lunch when you go to the park.
8. The ten students in the art class divided all of the construction paper and markers (*between, among*) themselves.
9. (*Who's, Whose*) going to show them how to use a fire extinguisher?
10. What some people call heat lightning is lightning that occurs too far away from people for them to hear (*its, it's*) accompanying thunder.

▶ EXERCISE 17 **Correcting Errors in Usage**

Each of the following sentences contains a usage error. Identify each error, and then write the correct usage.

EXAMPLE   **1.** Them fish are called sea horses.
          1. *Them—Those*

1. Where are sea horses found at?
2. Sea horses are found in tropical and temperate waters—but not anywheres that is very cold.
3. Baby sea horses often use they're tails to hold on to each other.
4. I just saw that there sea horse use its tail to grasp some seaweed.
5. Don't you think that it's head looks amazingly like a tiny horse's head?
6. The little fin on a sea horse's back moves so fast that you can't hardly see it.

7. Several students asked the teacher how come the eyes of a sea horse work independently of each other.
8. My stepsisters and I use to look for sea horses in the Pacific Ocean when we lived near the coast in California.
9. As we were leaving class, the teacher reminded us to bring home a parental approval form for the field trip to the city aquarium.
10. When your at the aquarium, remember to stop by the sea horse exhibit.

> EXERCISE 18   **Proofreading a Paragraph for Correct Usage**

Each of the sentences in the following paragraph contains an error in English usage. Identify each error. Then, write the correct usage.

EXAMPLE   [1] Do you all ready know about the area known as the Pantanal?
   1. *all ready—already*

[1] The Pantanal is the largest wetland anywheres in the world. [2] To get an idea of it's size, imagine an area about the size of Arkansas. [3] Most of the Pantanal is located inside of Brazil. [4] The area contains a enormous wealth of wildlife. [5] Our science teacher is learning us about the jaguar, the giant anteater, the giant otter, and other animals that live there. [6] The Pantanal may be more important for wading birds such as ducks and storks then any other place in South America. [7] In addition, alot of other birds, such as toucans and macaws, live there. [8] The Pantanal has many swamps, which from time to time have absorbed heavy rains that otherwise might of flooded nearby areas. [9] However, the Pantanal ain't all swamps; it also contains forests. [10] Although the Pantanal is a long ways from where I live, I hope to have a chance to explore it someday.

Grammar and Usage Test: Section 1

DIRECTIONS   Read the paragraph below. For each numbered blank, select the word or group of words that best completes the sentence. Indicate your response by shading in the appropriate oval on your answer sheet.

EXAMPLE

Two species of elephant __(1)__ today: the African elephant and the Asian elephant.

  1. (A) does exist
      (B) exists
      (C) have been existing
      (D) exist

SAMPLE ANSWER   1. (A) (B) (C) ●

Each of these species has __(1)__ own unique features; for example, the African elephant has __(2)__ ears and tusks than the Asian elephant. Although different in some ways, both species of elephant __(3)__ strong, intelligent, and social. Both have poor sight and are colorblind but can smell and hear quite __(4)__. Elephants can detect the scent of __(5)__ human who is over a mile away. __(6)__ hearing is so good that they can communicate over distances of more than two miles, using sounds __(7)__ any that humans can hear. Unfortunately, human population growth, farming, industry, and illegal hunting __(8)__ a decline in the elephant population. For instance, hunters have killed thousands of African elephants for their ivory tusks; in fact, from 1979 to the early 1990s, the number of elephants in Africa __(9)__ from 1,300,000 to fewer than 600,000. __(10)__ protect elephants, the trade of ivory was outlawed worldwide in 1989.

  1. (A) it
      (B) its'
      (C) it's
      (D) its

  2. (A) larger
      (B) more larger
      (C) the more larger
      (D) the most largest

  3. (A) they are
      (B) are
      (C) are being
      (D) is

  4. (A) well
      (B) good
      (C) better
      (D) alot

  5. (A) a
      (B) an
      (C) the
      (D) this

  6. (A) They're
      (B) There
      (C) Their
      (D) They

7. (A) more lower than
   (B) lower than
   (C) more low then
   (D) lower then

8. (A) will have caused
   (B) causes
   (C) are causing
   (D) does cause

9. (A) shrinks
   (B) shrank
   (C) shrunk
   (D) is shrinking

10. (A) To
    (B) Too
    (C) Two
    (D) 2

Grammar and Usage Test: Section 2

DIRECTIONS Either part or all of each of the following sentences is underlined. Using the rules of standard written English, choose the answer that most clearly expresses the meaning of the sentence. If there is no error, choose A. Indicate your response by shading in the appropriate oval on your answer sheet.

EXAMPLE

1. The fish smelled badly, so we didn't buy any.
   (A) smelled badly
   (B) smells badly
   (C) smelled bad
   (D) smelling bad

SAMPLE ANSWER 1.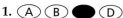

1. Roz and I catched fireflies in a jar.
   (A) I catched
   (B) me catched
   (C) I caught
   (D) me caught

2. Fun hiking in the wilderness preserve.
   (A) Fun hiking in the wilderness preserve.
   (B) While having fun hiking in the wilderness preserve.
   (C) Hiking in the wilderness preserve was fun.
   (D) Have had fun hiking in the wilderness preserve.

3. The election ended up in a runoff between he and I.
   (A) he and I
   (B) him and me
   (C) him and I
   (D) he and me

4. In bowling, a strike <u>is when</u> a bowler knocks down all ten pins on the first throw in a frame.
   - (A) is when
   - (B) occurs when
   - (C) is where
   - (D) is because

5. Have you heard of Lawrence and Lorne <u>Blair, two brothers who traveled in Indonesia for ten years?</u>
   - (A) Blair, two brothers who traveled in Indonesia for ten years?
   - (B) Blair? Two brothers who traveled in Indonesia for ten years.
   - (C) Blair, two brothers whom traveled in Indonesia for ten years?
   - (D) Blair and two brothers who traveled in Indonesia for ten years?

6. <u>Is this here</u> drill bit the right size?
   - (A) Is this here
   - (B) Is that there
   - (C) Is this here kind of
   - (D) Is this

7. <u>Here your car keys.</u>
   - (A) Here your car keys.
   - (B) Here are your car keys.
   - (C) Here's you're car keys.
   - (D) Here is your car keys.

8. <u>The dog barked the baby awoke.</u>
   - (A) The dog barked the baby awoke.
   - (B) The dog barked, the baby awoke.
   - (C) The dog barked, and the baby awoke.
   - (D) The dog barking and the baby awoke.

9. I <u>shouldn't of</u> waited to start my essay.
   - (A) shouldn't of
   - (B) shouldn't have
   - (C) ought not to of
   - (D) oughtn't not to have

10. Mrs. Levine asked Frederick <u>how come Darnell and he aren't</u> here yet.
    - (A) how come Darnell and he aren't
    - (B) how come Darnell and him aren't
    - (C) why Darnell and he isn't
    - (D) why Darnell and he aren't

EXERCISE 19 **Correcting Errors in Capitalization**

Each of the following groups of words contains at least one error in capitalization. Correct the errors either by changing capital letters to lowercase letters or by changing lowercase letters to capital letters.

EXAMPLE   **1.** abilene, texas
             1. *Abilene, Texas*

1. the smoky mountains
2. rutherford B. hayes
3. *Alice In Wonderland*
4. university of kansas
5. labor day
6. near lake Placid
7. it's already tuesday!
8. english or Art II
9. washington monument
10. marta Hinojosa, m.d.
11. neptune and other planets
12. second day of hanukkah
13. my Uncle Jack
14. *the Wizard of Oz*
15. a river running South
16. Bryce canyon national park
17. 912 valentine st.
18. president Cleveland
19. "i'm home!"
20. newbery medal

 EXERCISE 20 **Correcting Errors in Capitalization**

Correct the capitalization errors in the following sentences either by changing capital letters to lowercase letters or by changing lowercase letters to capital letters.

EXAMPLE   **1.** i went to see a Play last saturday.
             1. *I went to see a play last Saturday.*

1. Our drama teacher, ms. soto, took us to see it.

2. the play was performed by the south Texas performance company.
3. this theater group's founder and director is the translator, playwright, and theater scholar joe rosenberg.
4. He has established an exchange progam for theater students from the united states, mexico, and south america.
5. In addition, mr. rosenberg has written a full-length play titled *saturday stranger,* which was published in germany.
6. Mr. Rosenberg has also edited a Book called *¡aplauso! hispanic Children's theater.*
7. the book includes plays by héctor santiago, roy conboy, and lisa loomer, among others.
8. the plays are printed in both english and spanish.
9. these plays draw on hispanic literary traditions native to such places as mexico, puerto rico, and cuba.
10. Next month the southwest middle school drama club plans to perform one of the plays from this book.

> **EXERCISE 21** **Proofreading Sentences for the Correct Use of Commas**

Each of the following sentences is missing at least one comma. Write the word or numeral that comes before each missing comma, and add the comma.

EXAMPLE **1.** Oh I hope we win the track meet when we go to Salina Kansas next week.
   1. *Oh, Salina, Kansas,*

1. Sheila ran four laps around the track on Monday Tuesday and Wednesday.
2. On February 17 1997 my family had a reunion in Guadalajara Mexico.
3. Yes that is the dog they adopted from the animal shelter.

4. My father is going to teach me to play the guitar soon so he is showing me how to tune one now.
5. No I have never read *A Wrinkle in Time.*
6. Scissors pins tacks and other sharp items should be kept out of the reach of young children.
7. Athena the Greek goddess of crafts wisdom and war is often shown with an owl on her shoulder.
8. Douglas never leaves shopping carts in parking spaces set aside for people who have disabilities nor should anyone else do so.
9. My aunt and I bought nails lumber and paint for the birdhouses we plan to build.
10. Professor Chang will you explain the differences between these two kinds of cells?

EXERCISE 22 **Using End Marks Correctly**

For each of the following sentences, write each letter or word that should be followed by an end mark, and add the proper end mark.

EXAMPLE **1.** Will you please help me carry my books
1. *books?*

1. Please follow me
2. Senator Jackson, can you meet with our class at 8:15 A M
3. Where in the downtown library is the display of antique toys
4. Watch out for that falling rock
5. Yesterday Dr Williamson taught me how to fly a model helicopter
6. Anthony asked Rose if her favorite cartoonist is Charles M Schulz
7. One fossil recently discovered in these mountains dates back to 3 million B C
8. What a surprise that was
9. Have you ever brought your skateboard to school
10. The letter addressed to 4613 Sleepy Hollow Blvd , Kingston, NY 12401, must be for Mrs C R Smith

▶ EXERCISE 23 **Using Semicolons and Colons Correctly**

The following sentences lack necessary colons and semicolons. Write the words or numerals that come before and after the needed punctuation, and insert the proper punctuation.

EXAMPLE **1.** My grandmother is coming to visit we will meet her at the airport.
          1. *visit; we*

1. We picked subjects for our reports Richard and I chose sea turtles.
2. Our school day used to start at 8 15 now it starts at 8 00.
3. The following items will be needed for the new playground swings, slides, and picnic tables.
4. The rain just ended maybe we will get a chance to see a double rainbow.
5. We can save water in these ways turning off the faucet while brushing our teeth, pouring only as much as we plan to drink, and taking showers instead of baths.

▶ EXERCISE 24 **Punctuating and Capitalizing Quotations**

In the following numbered items, use quotation marks, other marks of punctuation, and capital letters where needed. If a sentence is correct, write *C*.

EXAMPLE **1.** I admire Marian Wright Edelman said Paul she has worked hard for children's rights.
          1. *"I admire Marian Wright Edelman," said Paul. "She has worked hard for children's rights."*

1. Edelman founded the Children's Defense Fund in 1973. That nonprofit organization has helped many people said Mr. Knepp.
2. Paul commented that just the other day he had read a newspaper article about Edelman titled The Children's Defender.

3. Justin said I'd like to work to protect children's rights, too, one day.
4. Edelman was born in 1939 Paul told us She grew up in Bennettsville, South Carolina.
5. Mr. Knepp said "that Marian Wright Edelman is one of our country's greatest civic leaders."
6. Please tell me more about Edelman's career as a lawyer, Ashley said.
7. She graduated from Yale Law School in 1963 he said and soon became the first African American woman licensed to practice law in Mississippi.
8. Mr. Knepp added Edelman has handled many civil rights cases and has always made community service a priority.
9. Did Edelman say that she had been taught as a child to make service a central part of her everyday life? Justin asked
10. Yes Ashley answered I think I read that in her autobiography, *The Measure of Our Success: A Letter to My Children and Yours.*

▶ EXERCISE 25 **Punctuating Dialogue**

Revise the following dialogue, adding quotation marks and other marks of punctuation and replacing lowercase letters with capital letters where necessary. Remember to begin a new paragraph each time the speaker changes.

EXAMPLE [1] The story of Greyfriars Bobby is so moving Jennifer exclaimed, that I'll never forget it.

1. *"The story of Greyfriars Bobby is so moving,"* Jennifer exclaimed, *"that I'll never forget it."*

[1] Bobby was a special dog, Jennifer said, and extremely loyal to his master. [2] Tony asked, "can you believe that Bobby actually lived by his master's grave for fourteen years?" [3] Jennifer said, My cousin went to Edinburgh, Scotland, and saw Bobby's grave. [4] It is in Greyfriars churchyard, near his master's grave.

[5] When did Bobby die? Tony asked. [6] He died in 1872, Jennifer replied. [7] "the people in the town fed Bobby and cared for him until his death."

[8] "Bobby slept during the day," Tony recalled "because, before his master died, they had worked together at night."

[9] Jennifer said, "yes, his master, old Jock, guarded cattle that were sold at the market." [10] Tony said, In Edinburgh there is a statue of Greyfriars Bobby on top of a drinking fountain for dogs.

EXERCISE 26 **Using Apostrophes Correctly**

Insert an apostrophe wherever one is needed in each of the following items.

EXAMPLE **1.** the womens class
         1. *the women's class*

1. if theyve gone
2. no ones fault
3. that statues condition
4. Lets try.
5. since youre going home
6. that giants castle
7. Theirs werent faded.
8. the Rockies highest peak
9. when there isnt time
10. these books authors

EXERCISE 27 **Correcting Spelling Errors**

If a word is not spelled correctly, write the correct spelling. If a word is spelled correctly, write *C*.

EXAMPLE **1.** mispeak
         1. *misspeak*

1. percieve
2. disolve
3. gladest
4. charging
5. comedies
6. sillyness

7. taxs
8. tryed
9. potatos
10. traceing
11. classes
12. sleigh
13. matchs
14. videoes
15. funnyer
16. toyes

17. schoolling
18. wieght
19. loosness
20. Gomezs
21. lovable
22. unatural
23. ladys
24. runing
25. finaly

▶ EXERCISE 28 **Choosing Between Words Often Confused**

For each of the following sentences, choose the word or words in parentheses that will make the sentence correct.

EXAMPLE **1.** Megan suggested that I (*altar, alter*) the first paragraph of my story.
1. *alter*

1. Have you (*all ready, already*) finished your latest painting?
2. (*Your, You're*) pets need food, water, shelter, and loving attention.
3. Be careful not to (*lose, loose*) any of those puzzle pieces.
4. Chuckwallas are harmless lizards that grow to two feet long and live in rocky (*desserts, deserts*) in the United States and Mexico.
5. Manuel dreamed of finding the sunken ship and (*it's, its*) treasure chest.
6. The school (*threw, through*) away tons of paper and cardboard before the recycling program was started.
7. (*Whose, Who's*) planning to bring food and drinks to the fiesta?
8. We drove (*passed, past*) the park and across the bridge.

9. Marcie's enthusiasm for playing in the band was (*plain, plane*) to see.
10. The guide (*lead, led*) the scouts through the museum.

▶ EXERCISE 29 **Proofreading Sentences for Spelling and Usage Errors**

For each of the following sentences, identify and correct any error in spelling or usage.

EXAMPLE 1. The Iroquois people's name for theirselves means "we longhouse builders."
1. *theirselves—themselves*

1. In our American history coarse, we learned that the Iroquois constructed large dwellings called longhouses.
2. Years ago, nearly all Iroquois lived in forests and built they're longhouses out of logs and strips of bark.
3. Several individual familys lived in each of these longhouses.
4. When a couple married, the husband would move into the longhouse of his wive's extended family, called a clan.
5. Each family had it's own separate area with a sleeping platform that was raised about a foot above the ground.
6. They kept the longhouse neat by storing many of their belongings on shelfs above their sleeping platforms.
7. Fires were made in hearths in a central corridor, and smoke rose threw holes cut in the longhouse roof.
8. When it rained or snowed, slideing panels were used to close the holes.
9. The bigest longhouses measured more than two hundred feet in length.
10. Such large longhouses could shelter 10 or more individual families.

▶ EXERCISE 30 **Proofreading a Business Letter for Correct Grammar, Usage, and Mechanics**

Correct the errors in grammar, usage, and mechanics in the numbered items in the following letter. Most items contain more than one error.

EXAMPLE [1] 254 Thirty second street
  1. *254 Thirty-second Street*

---

254 Thirty-second Street
Syracuse, NY 13210
[1] November 5 1997

Ms. Susan Loroupe
[2] Syracuse daily times
598 Seventh Avenue
Syracuse, NY 13208

[3] Dear Ms Loroupe

[4] Thank you for taking time during you're busy workday to show the Van Buren Middle School Journalism Club around the Newspaper's offices.

[5] Us club members are glad to have had the chance to see how newspaper articles are wrote and printed. [6] Especially enjoyed seeing the presses— even more then talking with the design artists and editors! [7] We were surprised that the presses were so loud and we were impressed by how quick and efficient everyone worked. [8] Please thank the artists, to, for showing us how they use computer's to arrange the art and photos on the pages.

Sincerely,

Carlos Lopez

Carlos Lopez
[9] journalism club Secretary
[10] Van Buren middle school

Mechanics Test: Section 1

DIRECTIONS Each numbered item below contains an underlined word or group of words. Choose the answer that shows the correct capitalization, punctuation, and spelling of the underlined part. If there is no error, choose answer D (Correct as is). Indicate your response by shading in the appropriate oval on your answer sheet.

EXAMPLE

[1] Quincy, MA 02158

1. (A)   Qunicy, Mass. 02158
   (B)   Quincy MA, 02158
   (C)   Quincy, M.A. 02158
   (D)   Correct as is

SAMPLE ANSWER   1. (A) (B) (C) ●

---

147 Hickory Lane
Quincy, MA 02158
[1] May 11 1997

The Hobby Shop
[2] 2013 forty-First Street
Los Angeles, CA 90924

[3] Dear Mr. Shaw

While I was visiting [4] my aunt Laura, who's house is near your store, she bought a model airplane from you. [5] Two of my freinds have [6] already tryed to help me get the plane to fly, but we haven't been able to. [7] Putting the plane together was not difficult; the problem is that the engine will not start. Also, I found no stickers in the box when I opened [8] it and the box says that there should be stickers for the plane's wings. I have enclosed the engine and my [9] aunt's reciept. I hope that [10] youre able to send me stickers and a new engine soon.

Sincerely,

Timothy Martin

---

1. (A) May, 11 1997
    (B) May 11, 1997
    (C) May, 11, 1997
    (D) Correct as is

2. (A) 2013 Forty First Street
    (B) 2013 Forty-first street
    (C) 2013 Forty-first Street
    (D) Correct as is

3. (A) Dear Mr. Shaw,
    (B) Dear Mr. Shaw:
    (C) Dear mr. shaw:
    (D) Correct as is

4. (A) my aunt Laura, whose
    (B) my Aunt Laura, whose
    (C) my Aunt Laura, who's
    (D) Correct as is

5. (A) Two of my friends
    (B) To of my freinds
    (C) Too of my friends
    (D) Correct as is

6. (A) all ready tryed
    (B) already tried
    (C) all ready tried
    (D) Correct as is

7. (A) Puting the plane
    (B) Puting the plain
    (C) Putting the plain
    (D) Correct as is

8. (A) it and the box says that their
    (B) it, and the box says that their
    (C) it, and the box says that there
    (D) Correct as is

9. (A) aunt's receipt
    (B) Aunt's receipt
    (C) aunts' reciept
    (D) Correct as is

10. (A) your
    (B) you're
    (C) your'
    (D) Correct as is

Mechanics Test: Section 2

DIRECTIONS Each of the following sentences contains an underlined word or group of words. Choose the answer that shows the correct capitalization, punctuation, and spelling of the underlined part. If there is no error, choose answer D (Correct as is). Indicate your response by shading in the appropriate oval on your answer sheet.

EXAMPLE

1. Today the school <u>librarian Mr Woods</u> will show us a film.
   - (A) librarian, Mr. Woods
   - (B) librarian, Mr. Woods,
   - (C) librarian Mr. Woods,
   - (D) Correct as is

SAMPLE ANSWER 1. Ⓐ ⬤ Ⓒ Ⓓ

1. I wonder what the <u>capital of Spain is?</u>
   - (A) capital of Spain is.
   - (B) capitol of Spain is.
   - (C) capitol of Spain is?
   - (D) Correct as is

2. The <u>mouses'</u> nest may be in the garage.
   - (A) mouses
   - (B) mices
   - (C) mice's
   - (D) Correct as is

3. "What did you <u>see at the park?" asked my grandfather.</u>
   - (A) see at the park"? asked my grandfather.
   - (B) see at the park," asked my grandfather?
   - (C) see at the park? asked my grandfather."
   - (D) Correct as is

4. Felix, you've been a naughty kitten this <u>passed week!</u>
   - (A) passed weak
   - (B) past weak
   - (C) past week
   - (D) Correct as is

5. Aisha <u>exclaimed, "see</u> how much these crystals have grown!"
   - (A) exclaimed, "See
   - (B) exclaimed! "See
   - (C) exclaimed "See
   - (D) Correct as is

6. The Olympic team waved at the <u>crowd, the audience</u> cheered.
   - (A) crowd; the audience
   - (B) crowd: the audience
   - (C) crowd, the audeince
   - (D) Correct as is

7. The <u>Kalahari Desert</u> is in southern Africa.
   - (A) Kalahari Dessert
   - (B) kalahari desert
   - (C) Kalahari desert
   - (D) Correct as is

8. <u>"Its snowing,"</u> observed Mrs. Daniels.
   - (A) "It's snowwing,"
   - (B) "It's snowing,"
   - (C) Its snowing,
   - (D) Correct as is

9. The Red Cross is asking <u>for: blankets,</u> sheets, and pillows.
   - (A) for; blankets,
   - (B) for, blankets,
   - (C) for blankets,
   - (D) Correct as is

10. Robert Frost's <u>poem The Road Not Taken</u> is famous.
    - (A) poem *The Road Not Taken,*
    - (B) poem "The Road Not Taken"
    - (C) poem "the Road not Taken"
    - (D) Correct as is

CORRECTING COMMON ERRORS

PART THREE

RESOURCES

RESOURCES

27 SPEAKING

Skills and Strategies

You probably enjoy chatting with people you know well, but you may have to speak in new and different situations. For example, you may need to leave a message on the telephone. You may give directions or instructions to someone. You may need to introduce people to one another. Or, in school, you may need to give an oral report or take part in a group discussion. These activities are also good practice for speaking in the workplace.

Communicating with Others

Communication is a two-way process. First, a person speaks, telling ideas or feelings to one or more listeners. Then the listeners react or respond to what the speaker says. This response is called *feedback.*

Listeners may respond in many ways. They may say something to the speaker, or they may communicate a message without words. For example, it's easy for a speaker to judge the meaning of feedback from listeners when they smile or applaud.

Speaking Socially

In many social situations, remember to speak politely and clearly.

Speaking on the Telephone

It is important to use the telephone courteously. Here are some suggestions.

GUIDELINES FOR TELEPHONING

1. Be sure to dial the correct number. If you get a wrong number, apologize for the error.
2. Call at a time that is convenient for the person you are calling.
3. Speak clearly. Say who you are when the person answers. If the person you're calling isn't there, you may wish to leave your name and number and perhaps a short message.
4. Don't stay on the telephone too long.

Giving Directions or Instructions

You may be asked to give directions or explain how to do something. Make sure your directions or instructions are clear and complete. Here are some pointers.

HOW TO GIVE DIRECTIONS OR INSTRUCTIONS

1. Before you give information, plan what you want to say. Think of the information as a series of steps.
2. Explain the steps to your listener in order. Be sure you haven't skipped any steps or left out any necessary information.
3. If necessary, repeat all of the directions or instructions so your listener can rehearse them.

RESOURCES

Making Introductions

Sometimes you may need to introduce other people who know you but not each other. Or, at other times, if no one present knows you or if no one is making introductions, you may need to introduce yourself. Here are suggestions for making introductions politely.

HOW TO MAKE INTRODUCTIONS

- When you introduce friends your own age, you can usually use first names. (For example, you can simply say, "Gina, this is Takai.")
- When you introduce a younger person to an older person, say the older person's name first. (For example, you might say, "Dad, I'd like you to meet my language arts teacher, Mrs. Schultz. Mrs. Schultz, this is my father, Michael Rosetti.")
- Introduce yourself to others if no one introduces you first. Start a conversation by mentioning something the person might talk to you about. (For example, "Hi, my name is Monica. I just moved here from Ohio. What's your name?")
- Don't present someone to a roomful of people all at once. Instead, introduce the person to small groups at a time. (For example, "Jamie, Sharria, Kim—I'd like you to meet Chris Polivka." Or, "Hey, group, this is our new classmate, Rico Morales. Rico, here are Anya, Suzette, and Li.")
- When you're introduced to someone your own age, you can offer a handshake if you think it is appropriate or friendly. If an older person extends a hand, it's polite for you to shake hands.
- If you are introducing two people and you know that there's something they have in common, you might mention it so that they have something that they can talk about. (For example, "Juana, this is my cousin Bill. Bill, Juana likes to play tennis, just like you do.")

Speaking Formally

Formal speaking is speaking that is planned. This means that a specific time and place are set aside for someone to speak. The purpose for this type of speaking is to inform, persuade, or entertain the audience. The most common types of formal speaking that you hear around you in school every day are announcements, introductions to a presentation, and oral reports.

Making Announcements

At times, you may need to make an *announcement*. An ***announcement*** is a short, formal speech that provides information to a group of listeners. An announcement often includes instructions about a situation or an event. An announcement should be clear and easy to understand.

HOW TO MAKE ANNOUNCEMENTS

1. Include all important facts that your audience will need to know. Most announcements include the following information:
   - the kind of event or occasion
   - who is involved
   - the time
   - the location where the event will take place
   - why the event is important
   - any special information, such as the amount of an admission fee
2. Add interesting details that will catch your listeners' attention.
3. Announce your message slowly, clearly, and briefly.
4. If necessary, repeat the most important facts.

Making an Introduction to a Presentation

An introduction is a special kind of announcement. An introduction is sometimes given to prepare an audience for a speaker's presentation. If you are introducing a speaker, you will need to attract your listeners' attention and provide brief information about the speaker or the speech topic. This information might include details about the speaker's background, experience, or accomplishments. Keep your introduction brief. Your introduction is meant to prepare the audience to hear what the speaker has to say.

Making an Oral Report

From time to time, you may be asked to give a short speech, or report. You might tell an interesting story, talk about a book you have read, or inform others how to do something. Sometimes the topic for your talk may be chosen for you. On other occasions, you may be allowed to choose your own topic.

Planning Your Report

Giving a successful oral report requires careful planning and preparation.

HOW TO PREPARE AN ORAL REPORT

1. *Choose a topic that will work well for your speech.* The best topic to choose is one that you are interested in talking about and that you think your audience is interested in hearing about.
2. *Make your topic as specific as possible.* Most oral reports have a time limit. This means you have to limit your topic to fit the time you're allowed.

(continued)

HOW TO PREPARE AN ORAL REPORT *(continued)*

3. *Think about your audience.* Before preparing a talk, ask yourself what your listeners already know about your topic. If they don't know very much about this topic, you'll need to give some background information. However, if they know a lot about your topic, you may need to talk only about information about the topic that you think they'd be less familiar with.

4. *Consider your purpose.* Think about *why* you are speaking. Do you want to *inform* your audience about some situation or process? Would you like to *persuade* them to accept your opinions or take some action? Or, maybe you want to *entertain* them by telling an amusing story.

5. *Gather information for your talk.* Look for material about your topic. Read books, newspapers, or magazines. Talk to people who know about the topic.

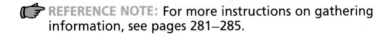 REFERENCE NOTE: For more instructions on gathering information, see pages 281–285.

Organizing Your Report

When you have decided the purpose and the length of your oral report, you can use the information you have gathered to organize and prepare your report. Organizing your ideas for an oral report is almost like writing them. Your best suggestions on deciding what you want to say can be found in the chapters of this textbook that help you write your ideas according to your purpose.

For example, if the purpose of your report is to inform, see pages 182–183 for ideas and suggestions about how to organize information. Or, if you plan to persuade your audience, you should see pages 202–232 for ideas about persuasive techniques.

RESOURCES

Preparing Your Report

Once you have decided exactly what you want to say, you can prepare for giving your report. Make a few notes on 3″ × 5″ note cards and refer to them while you are giving your report. Each note card should have one main idea, and perhaps a few notes about details you plan to mention. Number your note cards to help you keep them in order. Then practice giving your report, using your note cards until you are comfortable referring to them while you are speaking.

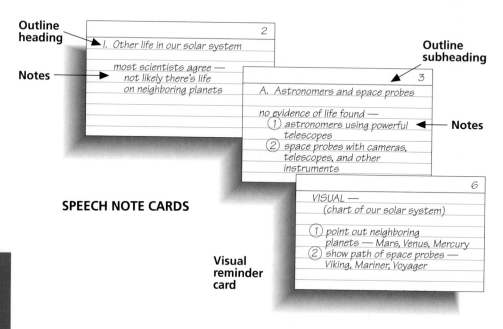

Outline heading

I. Other life in our solar system   2

Notes
most scientists agree —
not likely there's life
on neighboring planets

Outline subheading

A. Astronomers and space probes   3

no evidence of life found —
① astronomers using powerful   Notes
telescopes
② space probes with cameras,
telescopes, and other
instruments

SPEECH NOTE CARDS

VISUAL —   6
(chart of our solar system)

① point out neighboring
planets — Mars, Venus, Mercury
② show path of space probes —
Viking, Mariner, Voyager

Visual reminder card

RESOURCES

Giving Your Report

Most people feel nervous before speaking to an audience. Practice your talk until you feel confident with the material and your note cards. If you feel especially nervous before you speak, take a slow, deep breath. Hold it, then slowly let it out. Above all, pay attention to what you're saying.

HOW TO GIVE A REPORT

1. *Be confident.* Stand up straight but not stiffly. Look as if you're alert and interested in what you're saying.
2. *Look at your audience.* Try to make direct eye contact with your listeners. Speak directly to your audience.
3. *Use your voice effectively.* Use your voice to express your ideas. The way you speak adds interest to your talk and meaning to your message.
   - Speak loudly enough for everyone to hear.
   - To keep your listeners interested, your voice should rise and fall naturally as you speak.
   - Speak at a comfortable, relaxed rate. Pause for a moment before you go on to a different thought.
   - Pronounce your words clearly and carefully. Use a dictionary to find the pronunciation of unfamiliar words.

Group Discussions

Setting a Purpose

In many of your classes you probably work in groups. The purpose of group discussions is to accomplish a specific task or goal. This goal may be

- to discuss and share ideas
- to cooperate in group learning
- to solve a problem
- to arrive at a decision or to make a specific recommendation

To help your group decide about your purpose, identify what you'll need to accomplish within the time you are allowed.

RESOURCES

Assigning Roles

Each person involved in a group discussion has a role to play. Each role has special responsibilities. For example, your group may choose a chairperson to help keep the discussion moving smoothly. Someone else may be selected as the secretary, or reporter (recorder), who has the responsibility of taking notes during the discussion.

GUIDELINES FOR GROUP DISCUSSIONS

1. *Prepare for the discussion.* If you know what your group will talk about, spend some time before the discussion gathering information about the topic.
2. *Listen to what others say.* Be willing to learn from what other group members have to offer. Don't interrupt when others are speaking. Speak only when it's your turn to speak.
3. *Do your part.* Contribute to the discussion and share your ideas openly. Take only your fair share of time to talk. Be friendly and polite when it's someone else's turn to speak.
4. *Stay on the discussion topic.* Try not to wander away from the discussion topic. If necessary, politely remind others to stick to the subject.
5. *Ask questions.* If you don't understand something, ask questions.

Oral Interpretation

The purpose of an *oral interpretation* is to entertain. Sometimes, instead of talking about material you have written, you might be required to give an oral interpretation. An **oral interpretation** is a lively reading of someone else's written material.

Choosing a Selection

Short stories, novels, plays, and poems can provide you with good material for oral interpretation. Here are suggestions for finding a literary work that you can use for an oral interpretation.

| SELECTIONS FOR ORAL INTERPRETATION ||
TYPE OF LITERATURE	DESCRIPTION OF POSSIBLE SELECTION
poem	a poem that ■ tells a story, such as an epic or a narrative poem ■ has a speaker (using the word "I") ■ has a conversation between characters ■ is expressive of a particular emotion
short story	a brief story, or portion of a story, with ■ a beginning, middle, and end ■ characters whose words are expressed in a way that you can act out (such as a narrator who tells the story or characters who talk to one another, using dialogue in quotation marks)
play	a short play, or a scene from a play, with ■ a beginning, middle, and end ■ one or more characters with dialogue

When you choose a selection, think about the occasion. Determine how much time you will have for your presentation. Finally, consider your listeners. How will they respond to your selection? Will your audience find the selection interesting? Will they understand the meaning of your selection?

You may need to write an introduction for your interpretation. See page 698.

See page 698.

RESOURCES

Adapting Material

Sometimes you need to shorten a story, a poem, or a play for an oral interpretation. To make a shortened version, or *cutting,* follow these suggestions.

1. Decide where the story should begin and end.
2. Cut out parts that don't have anything to do with the portion of the story you are telling.
3. Cut dialogue tags such as *he cried.*

Presenting an Oral Interpretation

When you've chosen the piece of literature that you want to present, you can prepare a *reading script.* A *reading script* is a typed or neatly written copy of the selection that you can mark to show exactly how you want to present the material to your audience.

HOW TO MARK A READING SCRIPT

1. Underline any words or phrases you wish to stress.
2. Use a slash (/) to indicate a pause.
3. Make notes in the margin to show when you should vary the volume of your voice, show a special gesture, or suggest a particular tone.

Rehearse your selection carefully. Practice reading the material aloud, using voice tone, movements, and dramatic emphasis. Make the meaning of your selection clear to your audience. Use a practice audience, or practice in front of a mirror until you are satisfied with the way you give your presentation.

 COMPUTER NOTE: Use a word-processing program to prepare your reading script. The bold, italic, or underlining formats can be used for emphasis or for notes to yourself.

Review

▶ EXERCISE 1   **Practicing Telephone Dialogue**

Write down a brief telephone dialogue for this situation: A friend calls to ask for help with a class project. Your mother needs the phone first.

▶ EXERCISE 2   **Giving Directions or Instructions**

Prepare directions for this situation: Your parents plan to pick up a homework assignment you left in your locker at school. Explain how to find your locker, open it, and find the right paper.

▶ EXERCISE 3   **Making Introductions**

Explain what you might say in this situation: Your cousin Nick is visiting your English class. Introduce him to your teacher, then to a classmate.

▶ EXERCISE 4   **Preparing and Giving a Report**

Choose a topic for a short, three- to five-minute report on a topic that interests you. Gather information on your topic and make note cards. Then give your report.

▶ EXERCISE 5   **Participating in a Group Discussion**

Plan a group discussion on a topic provided by your teacher. Set a purpose and a time limit for your discussion. Try to accomplish your goal in the time allowed.

▶ EXERCISE 6   **Presenting an Oral Interpretation**

Select a piece of literature (a short story or play) that contains a scene with one or two characters. Prepare a reading script for a three-minute oral interpretation. Write a brief introduction.

RESOURCES

28 LISTENING AND VIEWING

Strategies for Listening and Viewing

Listening and viewing are not as simple as they seem. You constantly hear sounds and see images from many sources, but you probably don't really listen to or look carefully at very many of them. Active listening and viewing require you to think about what you hear and see.

It is important to develop good listening and viewing habits. They will help you learn more easily, remember what you hear and see, and become more aware of what is going on around you.

Listening with a Purpose

You will be a more effective listener if you remember your purpose for listening. Some common purposes for listening are

- for enjoyment or entertainment
- for information or explanation
- for understanding
- for forming opinions or evaluating ideas

Listening for Information

Listening for Details

When you're listening for details, try to sort out information that answers the basic *5W-How?* questions: *Who? What? When? Where? Why?* and *How?* As you listen, try to identify answers to these questions.

Listening to Instructions

Both at school and in the workplace, it's important to listen carefully when you are given assignments, instructions, or directions. Follow these guidelines.

1. Listen to each step. Listen for words that tell you when each step ends and the next one begins— for example, *first, second, next, then,* and *last.*
2. Listen for the number of steps required and the order to follow. Take notes if necessary.
3. Make an outline of the steps to follow in your own mind. Then picture yourself completing each step in order.
4. Make sure you have all the necessary information and understand the instructions. Ask questions if you are unclear about any step.

Listening and Responding Politely

Follow these guidelines to be a courteous and effective listener.

1. Look at the speaker and pay attention.
2. Don't interrupt the speaker. Don't whisper, fidget, or make distracting noises or movements.
3. Be tolerant of such differences as the speaker's race, accent, clothing, customs, or religion.
4. Try to understand the speaker's point of view. Your own point of view affects your judgment.

5. Listen to the speaker's entire message before you evaluate it.
6. Ask appropriate questions in a voice loud enough for all to hear. For better understanding, summarize or paraphrase the point you are questioning.
7. Use appropriate, effective language and gestures.

Using the LQ2R Method

The LQ2R study method is especially helpful when you are listening to a speaker who is giving information or instructions.

L   *Listen* carefully to information as it is being presented. Focus your attention on the speaker.

Q   *Question* yourself as you listen. Make a list of your questions as you think of them.

R   *Recite* to yourself in your own words the details of the information as the speaker presents them. Summarize information in your mind, or jot down notes as you listen.

R   *Relisten* as the speaker concludes the presentation. Major points may be repeated.

Taking Notes

Taking notes can help you remember what a speaker says. Don't try to write down every word. Just put down a few key ideas and important details.

Interviewing

An *interview* is a special listening situation. When you need firsthand information for a project or a report, set up an interview with someone who knows about your topic. Follow these suggestions.

Preparing for the Interview

1. Contact the person you would like to interview. Arrange to meet at a specific time and place.
2. Decide what information you most want to know.
3. Make a list of questions to ask. Avoid questions that require simple yes or no answers.

Conducting the Interview

1. Be on time for the interview.
2. Listen carefully. Be courteous and patient. Show respect for what the person has to say, even if you disagree with the person's opinion.
3. Take notes. If you don't understand something, ask questions.
4. As you finish, thank the person for granting you the interview.

Following the Interview

1. Go over your notes to be sure they are clear.
2. Write a summary as soon as you can.

 COMPUTER NOTE: Use your word-processing program's outline feature to organize your notes into an outline for your first draft.

Listening Critically

When you listen carefully, you can make decisions based on what you hear. Evaluating what you hear is known as *critical listening.* Critical listening is especially important when a speaker is trying to convince you to do something or to think in a certain way. The main purpose of critical listening is to be able to evaluate a speaker's ideas.

GUIDELINES FOR LISTENING CRITICALLY

1. *Listen for main ideas.* Identify the most important points. Listen for clue words, such as *major, minor, most important,* or similar words that help you to identify key ideas.
2. *Distinguish between facts and opinions.* Decide which of a speaker's remarks report facts and which express feelings or opinions. A **fact** is a statement of information that can be proved to be true. (For example, the saguaro is the state flower of Arizona.) An **opinion** is a belief or judgment about something. It cannot be proved to be true. (For example, if you say that chocolate is a better flavor than maple, that's an opinion, not a fact. It's a statement that can't be proved to be true.)
3. *Listen for the speaker's point of view.* Speakers may lean toward one point of view. They may sometimes present only one side of an issue and may not have enough real evidence to back up what they are saying.
4. *Determine the speaker's purpose.* A speaker may have a particular **motive,** or underlying reason, for persuading you. If a speaker has something to gain from convincing you to accept his or her opinions, weigh the speaker's arguments very carefully before you agree.

RESOURCES

Understanding Propaganda Techniques

To get you to believe in something or to take some action, speakers may use common *propaganda techniques. **Propaganda techniques** are ways of making an opinion seem very appealing. These techniques are often used in advertising in the mass media because they usually work. If you learn about these techniques, however, you are less likely to be swayed by speakers using them. You'll know the tricks!

COMMON PROPAGANDA TECHNIQUES

Bandwagon	You are urged to "jump on the bandwagon" because "everyone's doing it." This technique works when people like to join the crowd. ■ "Four out of five teens prefer Teen Scene jeans."
Testimonial	Well-known people sometimes give an endorsement of a product or idea. However, the person might not know much about that particular product. ■ "I'm football hero Joe Manly, recommending Whoosh brand vacuum cleaners."
Emotional appeals	This technique uses words that appeal to your emotions instead of your logic or reasoning. ■ "My political opponent is a dirty, rotten crook!"
"Plain folks"	People who seem to be like you may be used to persuade you. This technique works because people tend to trust those like themselves. ■ "Hey, folks! Come on down and see your friendly neighbors at Hometown Auto Sales."
False cause and effect	This technique is used to suggest that because one event happened first, it caused a second event to occur. However, the two events may not actually be related in any way. ■ "I'm sure the only reason I didn't win the prize was because I walked under a ladder in the parking lot."

RESOURCES

Viewing Critically

You see and hear advertisements almost everywhere you go. TV and radio programs broadcast ads at least every fifteen minutes. Magazines and newspapers print ads of all sizes. Advertising signs line many roads. Ads come in the mail and even appear on the Internet.

Why are there so many ads? Every ad has one aim—to get the viewer to buy or do something. Billions of purchasing dollars are involved. Before you go shopping, take a critical look at the ads you see every day. You may be surprised by the way they are designed and by the effect they have on you.

Analyzing Advertisements You See

Advertising uses complex techniques. Television ads flash by the viewer very quickly. Some ads are seen for only a few seconds. While you have more time to view print ads, you may not pay any attention to them at all if they do not catch your eye.

Because you view ads for such a short time, every image is designed for maximum effect. If you look at ads uncritically, you just react to the creative images. If you analyze ads, however, you see that their content and placement have been chosen very carefully.

Aiming at an Audience. What ads do you see when you watch your favorite TV programs? Are they ads for products that interest young people, or are they ads for baby powder and denture cleaner? When advertisers create an ad, they show it to people who might want the product. For example, they place an ad for a new toy with a children's TV program or magazine. This action is called *targeting an audience.*

Getting Your Attention. Advertisers must get your attention before they persuade you to buy.

What ads do you remember? Do the TV ads have a clever character or a catchy slogan? Do they have outstanding special effects or graphics? Do the magazine ads have images that stay in your mind? Do the radio ads feature a tune that you hum? Most successful ads have at least one of these. If you remember an ad, you are more likely to buy the product.

Delivering the Message. Advertisers often use the propaganda techniques discussed on page 711 to get you to buy, whether the ads are on TV or in print. Here are ways these techniques appeal to different needs that people have.

Bandwagon ads appeal to the need to belong. If you want to be like everyone else, you will buy the advertised product.

Testimonials appeal to the need to identify with people who are famous or who seem important or knowledgeable. If your favorite baseball player recommends a breakfast cereal, you may want to eat that cereal, too.

Ads may also use emotional appeals, such as *flattery.* "You wear the latest styles from the best stores. That's why you should shop at XYZ's. After all, you deserve the finest." These ads appeal to the need to feel good about yourself. They suggest that since you are terrific, you deserve the best product. Of course, that product is the one being advertised.

Making the Sale. Look critically at the next ad you see. Ask yourself, *What is the aim of this ad? Who is the target audience? How does the ad try to persuade me? Does it use a propaganda technique? If so, which one? Would I buy this product because it's better, or do I just like the ad?*

The ads you see and hear affect almost every part of your life: the food you eat, the clothes you wear, the music you hear, the sports you play, and even the way you style your hair. As you view ads, think about how they influence your choices.

RESOURCES

Review

▶ EXERCISE 1 **Listening for Information**

Make up five questions similar to the numbered items that follow. Read your questions aloud to your classmates, pausing about five seconds after reading each question to allow your listeners time to write down their answers. Then have your listeners check their answers to see how accurately they listened.

1. Here is a series of letters: *e–g–l–p–w.* What is the second letter?
2. Here is the order for pairs: first, Delmont and Rolo; then, Lucretia and Velma; last, Ling and Delia. What group is Rolo in?
3. Here is a list of colors: *blue, green, purple, orange, red.* What is the third color?
4. The White Mountains are in New Hampshire, the Great Smoky Mountains are in Tennessee, and the Cascade Mountains are in Washington. Where are the White Mountains?
5. Here is a list of starting times for movies and the theaters where they are showing: 6:30 at the Ritz, 7:15 at the Cinema West, 6:45 at the Film Palace, and 7:10 at the Movie Barn. What time is the show at the Film Palace?

▶ EXERCISE 2 **Preparing Interview Questions**

Think of someone famous (either living or dead) that you would like to interview. What specific topic or area of knowledge is this person an expert about? Prepare ten questions that you would like to ask in an interview with the person you have selected. Make sure that your questions require the person you're interviewing to give you more than a simple yes or no answer.

▶ EXERCISE 3 **Listening to a Speech**

Listen to a short speech presented by your teacher. Take brief notes. Then, respond to these questions.

1. What are the main ideas of the speech?
2. Does the speech contain details that support the main ideas in the speech? If so, identify them.

▶ EXERCISE 4 **Identifying Propaganda Techniques**

Identify the propaganda technique used in each of the following items.

1. Margo Lane for Bubble-O Bath Oil: "I'm always grateful for two things: all the little people who have made me a star and Bubble-O, the bath oil no tub should be without."
2. "Our mayor is a hard worker, just like you. He may be the mayor, but he's just an ordinary guy."
3. "Don't be out of touch! Listen to 950, the radio station more listeners tune in to."
4. "Our rivals use bad material in their products."
5. "Jolene wore a green dress on Tuesday. I told her green was unlucky and it would bring bad luck. Sure enough, she lost her watch on Thursday."

▶ EXERCISE 5 **Viewing Activity: Analyzing TV Advertising**

Watch a half-hour television program that is new to you. List the name of the program and the day and time you watched it. Then, list the product advertised in each commercial during that program, and answer the following questions. Discuss with your class-mates the ads you see.

1. What type of product is being advertised?
2. Who is featured in the ad?
3. Who is the target audience of the ad?
4. How does the ad try to persuade viewers? Which propaganda technique does it use?

RESOURCES

29 THE LIBRARY/ MEDIA CENTER

Finding and Using Information

All libraries, whether school, public, or workplace, collect information on many subjects. To find and use this information, learn about the library's contents and how they are arranged.

The Contents of the Library

The information in a library takes many forms. The resource you use depends on the type of information you need.

BOOKS	
Fiction	Stories (novels and short stories)
Nonfiction	Factual information about real people, events, and things; includes biographies and "how-to" books
Reference books	General information about many subjects

OTHER SOURCES	
Magazines and newspapers	Current events, commentaries, and important discoveries
Pamphlets	Brief summaries of facts about specific subjects
Audiotapes, records, films, filmstrips, slides, videotapes, CD-ROMs	Stories (narrated, illustrated, or acted out); music, instructions and educational material, facts and information about many specific subjects
Computers	Information stored electronically, allowing for easy access and frequent updates
Maps, globes, atlases, and almanacs	Geographic information, facts, dates, and statistics

The Arrangement of a Library

You can usually find a number and letter code on the spine of every book contained in a library. This code is a *call number.* The call number identifies the book and tells you where to find it on the shelves of the library.

Arrangement of Nonfiction

Most school libraries arrange nonfiction books using the *Dewey decimal system.* The **Dewey decimal system** assigns a number to each nonfiction book. These numbers are assigned according to the book's subject. Using this system of arrangement, books that contain factual information about similar subjects are placed near each other on the library shelves.

RESOURCES

Biographies describe the lives of real people. Most libraries place biographies in a separate section. Biographies are arranged in alphabetical order by the last name of the person the book is about. Biographies about the same person are in alphabetical order according to the last name of the author.

Arrangement of Fiction

Fiction books are not organized by subject like nonfiction books. Instead, fiction books are arranged alphabetically according to the last name of the author. For example, a novel by Maya Angelou would be arranged alphabetically before a novel by Ernesto Galarza. (Names of authors that begin with *Mc* and *St.* are alphabetized as if they were spelled out: *Mac* and *Saint.*)

If the library has more than one fiction book written by the same author, all these books are grouped together under the author's name. Then these books are arranged alphabetically by their titles. (Remember not to count the first word if it's *A, An,* or *The.*)

Types of Card Catalogs

The easiest way to locate a book in the library is to look up the call number in the library's card catalog. There are two kinds of card catalogs: the traditional card catalog and the online catalog.

The traditional *card catalog* is a cabinet of small drawers. Each drawer holds many small file cards. There are cards in this file for every book in the library. The cards are arranged in alphabetical order by title, author, or subject. Each fiction book has a *title card* and an *author card*. A nonfiction book will also have a *subject card*. Occasionally, you may find *"see"* or *"see also"* cards. These cards tell you where to go in the card catalog to find other books about the same subject.

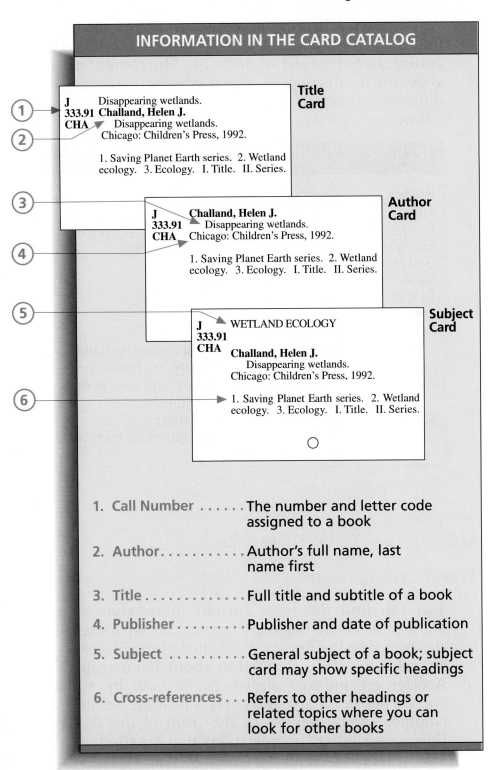

INFORMATION IN THE CARD CATALOG

(1) **(2)**

J
333.91
CHA

Disappearing wetlands.
Challand, Helen J.
   Disappearing wetlands.
Chicago: Children's Press, 1992.

1. Saving Planet Earth series. 2. Wetland
ecology. 3. Ecology. I. Title. II. Series.

Title Card

(3) **(4)**

J
333.91
CHA

Challand, Helen J.
   Disappearing wetlands.
Chicago: Children's Press, 1992.

1. Saving Planet Earth series. 2. Wetland
ecology. 3. Ecology. I. Title. II. Series.

Author Card

(5) **(6)**

J
333.91
CHA

WETLAND ECOLOGY

Challand, Helen J.
   Disappearing wetlands.
Chicago: Children's Press, 1992.

1. Saving Planet Earth series. 2. Wetland
ecology. 3. Ecology. I. Title. II. Series.

○

Subject Card

1. **Call Number** . . . . . . The number and letter code assigned to a book

2. **Author** . . . . Author's full name, last name first

3. **Title** . . . . Full title and subtitle of a book

4. **Publisher** . . . . Publisher and date of publication

5. **Subject** . . . . General subject of a book; subject card may show specific headings

6. **Cross-references** . . . Refers to other headings or related topics where you can look for other books

RESOURCES

The *online catalog* is stored on a computer. To find the call number for a book, type in the title, the author, or the subject of the book. The computer will show the results of your search. The results are a little different in each library, but the search results that follow are typical.

SEARCH RESULTS FROM ONLINE CATALOG	
Author:	Challand, Helen J.
Title:	Disappearing wetlands/Helen J. Challand; technical consultant, Milton W. Weller.
Published:	Chicago: Children's Press, © 1992.
Description:	127 p.: ill. (some col.); 25 cm.
Series:	Saving planet earth
LC Call No.:	QH87.3 .C43 1992
Dewey No.:	333.91816 20 CHA
Notes:	Includes index.
	Examines the ecological role of wetlands and discusses how they are formed, what life they support, and how people modify or destroy them.
Subjects:	Wetlands—Juvenile literature.
	Wetland conservation—Juvenile literature.
	Wetland ecology.

Using Reference Materials

The *Readers' Guide*

You can find the most current information about many subjects in magazine articles. Locate these articles by using the *Readers' Guide to Periodical Literature,* an index to articles printed in about 150 magazines. Articles are indexed alphabetically both by author and by subject. Each entry has a heading printed in boldface capital letters. In the front of the *Readers' Guide* is a guide to abbreviations that are used.

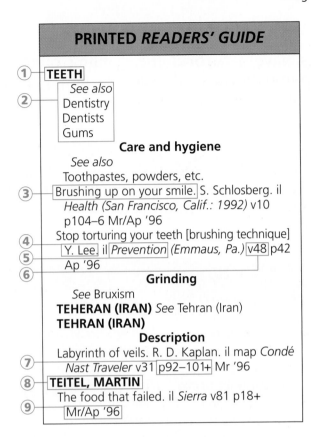

PRINTED *READERS' GUIDE*

① **Subject entry**

② **Subject cross-reference**

③ **Title of article**

④ **Author of article**

⑤ **Name of magazine**

⑥ **Volume number of magazine**

⑦ **Page reference**

⑧ **Author entry**

⑨ **Date of magazine**

Online Databases

You also can search for articles in magazines by using an ***online database.*** Search for specific topics by typing in a ***keyword*** or key phrase. You can print out the information you find. The results of a search for articles about teeth and brushing, using the Middle Search database, follow.

1. Subject: **TEETH**—Care & hygiene
   Title: Stop torturing your **teeth.**
   Source: (Prevention, Apr96, Vol. 48 Issue 4, p42, 1p, 1c)

2. Subject: Bacteria; **TEETH**—Care & hygiene
   Title: Bacteri-ahhh!
   Source: (321 Contact, Mar96 Issue 165, p2, 1/3p, 1c)

3. Subject: **TEETH**
   Title: The whole tooth.
   Source: (Owl, Jan96, Vol. 21 Issue 1, p20, 4p, 3c)

RESOURCES

The Vertical File

Many libraries have a *vertical file,* a filing cabinet containing up-to-date materials such as newspaper clippings, booklets, and pamphlets.

Reference Works

Most libraries devote an entire section to reference works. These sources contain information about a great number of subjects.

REFERENCE WORKS		
TYPE	**DESCRIPTION**	**EXAMPLES**
ENCYCLOPEDIAS	▪ many volumes ▪ articles arranged alphabetically by subject ▪ good source for general information	*Collier's Encyclopedia* *Compton's Encyclopedia* *The World Book Multimedia Encyclopedia*™
GENERAL BIOGRAPHICAL REFERENCES	▪ information about birth, nationality, and major accomplishments of outstanding people	*Current Biography* *Dictionary of American Biography* *The International Who's Who* *World Biographical Index on CD-ROM*
ATLASES	▪ maps and geographical information	*Atlas of World Cultures* *National Geographic Atlas of the World*

(continued)

RESOURCES

REFERENCE WORKS *(continued)*		
TYPE	DESCRIPTION	EXAMPLES
ALMANACS	■ up-to-date information about current events, facts, statistics, and dates	*The Information Please Almanac, Atlas and Yearbook* *The World Almanac and Book of Facts*
BOOKS OF SYNONYMS	■ lists of more interesting or more exact words to express ideas	*Roget's International Thesaurus* *Webster's New Dictionary of Synonyms*

Newspapers

Newspapers have many different types of reading materials that are often contained in several separate sections. As a reader, you probably read the various parts of a newspaper for different reasons.

WHAT'S IN A NEWSPAPER?		
TYPE OF WRITING/ EXAMPLES	READER'S PURPOSE	READING TECHNIQUE
informative news stories sports	to gain knowledge or information	Ask yourself the *5W-How?* questions (page 32).
persuasive editorials comics reviews ads	to gain knowledge, to make decisions, or to be entertained	Identify points you agree or disagree with. Find facts or reasons the writer uses.
creative or expressive comics columns	to be entertained	Identify ways the writer interests you or gives you a new viewpoint or ideas.

RESOURCES

Parts of a Book

Many books that you can use as sources are packed full of information. The specific information that you might need can sometimes be hard to find. You will find information more easily if you know how to use every part of a book. The following chart shows the types of information you will find in a book.

INFORMATION FOUND IN PARTS OF A BOOK	
PART	INFORMATION
Title page	gives the full title, the name of the author (or authors), the publisher, and the place of publication
Copyright page	gives the date of the first publication of the book and the date of any revisions
Table of contents	lists titles of chapters or sections of the book and their starting page numbers
Appendix	provides additional information about subjects found in the book; sometimes contains tables, maps, and charts
Glossary	defines, in alphabetical order, various difficult terms or important technical words used frequently in the book
Bibliography	lists sources used to write the book; provides names of books about related topics
Index	lists topics mentioned in the book, along with the page or pages on which they can be found; sometimes lists the page where a certain illustration may be found

Review

▶ EXERCISE 1 **Using the Library**

Answer the following questions about the information resources in the library.

1. Tell the order in which these fiction books would be arranged: *Big Red* by Jim Kjelgaard and *Bronzeville Boys and Girls* by Gwendolyn Brooks.
2. Using the sample *Readers' Guide* entry on page 721, find the article written by S. Schlosberg. In what magazine did this article appear?
3. Using the sample *Readers' Guide* entry on page 721, tell what heading you should look for if you want to find information about the care and hygiene of your teeth.
4. Use the card catalog or the online catalog in your library to find a nonfiction book. Write the title of the book, the author's name, and the call number.
5. What part of a book would you look in to find the meaning of a word you didn't understand?

▶ EXERCISE 2 **Using Reference Tools**

Answer the following questions about using printed or electronic reference sources in the library.

1. What kind of reference source might show you the number of miles between two cities?
2. What kind of reference source might tell you a list of words that mean the same as the word *large*?
3. What kind of reference source might tell you the population of the United States according to the most recent census?
4. What kind of reference source might you use to find information about pyramids?
5. What is your favorite part of a newspaper? Identify the type of writing, and explain why you like to read this specific part of the newspaper.

RESOURCES

30 THE DICTIONARY

Arrangement and Contents

A dictionary contains information about words. This information includes

- the meanings of a word
- how to spell a word
- how to pronounce, or say, a word
- how to use a word in speaking or writing

Arrangement of a Dictionary

Words found in a dictionary are called *entries.* Word entries in a dictionary are listed in alphabetical order. Each page of word entries in the dictionary has *guide words* to help you follow the alphabetical order. The first guide word tells you the first entry word found on that page. The second guide word tells you the last entry word found on that page.

 COMPUTER NOTE: Some spell-checking programs allow you to create a user dictionary. You can add the proper nouns and special terms you use often.

A SAMPLE ENTRY

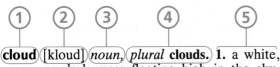

cloud [kloud] *noun, plural* **clouds.** **1.** a white, gray, or dark mass floating high in the sky. Clouds are made of tiny drops of water or ice hanging in the air. ◆ A **cloudburst** is a sudden, heavy rainfall. **2.** any mass or grouping of things like a cloud: *a cloud* of dust. A *cloud* of insects swarmed around the streetlight. —*verb,* **cloud-ed, clouding.** **1.** to cover or become covered with clouds: The morning sky was clear, but by noon it *clouded* over. **2.** to make or become darker or less clear: His face *clouded* when he heard the bad news.

cloud The majestic thunderhead, or *cumulonimbus* [kyo͞om′yə lō nim′bəs] cloud hanging over the woods is a sign that a storm is coming.

From *The Lincoln Writing Dictionary* © 1989 by **Harcourt Brace & Company.**

Contents of a Dictionary Entry

When you look up a word in a dictionary, you will find helpful information about how the word is used.

1. **Entry word.** The entry word is printed in boldface (dark) letters. It shows the way the word should be spelled and how to divide the word into syllables. It may also show if a word should be capitalized or if the word can be spelled in other ways.

RESOURCES

2. **Pronunciation.** The pronunciation of an entry word is shown with symbols. These symbols help you pronounce the word correctly. In the sample entry, look at the *k* symbol. It shows you that the *c* in *cloud* sounds more like the *c* in *can* than the *c* in *ice*. Special letters or markings that are used with letters to show a certain sound are called *phonetic symbols.* *Accent marks* show which syllables of the word are said more forcefully. Look in the front of your dictionary for an explanation of the symbols and marks your dictionary uses.

3. **Part-of-speech labels.** Some words may be used as more than one part of speech. For each meaning of a word, the dictionary shows the part of speech. In the sample entry, *cloud* can be used as a noun or as a verb, depending on the meaning.

4. **Other forms.** Sometimes your dictionary will show you how to spell other forms of the word. These may include the plural form of nouns, verb tenses, or adjective and adverb forms.

5. **Definitions.** The different meanings of a word are numbered. To help you understand the different meanings, dictionaries often include a sample phrase or sentence after a numbered definition.

6. **Related word forms.** Sometimes the dictionary may show forms of the entry word created by adding suffixes, prefixes, or other combining forms. Once you know the meaning of the main word (*cloud*), you can usually understand the meaning of the related word (*cloudburst*).

7. **Examples.** Examples show how the entry word is used in a sentence. The examples are often in the form of phrases or sentences using the word in context.

8. **Illustrations.** Sometimes dictionaries include pictures that show what a word means.

9. **Captions.** Illustrations may have a *caption,* a label that explains the picture or drawing. A caption may also give an example of how the word is used.

Review

▶ EXERCISE 1 **Dividing Words into Syllables**

Divide the following words into syllables. Use the same method to show syllable division that your dictionary uses.

1. manual
2. region
3. familiar

4. composure
5. incredible

▶ EXERCISE 2 **Using the Dictionary to Check Pronunciation**

Look up the following words in a dictionary. Write the pronunciation of the word the same way that your dictionary shows it.

1. next
2. hyphen
3. poncho

4. signature
5. designate

▶ EXERCISE 3 **Finding Part-of-Speech Labels**

Look up each of the following words in a dictionary. Give all the parts of speech listed for each word. Then write an example of how the word is used as each part of speech.

EXAMPLE **1.** graduate
　　　　1. *verb—He will graduate from high school.*
　　　　noun—He is a graduate of the state university.

1. flood
2. link
3. protest

4. beam
5. stack

RESOURCES

31 VOCABULARY

Learning and Using New Words

You come across new words all the time. You hear them when you talk with others and even when you hear people talk in movies, on TV, or on the radio. You also see new words when you read. This chapter shows many ways to learn new words. These methods will help you learn new words both now in school and later in the workplace.

Start a Word Bank

A good way to learn new words is by keeping a word bank. This can be as simple as making a vocabulary list in your notebook. When you read or hear an unfamiliar word, include the word and its definition in your list. Then, look it up in the dictionary to be sure you have the correct meaning.

 COMPUTER NOTE: Create a new vocabulary file on your computer. Add new words and their definitions to the end of the file. Then, use the Sort command to arrange the words in alphabetical order.

Using Words in Context

A dictionary is one of the best sources to find out the meaning of an unfamiliar word. However, when you read or listen, you can probably guess the meanings of many unfamiliar words from the *context,* or the way they are used. The ***context*** of a word includes all the other words and sentences that surround it. These surrounding words often provide clues to the word's meaning.

HOW TO USE CONTEXT CLUES	
TYPE OF CLUE	**EXPLANATION**
Definitions or Restatements	Look for words that can help you define an unfamiliar word or that restate the meaning of the unknown word, using terms that you already know. ■ Amado someday hopes to become an *architect*, a person who designs buildings. [The clues show you that *architect* can be defined as "a person who designs buildings."]
Examples	Look for one or more examples that show the meaning of an unfamiliar word. ■ Items of *apparel,* including sweaters, vests, pants, and gowns, were found in the old trunk. [The examples show that *apparel* means "clothing."]
Synonyms	Look for clues that show an unfamiliar word is similar in meaning to a more familiar word. ■ From the beginning, I always thought he was a faker, an *impostor!* [The clues show that *impostor* is similar in meaning to *faker.*]

RESOURCES

(continued)

HOW TO USE CONTEXT CLUES *(continued)*	
TYPE OF CLUE	EXPLANATION
Antonyms	Look for clues that show an unfamiliar word is opposite in meaning to a more familiar word. ■ On the tennis court, Elmore and Palani are *adversaries,* but off the court they are good friends. [The clues show that *adversaries* means the opposite of *good friends.*]
Cause and Effect	Look for clues that an unfamiliar word is related to the cause—or is the result—of an action, feeling, or idea. ■ Since the disease was easily spread, people in the stricken city had to be *quarantined.* [You can see that to *quarantine* people must mean to keep them away from others so they won't catch, or spread, a disease.]

Using the Dictionary

You may not always be able to figure out a word's meaning from its context. You may often need to look up the word in a dictionary. In the dictionary, you may find several meanings listed for a particular word. Then you'll need to read all the meanings to find the one that best fits the context of your sentence.

Synonyms and Antonyms

Synonyms are words that have nearly the same meaning, such as *happy* and *glad*. *Antonyms,* by contrast, are words that have nearly the opposite meaning, such as *bold* and *shy.* You can sometimes find synonyms in a dictionary, listed after the definitions for an entry word. Less often, dictionaries list antonyms for an entry word.

The best source to use to find synonyms is a *thesaurus.* A **thesaurus** is a special kind of reference book that has word entries like a dictionary. However, instead of definitions, a thesaurus lists synonyms— and sometimes antonyms—for its entry words.

Homographs

Homographs are words that are spelled the same but have different meanings. Although the words look the same, they may not be pronounced the same. To discover the meaning of a homograph in a sentence, you will need to use context clues. Or, you can read all the meanings listed for each homograph in a dictionary. Then choose the one that best fits the context of your sentence.

Using Word Parts

There are two main groups of words in English: those that cannot be divided into parts and those that can. Words that cannot be divided into parts are called **base words.** *Read, place,* and *great* are examples of base words.

Words that can be divided into parts, like *reject, happily,* and *unreadable,* are made up of **word parts.** The three types of word parts are

- roots
- prefixes
- suffixes

The *root* is the main part of the word. It carries the word's core meaning. A *prefix* is a word part added before a root. A *suffix* is a word part added after a root. In the word *unreadable, un–* is the prefix, *–read–* is the root, and *–able* is the suffix. Adding a suffix may change both a word's meaning and its part of speech, as in *joy/joyful*.

WORD	PREFIX	ROOT	SUFFIX
reflection	re–	–flect–	–ion
illegally	il–	–legal–	–ly
transportation	trans–	–port–	–ation
incredible	in–	–cred–	–ible

Knowing the meaning of word parts can help you figure out the meanings of many unfamiliar words.

COMMON PREFIXES		
PREFIX	MEANING	EXAMPLE
bi–	two	bicycle
dis–	away, opposing	disagree
in–	not	incomplete
mis–	wrong	misspell
non–	not	nonhuman
over–	above, too much	overdone
pre–	before	precook
re–	again	replace
semi–	half	semicircle
sub–	under	subtitle
un–	not	unhappy

☞ REFERENCE NOTE: For guidelines on spelling when adding prefixes, see page 639.

COMMON SUFFIXES

SUFFIX	MEANING	EXAMPLE
–able	able	respectable
–en	make	deepen
–ful	full of	stressful
–ion	action, condition	inspection
–less	without	penniless
–ly	characteristic of	quickly
–ness	quality	togetherness
–ous	characterized by	luxurious

☞ **REFERENCE NOTE:** For guidelines on spelling when adding suffixes, see pages 640–642.

Review

▶ EXERCISE 1 **Using Context Clues**

Use context clues to choose the word or phrase that best fits the meaning of each italicized word.

a. simple
b. life's work
c. easily broken
d. movement

e. attack
f. hard to locate
g. beautiful
h. earlier

1. The *migration*, or relocation, of the settlers moving to new lands was a terrible struggle.
2. Zane likes to work with his hands and wants a *career* as a carpenter or an auto mechanic.
3. Since we learned that rule in a *previous* lesson, we won't go over it again.
4. The brave men and women in the fort fought off the sudden *onslaught* of their enemies.
5. The vase was *fragile*, unlike the shatterproof plates.

RESOURCES

▶ EXERCISE 2 **Choosing the Best Synonym**

For each of the following sentences, write the word in parentheses that better fits the context of the sentence. Use a dictionary to check exact meanings.

1. In order to get a good night's sleep, Estelle asked everyone not to (*disturb, upset*) her until morning.
2. Shing certainly has a (*sincere, hearty*) appetite.
3. The police found a briefcase full of (*counterfeit, copied*) money in the car.
4. It is (*doubtful, suspicious*) that I will win the national spelling competition.
5. Oily rags in the basement are a fire (*risk, hazard*).

▶ EXERCISE 3 **Choosing Antonyms**

Select the antonym that is more appropriate for the italicized word in each sentence.

1. Vince felt *lazy,* but Kenesha felt (energetic, sleepy).
2. A child's first set of teeth is (temporary, important); the second set is *permanent.*
3. Paulo remained *calm* during the thunderstorm, but his little sister became (homesick, frantic).
4. In our national elections, we don't vote *publicly;* we cast our ballots (privately, separately).
5. The lion became a fierce *hunter;* a young antelope was her intended (partner, prey).

▶ EXERCISE 4 **Identifying Homographs**

Each of the following sentences contains a pair of homographs. Write a meaning for each homograph. You may use a dictionary to find exact meanings.

1. Tony will get a chance to *conduct* the chorus if his *conduct* in class improves.
2. The guide will *lead* us to the *lead* mine.

3. The ship's *bow* was decorated with a bright red *bow*.
4. When his well ran dry, the prospector was forced to *desert* his home in the *desert*.
5. The winter *wind* can somehow *wind* throughout the entire house.

EXERCISE 5   **Making New Words with Prefixes**

Combine each of the following words with the prefix whose meaning is shown in parentheses after the word. Use the prefix chart on page 734 to choose an appropriate prefix. Then, write the new word you have formed.

EXAMPLE   **1.** view (before)
            1. *preview*

1. monthly (two)
2. expensive (not)
3. historic (before)
4. handle (wrong)
5. organize (again)

6. marine (under)
7. locate (away)
8. fire (wrong)
9. place (again)
10. direct (not)

EXERCISE 6   **Making New Words with Suffixes**

Combine each of the following base words with the suffix that follows the plus sign. Write the new word. Use a dictionary to check your spelling.

EXAMPLE   **1.** victory + ous
            1. *victorious*

1. hope + less
2. love + able
3. demonstrate + ion
4. fury + ous

5. happy + ness
6. light + en
7. forget + ful
8. honorable + ly

RESOURCES

32 LETTERS AND FORMS

Style and Contents

Do you like to receive mail? Most people do. That's why you'll find it important to develop good letter-writing skills for social and business letters.

Kinds of Letters

There are several different kinds of letters. All of them have a purpose and an audience.

LETTERS		
TYPE OF LETTER	YOUR PURPOSE FOR WRITING	YOUR PROBABLE AUDIENCE
Personal	to tell about your ideas or feelings	close friends or relatives
Social	to be polite, to thank someone, or to tell some-one about a planned event	friends or social acquaintances
Business	to inform a business about a service you need or how a service was performed	a business or organization

Writing Letters

Personal Letters

A *personal letter,* also called a friendly letter, is a good way to communicate with a friend or relative. A friendly letter is like a conversation, only much better. Conversations may be interrupted or forgotten, but a friendly letter is often treasured and read many times.

A friendly letter is a token of friendship. It usually contains a personal message from you, the sender, to the person you are writing to, the receiver. For example, you might write a friend to send congratulations for receiving a school award. Or, you might write to tell a friend your reaction to news that the friend's family will be moving away. When you're sending a friendly letter, remember to write about a subject that interests both you and the person you're writing to.

Social Letters

Sometimes, to be very polite, you should write a social letter rather than use the telephone or speak to someone in person. A *social letter* is usually a courteous response to a specific event or occurrence. The kinds of social letters people write most often are thank-you letters, invitations, or letters of regret.

Thank-you Letters

When you receive a gift or a favor, you should write a thank-you letter. The purpose of a thank-you letter is to express your appreciation when someone has spent time, trouble, or money to do something for your benefit. In addition to thanking the person, you might include a paragraph or so of personal news or friendly, chatty information. Try to think of something about the person's effort or gift that made it special to you.

> 9300 Leon St.
> Burlington, VT 05401
> October 6, 1998
>
> Dear Grandpa,
>
>   Thank you so much for the wonderful beagle puppy you brought down from the farm. She must have been the smartest one in the litter. She already knows her name after only two days. We named her Waggles because her tail wags all the time. She's the greatest gift, Grandpa. Thanks!
>
> Love,
> Rita

Invitations

You write an invitation to ask someone to an event you're planning. Include specific information about the occasion, such as the type of event, time and place, and any other information your guests might need to know (such as how to dress and what to bring, if anything).

Letters of Regret

You will need to write a letter of regret whenever you receive an invitation to an event that you will not be able to attend. You should always respond in writing to invitations that include the letters *R.S.V.P.* (These letters are an abbreviation for the French words that mean "please reply.")

Business Letters

The Parts of a Business Letter

Business letters usually follow a standard form or style. There are six parts of a business letter:

(1) the heading
(2) the inside address
(3) the salutation
(4) the body
(5) the closing
(6) the signature

Block Style

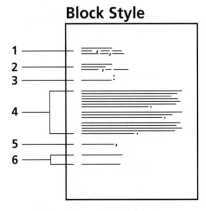

These six parts may be arranged in one of two styles.

In the *block form,* every part of the letter begins at the left margin of the page. A blank line is left between paragraphs, which are not indented.

In the *modified block form,* the heading, the closing, and your signature are placed to the right of an imaginary line down the center of the page. The middle parts of the letter begin at the left margin. Paragraphs are indented.

Modified Block Style

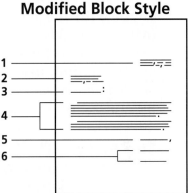

The Heading. The heading of a business letter has three lines:

- your street address
- your city, state, and ZIP Code
- the date you are writing the letter

The Inside Address. The inside address gives the name and address of the person you are writing.

■ If you're directing your letter to someone by name, use a courtesy title (such as *Mr., Ms., Mrs.,* or *Miss*) or a professional title (such as *Dr.* or *Professor*) in front of the person's name. After the person's name, include the person's business title (such as *Principal* or *Business Manager*).

■ If you don't have a person's name, use a business title (such as *Refunds Department* or *Editor in Chief*).

The Salutation. Your salutation is your greeting to the person you're writing. In a business letter, the salutation usually ends with a colon (such as in *Dear Professor Garcia:*).

If you are writing to a specific person, you can begin with the word *Dear.* Then, add a courtesy title (*Mr., Miss, Ms.,* or *Mrs.*) or a professional title (*Dr., Senator,* or others like these). If you don't have a specific name, use a general greeting (such as *Dear Sir or Madam:* or *Ladies and Gentlemen:*). You can also use a business title instead (*Dear Committee Leader:*).

The Body. The body contains the message of your letter. Leave a blank line between paragraphs in the body of the letter.

The Closing. Conclude your letter politely. The closing of a business letter often uses one of several common phrases (such as *Sincerely, Yours truly,* or *Respectfully yours*). Capitalize only the first word. End the closing with a comma.

The Signature. Sign your first and last name in ink directly below the closing. For a business letter, your name should be typed or printed neatly just below your signature.

Types of Business Letters

The Request or Order Letter. In a *request letter,* you ask for specific information about a product or service. An *order letter* tells a business about a product or service you want (such as a free brochure). Be sure to include all important information (such as the item number, size, color, brand name, and price).

The Complaint or Adjustment Letter. When you write a *complaint* or *adjustment letter,* you state a problem and how you think it should be corrected. For example, if you are unhappy with a product you bought, you might write a letter like the one below.

3400 Werner Drive
Charlotte, NC 28205
June 23, 1998

Customer Service Department
Barton Educational Products
1632 5th Street
Asheville, NC 28801

Dear Sir or Madam:

I am returning science kit #609 that was delivered yesterday. It arrived with a broken microscope.

Please replace the kit or refund my purchase price of $69.95 plus $4.30 that I paid for postage and handling.

Yours truly,

Lee Chin

Lee Chin

RESOURCES

The Appreciation Letter. Whenever you write an *appreciation letter,* you tell people in a business or organization that they did a good job. Give details about what they did that you liked. For example, perhaps a waiter or waitress gave you especially good service at a restaurant, and you want to tell the manager that you appreciate such good service.

GUIDELINES FOR WRITING BUSINESS LETTERS

1. *Decide on your purpose.* Are you ordering or returning merchandise? Or, are you asking for someone to send you information?
2. *Include all necessary information.* Your purpose for writing should be very clear to your readers. Be brief and get to the point quickly, but don't leave out any important details.
3. *Write your letter in a timely manner.* If you are requesting something, make your request well in advance. If you have a complaint, send your letter as soon as possible.
4. *Think about your choice of words.* A business letter should be clear, polite, and reasonable. If you have a complaint, tell what's wrong, but be courteous.

Appearance of a Business Letter

As your representative, your business letter should look its best. Use the following guidelines when writing a business letter.

- Use unlined $8\frac{1}{2}'' \times 11''$ white paper.
- Type your letter or write it neatly in blue or black ink. Always check your letter for errors, smudges, and misspellings.
- Center your letter on the paper to make the margins even all around.
- Do not write on the back. Use a second sheet of paper if necessary.

COMPUTER NOTE: As you compose your letters, remember to save your work every ten to fifteen minutes. Turn on the automatic Save if you have it.

Addressing an Envelope

To make sure that your letter arrives at its intended destination, address the envelope neatly and correctly.

- Place your return address in the top left-hand corner of the envelope.
- Write the name and address of the person to whom the letter is being sent in the center of the envelope. (For a business letter, the name and address on the envelope should match the inside address.)
- Use standard two-letter postal abbreviations for state names, followed by the ZIP Code.

Sudi Foster
63 Washington Ave.
Salem, OR 97305

Aola Washington
2119 Brushcreek Ave. #302
Independence, MO 64055

Completing Printed Forms

You are often required to fill out forms about yourself. You must fill out a form to get a library card, register for school, apply for a job, and for other reasons. These guidelines will help.

HINTS FOR FILLING OUT FORMS

1. Read all instructions before you begin. Look for special instructions to see whether you should use a pen or pencil.
2. Read each item carefully.
3. Print neatly all the information that is requested.
4. Proofread the form to make sure you didn't leave anything blank. Also, check for errors and correct them neatly.
5. Mail the form to the correct address or give it to the correct person.

Review

▶ EXERCISE 1   **Writing a Social Letter**

Write a social letter for one of the following situations. Make up your own situation if you prefer.

1. Your soccer team has just won its first game. Write a thank-you letter to your grandparents, thanking them for coming to the game.
2. You have been invited to spend a few days at the house of an out-of-town friend. Unfortunately, you cannot go because your family has already planned a vacation for that time.
3. You are planning a joint birthday party for two friends at your house. Write a letter of invitation, including all the information your guests will need to know.

▶ EXERCISE 2   **Writing a Business Letter**

Write a business letter for one of the situations that follow. Use white, unruled typewriter paper. Use your own return address, but make up any other information you need to write the letter. Address an envelope for your letter, but don't actually mail it.

1. You would like historical information about a city. Write to its Chamber of Commerce, requesting a pamphlet or brochure.
2. Write a letter to a nearby museum, asking for a schedule of exhibits. Tell why you are interested in this information.
3. Write a letter of appreciation to your city council, explaining why you are happy with a city service or program, such as a new park or an after-school recreation program for the young people in your community.

▶ EXERCISE 3 **Completing a Form**

For each of the numbered blanks on the following form, write what you would put on that blank line if you filled out this form.

INFORMATION FORM

NAME _(1)_____

NICKNAME _(2)_____ PHONE # _(3)_____

ADDRESS _____(4)_____

_____

PARENT OR GUARDIAN _(5)_____

RESOURCES

33 READING, STUDYING, AND TEST TAKING

Using Skills and Strategies

Good grades are usually the result of efficient study habits and good reading skills. Learning to study and read better doesn't always mean working harder. By making your study time count and by using appropriate reading strategies, you can improve your skills and get better grades.

Planning a Study Routine

Set up a study schedule that will help you earn the grades you want. Decide on a schedule and stick to it. Here are some suggestions.

1. *Know your assignments.* Write down your assignments and when each one is due. Be sure you understand the instructions for each assignment.
2. *Plan to finish your work on time.* Break larger assignments into smaller steps. Keep track of when you should be finished with each step.
3. *Study.* Set aside a time and a place to study. Focus your attention only on your assignments.

Strengthening Reading and Study Skills

Reading and Understanding

You read differently depending on what you're reading and why you are reading it. You should read at the rate that fits your purpose for reading. Here are some common purposes for reading.

READING RATES AND THEIR PURPOSE		
READING RATE	PURPOSE	EXAMPLE
Scanning	Reading for specific details	Looking in your English textbook for a poem by Gwendolyn Brooks
Skimming	Reading for main points or important ideas	Reviewing words in boldface or italics in a science chapter to prepare for a test on the parts of a flower
Reading for mastery	Reading closely to understand and remember	Reading a chapter in your history textbook to prepare an oral report on the ancient Incas

Writing to Learn

Writing helps you organize your thoughts to explore ideas, solve problems, or make plans. Here are some kinds of writing that can help you learn.

RESOURCES

TYPE OF WRITING	PURPOSE	EXAMPLE
Freewriting	To help you focus your thoughts	Writing for ten minutes to plan the plot of a short story
Autobiographies	To help you examine the meaning of important events in your life	Writing what you learned when you took on the responsibility for a new pet
Diaries	To help you recall thoughts and express your feelings	Writing your feelings when a good friend changed schools
Journals and Learning Logs	To help record observations, descriptions, and questions	Jotting notes after reading a poem, noting difficult parts
	To help you define or analyze information, or propose a solution	Listing and defining words you learned in Spanish class

Using Word-Processing Tools for Writing

Computer word-processing programs and word processors make every step of the writing process easier—from planning to publishing.

WRITING STEP	WORD-PROCESSOR BENEFITS
Prewriting	easy to type in rough notes
Writing a First Draft	easy to write, revise, and rearrange parts of what you're writing
Evaluating	easy to try out different versions

(continued)

WRITING STEP	WORD-PROCESSOR BENEFITS
Revising and Proofreading	easy to edit and make changes; some processors check spelling
Publishing	easy to print one or more clean, final copies

Using the SQ3R Reading Method

SQ3R is the name of a reading method. It is a series of steps for improving your ability to understand and remember learning materials. Developed by Francis Robinson, an educational psychologist, the SQ3R reading method includes five simple steps.

S *Survey* the entire assignment. For example, if you're studying a new chapter in a textbook, look quickly at the chapter headings, subheadings, terms in boldface and italics, charts, outlines, illustrations, and summaries.

Q *Question* yourself. Make a list of questions that you want to be able to answer when you have finished reading.

R *Read* the material carefully to find answers to all the questions you have listed. Take notes as you read.

R *Recite* answers to each of your questions in your own words.

R *Review* the material by rereading quickly, looking over your questions, and recalling the answers.

The SQ3R method will help you identify important information. Also, you are more likely to remember what you read if you ask yourself questions and analyze the material as you read it. This method also will be useful in the workplace.

RESOURCES

Interpreting and Analyzing What You Read

You can find patterns of organization in everything you read. You will better understand what you read if you can understand how the material is organized and how the ideas relate to one another.

Stated Main Idea. The main idea of a passage is the most important point the writer is making. The main idea may be stated. This means the author may write the main idea plainly in one or two sentences.

Implied Main Idea. Sometimes the main idea is not stated. The writer's major point may not be found in one or two specific sentences. Instead, the main idea may be implied. Look for clues to find the central idea that ties all the other ideas together.

HOW TO FIND THE MAIN IDEA

- Skim the passage. (What topic do the sentences have in common?)
- Identify the topic. (What is the passage about?)
- Identify what the passage says about the topic. (What's the message of the passage as a whole?)
- State the meaning of the passage in your own words.
- Review the passage. (If you have correctly identified the main idea, all the other ideas in the passage will support it.)

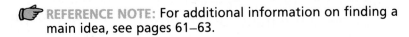 REFERENCE NOTE: For additional information on finding a main idea, see pages 61–63.

Reading to Find Relationships Among Details

To understand the meaning of a reading passage, you need to understand the main idea. Then you need to understand the relationship of details to the main idea and to each other.

FINDING RELATIONSHIPS AMONG DETAILS

Identify specific details.	What details answer questions such as *Who? What? When? Where? Why?* and *How?* (These are *5W-How?* questions.)
Distinguish between fact and opinion.	What statements can be shown to be true (facts) or false? What statements express a person's beliefs? (opinions)
Identify similarities and differences.	How are the details similar to one another? How are they different?
Understand cause and effect.	Do earlier events affect later ones?
Identify an order of organization.	In what kind of order are the details arranged? Are they in time order, order of importance, spatial order, or some other pattern of organization?

Reading Passage

In 1990, Antonia Novello became the first Hispanic and the first woman to be Surgeon General of the United States. Antonia Novello was born in Puerto Rico in 1945 with a serious health problem. Because of her illness, Antonia spent two weeks in the hospital every summer. At age eight, she was told that she could have surgery to correct her condition. However, the nearest hospital was too far away. For many years

Sample Analysis

DIFFERENCE: How was Antonia Novello different from previous Surgeons General?

ANSWER: *No other Surgeon General had been either Hispanic or female.*

FACT: Where was Antonia Novello born?

ANSWER: *She was born in Puerto Rico.*

RESOURCES

Antonia didn't have surgery. Her experiences made her interested in becoming a doctor and helping others, especially young people, who had health problems.

Antonia Novello entered the University of Puerto Rico when she was eighteen. Finally, she was able to have her surgery. Some problems that developed made a second surgery necessary. This time the surgery was successful.

Antonia missed a semester during her surgeries and her recovery, but she returned to school the very next semester. She graduated from the University of Puerto Rico School of Medicine in 1970. She then went to the University of Michigan, where she was chosen "Intern of the Year." Later, when she had already become a doctor, she went to graduate school, specializing in children's medicine and public health care.

Antonia Novello started working as a children's doctor with the U.S. Public Health Service (PHS) in 1978. There she learned skills in leadership that would help her as Surgeon General. Antonia's experience of living with sickness for many years made her determined to help people who needed health care but weren't getting it. As Surgeon General, she was especially concerned with the health problems of young people.

OPINION: Why do you think Antonia Novello cared so much about health problems of youth?
ANSWER: *As a child, she experienced health problems herself. This may have given her a special sympathy for young people with health problems.*

CAUSE AND EFFECT: Why did Antonia miss a semester of medical school?
ANSWER: *She had two surgeries to correct a health problem.*

DETAILS: What award did Antonia win in college?
ANSWER: *She was named "Intern of the Year."*

ORDER: In what kind of order are the details in this passage organized?
ANSWER: *They are in chronological (or time) order.*

Applying Reasoning Skills to Your Reading

To understand what you read, you have to think carefully about the ideas and details in the material you are reading. These are like clues, and you have to act like a detective to analyze all the evidence that you find in your reading. When you think critically as you read, you may draw *conclusions*. **Conclusions** are decisions based on facts and evidence that you find in your reading.

Sometimes important clues are hard to find. In some cases, this means that you must make *inferences*. **Inferences** are decisions you make that are based on evidence that may be only hinted at, or implied, in what you have read.

For example, when you analyze the reading passage on pages 753–754, you might draw conclusions or make inferences such as these:

> The health problem Antonia Novello had was serious. (Evidence: It required two surgeries to correct the problem, and her recovery made her miss a whole semester of college.)

> Antonia Novello is very dedicated to her profession. (Evidence: She won an award for her hard work as an intern. After she became a doctor, she returned to college for additional graduate study.)

A *valid conclusion* is one that is firmly supported by facts, evidence, or logic. However, a conclusion that is not supported by facts, evidence, or logic is called *invalid.* For example, it is invalid to conclude that Antonia Novello could not succeed until her health problem was cured. This conclusion can't be drawn from facts in the reading passage. Antonia Novello had already completed high school despite ten years of having to go to the hospital for two weeks every summer. She was already in college before she had her surgery.

RESOURCES

HOW TO DRAW CONCLUSIONS	
Gather all the evidence.	What facts or details have you learned about the subject?
Evaluate the evidence.	What do the facts and details you have gathered tell you about the subject?
Make appropriate connections.	What can you reasonably conclude from the evidence?

Reading Graphics and Illustrations

Many books and articles include visual information contained in diagrams, maps, graphs, and illustrations. Visual information is often clearer and easier to understand than information that is written.

A paragraph full of details can be difficult to understand. With graphics and illustrations, many of the relationships among sets of facts are more clear. For example, the following chart shows information about the depth of the world's oceans.

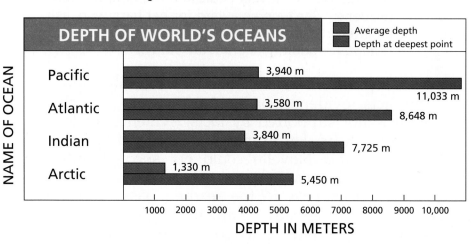

This chart quickly shows you information, such as which of the oceans has the greatest average depth or which ocean has the deepest point.

Applying Study and Reading Strategies

There are many different ways to read and study, because there are many different ways to organize and handle information. Some of the most common are

- taking notes
- classifying
- organizing information visually
- outlining
- paraphrasing
- summarizing
- memorizing

Taking Notes

Taking accurate notes is worth the extra effort. As you read at home or listen in class, your detailed information will be recorded in your notebook. Then you will be ready to study for even the most challenging tests.

HOW TO TAKE STUDY NOTES

1. Identify and write down the main ideas in class or your reading. These main ideas should be the headings in your notes. In class, listen for key words and phrases, such as *first, most important,* or *therefore.* These words often introduce main ideas and tell you how ideas are related. In a textbook, chapter headings and subheadings usually contain key ideas.
2. Keep your notes brief. Use abbreviations and sum up source material in your own words.
3. Include brief examples or details from the source material. Important examples or details can help you recall the key ideas more easily.
4. Look over your notes soon after you write them to be sure you have included the most important information.

RESOURCES

Here's an example of careful study notes about the reading passage on pages 753–754. The notes show the main ideas as headings. Underneath each main heading, you will find a group of important details that relate to that heading.

Dr. Antonia Novello

Childhood

- *1945—born in Puerto Rico*
- *Had serious health problem—2 wks. in hospital every yr.*
- *At 8 yrs. old—told she needed surgery*
- *Did not have surgery—hospital too far*
- *Decided to become a doctor to help others who had health problems*

Education

- *Grad.—Univ. of Puerto Rico School of Med., 1970*
- *Chosen as "Intern of the Year" at Univ. of Mich.*

Career

- *1978—started at Public Health Service (PHS) as children's doctor*
- *1990—became Surgeon General (1st Hispanic & 1st woman)*

Influences

- *PHS→ skills in leadership*
- *childhood illness→ desire to help others*
- *children's doctor→ concern with health problems of young people*

Classifying

Classifying is arranging information into categories or groups. When you classify items, you sort them so that the items in each category or group are related. The name or description of the category shows the relationship between the items in the group.

EXAMPLE   What do these creatures have in common?
giraffe, leopard, ladybug, Dalmatian
ANSWER   They all have spots.

You also use classification techniques when you identify patterns. For example, look at the relationship between the following sequence of numbers.

What's the next number in the series?

1   5   9   13   ?

ANSWER   The first number in this series is *1*. The difference between the first number, *1*, and the second number, *5*, is *4*. Add *4* to the second number to make the third number, *9*. Add *4* to the third number to get the fourth number, *13*. The pattern is to add *4* to each number in the series to get the next number. Therefore, to produce the next number in the series after *13*, you would again add *4*. The answer is *17*.

Organizing Information Visually

If you are learning new information, you may find it easier to understand if you organize it visually. A map, diagram, or chart is often easier to understand than a paragraph.

For example, the passage that follows compares Alaska and Hawaii.

RESOURCES

In some ways, Alaska and Hawaii are extremely different from each other. In other ways, the two states are more like each other than they are like the other forty-eight states.

Alaska is the largest state and the farthest north. One third of Alaska lies north of the Arctic Circle. By contrast, Hawaii is the fourth smallest state and the farthest south. Hawaii is located south of the Tropic of Cancer.

Yet Alaska and Hawaii have some similarities. They are the two newest states. Alaska was the forty-ninth state and Hawaii was the fiftieth. Both are located far from the other forty-eight states. Both states also have unique ethnic mixes. Alaska's population is about one-eighth Native American. Hawaii has great numbers of people with Japanese and Filipino ancestry, along with many native Polynesians. Both states are very expensive places to live, because many of their goods are shipped at great cost from the other states.

If you read this passage and tried to remember all the details, it would not be easy to compare the two states. However, making a chart like the one below would make the information easier to remember.

ALASKA	HAWAII
largest state	fourth smallest state
most northern state	most southern state
$\frac{1}{3}$ north of Arctic Circle	south of Tropic of Cancer
49th state	50th state
isolated from other 48 states	isolated from other 48 states
unique ethnic mix	unique ethnic mix
high cost of living	high cost of living

Outlining

An *outline* is another way to organize important information. When you make an outline, you arrange the ideas to show which are the main ideas and which are smaller parts of the main ideas. In this way, outlines make the relationship of ideas clear.

FORMAL OUTLINE FORM

I. Main Point
  A. Supporting Point
    1. Detail
      a. Information
        or detail

Sometimes you may need to use different types of outlines. For example, for a report you might use a formal outline, with Roman numerals for headings and capital letters for subheadings. However, when you take notes in class, an informal outline is easier and faster.

INFORMAL OUTLINE FORM

Main Idea
  Supporting detail
  Supporting detail
  Supporting detail

Paraphrasing

When you *paraphrase,* you express another person's ideas in your own words. A paraphrase can help you understand readings that are complicated or written with poetic or elaborate words.

A written paraphrase will usually be about the same length as the original. Therefore, paraphrasing is not very practical for long passages of writing. However, you may sometimes be asked (usually in language arts classes) to paraphrase a short passage, such as a poem.

Here is an excerpt from a poem.

> from A Poison Tree
> *by William Blake*
>
> I was angry with my friend
> I told my wrath, my wrath did end.
> I was angry with a foe:
> I told it not, my wrath did grow.

As an example, here is a possible paraphrase of this verse of the poem.

> The speaker in the poem was upset with a friend and told the friend about the problem. Before long, the speaker wasn't angry any more. However, the speaker was mad at an enemy and kept the anger inside. As a result, the speaker's bad feelings just kept getting worse.

Use these guidelines when you write a paraphrase.

HOW TO PARAPHRASE

1. Read the selection carefully before you begin.
2. Be sure you understand the main idea of the selection. Look up any unfamiliar words in a dictionary.
3. Determine the tone of the selection. (What is the attitude of the writer toward the subject of the selection?)
4. Identify the speaker in fictional material. (Is the poet or author speaking, or is it a character?)
5. Write your paraphrase in your own words. Shorten long sentences or stanzas. Use your own, familiar vocabulary, but keep the ideas in the same order as in the selection.
6. Be sure that the ideas in your paraphrase match the ideas expressed in the original.

Another common situation when you may find paraphrasing useful is when you are writing a research report. For example, whenever you get a set of facts from an encyclopedia and restate them in your own words, you are paraphrasing the encyclopedia's information. Make sure to name the source you paraphrase. It's very important to give credit for a quote or for a specific idea that you borrowed from someone else.

☞ REFERENCE NOTE: For more about giving credit to your sources when you are writing reports, see pages 283–286.

Summarizing

A *summary* is a brief restatement of the main ideas expressed in a piece of writing. A summary is similar to a paraphrase because when you summarize, you express another person's ideas in your own words. However, a summary is usually shorter than a paraphrase. Whenever you summarize, you shorten the original material and present only the most important points.

You think critically whenever you summarize. When you condense material, you make decisions and draw conclusions about what to include in the summary and what to leave out.

HOW TO SUMMARIZE

1. Skim the selection you wish to summarize.
2. Read the passage again closely. Look for main ideas and supporting details.
3. Write your summary in your own words. Include only the main ideas and the most important supporting points.
4. Evaluate and revise your summary. Check to see that you have covered the most important points. Make sure that the information is clearly expressed and that the reader can follow your ideas.

RESOURCES

Here's a sample summary of the reading passage found on pages 272–274.

> Water striders are insects that look similar to daddy longlegs. However, water striders live on the water. They walk, feed, breed, and are even born on the water. Water striders seek land only when the water is choppy or freezing. Their bodies repel water, so they don't absorb water and sink from the weight. Their legs are long and widely spaced to spread their weight. Water striders' lower legs and feet are covered with waterproof hairs that trap air bubbles to help keep them afloat. Water striders are also helped by the film that forms on the surface of water.

Memorizing

There are many times when you need to memorize information for tests and quizzes. It is not a good idea to "cram" information you are trying to memorize. You are more likely to remember the information more accurately and for a longer time if you practice recalling it in frequent, short, focused sessions. Here are some hints for memorizing effectively.

HOW TO MEMORIZE	
Memorize only the most important information.	Whenever possible, condense the material you need to remember.
Practice the material in different ways.	Copy the material by hand. Recite the material out loud.
Invent memory games.	Form a word from the first letters of important terms. Or, make up rhymes that help you remember facts and details.

Improving Test-Taking Skills

Preparing for Different Kinds of Tests

Nervousness before a test is normal. However, all the energy that comes from being nervous can help you do well on the test. Your attitude is the key.

HOW TO PREPARE FOR A TEST

Plan for success. Do everything you can to help you do your best on the test. Know what information will be covered on the test. Make a plan that gives you enough time to take notes, study, and review the material.

Be confident. If you have studied thoroughly, you know you are prepared. During the test, pay attention only to reading and answering the test questions.

Keep trying. Be determined to keep improving. Your commitment to keep learning will help you improve your study effectiveness.

Objective questions and *essay questions* are two basic ways that your knowledge can be tested. There are ways that you can prepare for each type of question.

Objective Tests

There are several kinds of objective test questions. Some examples are multiple-choice, true/false, matching, reasoning or logic, or short-answer questions. *Objective questions* always ask you for specific information. They may test you on information such as names, terms, dates, or definitions. Most objective test questions have only one correct answer. To prepare for objective tests, you will need to review specific information. The study skills listed earlier in this chapter will help you prepare for objective tests.

RESOURCES

HOW TO STUDY FOR OBJECTIVE TESTS

1. Identify important terms or facts in your textbook and class notes.
2. Review the information in more than one form. For example, you may need to learn the definitions for scientific terms. Make flashcards. Practice identifying the definition from the term, then the term from the definition.
3. Practice and repeat information to remember it. Go over difficult information more than once.
4. If possible, briefly review all the information shortly before the actual test.

You may change your study strategies for each type of objective test. For example, you might use flashcards to study definitions. Or, to study for a problem-solving type of test, you could work out practice problems and check them with your textbook.

Taking Different Kinds of Objective Tests

When you begin an objective test, quickly look over the questions. If you know the number of items on the test, you can decide how to budget your time for each item. Other strategies for handling specific kinds of objective test questions follow.

Multiple-Choice Questions. With a multiple-choice question, you will need to select a correct answer from a number of items that are provided for you.

EXAMPLE   **1.** Antonia Novello was born in
     A Mexico
     B Puerto Rico
     C El Salvador
     D Italy

HOW TO ANSWER MULTIPLE-CHOICE QUESTIONS

Read the question or statement carefully.	■ Make sure you understand the question or statement before you begin to look at the answer choices. ■ Look for words such as *not* or *only*. These words limit your choice of answers.
Read all the choices before selecting an answer.	■ Rule out all of the choices that you know are incorrect. ■ Think carefully about all of the remaining choices. Select only the one that makes the most sense.

True/False Questions. True/false questions ask you to decide whether the statement you are given is true or false.

EXAMPLE   **1.** T Ⓕ Hawaii is the smallest state in the United States.

HOW TO ANSWER TRUE/FALSE QUESTIONS

Read the statement carefully.	■ The whole statement is false if any part of the statement is false.
Look for word clues.	■ Words such as *always* or *never* limit the range of possibilities of a statement. ■ A statement is true only if it is entirely and always true.

Matching Questions. Matching questions ask you to match the items in one list with the items in another list.

> Directions: Match the name of the ocean in the left-hand column with the depth at its deepest point in the right-hand column.
>
> _C_ **1.** Indian **A** 8,648 meters
> _A_ **2.** Atlantic **B** 11,033 meters
> _D_ **3.** Arctic **C** 7,725 meters
> _B_ **4.** Pacific **D** 5,450 meters

HOW TO ANSWER MATCHING QUESTIONS	
Read the directions carefully.	Sometimes you may be told that you won't use all the items listed in one column. Other times items may be used more than once.
Scan the columns.	If you match items you know first, you'll have more time to think about difficult items you are less sure of answers for.
Complete the rest of the matching.	Make your best guess on remaining items.

Reasoning or Logic Questions. Reasoning or logic questions don't test your knowledge of a particular subject. These types of questions test your reasoning skills. A reasoning or logic question may ask you to identify the relationship between several items (usually words, pictures, or numbers).

Reasoning questions might ask you to identify a pattern in a number sequence (as in the example on page 759). Or you might be asked to predict the next item in a sequence.

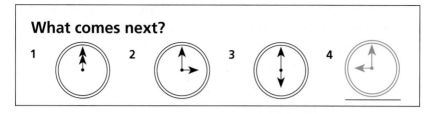

What comes next?

In this sequence of drawings, the time on the clock starts at noon and moves three hours forward each time. In the fourth position it will have reached the nine o'clock position.

HOW TO ANSWER REASONING OR LOGIC QUESTIONS	
Be sure you understand the instructions.	Reasoning or logic questions are often multiple-choice. On some tests, however, you may need to write a word or phrase, complete a number sequence, or even draw a picture for your answer.
Analyze the relationship implied in the question.	Look at the question carefully to gather information about the relationship of the items.
Draw reasonable conclusions.	Evaluate the relationship of the items to decide your answer.

RESOURCES

Short-Answer Questions. Short-answer questions require you to give brief, precise responses. Instead of choosing from among several choices, you must write the answer yourself.

Some short-answer questions ask you to give a

label or fill in a blank. This type of question can be answered with one or just a few words. However, other types of short-answer questions ask for a written response that may be several sentences in length.

EXAMPLE   Why do Alaska and Hawaii both have a high cost of living?

ANSWER   *Both states are isolated from the rest of the United States. Both need to have almost everything shipped to them from far away.*

HOW TO RESPOND TO SHORT-ANSWER QUESTIONS	
Read the question carefully.	Some questions have more than one part, so be sure to answer each part of the question in order to answer the entire item correctly.
Plan your answer.	Briefly decide what you need to include in the answer.
Be as specific as possible in your answers.	Write a full, exact answer.
Budget your time.	Begin by answering those questions you are sure you know. Save time for more difficult items.

Essay Tests

Essay tests require you to think critically about material you have learned. Then you express your understanding in your own words. Essay tests show how well you understand a subject. Essay answers are usually a paragraph or more in length.

HOW TO STUDY FOR ESSAY TESTS

1. Read the assigned material carefully.
2. Make an outline of the main points and important details.
3. Invent your own essay questions and practice writing out the answers.
4. Evaluate and revise your practice answers by checking your work against your notes and textbook. Also review the writing section of this textbook for help in writing.

Taking Essay Tests

Before you begin to answer an essay question, there are certain steps you should take. First, you should quickly scan the test questions. How many questions are you required to answer? Which of the questions do you think you can answer best? Next, you should plan how much time you can afford to spend on each answer. Then, as you begin to write your responses, stick with your plan.

Read each question carefully. Be sure you understand exactly what the question calls for before you plan your response. Remember that the question may be asking you to write an answer that contains several different parts.

Pay attention to important terms in the question. You always need to complete a specific task to answer an essay question well. You can tell what the task is by looking at the key verb that appears in the essay question.

If you know some of the key verbs and what answer pattern each one calls for, you can write a better essay response. Look at the list of key verbs in the following chart and pay attention to the task that each one asks you to perform.

ESSAY TEST QUESTIONS

KEY VERB	TASK	SAMPLE QUESTION
argue	Give your opinion about an issue and supply reasons to support this opinion.	Argue whether or not students who litter should have to clean up after school.
analyze	Examine something piece by piece to see how each part works.	Analyze the bad effects that smoking can have on people's health.
compare	Point out ways that things are alike.	Compare an apple and a crab apple.
contrast	Point out ways that things are different.	Contrast the aliens in *Independence Day* and *E.T.*
define	Give specific details that make something unique.	Define the term *simile.*
demonstrate	Give examples to support a point.	Demonstrate how water affects the frog's life cycle.
describe	Give a picture in words.	Describe the main characters in *Charlotte's Web.*
explain	Give reasons.	Explain how hail is formed.
identify	Point out specific characteristics.	Identify the three kinds of rocks.
list	Give all steps in order or all details about a subject.	List the food groups that make up a balanced diet.
summarize	Give a brief overview of the main points.	Summarize the story told in "Peter and the Wolf."

Use prewriting strategies. After you identify the key verbs in the question, jot down a few notes or an outline to help you decide what you want to say. Write notes or a rough outline on scratch paper.

Evaluate and revise as you write. You may not be able to redraft your whole essay, but you can edit your essay to strengthen it.

QUALITIES OF A GOOD ESSAY ANSWER

- The essay is well organized.
- The main ideas and supporting points are clearly presented.
- The sentences are complete and well written.
- There are no distracting errors in spelling, grammar, or punctuation.

Review

 EXERCISE 1   **Choosing an Appropriate Reading Rate**

Identify the reading rate that best fits each of the following situations.

1. You want to record a song on your new tape deck, so you start reading your owner's manual.
2. You are looking through an encyclopedia for information on Confucius.
3. You are looking for the chart of prime numbers in your math book.
4. You are reading Alfred Noyes' poem "The Highwayman" for an oral report tomorrow.
5. You need to write a summary of the two pages in your social studies textbook on the Ogallala Aquifer.

▶ EXERCISE 2   **Applying the SQ3R Reading Method**

Use the SQ3R method while reading a newspaper article or a chapter that you need to study for a class. List at least five questions and write a brief answer to each one.

▶ EXERCISE 3   **Reading: Analyzing Details in a Passage**

Answer the following questions about the reading passage on pages 753–754.

1. Before her surgery, how long did Antonia Novello stay in the hospital each summer?
2. In what year did Antonia Novello graduate from medical school in Puerto Rico?
3. How old was Antonia when she had her surgery?
4. What did Antonia do in 1978?
5. How many surgeries did Antonia have to correct her health problem?

▶ EXERCISE 4   **Reading: Drawing Conclusions and Making Inferences**

Using the reading passage on pages 753–754, identify the evidence or reasoning you might use to make the following inferences or draw the following conclusions.

1. Antonia Novello earned other people's respect.
2. Education is important to Antonia Novello.
3. As a doctor, Antonia Novello is sensitive to the patient's feelings.

▶ EXERCISE 5   **Reading Graphic Information**

Using the graph on page 756, answer the following questions.

1. Which ocean is the deepest?
2. What is the average depth of the Pacific Ocean?
3. Which ocean is the most shallow?

4. What is the difference between the Atlantic's average depth and the Pacific's?

5. How deep is the Pacific at its deepest point?

EXERCISE 6 **Analyzing Your Note-Taking Method**

Select a homework assignment your teacher has given you recently. Take study notes for this assignment, following the guidelines on page 757. Be prepared to share your notes in class and to explain how you took notes.

EXERCISE 7 **Identifying Classifications**

For each of the following groups, identify the category.

1. dog, cat, parakeet, goldfish
2. rose, daisy, lily, iris
3. Arabian, Clydesdale, appaloosa, mustang
4. country, jazz, classical, rap
5. Lincoln, Washington, Kennedy, Roosevelt

EXERCISE 8 **Reading: Applying Visual Organization**

After reading the paragraph below, make a numbered list of the steps in the metamorphosis of an insect.

> From birth to adulthood, most insects experience what is called complete metamorphosis. First, an adult insect produces an egg. Next, the egg hatches to produce the insect in its immature, larval stage. After spending a period of time as a larva, the insect becomes inactive. This inactive insect is called a pupa. While the insect is inactive, it begins its transformation. After the insect completes its metamorphosis, it emerges as a mature adult insect.

RESOURCES

EXERCISE 9   **Reading: Paraphrasing a Poem**

Read the following poem. Then, using the instructions for paraphrasing on page 762, write a paraphrase of the poem. Look in a dictionary for the meanings of unfamiliar words. (For example, a *crag* is a cliff, and *azure* means "sky blue.")

> The Eagle
> *by Alfred, Lord Tennyson*
>
> He clasps the crag with crooked hands;
> Close to the sun in lonely lands,
> Ringed with the azure world, he stands.
>
> The wrinkled sea beneath him crawls;
> He watches from his mountain walls,
> And like a thunderbolt he falls.

EXERCISE 10   **Analyzing Essay Questions**

Identify the key verb that states the specific task in each of the following essay questions. Do not write an essay. Just state briefly what you would need to do to answer the question. [Hint: Look at the middle column of the chart on page 772.]

1. Describe the personality of Melissa, the narrator of "The Glad Man" by Gloria Gonzalez.
2. Summarize the process of photosynthesis.
3. Explain the changes experienced by Wilbur and Marion, the main characters in "The Bear Hunt" by Gene Caesar.
4. Identify the major industries in the Republic of China.
5. Contrast a butterfly with a moth.

RESOURCES

DIAGRAMING SENTENCES

A *sentence diagram* is a picture of how the parts of a sentence fit together. It shows how the words in the sentence are related.

Subjects and Verbs (pages 342–357)

To diagram a sentence, first find the simple subject and the simple predicate, or verb, and write them on a horizontal line. Then separate the subject and verb with a vertical line. Keep the capital letters but leave out the punctuation marks.

EXAMPLES **Dogs bark.**   **Children were singing.**

Dogs	bark

Children	were singing

The preceding examples are easy because each sentence contains only a simple subject and a verb. Now look at a longer sentence.

EXAMPLE   **My older brother is studying Arabic in school.**

To diagram the simple subject and the verb of this sentence, follow these three steps.

Step 1: Separate the complete subject from the complete predicate.

complete subject	complete predicate
My older brother	**is studying Arabic in school.**

Step 2: Find the simple subject and the verb.

simple subject | verb
brother | is studying

Step 3: Draw the diagram.

brother | is studying

> EXERCISE 1 **Diagraming Simple Subjects and Verbs**

Diagram the simple subject and verb in each of the following sentences. Remember that simple subjects and verbs may consist of more than one word.

EXAMPLE **1.** Aunt Carmen is teaching me to cook.

1. Aunt Carmen | is teaching

1. My family goes to the store together every Saturday.
2. We shop the grocery store at the corner of our street.
3. I select the red beans, rice, meat, and cheese.
4. Grandma López must have written the shopping list.
5. Rosita is buying the chile peppers and cilantro.

Compound Subjects (pages 351–352)

To diagram a compound subject, put the subjects on parallel lines. Then put the connecting word (the conjunction, such as *and* or *but*) on a dotted line between the subject lines.

EXAMPLE **Koalas** and **kangaroos** are found in Australia.

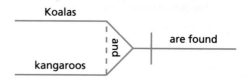

Compound Verbs (page 353)

To diagram a compound verb, put the two verbs on parallel lines. Then put the conjunction on a dotted line between the verbs.

EXAMPLE   Giraffes **look** skinny but **may weigh** a ton.

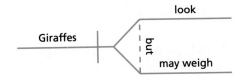

Compound Subjects and Compound Verbs
(pages 351–353)

A sentence with both a compound subject and a compound verb combines the two patterns.

EXAMPLE   The **cat** and her **kittens ate** and then **slept.**

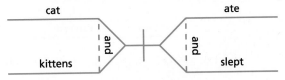

EXERCISE 2   **Diagraming Compound Subjects and Compound Verbs**

Diagram the simple subjects and verbs in the following sentences.

EXAMPLE   **1.** Spike Lee and Robert Townsend made and released movies last year.

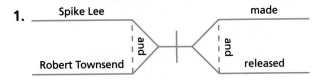

1. Ursula LeGuin and Nicholasa Mohr are my favorite authors.
2. Ms. Sánchez and Mr. Charles teach Spanish.

3. Bill Russell first played and later coached for the Boston Celtics.
4. The students and the teacher visited the museum but did not have time for a complete tour.
5. My friends and I hurried home and told our parents the news.

Compound Sentences (page 357)

A compound sentence contains two independent clauses. The second independent clause is diagramed below the first in the following way.

EXAMPLE **Ostriches seem** clumsy, but **they can run** fast.

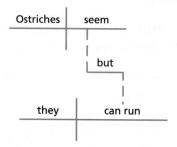

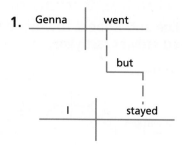 EXERCISE 3   **Diagraming Compound Sentences**

Diagram the simple subjects and verbs in the following compound sentences.

EXAMPLE **1.** Genna went to the mall, but I stayed home.

1. Chinese immigrants worked on the railroads in the West, but Irish immigrants built the railroads in the East.

2. Lisa likes roller-skating, but I prefer ice-skating.
3. Jewel will be class president, and Aaron will be vice-president.
4. Cactuses are desert plants, yet they can grow well in milder climates.
5. Gabriela Mistral is a poet, but she has also written essays.

Questions and Commands (page 360)

Questions (page 360)

To diagram a question, first make the question into a statement. Then, diagram the sentence. Remember that in a diagram, the subject always comes first, even if it does not come first in the sentence.

EXAMPLE   **Can all insects fly?** [question]
           All insects can fly. [statement]

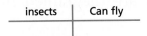

Notice that the diagram uses the capitalization of the original sentence.

Commands (page 360)

In an imperative sentence, or command, the subject is always understood to be *you*. Place the understood subject *you* in parentheses on the horizontal line.

EXAMPLE   **Look over there.**

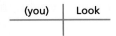

EXERCISE 4 **Diagraming Questions and Commands**

Diagram the simple subjects and verbs in the following sentences.

EXAMPLE **1.** Please wash the dishes, Jerome.

1.
| (you) | wash |

1. Eat the rest of your jambalaya.
2. Do you know much about the Jewish holidays?
3. Where is the driver going?
4. Please help me with these cartons.
5. Why are they standing in line?

Adjectives and Adverbs (pages 381–385 and 402–404)

Adjectives and adverbs are written on slanted lines connected to the words they modify. Notice that possessive pronouns are diagramed in the same way adjectives are.

Adjectives (pages 381–385)

EXAMPLES **yellow** bird **a playful** puppy **her best** blouse

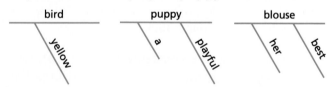

EXERCISE 5 **Diagraming Sentences with Adjectives**

Diagram the subjects, verbs, and adjectives in the following sentences.

EXAMPLE **1.** A strong, cold wind blew all night.

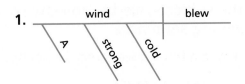

1. My favorite new rock group is coming to town.
2. The long, grueling hike was almost over.
3. The best album of the year is by Joan Osborne.
4. The two brave astronauts stepped into space.
5. A funny movie is playing downtown.

Adverbs (pages 402–404)

When an adverb modifies a verb, it is placed on a slanted line below the verb.

EXAMPLES **wrote quickly**   **walked there slowly**

When an adverb modifies an adjective or another adverb, it is placed on a line connected to the word it modifies.

EXAMPLES **incredibly** large poster   runs **very** fast

▶ EXERCISE 6   **Diagraming Sentences with Adverbs**

Diagram the subjects, verbs, adjectives, and adverbs in the following sentences.

EXAMPLE   **1.** We almost always recycle newspapers.

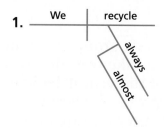

1. This song was recorded recently by Lena Horne.
2. That new band plays very loudly.
3. The busy librarian almost never leaves early.
4. Her two brothers visited Chinatown yesterday.
5. An extremely unusual program will be broadcast tonight.

Prepositional Phrases (pages 420–429)

Prepositional phrases are diagramed below the words they modify. Write the preposition on a slanting line. Then write the object of the preposition on a horizontal line connected to the slanting line. Notice that the slanting line extends a little way beyond the horizontal line.

Adjective Phrases (pages 423–425)

EXAMPLES   time **of day**   customs **of the Amish**

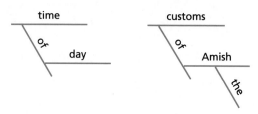

Adverb Phrases (pages 428–429)

EXAMPLES **walked on the moon**   **looked there for Skip**

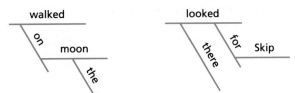

 EXERCISE 7 **Diagraming Sentences with Prepositional Phrases**

Diagram the following sentences.

EXAMPLE **1.** The freighter slowed for the first lock.

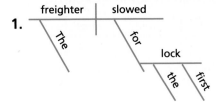

1. Olympia Dukakis and John Travolta starred in that new movie.
2. Tamales are wrapped in corn husks.
3. My friend from India wears a sari.
4. The students in Jill's class went to the library.
5. The soccer team from Brazil ran onto the field.

Direct and Indirect Objects (pages 439–442)

Direct Objects (page 439)

A direct object is diagramed on the horizontal line with the subject and verb. A short vertical line separates the direct object from the verb.

EXAMPLE **We have been playing tapes.**

We	have been playing	tapes

Compound Direct Objects (page 439)

EXAMPLE   Rachel enjoys **soccer** and **basketball**.

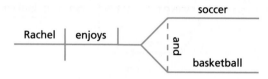

Indirect Objects (pages 441–442)

The indirect object is diagramed on a horizontal line beneath the verb. The verb and the indirect object are joined by a slanting line.

EXAMPLE   Dad fixed **us** some spaghetti.

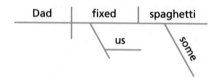

Compound Indirect Objects (page 442)

EXAMPLE   Marisa gave her **brother** and **me** some grapes.

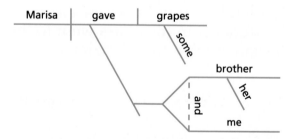

EXERCISE 8   **Diagraming Direct Objects and Indirect Objects**

Diagram the following sentences.

EXAMPLE   **1.** He handed her the report.

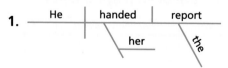

1. Marilyn won a bronze medal in the Special Olympics.
2. I bought Jolene and her sister a present.
3. My grandmother knitted me a sweater.
4. Marcus made a touchdown.
5. Amy Tan wrote that book.

Subject Complements (pages 446–448)

A subject complement is diagramed on the horizontal line with the subject and the verb. The complement comes after the verb. A line slanting toward the subject separates the subject complement from the verb.

Predicate Nominatives (page 447)

EXAMPLE   Mickey Leland was a famous **congressman** from Texas.

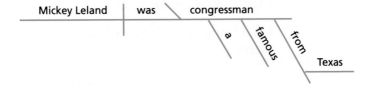

Compound Predicate Nominatives (page 447)

EXAMPLE   Paula Abdul is a **singer** and a **dancer**.

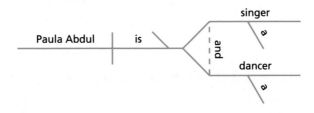

Predicate Adjectives (page 448)

EXAMPLE   The guitarist was very **skillful.**

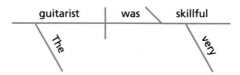

Compound Predicate Adjectives (page 448)

EXAMPLE   They were **weary** but **patient.**

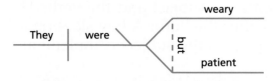

 EXERCISE 9   **Diagraming Sentences with Subject Complements**

Diagram the following sentences.

EXAMPLE   **1.** Ms. Chang is an excellent teacher and a fine lawyer.

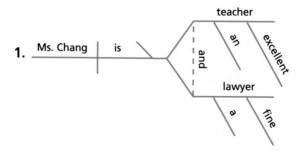

1. Coyote is a trickster in Native American mythology.
2. The library is full of interesting books.
3. These CDs are oldies but goodies.
4. Ossie Davis is an actor and a playwright.
5. Your little brother looks quite sleepy.

Glossary of Terms

Action verb An action verb is a verb that expresses physical or mental action. (See page 391.)

Adjective An adjective is a word that modifies a noun or a pronoun. (See page 381.)

Adjective phrase An adjective phrase is a prepositional phrase that modifies a noun or a pronoun. (See page 423.)

Adverb An adverb is a word that modifies a verb, an adjective, or another adverb. (See page 402.)

Adverb phrase An adverb phrase is a prepositional phrase that modifies a verb, an adjective, or another adverb. (See page 428.)

Aim An aim is one of the four basic purposes, or reasons, for writing. (See pages 7 and 24.)

Antecedent An antecedent is a noun or pronoun to which a pronoun refers. (See page 373.)

Appositive An appositive is a noun or a pronoun that explains or identifies another noun or pronoun. (See pages 520 and 600.)

B

Base form The base form, or **infinitive**, is one of the four principal, or basic, parts of a verb. (See page 476.)

Brainstorming Brainstorming is a way a writer finds ideas for writing by listing all thoughts about a subject without stopping to judge the ideas. (See page 29.)

C

Chronological order Chronological order is a way of arranging details according to when events or actions take place. (See page 39.)

Clustering Clustering, or **webbing**, is a way a writer finds writing ideas and gathers information by breaking a large subject into its smaller parts, using circles and lines. (See page 30.)

Comparing Comparing means telling how things are alike. (See page 73.)

Complement A complement is a word or group of words that completes the meaning of a verb. (See page 438.)

Complex sentence A complex sentence is made of two sentences joined by a connecting word that shows their special relationship to each other. (See page 318.)

Compound sentence A compound sentence consists of two or more simple sentences, usually joined by a connecting word. (See pages 318 and 357.)

Conjunction A conjunction is a word that joins words or groups of words. (See page 411.)

Contrasting Contrasting means telling how things are different from one another. (See page 73.)

Creative writing Creative writing is writing that aims at creating something new with language: stories, poems, songs, and plays. (See pages 7 and 24.)

D

Declarative sentence A declarative sentence makes a statement and is followed by a period. (See page 360.)

Description Description is a way a writer develops a paragraph or composition by using sensory details to describe something. (See page 69.)

Direct object A direct object receives the action of a transitive verb. (See page 439.)

Double negative A double negative is the use of two negative words to express one negative idea. (See page 538.)

Evaluating Evaluating is the stage in the writing process in which a writer goes over a draft, making judgments about it. (See pages 6 and 25.)

Evaluation Evaluation is a way a writer develops a paragraph or composition by making judgments, telling what is good or bad about a subject. (See page 75.)

Exclamatory sentence An exclamatory sentence shows excitement or expresses strong feeling and is followed by an exclamation point. (See page 360.)

Expository writing *See* Informative writing.

Expressive writing Expressive writing is writing that aims at expressing a writer's feelings and thoughts. (See pages 7 and 24.)

5W-How? questions The *5W-How?* questions—*Who? What? Where? When? Why? How?*—are questions a writer uses to collect information about a subject. (See page 32.)

Freewriting Freewriting is a way of finding ideas for writing in which a writer writes for a few minutes on whatever comes to mind. (See page 27.)

Helping verb A helping, or **auxiliary,** verb helps the main verb to

express action or a state of being. (See page 397.)

"How-to" process writing "How-to" process writing is a step-by-step story of how to do something. (See Chapter 6.)

Imperative sentence An imperative sentence gives a command or makes a request and is followed by either a period or an exclamation point. (See page 360.)

Indirect object An indirect object is a noun or pronoun that comes between the verb and the direct object. (See page 441.)

Inference An inference is a decision that is made based on clues the writer supplies. (See page 250.)

Informative writing Informative writing is writing that aims at giving facts or information, or explaining something. (See pages 7 and 24.)

Interjection An interjection is a word used to express emotion. (See page 412.)

Interrogative sentence An interrogative sentence asks a question and is followed by a question mark. (See page 360.)

Intransitive verb An intransitive verb expresses action (or tells something about the subject) without passing the action to a receiver. (See page 393.)

Linking verb A linking verb is a verb that expresses a state of being and connects the subject of a sentence with a word in the predicate that explains or describes the subject. (See page 394.)

Logical order Logical order is a way of grouping related ideas by what makes sense. (See pages 39 and 73.)

M

Main idea A main idea is the idea that a paragraph or composition is organized around. (See pages 6 and 24.)

Modifier A modifier is a word or a phrase that describes or limits the meaning of another word. (See page 527.)

N

Narration Narration is a way a writer develops a paragraph or composition by telling about events or actions as they change over a period of time. (See page 71.)

Noun A noun is a word that names a person, place, thing, or idea. (See page 368.)

O

Object of the preposition The noun or pronoun that ends a prepositional phrase is the object of the preposition that begins the phrase. (See pages 408 and 420.)

Order of importance Order of importance is a way of arranging details in a paragraph or composition according to the details' importance. (See pages 39 and 75.)

P

Personal narrative A personal narrative is a form of writing in which an author explores and shares the meaning of an experience that was especially important to him or her. (See Chapter 3.)

Persuasive essay A persuasive essay is a form of writing in which a writer supports an opinion and tries to persuade an audience. (See Chapter 7.)

Persuasive writing Persuasive writing is writing that aims at convincing people to think or act in a certain way. (See pages 7 and 24.)

Phrase A phrase is a group of related words that is used as a single part of speech and does not contain both a subject and a verb. (See page 419.)

Predicate The predicate is the part of a sentence that says something about the subject. (See page 345.)

Predicate adjective A predicate adjective is an adjective that follows a linking verb and describes the subject of a sentence. (See page 448.)

Predicate nominative A predicate nominative is a noun or pronoun that identifies or explains the subject of a sentence. (See page 447.)

Preposition A preposition is a word that shows the relationship between a noun or pronoun and some other word in the sentence. (See page 406.)

Prepositional phrase A prepositional phrase begins with a preposition and ends with a noun or a pronoun. (See pages 408 and 420.)

Prewriting Prewriting is the first stage in the writing process. In this stage, a writer thinks and plans, decides what to write about, collects ideas and details, and makes a plan for presenting ideas. (See pages 6 and 25.)

Pronoun A pronoun is a word used in place of a noun or more than one noun. (See page 373.)

Proofreading Proofreading is the stage of the writing process in which a writer carefully reads a revised draft to correct mistakes in grammar, usage, and mechanics. (See pages 6 and 25.)

Publishing Publishing is the last stage of the writing process. In this stage, a writer makes a final, clean copy of a paper and shares it with an audience. (See pages 6 and 25.)

Purpose Purpose, or **aim,** is the reason for writing or speaking. (See pages 7, 37, and 76.)

R

Report A report is a form of writing in which a writer presents factual information that he or she has discovered through reading and asking questions about a topic. (See Chapter 9.)

Revising Revising is the stage of the writing process in which a writer goes over a draft, making changes in its content, organization, and style in order to improve it. (See pages 6 and 25.)

Run-on sentence A run-on sentence is two or more complete sentences run together as one. (See page 307.)

S

Sentence A sentence is a group of words that expresses a complete thought. (See pages 304 and 340.)

Sentence fragment A sentence fragment is a group of words that looks like a sentence but does not express a complete thought. (See pages 304 and 340.)

Simple sentence A simple sentence has one subject and one verb. (See page 357.)

Spatial order Spatial order is a way of arranging details in a paragraph or composition by ordering them according to their location—from near to far, left to right, and so on. (See pages 39 and 69.)

Subject The subject is the part of a sentence that tells who or what the sentence is about. (See page 342.)

Subject complement A subject complement completes the meaning of a linking verb and identifies or describes the subject. (See page 446.)

T

Topic sentence A topic sentence is the sentence that states the main idea of a paragraph. (See page 61.)

Transitional words and phrases Transitional words and phrases connect ideas in a paragraph or composition by showing why and how ideas and details are related. (See page 66.)

Transitive verb A transitive verb is an action verb that expresses an action directed toward a person, place, or thing. (See page 392.)

V

Verb A verb is a word that expresses an action or a state of being. (See page 391.)

Verb phrase A verb phrase contains one main verb and one or more helping verbs. (See pages 349 and 397.)

W

"What if?" questions Asking "What if?" questions can help a writer spark his or her imagination to explore ideas for writing. (See page 33.)

Writer's journal A writer's journal is a written record of what happens in a person's life, and how he or she feels and thinks. (See page 26.)

Writing Writing is the stage in the writing process in which a writer puts his or her ideas into sentences and paragraphs, following a plan for presenting the ideas. (See pages 6 and 25.)

Writing process The writing process is the series of stages or steps that a writer goes through to develop ideas and to communicate them clearly in a piece of writing. (See pages 6 and 25.)

Glossary

This glossary is a short dictionary of words found in the professional writing models in this textbook. The words are defined according to their meanings in the context of the writing models.

Pronunciation Key

Symbol	Key Words	Symbol	Key Words
a	asp, fat, parrot	b	bed, fable, dub, ebb
ā	ape, date, play, break, fail	d	dip, beadle, had, dodder
ä	ah, car, father, cot	f	fall, after, off, phone
e	elf, ten, berry	g	get, haggle, dog
ē	even, meet, money, flea, grieve	h	he, ahead, hotel
i	is, hit, mirror	j	joy, agile, badge
ī	ice, bite, high, sky	k	kill, tackle, bake, coat, quick
		l	let, yellow, ball
ō	open, tone, go, boat	m	met, camel, trim, summer
ô	all, horn, law, oar	n	not, flannel, ton
oo	look, pull, moor, wolf	p	put, apple, tap
ōō	ooze, tool, crew, rule	r	red, port, dear, purr
yōō	use, cute, few	s	sell, castle, pass, nice
yoo	cure, globule	t	top, cattle, hat
oi	oil, point, toy	v	vat, hovel, have
ou	out, crowd, plow	w	will, always, swear, quick
u	up, cut, color, flood	y	yet, onion, yard
ur	urn, fur, deter, irk	z	zebra, dazzle, haze, rise
ə	a in ago	ch	chin, catcher, arch, nature
	e in agent	sh	she, cushion, dash, machine
	i in sanity	th	thin, nothing, truth
	o in comply	*th*	then, father, lathe
	u in focus	zh	azure, leisure, beige
ər	perhaps, murder	ŋ	ring, anger, drink

Abbreviation Key

adj.	adjective	*pl.*	plural
adv.	adverb	*prep.*	preposition
conj.	conjunction	*vi.*	intransitive verb
n.	noun	*vt.*	transitive verb

A

al·gae [al'jē] *n.* Simple plants with no root system that grow in damp places.

Aston Martin [as'tən märt''n] *n.* An expensive sports car.

B

be·hest [bē hest'] *n.* A command or order.

buoy [bɔi] *vt.* To keep afloat.

C

churl [churl] *n.* A selfish, mean person.

con·do·min·i·um [kän'də min'ē əm] *n.* An apartment building.

cre·ma·tion [krē mā'shən] *n.* The burning of a dead body.

cur·mudg·eon [kər muj'ən] *n.* A rude, bad-tempered person.

D

de·lin·quent [di liŋ'kwənt] *adj.* Not obeying the law.

dike [dīk] *n.* A barrier made of dirt to keep water in or out of an area.

dour [dɔor] *adj.* Severe; sullen.

dredge [drej] *vt.* To clear out the bottom of a river or other waterway.

driv·el [driv'əl] *n.* Silly or meaningless talk.

du·ly [dōo'lē] *adv.* As required or expected.

E

en·crust·ed [en krust'id] *adj.* Covered with a hard coating.

er·go [er'gō] *conj.* Therefore.

F

feat [fēt] *n.* An act showing unusual skill.

foi·ble [fɔi'bəl] *n.* A fault.

for·get-me-not [fər get'mē nät'] *n.* A plant with clusters of small pink, white, or blue flowers.

G

gall [gôl] *vt.* To annoy.

H

heir [er] *n.* One who receives property from a relative who dies.

hog·fish [hôg'fish'] *n.* A fish whose head resembles a pig.

I

in·stinc·tive·ly [in stiŋk'tiv lē] *adv.* Done in a natural way, without thinking.

M

man·a·tee [man'ə tē'] *n.* A large sea cow that lives in warm, shallow tropical waters.

mem·oir [mem'wär] *n.* The story of one's life written by oneself.

min·gy [min'jē] *adj.* Mean and stingy.

N

nom·i·nal [näm'ə nəl] *adj.* Small, compared to what is expected.

par·a·site [par′ə sīt] *n.* A plant or animal that lives on another plant or animal and takes food from it.

par·si·mo·ni·ous [pär′ sə mō′nē əs] *adj.* Being over-careful about one's money; stingy.

plod [pläd] *vi.* To walk heavily with great effort.

prey [prā] *n.* An animal killed for food by another animal.

pum·ice [pum′is] *n.* A light rock full of tiny holes made from hardened volcanic lava.

quea·sy [kwē′zē] *adj.* Feeling as if one might vomit.

re·gard·less [ri gärd′lis] *adv.* Anyway; no matter what.

re·past [ri past′] *n.* A meal.

score [skôr] *vt.* To partly cut lines in something for easy tearing.

se·rum [sir′əm] *n.* The part of an animal's blood often used for preventing diseases in humans.

skin·flint [skin′flint′] *n.* A stingy person.

tat·ty [tat′ē] *adj.* Shabby; in bad condition.

tax [taks] *vt.* To question in an accusing way.

Trans·vaal [trans väl′] *n.* A territory in the northeastern part of South Africa.

u·nan·i·mous [yo͞o nan′ə məs] *adj.* Everyone agreeing.

u·su·rer [yo͞o′zhər ər] *n.* A person who lends money and expects much more in return.

Index

M

INDEX

S

INDEX

Y

Z

Acknowledgments

For permission to reprint copyrighted material, grateful acknowledgment is made to the following sources:

Atheneum Books for Young Readers, an imprint of Simon & Schuster: "How Can Water Striders Walk on Water?" from *How Do Ants Know When You're Having a Picnic?* by Joanne Settel with Nancy Baggett. Text copyright © 1986 by Joanne Settel and Nancy Baggett.

Ballantine Books, a division of Random House, Inc.: From "The Journey to Anar" from *The Sword of Shannara* by Terry Brooks. Copyright © 1977 by Terry Brooks. Map from *The Sword of Shannara* by Terry Brooks, illustrated by The Brothers Hildebrandt. Illustrations copyright © 1977 by Random House, Inc.

Susan Bergholz Literary Services, New York: From *Tortuga* by Rudolfo A. Anaya. Copyright © 1979 by Rudolfo A. Anaya. Published by the University of New Mexico Press. All rights reserved.

Cobblestone Publishing, Inc., 7 School St., Peterborough, NH 03458: From "Making a Flying Fish" by Paula Morrow from *Faces: Happy Holidays*, vol. 7, no. 4, December 1990. Copyright © 1990 by Cobblestone Publishing, Inc.

Compton's Learning Company: From entry "Lava and Magma" from *Compton's Interactive Encyclopedia.* Copyright © 1997 by Compton's Learning Company.

Dial Books for Young Readers, a division of Penguin Books USA Inc.: "Brer Billy Goat Tricks Brer Wolf" from *Further Tales of Uncle Remus* by Julius Lester. Copyright © 1990 by Julius Lester.

Doubleday, a division of Bantam Doubleday Dell Publishing Group, Inc.: From "The Sky Is Gray" from *Bloodline* by Ernest J. Gaines.

Copyright © 1963 by Ernest J. Gaines.

EBSCO: "Teeth" from *EBSCO CD-ROM Middle Search.*

Margery Facklam: From *Wild Animals, Gentle Women* by Margery Facklam. Copyright © 1978 by Margery Facklam.

Harcourt Brace & Company: From Riddle #11 from *When I Dance* by James Berry. Copyright © 1991, 1988 by James Berry. Entry for "cloud" from *The Lincoln Writing Dictionary,* edited by Christopher Morris. Copyright © 1989 by Harcourt Brace & Company. From *The Pride of Puerto Rico: The Life of Roberto Clemente* by Paul Robert Walker. Copyright © 1988 by Harcourt Brace & Company.

HarperCollins Publishers: From *Women Who Made America Great* by Harry Gersh. Copyright © 1962 by Harry Gersh. From *The Land I Lost: Adventures of a Boy in Vietnam* by Huynh Quang Nhuong. Copyright © 1982 by Huynh Quang Nhuong.

Henry Holt and Company, Inc.: From *Scissor Cutting for Beginners* by Cheng Hou-tien. Copyright © 1978 by Cheng Hou-tien.

Alfred A. Knopf, Inc.: "April Rain Song" and "Poem" from *The Dream Keeper and Other Poems* by Langston Hughes. Copyright 1932 by Alfred A. Knopf, Inc.; copyright renewed © 1960 by Langston Hughes.

Sterling Lord Literistic, Inc.: From *Arctic Dreams* by Barry Lopez. Copyright © 1986 by Barry Holstun Lopez.

Lothrop, Lee and Shepard Books, a division of William Morrow & Company, Inc.: From "Man and Manatee" from *Manatee: On Location* by Kathy Darling. Copyright © 1991 by Kathy Darling.

Macmillan USA, a Simon & Schuster Macmillan Company: From "Pronunciation Key" from *Webster's New World College Dictionary*, Third Edition. Copyright © 1996, 1994, 1991, 1988 by Simon & Schuster, Inc.

Morrow Junior Books, a division of William Morrow & Company, Inc.: From *A Girl from Yamhill, A Memoir* by Beverly Cleary. Copyright © 1988 by Beverly Cleary. From "Picky-picky" from *Ramona Forever* by Beverly Cleary. Copyright © 1988 by Beverly Cleary. From *A Cat's Body* by Joanna Cole. Copyright © 1982 by Joanna Cole.

Naomi Shihab Nye: From "The Rider" and Poet's Comments from *The Place My Words Are Looking For* by Naomi Shihab Nye, selected by Paul B. Janeczko. Copyright © 1990 by Naomi Shihab Nye.

The Octagon Press, Ltd.: "Camel fodder" from *The Subtleties of the Inimitable Mulla Nasrudin* by Idries Shah. Copyright © 1983 by Designist Communications.

The Putnam Publishing Group: From *Oral History* by Lee Smith. Copyright © 1983 by Lee Smith.

Random House, Inc.: From "Banana Surprise" from *Mr. Wizard's Supermarket Science* by Don Herbert. Text copyright © 1980 by Don Herbert; illustrations copyright © 1980 by Roy McKie.

The James Reeves Estate: From "The Sea" from *The Complete Poems for Children* by James Reeves. Copyright © 1950 by James Reeves. Published by Heinemann.

Simon & Schuster Books for Young Readers, an imprint of Simon & Schuster Children's Publishing Division: From "Survivors and Colonizers" from *Volcano: The Eruption and Healing of Mount St. Helens* by Patricia Lauber. Copyright © 1986 by Patricia Lauber.

Simon & Schuster Books for Young Readers, an imprint of Simon & Schuster Children's Publishing Division: "Boar Out There" from *Every Living Thing* by Cynthia Rylant. Text copyright © 1985 by Cynthia Rylant. From "The Outsider" from *The Lost Garden* by Laurence Yep. Copyright © 1991 by Laurence Yep.

Larry Sternig & Jack Byrne Literary Agency: From "Zoo" by Edward D. Hoch. Copyright © 1958 by King Size Publications.

John Updike: Quotation by John Updike.

Viking Penguin, a division of Penguin Books USA Inc.: From *Henry Reed, Inc.* by Keith Robertson. Copyright © 1958 and renewed © 1986 by Keith Robertson. From "You Can't Take It with You" from *Escape If You Can* by Eva-Lis Wuorio. Copyright © 1977 by Eva-Lis Wuorio.

Walker and Company: From *How Did We Find Out About Coal?* by Isaac Asimov. Copyright © 1980 by Isaac Asimov.

Wayland Publishers Limited: From "Which Are Rabbits and Which Are Hares?" from *Rabbits and Hares* by Ralph Whitlock. Copyright © 1974 by Priory Press Ltd.

The H. W. Wilson Company: Entries for "Teeth" through "Teitel, Martin" from *Readers' Guide to Periodical Literature*. Copyright © 1996 by The H. W. Wilson Company, 950 University Avenue, Bronx, NY 10452. All rights reserved.

The World Book, Inc.: From "Massasoit" from *The World Book Encyclopedia*. Copyright © 1996 by World Book, Inc.

William K. Zinsser: From "Writing About Places: The Travel Article" from *On Writing Well*, Fifth Edition by William Zinsser. Copyright © 1976, 1980, 1985, 1988, 1990, 1994 by William K. Zinsser.

Photo Credits

ILLUSTRATION CREDITS

Kate Beetle—265

Linda Blackwell—116, 241

Keith Bowden—150, 155, 201, 332, 408, 424

Lee Christiansen—114–115

Chi Chung—137

Rondi Collette—134, 174–175, 177, 183, 400, 410, 427, 516, 530, 541, 631

Chris Ellison—13, 15, 16, 242, 243, 244, 245, 258, 452, 497

Richard Erickson—52, 97, 149, 159, 161, 327

Janice Fried—187, 188, 236, 239, 351, 651

Gerhold/Smith—202–203

Tom Gianni—266, 460, 556

John Hanley—64, 627, 628, 647

Mary Jones—178, 232, 331

Linda Kelen—163, 164, 172, 230, 231, 255, 261, 302, 324, 394, 413, 523

Susan Kemnitz—vi, 20, 21, 22, 99, 100

Rich Lo—xi, xii, xix, 30, 36, 167, 181, 184, 185, 204, 205, 206, 207, 221, 347, 422, 443, 533, 555, 604

Yoshi Miyake—xvii, 355, 631

Richard Murdock—x, 145

Precision Graphics—458, 558, 575, 660

Jack Scott—xvi, 320, 322, 334, 335

Steve Shock—viii, 84–85, 86, 87

Chuck Solway—xiii, 237

Nancy Tucker—42, 304, 319